SS

Programming
Microsoft
Office 2000
Web
Components

Dave Stearns

PUBLISHED BY
Microsoft Press
A Division of Microsoft Corporation
One Microsoft Way
Redmond, Washington 98052-6399

Library of Congress Cataloging-in-Publication Data
Stearns, Dave.
    Programming Microsoft Office 2000 Web Components / Dave Stearns.
        p.   cm.
    Includes index.
    ISBN 0-7356-0794-X
    1. Internet programming.   2. Microsoft Office.   3. Web site
development.
    QA76.625.S74   1999
    005.2'76--dc21   99-36327
                                                          CIP

Printed and bound in the United States of America.

1 2 3 4 5 6 7 8 9   WCWC   4 3 2 1 0 9

Distributed in Canada by Penguin Books Canada Limited.

A CIP catalogue record for this book is available from the British Library.

Microsoft Press books are available through booksellers and distributors worldwide. For
further information about international editions, contact your local Microsoft Corporation
office or contact Microsoft Press International directly at fax (425) 936-7329. Visit our Web
site at mspress.microsoft.com.

TrueType fonts is a registered trademark of Apple Computer, Inc. ActiveX, FrontPage, JScript,
Microsoft, Microsoft Press, MSDN, Outlook, PivotTable, PowerPoint, Visual Basic, Visual C++,
Visual FoxPro, Visual InterDev, Visual J++, Windows, and Windows NT are either registered trademarks or trademarks of Microsoft Corporation in the United States and/or other countries. Other
product and company names mentioned herein may be the trademarks of their respective owners.

The example companies, organizations, products, people, and events depicted herein are
fictitious. No association with any real company, organization, product, person, or event is
intended or should be inferred.

Acquisitions Editor: Eric Stroo
Project Editor: Michelle Goodman
Technical Editor: Steve Perry

"...that book would be, like my heart and me, dedicated to you..."
from "If I Should Write a Book" by Cahn-Chaplin,
recorded by John Coltrane and Johnny Hartman

To my one and only love, Chelle.

*And to the memory of Arlene Myers, the magical grandmother of
Microsoft Press and a dear friend.*

Soli Deo Gloria!

Contents

Contents

Contents

Contents

Acknowledgments

This book is not solely the product of my own work. A number of people contributed information, helpful tips, review comments, and even some source code. Although the full list of people I would like to thank is longer than this book, I do want to recognize the following people and their contributions to its creation.

My coworkers on the Office Web Components program management team—Jason Cahill, Mark Igra, Kent Lowry, Jay Massena, Peter Hussey, Paul Davies, and George Snelling—all provided volumes of information and review comments. Jason also developed some of the scriptlets and ancillary controls used in Part II of the book.

I can't thank the OWC development team enough, both for their hard work in creating the Office Web Components and for the constant technical and debugging help they provided while I developed the solutions. Amit Dekate, Andy Milton, David Wortendyke, Eric Matteson, Jason Allen, Jeff Couckuyt, Kevin Grealish, Matt Reynolds, Matt Androski, Mike Coulson, Randy Davis, Wes Cherry, Anatoly Grabar, Matt Bellew, Chris Brown, Will Pugh, Andrew Miller, Less Wright, and Cesar Alvarez made up this team, and they are by far the best developers on the face of the Earth.

Special thanks goes to Erik Christensen for his explanation of how Microsoft Visual Basic implements IPropertyNotifySink, as well as all the other great help he's given me over the years. Erik is the brainchild behind most of Visual Basic's most successful features.

I would also like to thank the OWC testers that assisted me in reviewing the chapters: Chad Foley, Dan Ricker, and our esteemed and ever-capable test lead Aaron Bregel.

Thanks also to Corey Salka, Amir Netz, Ariel Netz, Eric Jacobsen, and the whole SQL Server OLAP Services team for their assistance and for their permission to include the Foodmart sample cube on the book's companion CD. The OLAP Services team is one of the best at Microsoft (second to the OWC team of course...☺).

Special thanks to George Snelling, Richard McAnnif, and Steve Sinofsky for giving me permission to work on the book. It didn't affect my job performance—I promise.

Many thanks to Jen Hoffey for taking my picture for the book.

Of course, many thanks have to go to Eric Stroo, Michelle Goodman, Linda Harmony, and Steve Perry, my editors at Microsoft Press. Without them, this project would certainly never have come to fruition.

Acknowledgments

Lastly, no amount of thanks to my wife Chelle and all my friends could be enough. Without their support and encouragement, I would have never embarked on this hefty endeavor, nor ever completed it. Luckily, my wife and friends are the most patient people in the universe and don't hate me for the many times I ignored them while finishing a chapter!

Dave Stearns
Seattle, Washington
June 1999

Introduction

When I first started developing information systems at Microsoft, I often looked at Microsoft Excel and lamented that it was not packaged as a collection of reusable components that I could simply pick up and integrate into my applications. At that time, the current version of Excel had a new revolutionary user interface element called a "toolbar," and everyone loved it. When the Microsoft engineers integrated toolbars into the new operating system shell, Microsoft Windows 95, they built the toolbar as a reusable control—part of the Windows common controls. However, Microsoft Office still remained a set of large, monolithic applications, reusable only through cross-process automation. Soon after that, the Office applications integrated Microsoft Visual Basic for Applications (VBA), allowing developers to build solutions *within* the applications; however, that did not help developers who were writing custom applications in Microsoft Visual Basic or C++. Those developers needed the power of Excel's recalculation, charting, and PivotTable services *inside* their applications, hosted on their forms, and integrated with their data.

With the release of Office 2000, this dream of mine has finally become a reality. In this version of Office, our team released a new set of reusable services named the Office Web Components (OWC), which encapsulate the basic data analysis and reporting features found in Excel and Microsoft Access. However, as with most first-version technologies, developers will need help understanding what these components offer and how they can successfully incorporate OWC into their custom solutions. That is why I wrote this book. This book is the definitive resource on the Office Web Components, and it comes straight from a member of the team that built them.

ABOUT THE BOOK

I believe that to learn a new technology, you need both a conceptual overview and examples of the technology used in a larger context. Conceptual information is critical to your general understanding of the technological principles at work, but to be truly successful at applying a new technology, you must also see it at work in a real-world solution and not just in conveniently packaged demonstrations that exist in a vacuum.

Only then can you see how the technology interacts with related technologies and how to overcome the sometimes confusing quirks that all technologies have.

For this reason, I divided this book into two parts. Part I contains a conceptual overview of the Office Web Components, and Part II documents a number of solutions I built using OWC and related technologies. Part II also contains a final chapter on deployment. The chapters in Part II build on the conceptual foundation laid in Part I, so even if you have some familiarity with the Office Web Components, you should at least browse through Part I to ensure that you know all the concepts.

Chapter 1 discusses the OWC library as a whole, explaining why it was created and for what uses it was intended. It provides a brief introduction to each of the components in the library and lists the supported containers in which you can use them.

Chapters 2 through 5 cover the Spreadsheet, Chart, PivotTable, and Data Source components. Each chapter discusses its respective component in depth, listing relevant features, describing how to accomplish the most common programming tasks with sample source code, and describing some powerful advanced functionality that you might not notice at first glance.

Chapter 6 begins the second part of the book. This chapter shows you how to build interactive web sites that display critical business metrics in graphical form. Most businesses have a set of critical metrics by which executives measure the health of the company or its processes, and this chapter shows you how to present those metrics in easy-to-read charts—a key element in an executive's information dashboard.

Chapter 7 shows you how to use the PivotTable and Chart components to create an interactive data analysis system. This solution shows you how to connect the Office Web Components to an OLAP (Online Analytical Processing) data source and provide rich data analysis right in a web browser. It also demonstrates a few tricks, such as saving and reloading reports, adjusting chart types to display all the totals in your report, and combining the multidimensional extensions to ADO (Microsoft ActiveX Data Objects) with the PivotTable component to enable more sophisticated data analysis. The techniques you learn in this chapter apply equally well to the analysis of other kinds of data.

Chapter 8 describes how to build solutions that not only provide analytical capabilities, but also involve grid-based data entry. The solution in this chapter is a system for creating and tracking timesheets, showing you how to use the Spreadsheet component in the context of data entry. The techniques you learn in this chapter are similar to those used when developing an expense reporting or budgeting system.

Chapter 9 teaches you how to leverage new or existing spreadsheet models using the Spreadsheet component. The solution in this chapter illustrates how to use a mortgage calculation model both on a web server and in an interactive Spreadsheet control on the client. The techniques you learn in this chapter apply equally well to any system in which you want to employ spreadsheet models.

Chapter 10 shows you how to feed real-time data into the Spreadsheet component. It describes a real-time data source I built for returning stock information and demonstrates how you can bind cells in a spreadsheet model to properties of a real-time data source. The techniques you will learn in this chapter are the same ones you would use when loading any kind of real-time data into the Spreadsheet component.

Chapter 11 discusses how to build custom function add-ins for the Spreadsheet component. A function add-in is an incredibly powerful mechanism that allows you to offer any kind of custom calculation to your users, including calculations that access other network resources or data sources.

Chapter 12, the final chapter in the book, discusses how to deploy the Office Web Components with your solution. The components come with a special Web Installer that you can use to deploy the components to users who do not already have Office 2000. This chapter also lists all the files installed by the Web Installer.

Woven throughout the chapters are tips on the components' more esoteric features and stories about how we developed the Office Web Components. These tips and anecdotes appear as sidebars in the text, so you can read those that interest you and skip the ones that don't.

ABOUT THE CODE

Nearly all the code in this book is written in Microsoft Visual Basic Scripting Edition (VBScript) and exists as client-side script in a web page or as script in an ASP (Microsoft Active Server Pages) page. (However, Chapter 11 contains code written in Visual Basic.) This is not meant to imply that the Office Web Components can be scripted only in web or ASP pages, nor is it meant to imply that you cannot use JavaScript, C++, or other COM-enabled languages. My choice of VBScript was based on two considerations:

- Developers familiar with programming Office will be more familiar with VBScript than with other languages because VBScript is a subset of VBA, which is the programming language embedded in Office applications.

- VBScript has more functionality and far better error-handling capabilities than JavaScript. This enabled me to write better examples and more robust solutions.

My choice of web and ASP pages (as opposed to Visual Basic or C++ applications) as the execution context was primarily due to developers' current excitement about these environments. Many developers recognize the benefits presented by Internet technologies, and I wanted this book to illustrate how the Office Web Components work in that environment.

My naming and coding conventions might be slightly different than what you have seen before. I developed them when implementing information systems in Microsoft's Information Technology group. My conventions are similar to most naming conventions evangelized by others, using consistent prefixes to variable names to denote their purpose in the code. However, while others base prefixes solely on a variable's data type, I prefer to encode a bit more meaning into my prefixes. For example, instead of giving a prefix of "l" or "n" to all Long number variables, I use a prefix that denotes the variable's *purpose,* such as "ct" for counter or "id" for unique identifier.

USING THE CD

The companion CD for this book contains numerous code samples, as well as the complete source code to all the solutions discussed in Part II. I highly encourage you to examine and run these samples and solutions while you read the chapters, as this will help illustrate the concepts you are learning. Feel free to reuse the sample code in your own applications.

To run the code samples from Part I, browse the files on the companion CD and double-click them. These files were designed to run directly from the CD, so they use relative paths for finding databases and style sheets. If you copy the CD folders to your hard disk, make sure to copy all the folders and keep them in the same relative locations. This will happen automatically if you run the Setup program on the CD.

Most of the solutions in Part II require a web server capable of executing ASP scripts. Microsoft Internet Information Server (IIS) and Microsoft Personal Web Server are both capable of executing ASP scripts, so you can use either product. Determining how to install these products can be challenging, so refer to the following table to ascertain the appropriate place from which to install them given your operating system.

Operating System	*How to Install*
Windows 98	Run the Personal Web Server Setup program from the add-ons\pws folder on your Windows 98 CD.
Windows NT Workstation	Run the Setup program for the Windows NT Option Pack. This will install Personal Web Server. The Windows NT Option Pack can be downloaded from Microsoft's web site.
Windows NT Server and Advanced Server	Run the Setup program for the Windows NT Option Pack. This will install IIS. The Windows NT Option Pack can be downloaded from Microsoft's web site.

SUPPORT

I am quite interested in receiving feedback on this book. If you have constructive feedback, please send me e-mail at davesowcbook@hotmail.com.

Every effort has been made to ensure the accuracy of this book and the contents of the companion CD. Microsoft Press provides corrections for books through the Web at http://mspress.microsoft.com/support/.

If you have questions about this book or the companion CD, please send them to Microsoft Press using postal mail or e-mail:

Microsoft Press
Attn: Programming Microsoft Office 2000 Web Components Editor
One Microsoft Way
Redmond, WA 98052-6399
mspinput@microsoft.com

Please note that product support is not offered through the above mail addresses. For support information regarding Microsoft Office 2000, you can call Standard Support at (425) 635-7011 weekdays between 6 A.M. and 6 P.M. Pacific Time. You can also search Microsoft's Support Online at http://support.microsoft.com/support.

Part I

Overview of the Office Web Components

Chapter 1

Introducing the Office Web Components

Microsoft Office 2000 includes a new set of controls called the Office Web Components (OWC). Using these components, you can build many useful data analysis and reporting solutions, both in the web browser and in traditional programming environments. In this chapter, I will explain why the Office Web Components were created, what they are, and where you can use them. I will also give you a few initial ideas for their use in business solutions. Part II of the book will provide some common, practical uses of the components and will take you on a step-by-step tour of the techniques used in those solutions.

If you don't know anything about these controls, read on, as this chapter will serve as the foundation for the rest of the book. If you are already familiar with the components and just want to see how to use them in business solutions, skip ahead to Chapter 6.

WHY WERE THE OFFICE WEB COMPONENTS CREATED?

The technologies developed for the World Wide Web are taking both large and small businesses by storm. Companies now see the Internet and the Web as key mechanisms for reaching their customers and for distributing information among customers, suppliers, and vendors. Companies are also realizing that the same technologies used internally on their LANs or WANs (known as intranets) provide scalable, flexible, easy-to-use mechanisms for sharing information and for developing and deploying tools to run their businesses.

Not so long ago, setting up and managing content on an intranet was a black art relegated to "webmasters." With the advent of site management and content creation tools such as Microsoft FrontPage, ordinary mortals could create web-ready documents and manage them much like they managed files on their local computers. Tools such as these made it possible for semitechnical individuals to set up web sites and share information with their coworkers.

Documents full of text lend themselves well to HTML and web browser technologies, but not all documents are useful when viewed as static text only. Authors who create spreadsheets, databases, and database reports encounter special problems and opportunities when sharing these on their corporate intranets. Much of the value of sharing a spreadsheet or database report lies in letting other users interact with it and tailor the model to their own needs. For example, if you create a spreadsheet to analyze a product's profitability given various input costs, an important aspect of sharing that spreadsheet is enabling other users to change or enter new assumptions and view the recalculated results. Likewise, if you create a Microsoft Excel PivotTable report (more commonly known as a *crosstab report*), allowing other people to sort, filter, group, reorganize, or drill down to more detail is an essential part of sharing these documents. In other words, publishing a spreadsheet or database document on a web is only half the story. The other half is enabling others to interact with the published document and garner information that's meaningful to them, not just to the publisher.

Corporate information technology (IT) groups are also realizing the benefits of web and Internet technologies. Many information systems are much easier to develop, deploy, use, and support when created with web technologies on the corporation's intranet. Two such classes of systems exist: *decision support systems (DSS),* also known as *executive information systems (EIS)* or the more recent name *online analytical processing (OLAP),* and *transactional systems,* which are used infrequently or by large audiences. The Sales Analysis and Reporting solution in Chapter 7 gives an example of OLAP in a web browser, and the Timesheet solution described in Chapter 8 shows an example of a transactional tool commonly used by a large audience.

Decision support systems lend themselves incredibly well to the technologies and user metaphors of the web. Want to know how many units of your product were sold last month? Open your web browser, and click a particular hyperlink. Need to see a list of customers in your district? Again, it's just a click away from your team's intranet home page. Technologies such as Common Gateway Interface (CGI) and Microsoft Active Server Pages (ASP) have made it possible for IT groups to deliver live reports on demand in a format that can be viewed, printed, or imported into a variety of analysis tools.

However, often the person viewing the report wants to see it in a slightly different way, sort it by a different value, group the data in a different order, drill down and see more detail about a number, or see the data organized into a chart. When any of these scenarios occurs, IT groups return to the same problem they have always had to deal with: how do they build a flexible, robust, and easy-to-use reporting system that satisfies everyone's needs?

The second class of systems—transactional systems—also benefits from the technologies of the web. Need to change your 401(k) contribution? Just follow a hyperlink on the human resources home page, enter the new value, and click the Submit button. Need help fixing your computer? Navigate to the helpdesk site, fill out the form describing your problem, and click Submit. There's no install program to run, no complex application to execute, and little to no client-side disk space needed.

Sometimes these applications demand a richer client interface, one that will provide gridlike data entry, recalculation, updates to charts showing the impact of the current value, and so on. To keep the deployment benefits, an IT group would need to use an active component in the page; however, they often lack the resources to develop such components themselves.

THE SUBTLER SIDE OF BUZZWORDS

To be precise, the terms "decision support systems," "executive information systems," and "OLAP" are not quite synonymous—each has a slant that makes it a little unique. The term "executive information systems" is hardly used today since information systems aren't used only by executives anymore; however, once upon a time the phrase described information systems that delivered critical, high-level business information to executives who were monitoring the health of the company. The term "decision support systems" is more encompassing and applies to systems that aid in decision making, often focusing on delivering ad hoc data analysis. "OLAP" is a hot buzzword today, and it's more often used to describe a class of technologies than the solutions built around them. Alas, our friends in the trade press often use all these terms interchangeably.

So how do you deliver an interactive experience on the corporate intranet? How do you make a spreadsheet or database report come to life in the web browser? How can you develop and deploy solutions that provide rich data analysis and data visualization capabilities? How can you build transactional solutions with richer client interfaces? The answer is the Office Web Components.

WHAT ARE THE OFFICE WEB COMPONENTS?

The Office Web Components are a set of Component Object Model (COM) controls designed to bring interactive spreadsheet modeling, database reporting, and data visualization to a number of control containers. The OWC library contains four principal components: Spreadsheet, Chart, PivotTable, and Data Source. We'll discuss each of these controls briefly in this section and in much more detail in the following chapters.

> NOTE COM is also known as ActiveX. I was on the Visual Basic team when Microsoft invented the term "ActiveX" to describe the COM technologies, throwing most of our customers for a loop since they had just gotten used to saying COM after we stopped using the term "OLE." Since I'm not a marketing person, I'll just use the term COM in this book to describe the Component Object Model technologies.

The word "Office" in the name "Office Web Components" indicates that the controls were developed by some of the same programmers who created Microsoft Excel and Microsoft Access and that the controls were made to look, feel, and behave like small versions of their Microsoft Office siblings. These controls definitely don't have all the features found in Excel and Access—in other words, you wouldn't want to dynamically download all of Excel and Access to view a report in your browser! However, the controls do contain many of the commonly used features, especially those needed when interacting with content that's already been created. Plus, they can read and write the HTML file format of Excel 2000, allowing the user to click a button and load the current data into Excel for more powerful analysis. In this book, I'll detail the noteworthy Excel or Access features that are and aren't supported by each component. I'll also show you how to add some of these missing features with your own code.

The "Web" part of OWC's name is often misleading. The controls are standard COM controls and can be used in many control containers such as Microsoft Internet Explorer, Microsoft Visual Basic, Microsoft Visual C++, Microsoft Visual FoxPro, or Microsoft Office UserForms. However, the controls have a few behaviors that make them especially suited to the unique environment of Internet Explorer. For example, web browsers automatically support scrolling along a document, and it's often annoying for a control in the page to have its own set of scroll bars. The Spreadsheet and PivotTable controls can be set to automatically adjust themselves to fit their current content without requiring internal scroll bars. Also, all the controls support the color names available in Internet Explorer in addition to supporting numeric RGB values. That means you can set the background color of an element to "CornSilk" or "PapayaWhip" (my personal favorite), and the control will convert the color to the appropriate RGB value just as Internet Explorer would.

The "Components" part of OWC's name is a touch confusing, although it's more accurate than using the word "Controls" (though I will often refer to OWC as "controls" for convenience throughout this book). The Office Web Components are unusual in that they can be used in control containers like web pages, Visual Basic forms, and so on, as well as in memory as invisible objects. Most COM controls can be used only as visible controls in control containers, and most invisible objects, such as those accessed via the Microsoft ActiveX Data Objects (ADO) interface, can be used only in memory and cannot be put on a form or web page. The OWC library was built so that its components could be used either way, which enables you to use the controls with the user interfaces they expose or for their base services, such as spreadsheet recalculation. The ability to use the components as invisible objects also enables you to use the library on a server to easily generate static content that users can view in any web browser (more on that later in the chapter).

All the controls support a rich set of programming interfaces that you can call from Microsoft VBScript (Visual Basic Scripting Edition), Microsoft JScript, Microsoft VBA (Visual Basic for Applications), Java, C++, and any other language capable of calling a dual or dispatch COM interface. That means you can weave the components into a custom solution and make them look and act the way you want. I will discuss most of the important properties, methods, and events in the subsequent chapters and will cover many more of these in the chapters describing the various solutions found on the companion CD.

> **SEE ALSO** If you are looking for a definitive reference on COM, I'd recommend picking up a copy of David Chappell's *Understanding ActiveX and OLE* (Microsoft Press, 1996).

Let's take a brief look at each of the components and discuss what kinds of solutions you can build with them. As already mentioned, the next four chapters will cover each component in more depth.

The Spreadsheet Component

The Spreadsheet component (shown in Figure 1-1) is like a small version of an Excel spreadsheet, complete with a spreadsheet user interface and a recalculation engine that supports nearly all the calculation functions in Excel 2000. With this control, you can change or recalculate values; sort, filter, and scroll data; protect cells; and even reload the data into Excel 2000 for further manipulation. The Spreadsheet control can load its data from an embedded parameter or from any URL that points to an Excel spreadsheet saved in HTML file format.

	A	B	C	D
1		Promotional Keychains Ltd.		
2		Break-Even Analysis		
4		Cost	Production Level	
5		Per Unit	100,000	500,000
6	Raw Materials	$ 0.23	$ 23,000.00	$ 115,000.00
7	Assembly Labor	$ 0.14	$ 14,000.00	$ 70,000.00
8	Packaging Materials	$ 0.03	$ 3,000.00	$ 15,000.00
9	Packaging Labor	$ 0.04	$ 4,000.00	$ 20,000.00
10	Subtotal Direct Costs	$ 0.44	$ 44,000.00	$ 220,000.00
11				
12	G&A expenses		$ 68,000.00	$ 68,000.00
13	Allocated Mfg. Overhead		$ 85,000.00	$ 85,000.00
14	Subtotal Fixed Costs		$ 153,000.00	$ 153,000.00
15	Total Costs		$ 197,000.00	$ 373,000.00
16				
17	Selling Price Per Unit		1.29	0.99
18	Revenue		$ 129,000.00	$ 495,000.00
19	Net Income		($68,000.00)	$122,000.00

Figure 1-1. *The Spreadsheet component.*

The Spreadsheet control is useful anytime you want to make a spreadsheet model available on your intranet so that others can change the input and instantly view the recalculated results. Examples include a mortgage calculator and payment schedule model, a product break-even model, and a sales forecasting model.

This control is also useful for any kind of cross-tabulated or grid-based data entry, especially when you need to use formulas with automatic recalculation. Examples include expense reports, timesheets, and budgets.

The Spreadsheet control has the ability to bind cells to properties of other objects on the page and then automatically update the cell and its dependents when the source indicates that the property value has changed. This makes it possible to feed real-time data into the spreadsheet for scenarios such as a stock portfolio. The Spreadsheet control is specifically designed to keep listening for new values and recalculating even when you are editing other formulas or formatting other cells in the spreadsheet you're working on.

The Chart Component

The Chart component (shown in Figure 1-2) is comparable to a small version of Excel charting, supporting most of the two-dimensional chart types in Excel 2000 as well as a Polar chart type. Another big feature is that the Chart control can display many plots at once, allowing you to create a *small-multiple design*—in other words, a collection of plots that vary by one property and can be compared at a glance. A chart can be data-bound to the Spreadsheet control, the PivotTable control, or an ADO Recordset object, or it can be filled with literal data values. When bound to a data source, a Chart control will update whenever the source data changes.

SEE ALSO   For more information on the power of small-multiple designs, see Edward Tufte's book *Envisioning Information* (Graphics Press, 1990).

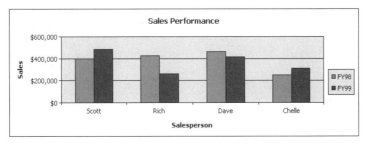

Figure 1-2. *The Chart component.*

The Chart control is primarily useful any time you need to chart live data or monitor a specific metric critical to your business. Because it supports a rich programming model, you can also add many effects to a chart with this control, such as zooming and panning on large axes, dynamically changing other content in the application based on the mouse's location, or letting users double-click to link to a new page displaying more information about the selected data point.

The PivotTable Component

Designed to deliver interactive data reporting and analysis, the PivotTable component (shown in Figure 1-3) provides all the functionality found in Excel PivotTables and external data ranges. It can retrieve data from tabular, relational databases through OLE DB, as well as from OLAP server cubes and cube files through OLE DB for OLAP. Using this control, you can view data grouped, sliced, and sorted in a variety of ways, creating polished reports and interactive analysis on live data.

You can use this control for many tasks, although it's best suited for database reporting and data analysis solutions. When bound to an OLAP cube, the PivotTable control can provide the user with a flexible, high-performing analysis surface. IT groups can concentrate on collecting and cleaning data and loading it into cubes that reflect the way their company thinks about the data, while users working with this control can create slices of the data to fit their own needs.

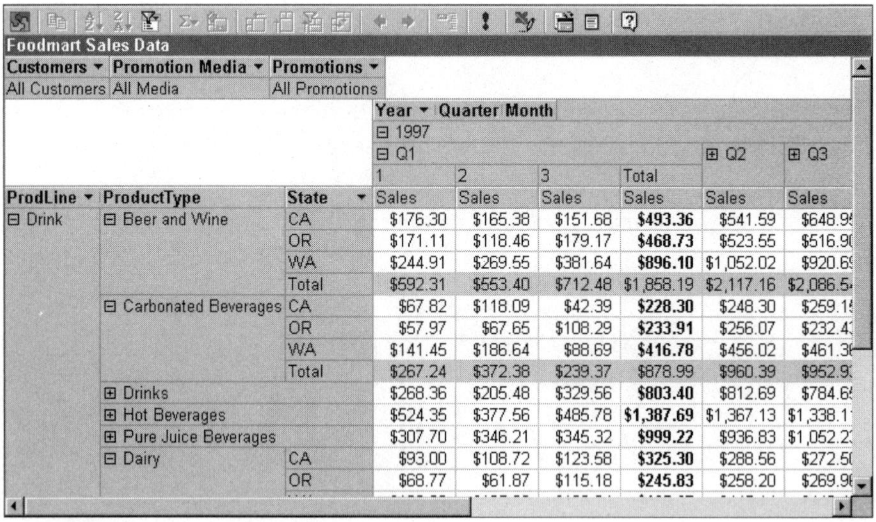

Foodmart Sales Data

Customers	Promotion Media	Promotions
All Customers	All Media	All Promotions

ProdLine	ProductType	State	1997 Q1 1 Sales	1997 Q1 2 Sales	1997 Q1 3 Sales	1997 Q1 Total Sales	1997 Q2 Sales	1997 Q3 Sales
⊟ Drink	⊟ Beer and Wine	CA	$176.30	$165.38	$151.68	**$493.36**	$541.59	$648.9
		OR	$171.11	$118.46	$179.17	**$468.73**	$523.55	$516.9
		WA	$244.91	$269.55	$381.64	**$896.10**	$1,052.02	$920.6
		Total	$592.31	$553.40	$712.48	$1,858.19	$2,117.16	$2,086.5
	⊟ Carbonated Beverages	CA	$67.82	$118.09	$42.39	**$228.30**	$248.30	$259.1
		OR	$57.97	$67.65	$108.29	**$233.91**	$256.07	$232.4
		WA	$141.45	$186.64	$88.69	**$416.78**	$456.02	$461.3
		Total	$267.24	$372.38	$239.37	$878.99	$960.39	$952.9
	⊞ Drinks		$268.36	$205.48	$329.56	**$803.40**	$812.69	$784.6
	⊞ Hot Beverages		$524.35	$377.56	$485.78	**$1,387.69**	$1,367.13	$1,338.1
	⊞ Pure Juice Beverages		$307.70	$346.21	$345.32	**$999.22**	$936.83	$1,052.2
	⊟ Dairy	CA	$93.00	$108.72	$123.58	**$325.30**	$288.56	$272.5
		OR	$68.77	$61.87	$115.18	**$245.83**	$258.20	$269.9

Figure 1-3. *The PivotTable component.*

The PivotTable control can also perform the same operations directly on a relational database, so you can use it even if you don't have an investment in an OLAP system. However, the performance when using an OLAP data source is always much faster because of the nature of the technology. OLAP has other logical benefits that we'll discuss further when we explore the Sales Analysis and Reporting solution in Chapter 7.

The Data Source Component

The Data Source component (DSC) is the backbone for controls that require data from external sources. Although this control is invisible, it is widely used to retrieve data, manipulate data into hierarchies or temporary OLAP cubes (more on this in Chapter 4), and establish data bindings between the various controls. Since the DSC supports the same standard interfaces as other data source controls found in Internet Explorer and Visual Basic, it will interoperate in those environments. The DSC is used heavily in Access 2000's data access pages feature and encapsulates much of the functionality found in the Access reporting engine.

The DSC is involved almost any time the other components retrieve data from an external database. However, it also supports a programming model of its own, and you can use it to build or manipulate hierarchical Recordset objects. In general, you don't need to think much about the DSC since the other components and the Access 2000 Data Access Page Designer will set it up and implement it for you.

WHERE CAN YOU USE THE COMPONENTS?

Since the Office Web Components are COM controls, you'd naturally expect them to work in any environment that called itself a COM control container. However, theory and reality don't always match up, especially in the world of software. Microsoft makes many environments that can contain controls (16 that our team could recall off the top of our heads), and various other companies create many others.

To keep the Office test team from going mad, we tested the Office Web Components at different levels in different containers. First, we picked the containers we thought people would use most and performed full test passes on them. We then performed basic, ad hoc testing on the containers used less often. And finally, we grouped a few containers into the "not formally tested but doesn't cause a nuclear meltdown when tried" category. Table 1-1 shows which containers fell into what category.

Container	*Test Coverage*
Microsoft Internet Explorer 5.0	Full
Microsoft Internet Explorer 4.01	Full
Microsoft Internet Explorer 3.x	Not supported
Microsoft Visual Basic 6.0	Full
Microsoft Visual Basic 5.0	Basic
Microsoft Visual InterDev	Basic
Microsoft Access Forms	Basic
Microsoft Office UserForms	Basic
Microsoft FrontPage 99	Full
Microsoft FrontPage 98	Basic
Microsoft Access 2000 Data Access Page Designer	Full
Microsoft Script Editor	Full
Microsoft Word 2000	Basic
Microsoft Excel 2000	Basic
Microsoft PowerPoint 2000	Basic
Microsoft Outlook 2000	Basic
Microsoft Visual C++/MFC Projects	None
Microsoft Visual J++	None

Table 1-1. *Tested containers.*

Also note that the design-time activation of the controls varies quite a bit from container to container. Since the Office Web Components are fairly complex controls, it is often necessary to select elements within a control (such as a cell in a spreadsheet, a pivot field in a PivotTable report, or a series of data points in a chart) and format or perform operations on them. To enable this functionality, the controls will become *UI active* in containers that allow this, meaning they will respond to mouse and keyboard events. Any changes made to the controls in design mode will persist with the document or form when it is reloaded at runtime, resetting the controls to look exactly as they did when you saved them. Some containers make the controls UI active as soon as you click them. Others require that you double-click the control before it becomes UI active. Still other containers require you to single-click them twice to activate them. This behavior is entirely determined by the container, so refer to the container's documentation to see how it deals with COM controls at design time.

Note that this does not affect a control's runtime behavior. At runtime, all containers make the controls UI active after loading them. But some environments, such as Office documents, never get into a runtime state because you are always editing the document that's currently loaded. Internet Explorer, Visual Basic, Visual C++, Access Forms, and Office UserForms all have a runtime mode in which the controls are immediately active.

Data Access Pages and Internet Explorer 5

If you read any of the Access 2000 documentation, you will likely see statements that say you can view data access pages only in Internet Explorer version 5 and above. Although true, that statement does *not* apply to the Office Web Components in general. The components will function in Internet Explorer 4.01 and above, though they won't function in any earlier versions (4.0, 3.x, 2.x, and so on). This applies to any interactive content created with Excel 2000 (which uses the Office Web Components) and to custom solutions developed using the components.

Data access pages rely on a few specific features in Internet Explorer 5, which is why they only run in that environment. However, the Office Web Components themselves can run quite happily in the tested containers listed earlier.

Using the Office Web Components on a Server

As mentioned before, the Office Web Components were designed to run both as controls "sited" within a form, document, or web page, and as objects in memory with no user interface. Each of the controls exposes a property or method that returns a static representation of its current content. The Chart and PivotTable controls can create GIF images of their content, and the Spreadsheet control can return an HTML table fragment or full page that can be rendered by any browser that's compatible with HTML 3.2. All of this means you can use the components on a web server to perform server-side generation of chart images and PivotTable reports or server-side recalculation of a spreadsheet model. I'll demonstrate a few of these techniques in Part II of the book.

Besides discussing the how-to of using the components on the server, we'll examine a number of more subtle issues related to performance, scalability, and reliability later in the book.

Deployment

One of the more attractive aspects of web-based solutions is that they don't require explicit setup of an application. Anything needed is either included with the web page in the form of scripts or is automatically downloaded as applets or COM controls. The Office Web Components enable a no-install deployment and automatic upgrade mechanism by using the codebase feature of Internet Explorer. The components also include a sophisticated web installing control that makes the download experience much more attractive. Furthermore, OWC has no technological dependency on Office 2000, so it can coexist in an Office 97 environment or be used on a machine that doesn't have any other part of Office installed.

I'll cover all the aspects of deployment and how you can build your solutions to automatically deploy OWC in Chapter 12.

What About Netscape Navigator?

When I talk about the Office Web Components at conferences or other customer gatherings, invariably someone asks the question, "Do these run in Netscape Navigator?" The answer is essentially "no," but it has a few caveats.

Netscape Navigator 4.5 does not natively support COM controls, so without any plug-ins, the Office Web Components won't even be loaded by Netscape Navigator. However, a company called NCompass Labs, Inc. makes a plug-in for Netscape Navigator that can host COM controls in a web page. So if you installed this plug-in, could you use the components in Netscape Navigator? The answer is "it depends" and, again, has a few caveats.

Many solutions you might build with OWC involve communication between the components—for instance, a chart bound to a PivotTable or spreadsheet, or a spreadsheet cell bound to the property of another element on the page. These solutions depend on functionality provided in Internet Explorer that isn't present in Netscape Navigator even with the NCompass plug-in, so they simply won't work in Netscape Navigator.

Using a single component or multiple components that do not communicate with one another *is* possible in Netscape Navigator. However, this is one of the containers that our test team did not research, so I can't guarantee that it will work.

You should always remember, however, that static content generated by the controls on the server can be rendered in either Netscape Navigator or Internet Explorer. So if your runtime environment requires that you support both browsers, you probably will be more interested in using the components on your web server and in the solutions that show the techniques that do so.

Chapter 2

The Spreadsheet Component

This chapter will delve into the functionality and the programming model of the Microsoft Office Spreadsheet component. Since this book focuses on building real solutions, I'll present a few interesting uses of each component feature along with its description. In Part II of the book, you'll see many of these ideas actually implemented.

This chapter will give you an understanding of what the Spreadsheet component can and cannot do, suggest clever ways you can use your own code to add functionality to the component, and show the key elements of the programming model that will get you started.

THE BASICS OF THE SPREADSHEET COMPONENT

Before we get too detailed, let's examine the basic features of the Spreadsheet component and describe the various ways it can load and save data.

Recalculation Engine

The recalculation engine lies at the heart of the Spreadsheet component—making this component more than just a typical grid control. Designed by the same developers who built the recalculation engine for Microsoft Excel, the Spreadsheet component supports nearly all the functions in Excel 2000, including most of those in the Analysis ToolPak (ATP).

> **NOTE**   For those who are curious, the following functions are not supported
> by the Spreadsheet component: ASC, CALL, DATEDIF, FINDB, FREQUENCY,
> GETPIVOTDATA, GROWTH, INFO, ISPMT, JIS, LEFTB, LENB, LINEST,
> LOGEST, MDETERM, MIDB, MINVERSE, MMULT, PHONETIC, REGISTER.ID,
> REPLACEB, RIGHTB, SEARCHB, SQL.REQUEST, TRANSPOSE, TREND,
> and YEN. All the functions ending in the letter "B" operate at the byte level in-
> stead of the character level in a double-byte character set (DBCS) system.
>
> Refer to the sections on property binding and function add-ins later in this
> chapter to see how to use the VBA or VBScript equivalents of these functions.
> Also, the INDEX and LOOKUP functions each have two forms in Excel, one using
> arrays and one using vectors (single-dimension ranges). The Spreadsheet con-
> trol supports the vector forms but not the array forms.

Any use of the Spreadsheet component that involves formulas will naturally
require the recalculation engine—for example, a solution allowing users to view a
product break-even model, change assumptions, and see the recalculated results.
Recalculation is the backbone of spreadsheet "what if" analysis and the core feature
of any spreadsheet product. The recalculation engine can also take advantage of some
of the advanced features discussed later in the chapter, such as property binding and
function add-ins.

When the Spreadsheet component is used without a user interface (that is, as
an in-memory object), the recalculation engine becomes its primary service. The
recalculation engine can perform any complex calculation that's easily expressed in
a spreadsheet model. It can also recalculate an existing model on the server and then
send the output to a web browser or into an e-mail message. Many calculations can
be cumbersome to construct in script or C code but can be expressed rather easily
in a spreadsheet model.

For example, a bank or lending institution might develop a spreadsheet model
to assess the risk of a particular type of loan. Since loan underwriters typically are
not programmers, developing a loan assessment function to run on the server probably would be difficult—just as it would be for the programmer who doesn't understand the complicated calculations the loan underwriter uses. However, using the
Spreadsheet component's recalculation engine, the programmer can load the underwriter's published spreadsheet model, change the inputs, and grab the new risk assessment as the output.

The Spreadsheet component supports a worksheet with a maximum of 65,536
rows by 702 columns (A through ZZ) but supports only one worksheet per instance
of the component. This is the same number of rows that Excel 2000 offers but nearly
three times the number of columns. (Excel supports only 256 columns.)

WARNING If you try to load all 65,536 rows and 702 columns, you'll be waiting quite a while. Since the Spreadsheet control loads its content from HTML, the load operation is naturally slower than that of loading binary data, such as when Excel loads an XLS file. Although you can generally load files with hundreds of rows fairly quickly, large models will not load quickly in the Spreadsheet component.

The Spreadsheet control supports both absolute ($A$1) and relative (A1) cell references in formulas and, just like Excel, it automatically adjusts these references when you move, insert, or delete rows or columns. Using both absolute and relative references can be especially useful when copying cells containing formulas from one part of a range to another. For example, you would use an absolute cell reference if that reference must remain the same regardless of which row and column contains the formula. A reference that must refer to the current row and column, however, needs to be relative. In other words, $A$1 will remain $A$1 after the copy operation, while A1 will be converted to the current row and column into which you have copied.

NOTE The Spreadsheet component does not support the old R1C1 reference style. It also doesn't support English language formulas, which attempt to let you build formulas based on named ranges. While this was a wonderful goal, it seldom works as expected.

Unfortunately, the Spreadsheet component doesn't support named ranges in this version of Office. When Excel publishes a spreadsheet model with *interactivity* (in other words, publishes a page containing the Spreadsheet control), it automatically converts named range references to absolute range references. This also occurs when you copy and paste cells from Excel to the Spreadsheet control. If you want to use a named range in the code around the Spreadsheet component, consider using the Dictionary object (Scripting.Dictionary) as an easy way to store and retrieve the actual references for a given name. (The Dictionary object is implemented in the Microsoft Scripting Runtime library.)

For example, if you want to define a named range that refers to a list of data in the spreadsheet and want to use that range in script to perform a sort, you can write code like this:

```
Set dict = CreateObject("Scripting.Dictionary")
dict.Add "MyName", "A1:F20"
Set rng = Spreadsheet1.Range(dict("MyName"))
```

The Dictionary object is an associative array. You add key/value pairs to it and, given the key, you can efficiently retrieve any value. You can easily keep track of named ranges with this object, and any time you need to pass a reference to the spreadsheet, you can use the method shown in the last line of code on the preceding page to retrieve the real reference for a given name.

Spreadsheet Component User Interface

On top of the recalculation engine sits the Spreadsheet component user interface. The user interface is, of course, similar to that of Excel but is specifically designed to favor activities you'd need to perform when interacting with an existing spreadsheet model. Many of the features found in Excel that make authoring a new spreadsheet easy do not yet exist in the Spreadsheet control; however, there are enough so that you can create new spreadsheets for your solutions as needed. Plus, you can copy and paste from Excel to the Spreadsheet component—meaning you can do most of your authoring in Excel. Figure 2-1 shows an example of a basic Spreadsheet component.

SPREADSHEET REFERENCE MADNESS

While reviewing this chapter, one of our capable Spreadsheet component developers, Andrew Milton, showed me many other types of range references supported by Excel but not supported by the Spreadsheet component. However, I had never seen most of these references and didn't even know they were possible in Excel. Try this:

1. Type *1, 2, 3, 4, 5* into the cells A1:A5.

2. Next, type the value *2* in cell B1.

3. Finally, enter the formula *=SUM(A1:CHOOSE(B1, A1, A2, A3, A4, A5))* into cell C1. You should get *3* as the result.

4. Now change cell B1 to *3*. The formula will recalculate to *6*.

The CHOOSE function acts like a Select Case statement in VBA and can be used in the middle of a range reference to define the range's end point dynamically. Defining a range dynamically also works with the INDIRECT function, but the Spreadsheet component simply doesn't support such dynamic range definition.

Range intersection is another interesting construct. On the same spreadsheet you used for the last example, type the formula *=A1:A5 A1:B1* into cell D1. You should get 1. This type of reference makes Excel perform an intersection of the two ranges, resolving to a reference of A1. The Spreadsheet component lets you enter a formula like this, but it resolves the formula to =A1, while Excel leaves the formula as you originally entered it.

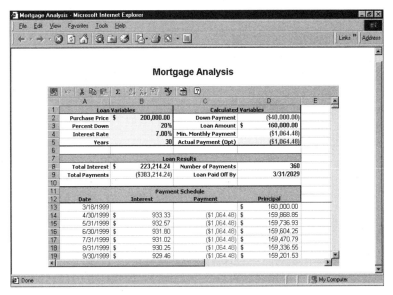

Figure 2-1. *A basic Spreadsheet component.*

The Spreadsheet component user interface contains a great number of spreadsheet features that people now take for granted. Rather than list every last one here, I'll leave you to discover most of them as you play with the control. Although the following list is not exhaustive, it should give you an idea of the level of user interface features supported by the Spreadsheet control:

- Column and row resizing
- See-through selection
- Semiselect when entering formulas
- Multilevel undo
- Insert and remove columns and rows
- Cut, copy, and paste
- Per-cell formatting, including font, background, alignment, and so on
- Full set of number formats, including euro support
- AutoFilter
- AutoSum

- Sort ranges
- Find
- Cell borders
- Hide or Show toolbar, row and column headers, and gridlines
- Merged cells
- Optional title bar
- Manual or automatic recalculation switch
- Protected cells and ability to disable insertion and deletion of rows and columns
- Viewable range and AutoFit

- Percent sizing and maximum size in Microsoft Internet Explorer
- Built-in online help
- Frozen panes
- Full keyboard support
- Control over the existence of scroll bars
- Control over current cell selection after return
- Worldwide, multilanguage, and right-to-left support

Since the Spreadsheet component is just a control and not an application unto itself, most of the formatting capabilities are exposed through a modeless tool window called the *Property Toolbox*. This part of the user interface is actually shared among all the components and used whenever the developer or user wants to change the formatting of an element in the control. A developer that wants to supply a custom runtime user interface or disable runtime changes altogether can disable the Property Toolbox at runtime by changing a property in the programming model. (I'll describe this process later in the chapter.)

Interestingly enough, the Property Toolbox was written entirely in Dynamic HTML (DHTML). The Office Web Components host an instance of the Internet Explorer control to render the Property Toolbox and execute its code when you interact with the elements on the web page. The Property Toolbox merely executes script against the component's programming model so that anything the Property Toolbox does, you can do in code too.

The Spreadsheet control, along with the other Office Web Components, supports the Office 2000 language settings that enable users to set the user interface language used in the Office applications without having to reset the underlying system regional settings. If these language settings have been changed from their defaults, the controls will automatically adjust their user interfaces to show the selected language. This also affects currency, date, and number formatting. The Spreadsheet component supports Unicode characters in cells, as well as right-to-left layout for those locales that require it.

Sorting and Filtering

While you are reading this section, you might find it useful to open the Samples\ Chap02\SortFilterExample.htm file on the companion CD. The code shown in this section and the scenario described stem from that file.

The Spreadsheet component supports the basic sorting and filtering functionality found in Excel and exposes it through the programming model and the user interface. However, the sort and filter user interface in the Spreadsheet control is somewhat improved over that in Excel. Let's look at an example.

ADVENTURES IN DHTML

The Property Toolbox is an incredible piece of work created by two of OWC's talented developers, Eric Matteson and Cesar Alvarez. The Property Toolbox is also proof that attempting to emulate Office user interface conventions in DHTML is just asking for trouble. Early on, we decided that we should make the Property Toolbox look as much like the standard Office user interface as possible, and Eric and Cesar faithfully spent many months twisting and contorting HTML and Internet Explorer to make it comply. Most people can't believe that the result is actually in HTML. However, the jury's still out on whether emulating the Office user interface in HTML makes it any easier to use, considering that the average person can use web sites quite effectively but is still befuddled by many of the advanced dialog boxes in the Office applications.

I think everyone would agree that it would have been much easier to follow the user interface conventions made popular on the Web and present a new kind of command interface born and bred in HTML. For developers intending to use the Office Web Components in web pages, my advice is not to spend your time trying to wrangle HTML into a traditional Microsoft Windows application user interface. Instead, use HTML's simplicity and dynamic layout strengths to develop a more natural, easy-to-use interface for your application.

Suppose you have developed a spreadsheet that lists your current product line, showing each product's unit price, quantity in stock, and quantity on order, as well as a calculated column showing a potential worth given a sell-through rate. Now the user wants to sort the list of products by their potential worth in descending order. Through the Spreadsheet component user interface, the user simply selects the range to sort (or selects any cell in the range) and clicks the Sort Descending toolbar button. When this button is clicked, a menu appears below it that does not appear in Excel, as Figure 2-2 depicts.

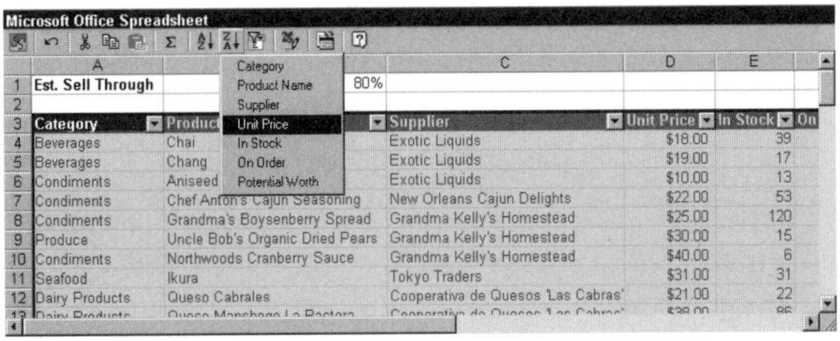

Figure 2-2. *The Spreadsheet component user interface in action.*

One of the common problems users encounter while sorting Excel ranges is selecting the range to sort and the column to sort by. The Spreadsheet component lets users easily select the range to sort, and it lets them choose the column to sort by from a list of column names that appears when the Sort Ascending Or Sort Descending toolbar button is clicked. The sorting functionality is also available through the programming model via the Sort method of the Range object. This allows the developer to easily enable list sorting when the user clicks or double-clicks a column heading.

You might notice that the Spreadsheet component lets you sort the list only one column at a time. Excel offers a Sort dialog box that lets you sort by up to three keys at once (for example, sort by category, then by shipper, and then by potential worth). The Spreadsheet component has no user interface for doing this, but the underlying engine does support it. To emulate multicolumn sorting, you can use the following routine:

```
' - - - - - - - - - - - - - - - - - - - - - - - - - - - - - - - - - - - - - - - - - - - - - - - - - -
' MultiColumnSort
' Purpose: Sorts the spreadsheet by many columns at once
' In:       References to the spreadsheet and range to sort,
'           an array of column numbers on which to sort,
'           and an array (same size) of direction indicators
' Out:      Nothing (performs the sort)
'
Sub MultiColumnSort(Spreadsheet, Range, Columns, Directions)
    ' Start an undo unit so that this can undo as a whole unit of work
    Spreadsheet.BeginUndo()

    ' Turn ScreenUpdating off so that the spreadsheet does not redraw
    ' while we are resetting filters, sorting, and reapplying filters
    Spreadsheet.ScreenUpdating = False

    ' Now loop over the Columns and Directions arrays backwards,
    ' which will give us the effect we want
    For ct = ubound(Columns) To lbound(Columns) Step -1
        ' 0 is a guess for column headings
        Range.Sort Columns(ct), Directions(ct), 0
    Next 'ct

    ' Turn ScreenUpdating back on so that the spreadsheet redraws
    Spreadsheet.ScreenUpdating = True

    ' End the undo unit
    Spreadsheet.EndUndo()

End Sub 'MultiColumnSort()
```

The trick to multicolumn sorts is to actually perform the sorts in the opposite order they're defined in. If you want to sort first by category and then by shipper, the routine first sorts the list by shipper and again by category. When the spreadsheet sorts a list by a new column, the previous ordering in another column is preserved within each item in the new column. The routine we just looked at accepts a range to sort, an array of column numbers, and an array of direction values (ascending or descending). The routine walks backwards along the two arrays, giving the effect of a multicolumn sort. Note that it also uses the BeginUndo and EndUndo methods to make all the sort operations part of one undo block so that they're undone together when the user chooses the Undo command.

The Spreadsheet component also sports a new AutoFilter user interface. The filtering functionality is similar to that found in Excel, but the AutoFilter drop-down lists in the user interface are a little different. Suppose that in the list of products we examined in Figure 2-2 you want to filter out some product categories to see how it would affect the products with high potential worth. The developer or user could turn on AutoFilter, click the AutoFilter arrow for the Category column, and see the screen shown in Figure 2-3.

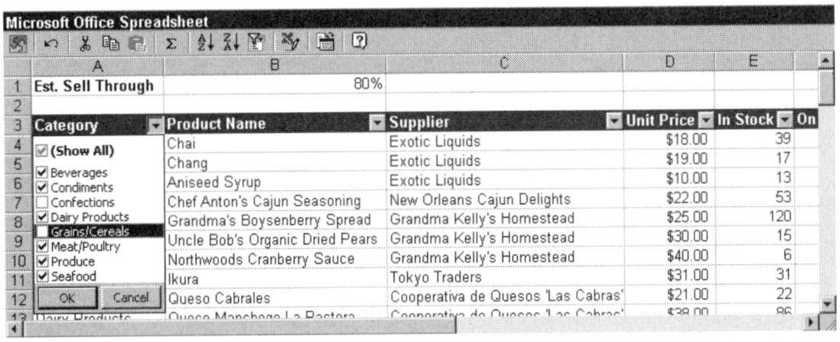

Figure 2-3. *The Spreadsheet component's AutoFilter user interface.*

In Excel, you can choose a single item quite easily; however, selecting more than one item requires using the Custom AutoFilter dialog box, which can be quite arduous when you simply want to exclude four or five items. In the Spreadsheet component, the AutoFilter drop-down list has check boxes next to each item, as well as a Show All item at the top that lets you quickly toggle all items between the checked and unchecked states.

The astute reader will notice that the AutoFilter drop-down lists do not include two of the useful settings found in Excel. For instance, you won't find a Top 10 item, which allows you to quickly filter for the top 10 (or any other number of) items. Nor will you find a Custom item, which you can use to perform more complex filtering than simple include and exclude filters allow. Unfortunately, these higher-level functions aren't built in to the Spreadsheet component yet. However, you can easily emulate them by making a few calls to the Spreadsheet control's programming model.

To emulate top *N* filtering, you can use the following routine:

```
'--------------------------------------------------------------------
' TopNFilter
' Purpose: Filters for the top N items in the list given a column number
' In:      References to the spreadsheet and range, column number,
'          number of rows, and direction value that indicates
'          top N or bottom N filtering
' Out:     Nothing (performs the top N filter)
'
Sub TopNFilter(Spreadsheet, Range, ColumnNum, N, Direction)
    Set c = Spreadsheet.Constants
    Set rngData = Range
    Set af = Spreadsheet.ActiveSheet.AutoFilter

    ' Start an undo unit so that this can undo as a whole unit of work
    Spreadsheet.BeginUndo()

    ' Turn ScreenUpdating off so that the spreadsheet does not redraw
    ' while we are resetting filters, sorting, and reapplying filters
    Spreadsheet.ScreenUpdating = False

    ' Clear any existing filters
    ClearFilters Spreadsheet

    ' Sort the list in the data range by the column number
    If LCase(Direction) = "bottom" Then
        rngData.Sort ColumnNum, c.ssAscending, c.ssNo
    Else
        rngData.Sort ColumnNum, c.ssDescending, c.ssNo
    End If

    ' Top N can actually include more than N rows if the N+1, N+2,
    ' and so on rows have the same value as the Nth row.
    ' Go to the N+1 row and see if it's the same as the Nth.
    ' Loop until there is a different value.
    vNValue = rngData.Cells(N,ColumnNum).Value

    While rngData.Cells(N+1,ColumnNum).Value = vNValue
        N = N + 1
    Wend

    ' N is now set to the number of rows we want to include in the filter
    Set fltr = af.Filters(ColumnNum)
    fltr.Criteria.FilterFunction = c.ssFilterFunctionInclude

    For ct = 1 To N
        fltr.Criteria.Add(rngData.Cells(ct,ColumnNum).Text)
    Next
```

```
' Finally apply the AutoFilter
af.Apply

' Turn ScreenUpdating back on so that the spreadsheet redraws
Spreadsheet.ScreenUpdating = True

' End the undo unit
Spreadsheet.EndUndo()

End Sub 'TopNFilter()
```

Top *N* filtering might seem as easy as sorting and then viewing the first *N* rows. But true top *N* filtering can return more than *N* rows because it really means "include the top *N* values." If the tenth and eleventh values are identical after the sort, a top 10 filter will return both products since they are among the top 10 values. The previous code can perform both top and bottom *N* filters by merely changing the sort direction from descending to ascending.

Similarly, you can emulate expression-based filtering using a routine like this:

```
'- - - - - - - - - - - - - - - - - - - - - - - - - - - - - - - - - - - - - - - - - - - - - - - - - - - - - - - - -
' ExpressionFilter
' Purpose: Filters a list on a given column using an arbitrary expression
'          that can be evaluated by VBScript
' In:      References to the spreadsheet and range, column number to
'          filter upon, and expression to use for evaluation
' Out:     None (list is filtered)
'
Sub ExpressionFilter(Spreadsheet, Range, ColumnNum, Expression)
    Dim sExp        ' Temporary expression variable
    Dim vValue      ' Temporary value holder

    Set c = Spreadsheet.Constants
    Set rngData = Range
    Set af = Spreadsheet.ActiveSheet.AutoFilter

    ' Start an undo unit so that this can undo as a whole unit of work
    Spreadsheet.BeginUndo()

    ' Turn ScreenUpdating off so that the spreadsheet does not redraw
    ' while we are resetting filters, sorting, and reapplying filters
    Spreadsheet.ScreenUpdating = False

    ' Clear any existing filters
    ClearFilters Spreadsheet

    ' Get the filter object for the specified column,
    ' and set the filter function to "include"
    Set fltr = af.Filters(ColumnNum)
    fltr.Criteria.FilterFunction = c.ssFilterFunctionInclude
```

(continued)

```
' Check whether the expression contains the column value token,
' and set a flag if it does
fValueToken = cbool( _
    instr(1, Expression, g_sValueToken, vbTextCompare) > 0)

' Loop over the column values in all the rows
For Each cell In rngData.Columns(ColumnNum).Cells
    ' Get the current row's value
    vValue = cell.Value

    ' If vValue is a string, we need to wrap quotes around it in
    ' case it contains spaces
    If vartype(vValue) = vbString Then
        vValue = """" & vValue & """"
    End If

    ' Build the expression we need to execute by inserting the
    ' current row's value in the right place
    If fValueToken Then
        sExp = "g_fEval = cbool(" & Replace(Expression, _
            g_sValueToken, vValue, 1, -1, vbTextCompare) & ")"
    Else
        sExp = "g_fEval = cbool(" & vValue & " " & Expression & ")"
    End If

    ' Execute the expression
    window.execScript sExp, "VBScript"

    ' The global g_fEval will now be set to True or False.
    ' If True, the row should be included in the filter.
    If g_fEval Then
        fltr.Criteria.Add cell.Text
    End If
Next 'ct

' Finally apply the AutoFilter
af.Apply

' Turn ScreenUpdating back on so that the spreadsheet redraws
Spreadsheet.ScreenUpdating = True

' End the undo unit
Spreadsheet.EndUndo()

End Sub 'ExpressionFilter()
```

This routine uses a Document Object Model (DOM) method named execScript to evaluate expressions. (DOM is the programming model exposed to scripting in Internet Explorer.) This method passes the script code in string form to the Active Scripting Engine (in this case, VBScript) for evaluation. The script code stores the result of the expression in a global variable that is then used to determine whether the expression is True or False. If the expression is True, the row is included in the filtered set; if False, the row is not included.

Alternatively, you can evaluate expressions by using the Eval method of the Spreadsheet component's Worksheet object. Eval uses the Spreadsheet component's function libraries and expression evaluator instead of the active scripting engine, meaning it's useful in containers other than Internet Explorer or when you want to let users include spreadsheet functions or range references in the expression. However, the active scripting engine can give you a powerful expression evaluator. Plus, it allows you to use other scripting languages, such as ECMA Script (also known as JavaScript).

Loading Data

Since the Spreadsheet component is not an application, the questions "Where does it get data from?" and "How can I save its data?" are crucial. Yet the answers to these questions are much more complicated than they would be for an application. The good news is that the Spreadsheet component can load and save data in a variety of ways that you can use creatively in your solutions.

Unlike an application, a component does not "own" the storage mechanism used by the container. It is the container's responsibility to save the entire form or document into a persistence mechanism and to reload it. A container usually asks the component to save its current state into a stream or *property bag;* the container then inserts the data into the middle of the form or document it is saving. Because of this, any component is somewhat at the mercy of its container to make loading and saving data easy. Needless to say, not all containers are created equal; some do a better job than others. Recognizing this, we designed the Spreadsheet component to be flexible in how it loads and saves data. In fact, you've got four ways to get data into the Spreadsheet control:

- Publish a spreadsheet or range from Excel 2000 with interactivity.

- Copy a range from Excel 2000, and paste it into the Spreadsheet control.

- Type data or a new set of formulas directly into the Spreadsheet control while it's in a designer such as Microsoft FrontPage 2000, Microsoft Script Editor, Microsoft Visual InterDev, or Microsoft Visual Basic.

■ Specify a URL to load data from, one that returns an HTML document with at least one HTML table in it. Alternatively, you can load Comma Separated Values (CSV) data from a URL.

Publishing from Excel

Publishing a spreadsheet or range from Excel 2000 with interactivity will prompt Excel to create an HTML file with an <object> tag for the Spreadsheet component. Excel copies the content of the selected spreadsheet or range into the HTML page as a parameter to the <object> tag, so once the data is published, it no longer refers to the source spreadsheet. However, you can easily republish content from Excel, and Excel will replace the previous content with the new content, preserving any other changes you made to the surrounding page.

To try publishing from Excel 2000, open your favorite workbook and choose the Save As Web Page command from the File menu. You will then see the dialog box depicted in Figure 2-4.

Figure 2-4. *Choose Save As Web Page to display this dialog box.*

Choose the Selection option, and check the Add Interactivity check box. When you save, instead of saving the content as static HTML, Excel will write a page containing the Spreadsheet control and a copy of the selected content. For more advanced control over what is published, click the Publish button to display the Publish As Web Page dialog box.

You might encounter an error message when attempting to publish certain spreadsheets to HTML. If the source spreadsheet is protected with a password (using the Tools|Protection|Protect Sheet command), Excel won't let you publish the spreadsheet or any range on it to a web page. Doing so is a breach of security since a web page is only plain text that anyone can open, view, and modify in any text editor. Spreadsheets are often protected with passwords when authors want to keep users from modifying certain parts. For example, a company expense report created in Excel is typically password protected so that employees can't adjust the formulas or validation rules.

Note that you can still use protection to lock most cells and let users change only the cells you've designated as updateable. As long as you don't use a password when protecting the spreadsheet, you can publish or copy the spreadsheet to the Spreadsheet component and all the protection settings will be preserved.

Copying and Pasting

Excel 2000 and the Spreadsheet component are both capable of reading and writing ranges in HTML table format, augmented with extra attributes and XML (Extensible Markup Language) code that conveys information specific to Excel. This means you can copy ranges from Excel 2000 and paste them into the Spreadsheet control and vice versa, which is useful for both authoring spreadsheets and copying data seen in a Spreadsheet control to Excel for further analysis.

You should note a few things when copying and pasting ranges. First, if a cell in the range has a formula referring to a cell that's not in the range, that's on another worksheet, or that's in another workbook, Excel will simply copy the current value for that cell but not the formula. Consider the problem for a moment: If you paste a formula referring to a cell that is outside the range of the copied cell into the Spreadsheet control, the Spreadsheet control has no way to resolve that reference and can't show any data. So any reference to a cell outside the copied range turns into a literal value that equals the value of the reference when it was copied.

Second, a more advanced structure in an Excel spreadsheet, such as a PivotTable, will paste only as literal data cells and not as a PivotTable structure. (In other words, you won't be able to pivot or drill to more detail.) The Office Web Components do, however, include the PivotTable component for performing PivotTable functionality. Charts will not paste at all since the Spreadsheet component isn't capable of hosting other controls or floating images.

Third, spreadsheet protection settings affect not only how the content gets published but also how it gets pasted into the Spreadsheet control. If the source spreadsheet is password protected, the range will still copy and paste, but only literal values will be pasted into the Spreadsheet component. If the spreadsheet is protected, but not with a password, the range will paste normally.

It's also interesting to note that the format of data pasted into the Spreadsheet component is HTML, so any application that can copy an HTML table to the clipboard can be used to get data into the Spreadsheet control. Excel 2000 does embed other information in the clipboard data, such as the formula and full-precision value for a given cell. However, if another application copies an HTML table to the clipboard without this extra information, the table will still be pasted into the Spreadsheet control as literal data with formatting.

Typing Directly into the Spreadsheet Component

There isn't much to say about this approach, except that you will find many of the features that make authoring spreadsheets easy in Excel missing in the Spreadsheet component. Nevertheless, you can still select cells while entering formulas to quickly enter cell references, set formatting information through the Property Toolbox, and hide or show various elements such as the title bar, toolbar, column and row headings, and gridlines. It's much more practical to author your spreadsheets in Excel 2000 and then publish or copy the content into the Spreadsheet component when done. But for simple spreadsheets, you might find it easier to type the model directly into the Spreadsheet control.

As noted earlier, not all containers make it easy to activate controls at design time and interact with them. Typing directly into the Spreadsheet component will work only in containers that allow controls to activate and that persist the control's content when saving.

USING THE SPREADSHEET COMPONENT IN VISUAL BASIC AND FRONTPAGE

Both Visual Basic and FrontPage make excellent containers for the Spreadsheet component; however, a few tips can help make the editing experience much easier.

In Visual Basic, the Spreadsheet control will be UI active as soon as you click it. This makes it hard to move the control around the form since clicking and dragging will simply select ranges of cells. However, you can move the entire control by clicking the title bar and then dragging the control. If the title bar isn't visible, set the DisplayTitleBar property to True to temporarily show it, and then set it to False to hide it.

When editing the Spreadsheet control in Visual Basic or FrontPage, you should also avoid using the AutoFit property (leave it set to False). Using AutoFit in Visual Basic is dangerous because the Spreadsheet control will resize to fit whatever content is loaded into it without scroll bars. If that content is larger than your Visual Basic form, the control will resize right off the edge of the form. However, if you know that the content will be smaller than the form and that it will never receive larger content, it's safe to use AutoFit.

In FrontPage 2000, the AutoFit behavior will not work in the Normal view; however, it will work correctly in the Preview view or in the web browser.

Loading from a URL

A URL is the most curious yet powerful mechanism for loading data into the Spreadsheet component. Using the Property Toolbox or the programming model, you can tell the Spreadsheet control to load its content by opening a specific URL and loading the first HTML table encountered. Alternatively, you can load CSV data returned from a URL. However, CSV lacks any formatting or formula information, so you will load only raw data values from a CSV stream. The data remains stored in the file the URL points to, and the Spreadsheet control loads the data every time it is initialized. Of course, this URL could easily point to a Microsoft Active Server Pages (ASP) page or a CGI program that generates HTML tables from an enterprise database or another storage system on the fly, enabling you to load the Spreadsheet control with dynamic, up-to-the-minute data.

Note that the Spreadsheet component uses the security mechanism in Internet Explorer to make sure that it doesn't load data from a domain other than the one where the first page originated (depending on your Internet Explorer security settings). This feature prevents malicious developers from sending you a web page containing the Spreadsheet control and the script that ran as the page loaded. If the security feature is not in place, a hacker can use your credentials to load sensitive data and then send that data to another location for his or her examination.

This feature uses the security settings the client specifies in Internet Explorer, so users can turn off cross-domain access warnings if they think the site the page originated from is "trusted." If the site is not in the trusted sites zone or has anything but the lowest security setting, the Spreadsheet control will warn the user before accessing a URL from any domain other than the one the original page came from. If the original page and the URL from which to load come from the same domain, the Spreadsheet component won't show any warnings because the situation is considered safe.

I'll discuss security a bit more in the chapters ahead. The Spreadsheet component's security mechanism is slightly different from security used when accessing databases (more on this in Chapter 5): it will never give the user the opportunity to permit cross-domain access when the URL refers to a site not in the trusted sites zone. The Spreadsheet control merely returns an error and says that it's not allowed, whereas in the database access scenario, the user can approve the cross-domain access if he or she chooses.

Unfortunately, the Spreadsheet control cannot load data directly from a binary XLS file, but it can load from an Excel file saved in HTML format by loading from a URL as described above. This allows developers building a spreadsheet model to use Excel 2000 for creation and maintenance. Plus, it lets developers load that model directly into the Spreadsheet control at runtime.

Is a Different Share on the Same File Server a Different Domain?

Near the end of the OWC product cycle, a tester posted a bug against the Spreadsheet component that said it was showing the security warning message even though the URL it was getting data from was on the same file server as the original HTML page. We were perplexed since it did seem that this should be a trusted scenario, but because we used Internet Explorer's security code to determine whether two URLs were from the same domain, we pushed the bug over to the Internet Explorer team.

It turns out that the page's URL and the data's URL were indeed pointing to the same file server but were pointing to different *shares* on that file server. The Internet Explorer team explained that technically these are two different domains since it's common to use mammoth file servers for many different groups in an organization, and those that have permissions to one share might not have the same permissions on the other share.

So if you are using file share access instead of a web server, keep in mind that different shares on the same file server are different domains as far as security is concerned. However, this applies only to file share access, not HTTP access to a web server.

Saving Data

Just as loading data into the Spreadsheet component is not as straightforward as in the Excel application, saving data from the Spreadsheet control can take place in various ways, making it difficult to explain.

Most containers don't allow the user to save the form or document while it is in a runtime state. For example, a Visual Basic form has no direct saving mechanism when it is running. Internet Explorer is slightly different: it offers a "save as" mechanism for running pages, but it doesn't allow users to alter the original page from the web server. (If that were possible, any hacker could alter your company's home page!) Often, when we show the Office Web Components to customers, one of their first assumptions is that they can change the content of a Spreadsheet control and resave it to the web server like a shared file. Because of the way the Web works, this isn't possible—unless Internet Explorer can return a new version of the page to the web server, which most servers wouldn't allow anyway.

To overcome these issues, we developed four ways to save data from the Spreadsheet control:

■ Use a tool such as FrontPage 2000 to open the web page for editing, make changes, and save the page to the web server. Internet Explorer 5 offers a new Edit With command on the File menu that quickly loads a page you're viewing into a registered HTML editor.

■ Use the Export To Excel toolbar button on the Spreadsheet control to quickly export its content to Excel 2000, where you can save it in an Excel workbook or republish it to the original file on the web server.

■ Copy the content of the Spreadsheet control to the clipboard, and paste it into Excel 2000.

■ As a developer, use the HTMLData property to retrieve the current content as a text stream and post it to an ASP page or a CGI program that saves it on the server. I'll demonstrate this technique in Chapter 8.

ADVANCED FUNCTIONALITY OF THE SPREADSHEET COMPONENT

Now that we've discussed the more basic features of the Spreadsheet component, let's move on to some of the advanced ones. Most of these do not exist in Excel 2000 since they enable specific functionality that is desirable in a component. Those that do exist in Excel 2000 have been enhanced to enable some new capabilities.

Property Binding and Real-Time Data

One of the most curious new features in the Spreadsheet component is *property binding,* which refers to the control's ability to use properties and methods of other objects on the same web page as cell values or formula arguments. The Spreadsheet control uses a standard COM mechanism for binding to properties, and when the source object notifies the control that the property's value has changed, the control automatically retrieves the new value and recalculates any dependent cells.

For example, if you develop a component that exposes properties and methods returning the last sale price for a given stock symbol, you can use the Spreadsheet control to view this information and see it change when the value updates. If other parts of the spreadsheet—such as the current user's portfolio information—refer to that last sale value, the Spreadsheet control also will recalculate those cells when the value changes.

To set up property binding, enter a function like this into a cell:

```
=document.StockTicker.Quote("msft").LastSale
```

Whenever the first part of the formula contains *=document.*, the Spreadsheet component knows that a property binding follows. The Spreadsheet control will expect the next part of the expression to be the ID of another element on the page, and the rest of the expression will resolve to a property of that element or of another element returned by a method. You can use a cell reference as an argument in a method call, and the Spreadsheet control will make sure to pass the real value to the method.

The object the cell is bound to can either be another COM object or any HTML element on the page, such as an edit box or a drop-down list. This allows you to include other data on the page in the recalculation model without having to write script to push the HTML element's value into a spreadsheet cell.

The property binding mechanism is often discussed in the context of real-time data feeds because it includes two necessary features for working with live data feeds:

- When notified that the property has changed, the Spreadsheet component updates the cell immediately, rather than on a fixed polling interval.

- The Spreadsheet component continues to listen for new values and updates cells *even while the user is editing other cells or invoking commands.* A common complaint about Excel's DDE links mechanism is that it doesn't do this, so we made sure to avoid the same mistake in the Spreadsheet control's property binding feature.

CAN A PROPERTY BINDING REFER TO THE SPREADSHEET COMPONENT ITSELF?

Adventurous readers are probably thinking wildly about the possibilities of binding cells in the Spreadsheet component back to the component itself or perhaps to another Spreadsheet component. On the surface, it might seem that you can support the dependence of cells in one spreadsheet upon cells in another spreadsheet simply by using this mechanism.

But alas, this is not possible. The Spreadsheet control itself prohibits such support because the reentrancy and circular reference possibilities are absolutely frightening. The Spreadsheet control only knows it is bound to another object—not to itself or another Spreadsheet control—so it cannot check that a reference doesn't create a circular dependency that would hang the recalculation chain.

To have cells dependent on cells in another Spreadsheet component, you must write code in the other component that responds to the Change event and pushes new values into the dependent cells.

Of course, keep in mind that the Spreadsheet component's ability to process property change notifications is entirely dependent on how long it takes to recalculate the current model. For small and medium-sized models, this usually isn't a concern since recalculation takes one second or less—far faster than most people want to see new data flash before their eyes. However, if the model is quite large, the Spreadsheet control can only process new values as fast as it can recalculate, which might be slower than the rate at which new values arrive.

I'll cover property binding in greater detail in Chapter 10, where you'll see how to build a stock ticker control in Visual Basic that feeds real-time quotes to a stock portfolio spreadsheet.

Function Add-Ins

As in Excel, developers can use function add-ins to incorporate new functions into the Spreadsheet component. Unlike the add-ins that follow Excel's proprietary XLL model, function add-ins for the Spreadsheet component are created as COM objects. Any method exposed by such an object is added as a potential function that you can use in formulas, just as you would do using the intrinsic Excel functions.

For example, if you develop a COM object with a method called SumTopN that takes a range of values and returns the sum of the top N numbers, you can make that function available in the Spreadsheet component by executing the following code, most likely in the Window_onLoad event:

```
Spreadsheet1.AddIn MyObject
```

The MyObject variable should point to an instance of the custom function object. To ensure that your object is available, use an <object> tag on the page and pass the value of the id attribute to the Spreadsheet control's AddIn method, like so:

```
<object classid="clsid:0002E510-0000-0000-C000-000000000046"
    id=Spreadsheet1>
</object>
<object classid="clsid:ClsidOfYourObject"
    codebase=PathToCABfileOfYourObject id=MyObject>
<script language=VBScript>
Spreadsheet1.AddIn MyObject.Object
</script>
```

The codebase attribute in the <object> tag tells Internet Explorer where to install the object from if the object referenced by the class ID isn't on the client's machine. To learn more about the codebase attribute, see the Internet Explorer and DHTML topics in the Microsoft Developer Network (MSDN) Libraries.

Using the Object property is necessary only in Internet Explorer or other containers that wrap objects with a different interface. In the HTML file we just examined, MyObject actually refers to a COM object type known as *object*, which represents the <object> tag, not the actual COM object that the tag created. The Object property returns the pointer to the real COM object.

In Visual Basic, you would still call the AddIn method but would pass a variable that refers to an instance of a class you created. For example:

```
Dim MyAddIn As New FunctionLib
Spreadsheet1.AddIn MyAddIn
```

In C++, the technique is exactly the same, but you would of course use the coCreateInstance function and pass a reference to the IDispatch interface of your object to the AddIn method.

The Spreadsheet component actually uses this add-in mechanism for loading the functions used less often. Not all the Spreadsheet control's functions are implemented in the primary Office Web Components DLL file, named Msowc.dll. The ones used less often are actually implemented in Msowcf.dll (the "f" stands for *extended function library*); the Spreadsheet component automatically adds them to the add-in list the first time you use them. The extended functions are implemented as COM objects with a series of methods, one for each function exposed.

You might be wondering if function add-ins are any different than the property binding mechanism described earlier. The answer is yes. Property bindings listen for source notification that a value has changed, whereas function add-ins are called only when an input to the function (or a cell affecting the input) changes. This is essentially the difference between a push model and a pull model: Property binding is like a push model; it can push new values into the Spreadsheet control whenever it deems this necessary. Function add-ins, on the other hand, have no communication channel back to the Spreadsheet component; the Spreadsheet component determines when it needs to call the function add-in to calculate a new value.

The line between push and pull can get fuzzy sometimes, especially when you consider the strange and rather interesting side effect caused by Internet Explorer's ability to expose script functions on the page as an object. All the various <script> blocks on your page are exposed as a DOM object called Script, and each function or subroutine defined in those <script> blocks is exposed as a method of that Script object. This means you can use script functions on your page as functions in your spreadsheet, but the mechanism you use to do this is more akin to property binding than to using function add-ins.

For example, suppose you have a <script> block on the page like this:

```
<script language="VBScript">
Function VBDateAdd(interval, number, date)
    On Error Resume Next
    VBDateAdd = DateAdd(interval, number, date)
End Function
</script>
```

The Spreadsheet component doesn't have terrific date manipulation functions. However, VBScript offers the flexible DateAdd function that lets you add (or subtract, by using a negative number for the interval argument) any number of intervals to a given date. To enable the Spreadsheet component to use this function, the previous <script> block defines a function called VBDateAdd that returns the results of the VBScript function DateAdd. To use VBDateAdd in your spreadsheet, enter the following formula into a cell in which you want the result placed:

```
=document.script.VBDateAdd(B1, B2, B3)
```

This will use the current values in cells B1, B2, and B3 for the interval, number, and date arguments, respectively. The formula is put into the dependency chain just as any other formula, and any time one of those input cells changes, the Spreadsheet component will call this function, passing the new input values and displaying the new result.

Using script functions has its advantages and disadvantages. Scripts are executed in an interpreted manner, meaning they will usually be slower than compiled code. Scripts also are limited to the capabilities of the scripting language and are limited in their interaction with the client computer and the network because of security restrictions. However, compiled objects require downloading and installation on the client machine, which might not be allowed in certain organizations and can have a potentially negative impact on the client machine if the object wasn't implemented and tested well. By definition, scripts in web pages are "safe," and since they are interpreted on the fly, they don't require additional files to be downloaded or installed.

Of course, script functions are only relevant when the container is Internet Explorer. For example, if you are using the Spreadsheet component in a Visual Basic form, you can still use function add-ins, but there is no concept of script blocks in a page. Note that the AddIn method takes a reference to a COM object, so if you are using Visual Basic for your application, you can use any public class in the same project as a function add-in object. Just create an instance of it, and pass a reference to the Spreadsheet control's AddIn method.

Viewable Range and AutoFit

Spreadsheet applications often display just a portion of the spreadsheet surface rather than show all the columns and rows. For example, a timesheet application will show enough columns and rows so that the user can enter his or her work times without having to see numerous blank columns and rows surrounding the data. The Spreadsheet control lets you do this through its ViewableRange property, which you can also set through the Property Toolbox at design time.

The *viewable range* defines how many columns and rows the spreadsheet displays. The default value is to show all columns and rows, but you can change this—either in script or in the Property Toolbox at design time—to any valid range reference. For example, setting the range to A1:D6 makes the spreadsheet show only four columns and six rows. The rest of the spreadsheet appears as a blank gray area; the user cannot select or move anywhere outside the viewable range. The cells outside the viewable range still exist and can be referenced in script code, but the user cannot see or interact with them. This is an excellent way to hide lookup tables or intermediate calculated values that you don't want your users to see.

The viewable range can be adjusted dynamically through code, so you can adjust the viewable range in reaction to other user events. Also note that the viewable range has the same auto-adjustment characteristics that normal ranges do—if the developer or user inserts a column or row inside the viewable range, the viewable range will extend by one column or row. Also, remember that the ViewableRange property is a String rather than a Range object, so if you want to retrieve a Range object for the entire viewable range, you need to write code like this:

```
Set rngViewable = Spreadsheet1.Range(Spreadsheet1.ViewableRange)
```

Setting the viewable range does not automatically alter the size of the Spreadsheet control within its container. However, once you have defined a viewable range, you can set the AutoFit property to True, which will cause the spreadsheet to resize itself so that it can show the entire viewable range without scroll bars. If the viewable range is smaller than the current size, it will shrink; if it's larger, it will grow.

Two other properties govern how large the Spreadsheet control can grow so that it does not become ridiculously huge. The MaxHeight and MaxWidth properties determine the height and width thresholds for the spreadsheet. If the viewable range is larger than the maximum height and width allow for, the spreadsheet will show the internal scroll bars so that the user can navigate over the entire range.

The MaxHeight and MaxWidth properties can be set to percentages when running in Internet Explorer. For example, if MaxWidth is set to 80 percent, the spreadsheet will allow itself to grow to 80 percent of the size of the containing element. If the spreadsheet is inside the <body> element, for example, the spreadsheet can grow to 80 percent of the document width. If it is inside a table cell, the spreadsheet can grow to 80 percent of the table cell's width. This percent sizing capability also applies to the normal Width and Height properties of Internet Explorer. Such a capability can be extremely useful in the world of dynamic HTML layout and can be used to make sure the spreadsheet looks correct on the page regardless of window size or monitor resolution.

The Spreadsheet Component as a Data Source

One of the most common requests heard in the Excel group is for Excel to be an OLE DB provider for data contained in an XLS file. When we built the Spreadsheet component, we knew that we had to provide a way for the Chart component to retrieve ranges of data from the Spreadsheet component to chart them. The Chart component also had to know when those values changed so that it could update the chart. Happily, these requirements match those for OLE DB data binding, so we decided to make the Spreadsheet control a real OLE DB data source. I'll discuss exactly what this means from a technical perspective in a moment. But first, an example will help clarify this point.

In Internet Explorer, you can data-bind a number of HTML elements to any control that is a valid *data source*. Internet Explorer 5 has the ability to bind elements to a particular *data member* within a data source in cases where the data source has one or more data members. For example, if you have a data source control on the page named tdcComposers, you can bind an HTML table to it using the following HTML fragment:

```
<table datasrc=#tdcComposers>
<thead>
    <tr style="font-weight:bold">
        <td>First</td><td>Last</td>
        <td>Birth</td><td>Death</td><td>Origin</td>
    </tr>
</thead>
<tbody>
    <tr>
        <td><div datafld="compsr_first"></div></td>
        <td><div datafld="compsr_last"></div></td>
        <td><div datafld="compsr_birth"></div></td>
        <td><div datafld="compsr_death"></div></td>
        <td><div datafld="origin"></div></td>
    </tr>
</tbody>
</table>
```

In the same manner, you can bind an HTML table to the contents of a range in the Spreadsheet component. The following HTML fragment is taken from the file SpreadsheetDS.htm on the companion CD:

```
<table datasrc=#Spreadsheet1.A2:D7 border=1>
<thead>
    <tr>
        <th>Salesperson</th>
        <th>FY98 Sales</th>
        <th>Projected Growth</th>
        <th>Est. FY99 Sales</th>
    </tr>
</thead>
<tbody>
    <tr>
        <td><div datafld="A"></div></td>
        <td><div datafld="B"></div></td>
        <td><div datafld="C"></div></td>
        <td><div datafld="D"></div></td>
    </tr>
</tbody>
</table>
```

The Spreadsheet control implements the IDataSource interface, which is the standard data source interface defined and supported by Internet Explorer and Visual Basic version 6 and later. These containers consider any control implementing this interface to be a valid source of data to other data-bound controls on the page or form. A data source control can expose any number of data members, each of which is identified by a string and returns an OLE DB Rowset. The Spreadsheet control exposes a nearly limitless number of data members because any valid range reference is a valid data member. For example, the previous HTML fragment asks for a data member named A2:D7 and gets a Rowset of two columns and seven rows. The magic syntax in Internet Explorer 5 for specifying the data member is <ID of Data Source Control>.<Data Member Name>. The ID is preceded by a hash symbol (#) to indicate that the source is a control on the same page. For the Spreadsheet component, any valid range reference can be passed for the data member name.

The Spreadsheet component also implements the OLE DB Simple Provider interface, sometimes known as OSP, when exposing ranges of data. This interface was defined to make exposing data in OLE DB a tad easier than implementing IRowset and the other interfaces of OLE DB, and the OLE DB Simple Provider toolkit provider will map OSP into a full IRowset interface for data-bound controls that want to work with the IRowset interface. In fact, Internet Explorer will automatically use these mappers when the bound control requests an IRowset interface but the source returns an OSP interface.

The Spreadsheet component's implementation of the OLE DB Simple Provider interface is read/write, and it will raise the appropriate notifications when data in the source range changes so that bound controls know to refresh their contents with new values.

KEY ELEMENTS OF THE PROGRAMMING MODEL

To conclude our introduction to the Spreadsheet component, I'll cover the key elements of the control's programming model so that you'll know how to get the control working and where to go when you want to write script for different functionality. This section is not a full reference to the programming model—that would be a book unto itself. Instead, the properties and methods you'll commonly use are presented here, along with a brief description of each. For more information on any part of the programming model, refer to the online help in the Msowcvba.chm file, which you can find in the local folder under the Office folder (generally Program Files\Microsoft Office\Office\1033 for English-speaking people).

If you are at all familiar with the Excel programming model, you will notice that the Spreadsheet component's programming model is quite similar.

Working with Enumerations in Script

COM and OLE Automation enable components to define *enumerations,* each of which is a named set of constant values that acts like a type declaration in a programming language. A property or method argument can be typed as an enumeration, which causes environments such as Visual Basic and Microsoft Visual C++ to display the statement completion drop-down list containing the valid constants for that enumeration. The Office Web Components, like many other ActiveX controls, have a predefined set of enumerations.

However, in scripting environments such as a web page or an ASP page, no notion of types exists. Therefore, no ability to use enumeration member names in script languages exists since these languages have no way of knowing what a particular constant, such as ssHAlignLeft, evaluates to. This means your VBScript or ECMA Script code can get littered with magical numbers that are not self-describing.

To alleviate this problem, all the Office Web Components have a top-level property called Constants that can be used in scripting languages to access their various enumeration members. For example, if you want to use ssHAlignLeft in VBScript code to align a cell's contents to the left, you can write code like this:

```
MyRange.HAlignment = Spreadsheet1.Constants.ssHAlignLeft
```

To use an enumeration constant, you refer to it as though it were a property of the Constants object, and the object will return the correct enumeration member value.

41

Note that it's useful to set a variable equal to the Constants object if you plan on using it in more than one line of your function, both to avoid unnecessary typing and for better performance. For example, you can write something like this:

```
Set c = Spreadsheet1.Constants
MyRange.HAlignment = c.ssHAlignRight
MyRange.VAlignment = c.ssVAlignBottom
```

This Constants object is meant only for scripting languages that have no concept of enumerations. If you are writing code in Visual Basic, VBA, or C++, simply use the enumerations as you normally would and ignore the Constants object.

Getting Data into the Component

I discussed a number of techniques for getting data into the Spreadsheet component earlier. I'll describe those that involve the programming model in more detail here. Table 2-1 lists the relevant properties and methods for loading data, all of which are exposed from the Spreadsheet object's interface.

Property or Method	Description
Spreadsheet.DataType	A string-based property that tells the Spreadsheet component which of the properties to use for loading data if more than one is set. The value to which you set this property is the name of the other property you want it to use—for example, setting it to HTMLURL will cause the component to load the data returned from the URL in the HTMLURL property.
Spreadsheet.HTMLData	A string-based property that can be used to get or set the spreadsheet's contents in an HTML table format. The format also contains extra attributes and XML tags that are used to keep information that is necessary to reconstruct the spreadsheet model (such as a cell formula) but that is not part of the HTML 3.2 table format. You can set this property to a string containing an HTML table, or you can get the value of this property to obtain the entire contents of the spreadsheet when necessary for persistence.
Spreadsheet.HTMLURL	A string-based property that contains a URL from which to load the spreadsheet. The URL must return an HTML document with a table in it. A spreadsheet saved in HTML format from Excel 2000 can be loaded using this property, or this property can refer to an ASP page or a CGI program that builds tables from a database on the fly.

Table 2-1. *Properties and methods for loading data.*

Property or Method	*Description*
Spreadsheet.CSVData	A string-based property similar to the HTMLData property, except that the format of the data it accepts or returns is CSV. This property is useful when trying to load data from older systems that aren't capable of emitting HTML.
Spreadsheet.CSVURL	A string-based property similar to the HTMLURL property, except that the format it expects from the URL is again CSV. Just as in the HTMLURL case, this URL can be an ASP page or a CGI program that gets data from a mainframe or minicomputer and returns it to the caller.
Spreadsheet.LoadText	A method used to load a delimited text file into the spreadsheet. Unlike the CSV format, the text file format can use any set of field delimiters. LoadText and its cousin ParseText are also available for the Range object for loading text into a specific range of the spreadsheet. LoadText can refer to a file in your file system or to a URL.

Working with Ranges

The most commonly used programming interface in the Spreadsheet component is that of the Range object. Range objects are returned from many methods and are used whenever you want to modify the contents, formatting, sort order, or filter settings of a range of cells. Table 2-2 shows the properties and methods of the Range object that you should know about when building solutions with the Spreadsheet component.

Property or Method	*Description*
Spreadsheet.Range	This method returns a Range object given a range reference (such as A1:B2 or A:B). Because a range can be just one cell, you can also pass a single cell reference (such as A1). The Range method can also take two different cell references and return a bounding range.
Range.Address	This property returns the address of the range (for example, A1:B2).

Table 2-2. *Principal Range object properties and methods.* *(continued)*

Table 2-2. *continued*

Property or Method	Description
Range.Cells	I was highly confused by this property when I first saw it because it's typed to return another Range object. However, you can use this property as a collection of cells, meaning that you can access the individual cells using a For Each loop. The property can also be accessed as a two-dimensional array. For example, MyRange.Cells(1,3).Value will return the value from row 1, column 3 in the range. There is also a Cells property for the Spreadsheet and Worksheet objects, so you can use it instead of the Range method (described earlier) to access specific cells.
Range.Column, Range.Row	These properties indicate the number of the first column and first row in the range. They are useful when you're iterating over a range of columns or rows and want to know what column or row you're at.
Range.Columns, Range.Rows	Although strikingly similar in name to the previous two properties, this duo returns a collection of columns or rows contained in the Range object. Range.Columns.Count and Range.Rows.Count tell you the number of columns and rows in the current range.
Range.HTMLData	This property is similar to Spreadsheet.HTMLData, except that it is read-only for the Range object. Use it to quickly get an HTML table representation of the data in a given range.
Range.Value	This property gets or sets a variant value for the range. Although the help file states that Range.Value returns a two-dimensional array of variants if the range constitutes more than one cell, it actually isn't implemented in this version. However, Range.Value can accept a two-dimensional array of variants for putting data into the range. Use this property when you want to set the cell or cells to a literal value or when you want to get a cell's current unformatted value.

Property or Method	Description
Range.Formula	This property is used to read or write the formula string for a cell. Use it when you want to get or set the formula for a cell or cells in a range, and remember to use the equals sign (=) at the beginning of the formula.
Range.Text	The Range.Text property returns the formatted version of the Range.Value property. It is useful when you need to present the formatted value in a message box or another user interface element, and it's the value you pass when adding AutoFilter criteria.

Formatting

Once you have loaded data into the spreadsheet, you might want to apply formatting programmatically. Each cell can have its own font, alignment, border, color, and number formatting, and all these aspects are set using the properties shown in Table 2-3.

Property	Description
Range.NumberFormat	A string-based property that controls the formatting used for a cell's numeric value. A number of built-in formats that you can use by name exist (such as Currency). You can also construct your own format definitions (for example, #,###, which makes 1000 appear as 1,000).
Range.Font	A property that returns the common Font object used by many of the components. Range.Font lets you set various properties of the Font object such as Name, Size, Bold, Italic, Color, and Underline. Note that you can use the Internet Explorer color names with the Font.Color property if you want.
Range.Halignment, Range.Valignment	Two properties that control the horizontal and vertical text alignment within the range's cells. Enumerations that contain the possible alignment values are defined for each of these properties.
Range.Borders	A property returning the Borders object that lets you set the various aspects of each cell border, such as line weight, line style, and line color.

Table 2-3. *Formatting properties.*

Component-Level Appearance and Behavior

A number of properties and methods affect the entire Spreadsheet component. Table 2-4 shows the most interesting ones for custom solutions.

Property	Description
Spreadsheet.AllowPropertyToolbox	Controls whether the Property Toolbox can be shown. If AllowProperty-Toolbox is set to False, the Property Toolbox toolbar icon and context menu command are disabled. You use this property any time you want to disable the default formatting user interface and supply your own.
Spreadsheet.AutoFit	Determines whether the control is in AutoFit mode. See the section earlier on AutoFit for more details on how this feature works.
Spreadsheet.Dirty	Tells you if anything has changed in the control. If any cell has been modified, this property returns True. You commonly use the Dirty property to determine whether you need to save the contents in some way. Note that this is a read/write property, so you can also reset it to make the spreadsheet "clean" again.
Spreadsheet.DisplayColHeaders, Spreadsheet.DisplayRowHeaders	Control whether the column and row headers are displayed. These two properties are True by default. Normally, you set them to False if you want to have total control over the spreadsheet surface from your code.
Spreadsheet.DisplayGridlines	Controls whether gridlines are displayed. By default they are, and it's common to turn them off for custom solutions that use borders in specific places where you want cell separator lines.
Spreadsheet.DisplayPropertyToolbox	Controls whether the Property Toolbox is displayed. Set this to True to display it or False to hide it.

Table 2-4. *Principal properties that affect the spreadsheet as a whole.*

Property	*Description*
Spreadsheet.DisplayTitleBar	Controls whether the title bar is displayed. The title bar is displayed by default. Use the TitleBar property described below to modify the contents and formatting of the title bar.
Spreadsheet.DisplayToolbar	Controls whether the toolbar is displayed. The toolbar is displayed by default.
Spreadsheet.EnableAutoCalculate	Controls how the spreadsheet model recalculates. If this property is set to False, the spreadsheet model will not automatically recalculate; you must call the Calculate method of the Worksheet object to see new results for changed inputs. This property can be useful if you plan to make many changes to a set of inputs and want to recalculate the model only when you're done with all the changes. By default, this property is True—models will automatically recalculate when changed.
Spreadsheet.ScreenUpdating	By default, the screen display of the spreadsheet always reflects the most current data, but you can set this property to False if you plan to perform a number of operations and don't want the spreadsheet to flicker after each one. Setting this property back to True causes a full repaint.
Spreadsheet.Selection	Returns the currently selected object. You can use the TypeName function in VBA or VBScript to determine what type of object it is.
Spreadsheet.TitleBar	Gives you access to the Spreadsheet control's title bar, which you can change the text and formatting of.
Spreadsheet.ViewableRange	Controls what part of the spreadsheet is actually visible. See the earlier discussions of ViewableRange and Auto-Fit for more details on how this works.

Sorting and Filtering

Table 2-5 lists the properties and methods you will use when sorting and filtering data in the Spreadsheet component.

Property or Method	Description
Range.Sort	This method sorts the range given a column and sort direction.
Worksheet.AutoFilter	This property returns the AutoFilter object that can be used to set up the details of a current filter.
AutoFilter.Filters	This property returns the Filters collection for the current AutoFilter range. One Filter object applies to each column in the AutoFilter range, and the index of the Filter object matches the column index in the range.
AutoFilter.Apply	This method applies a new AutoFilter. After you've set up the criteria, you must call this method to actually apply the filter.
Criteria.FilterFunction	This property controls whether the criteria is included in the filter or excluded from it. Include filters include exactly the items in the criteria set, while exclude filters exclude the items in the criteria set but include everything else.
Criteria.ShowAll	This property determines whether all data will be shown. When set to True, the property resets a filter to show all data. When set to False, assuming there are no filter criteria, it shows no data.
Criteria.Add	This method is used to add new criteria to a filter.
Range.AutoFilter	This method is used to turn AutoFilter on for a given range. Call this method first, and then use the Worksheet.AutoFilter property (described above) to access the filters and set up the criteria.

Table 2-5. *Properties and methods for sorting and filtering.*

Protection

If you want to protect part of the spreadsheet so that your users cannot modify cell contents or change cell formatting, you need to work with the properties that control protection. Table 2-6 lists the common protection properties and gives a brief description of how each is used.

Note that the protection settings apply to user interactions through the user interface and to operations performed in code. If you want to delete rows while a protection option is enabled, you must set the Enabled property of the Protection object to False before performing the operation, and then set it back to True to return to the protected state.

Property	*Description*
Worksheet.Protection	Returns the Protection object for which you set the various protection options that enable global actions such as inserting or deleting rows.
Protection.Enabled	Controls whether protection in general is enabled. To use the protection options or lock cells, first set the option or lock the cells and then set this property to True. You can set this property to False to temporarily disable protection while you perform operations in code.
Protection.AllowInsertingColumns, Protection.AllowInsertingRows, Protection.AllowDeletingColumns, Protection.AllowDeletingRows	Enable or disable the ability to insert or delete columns or rows in the spreadsheet. For example, if AllowInsertingRows is set to False, the spreadsheet will disable all commands that can be used to insert a row, including those in the programming model.
Protection.AllowSizingAllColumns, Protection.AllowSizingAllRows	Enable or disable the ability to resize columns or rows. For example, if AllowSizingAllRows is set to False, the spreadsheet won't allow the user to resize the rows, nor will it let you do so through code.
Protection.AllowSorting	Allows or prohibits the sorting of data in the spreadsheet. Set AllowSorting to False to prohibit users from sorting the contents of any range.
Protection.AllowFiltering	Allows or prohibits the use of the AutoFilter feature. Set this property to False to prohibit users from enabling the AutoFilter feature.

Table 2-6. *Common protection properties.*

Undo

Table 2-7 lists the relevant properties and methods you will use when controlling the Undo mechanism of the Spreadsheet component.

Property or Method	Description
Spreadsheet.BeginUndo	A method that enables you to treat a number of operations as one undo operation. For example, if you call BeginUndo and then perform three different sorts or change many cells, you can undo all these operations at once.
Spreadsheet.EndUndo	A method that marks the end of your logical undo unit. All operations performed between the BeginUndo call and the EndUndo call will be undone as a single unit.
Spreadsheet.EnableUndo	A property that controls whether the undo feature is available. By default, it is. You might want to temporarily disable this feature to save memory or perform a number of operations in code.

Table 2-7. *Properties and methods for controlling undo.*

Useful Events

A number of events are exposed from the top-level Spreadsheet object, more than from any other control in the OWC library. Table 2-8 lists several of the key events you likely will want to use when developing custom solutions around the Spreadsheet component.

Nearly all the events in the Spreadsheet control pass a single parameter of type SpreadsheetEventInfo to the event handler. SpreadsheetEventInfo is a COM object that you can use to retrieve all kinds of information about the state of the application when the event was fired, including what was selected, what range was affected, where the mouse was, what keys were pressed, and so on. This mirrors the treatment of event information in the DOM.

The biggest reason to use an object as the parameter is to support cancelable events in JavaScript. Parameters passed to an event in JavaScript are always passed by value unless they are object pointers. In other words, if the OWC team had designed the events with a ReturnValue *parameter* that the script set to True to cancel the event, it wouldn't work in JavaScript because of the parameter being passed by value. However, if the script sets an object's ReturnValue *property* to True, the control raising the event will see it. So if you want to cancel an event (most of the events whose names begin with "Before" can be canceled), set the ReturnValue property of the SpreadsheetEventInfo object to False.

Event	Description
Spreadsheet.Change	Fires any time a change is made to a cell or cells in the spreadsheet. Use the Range property of the SpreadsheetEventInfo object to determine the range affected.
StartEdit, EndEdit, CancelEdit	Raised whenever a cell is about to be edited, was just edited, or just had its edit canceled. You can perform data validation in the EndEdit event and set the ReturnValue property of the SpreadsheetEventInfo object to True to deny the new value. Use the EditData property of the SpreadsheetEventInfo object to get the new value for the cell. Use the StartEdit event to replace a displayed value with another element for editing purposes, such as using a TrueType font for displaying a special symbol instead of a text description.
BeforeCommand, Command	Raised just before and after a command—an action such as sorting; filtering; inserting or deleting rows or columns; showing help; and cutting, copying, or pasting—is processed. See the list of Sheet-CommandEnum constants in the Msowcvba.chm file or in your object browser for all the possible commands you can catch using these events. Again, set the ReturnValue property to False in the BeforeCommand event if you want to cancel the default behavior for an event. For example, you might want to show your own help page when the user clicks the Help button on the spreadsheet toolbar.

Table 2-8. *Useful events.*

Retrieving Version Information

Sometimes you need to find out the version of the control you're working with so that you can either take advantage of new features or use workaround code to solve problems in an older version. Most software programs have service releases between their major version releases, so you often need to verify that the version your code is talking to is indeed the version you expect.

To help you do so, we added the properties listed in Table 2-9 to every control in the Office Web Components library. You can use them to determine the version of the control you're coding against and take the appropriate action.

Property	Description
MajorVersion	A long integer value that indicates the major version number of the component. For the Office 2000 release, this number is 9.
MinorVersion	A string-based value that indicates the minor version number of the component. For the Office 2000 release, this number is 0 and will be incremented if any minor releases occur before the next major version release. Note that MinorVersion is a string value in case an "a" release occurs. It's best to perform an equality comparison on this value rather than a greater-than or less-than comparison.
BuildNumber	A string-based value that indicates the build number of the component. The build number is incremented with every build of the component DLL, and the value for the Office 2000 release wasn't yet available at the time of this writing. Again, this is a string value, so it can handle cases in which a letter is added to a version number in the event of a minor release.
Version	A string-based value that returns the entire version number. Use the Version property when displaying the version, but use the other properties for determining whether the version is the one you want.

Table 2-9. *Version information properties for all Office Web Components.*

SUMMARY

We've covered a lot of ground on the Spreadsheet component in this chapter; however, we've got plenty left to discuss in the solution chapters involving this control. So far, I've explained all the necessary conceptual information. In Part II of the book, you'll see these concepts put to work in real-world examples.

Chapter 3

The Chart Component

Now that you have an understanding of the Spreadsheet component, let's examine the functionality and programming model of the Chart component. As in the previous chapter, after describing a given feature, I will present a few interesting uses for it. In Part II of the book, you will see many of these ideas actually implemented.

This chapter will also show you some clever ways to add functionality to the Chart component using your own code. The Chart component might seem a bit less complex than the Spreadsheet or PivotTable components at first, but it has some powerful features that you can use in your solutions. Plus, it offers many "knobs" that you can adjust to customize a chart to your liking.

THE BASICS OF THE CHART COMPONENT

The Chart component is a COM control that was built by the same team that developed charting in Microsoft Excel 2000. It provides basic business charting both as an onscreen COM control and as an in-memory, GIF-generating engine. In this first version, the Chart control supports all the two-dimensional chart types found in Excel (except for the Contour type) with the addition of the Polar, Stacked Pie, and Filled Scatter chart types. This version does not contain any three-dimensional chart types or effects.

One new feature that I will discuss in this chapter is the Chart control's ability to display more than one chart within the overall *chart space* of the component. The Chart control is actually composed of an entire chart space containing one or more charts that all share the same set of categories. (I will explain the term "categories" in more detail later in this section.) Normally, you will have only one chart in the control at a time; however, having multiple charts in the same chart space makes it easier to compare similar information at a glance. I will describe chart spaces in more detail toward the end of the chapter.

Like the Spreadsheet component, the Chart component has a number of basic features and some distinct terminology that you should become familiar with before we move on to more advanced topics.

The Nomenclature of Charting

During the development of a new feature in Excel 2000 charting, the OWC team conducted a number of usability tests to determine whether our design was easy to use. For those who have never heard of such tests, we take real customers from companies and homes throughout the Seattle area and put them in front of a prototype for a new feature. We ask the people to perform a number of tasks and watch to see how they approach them and whether the design was effective in helping them accomplish the assignment. Often, we find that our expectations were far from reality— meaning we have to go back and redesign the feature.

In one particular test, we showed people various charts we created in Excel with certain parts circled. We asked them to tell us what they thought the name of the circled part should be. Logically, you would expect us to find some commonality and discover the "name" that most people already associate with a particular element. We could then use that name in our documentation, programming models, onscreen user interface, and so on. Much to our dismay, we discovered absolutely no standard names for elements within a chart. You might expect that people would know which is the X axis and which is the Y axis, but many people don't remember much from their math classes and commonly mix them up.

> **NOTE**   For those whose minds are now racing to remember which is which, the X axis is horizontal and the Y axis is vertical. Of course, most charts have what's called a *category axis* and a *value axis,* and their orientation depends on the particular chart type. Scatter and Bubble charts have X and Y axes since they compare two (or three) values against each other. In chart types such as Radar or Polar, the axes actually extend from the center of the chart, so X and Y are meaningless.

Since no common language seems to exist for describing elements of a chart, it is quite hard to talk about creating and manipulating charts. To gain any understanding of the Chart component's features and programming model, we must first define a number of key terms used in the component and look at what elements they represent. Many of the terms have specific connotations in different chart types, so if you see a chart type in the following discussion that you are not familiar with, refer to the "Supported Chart Types" section on page 61 for a screen shot and a description.

Series

A *series* is one of the most important constructs of the Chart component. In fact, most of the internal structures in this component are oriented around the series. Figure 3-1 points out the series in a Column chart. Notice that each series correlates to an entry in the chart's legend.

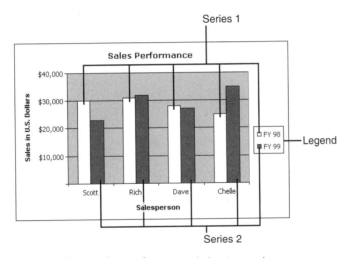

Figure 3-1. *A Column chart containing two series.*

A series represents a sequence of *data points* that you want to display in a certain manner. People commonly think that a chart has a particular type (such as a Line chart, Bar chart, or Pie chart). But in the Chart control, it's the series that has a particular type—which means you can create a combination chart by setting one series as a Line type and another as a Column type. All the data points in a series commonly have the same color (though you can override this, as we will see later). Plus, elements such as trendlines and error bars are attached to particular series.

By default, an entry in the legend exists for each series, but you can hide specific entries in the legend if you want. (I will explain how to do that later.)

Categories

Categories are a little harder to explain than series. Figure 3-2 points out the category labels contained in a Column chart.

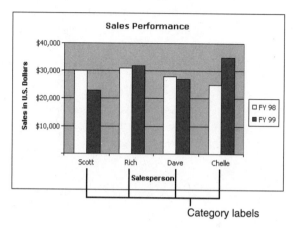

Figure 3-2. *Categories in a Column chart.*

All charts have a notion of categories, but not all charts have a category axis. In Figure 3-2, the sales representatives' names are the categories, and each series contains a single data point in each category. In most charts, the intersection of a category and a series creates a data point. Note, however, that a particular series might not have a data point for a given category although the other series do. When this is the case, the Chart control merges all categories from all series and simply does not plot a data point at that series-category intersection.

Category axes differ from value axes in three important ways:

- There is no inherent ordering of categories.

- There is no minimum and no maximum category.

- Data points are neatly assigned to a specific category.

If Salesperson is your category axis, specific sale amounts are naturally attributed to specific salespeople, and no data points sit between salespeople. A value axis has a defined minimum and maximum, and the space along the axis is evenly divided into units that increase as you move from the minimum to the maximum. Each data point is therefore plotted wherever it lies along the axis.

A Scatter or Bubble chart does not have a category axis because its data points are defined by X and Y coordinates as well as a bubble size for Bubble charts. Although these chart types do not have category axes, the data points can still belong to specific categories and you can retrieve the category name for a given data point.

This mechanism is useful for encoding extra information into the data points of a Scatter or Bubble chart, allowing you to display that information when the user's mouse hovers over a data point.

> **NOTE** Of course, in the real world, sales often can be attributed to more than one sales representative. However, most sales information systems perform an allocation and store each representative's contribution to the sale as a specific value that is then plotted on the chart. The point about data fitting neatly into a category is made to contrast discrete categories from continuous values. For example, a value of 1.4567454 can be plotted along a value axis between 0 and 2, but it does not fit into a discrete "bucket" on the axis the way data in categories do.

Values, Values, Values

In most of the simpler chart types, you have only one set of values to worry about. Figure 3-3 shows the sales values plotted by year by salesperson. This chart contains only one value per data point—which holds true for most of the simple chart types.

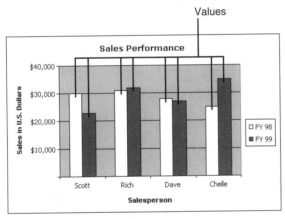

Figure 3-3. *Values in a Column chart.*

Scatter and Bubble charts, on the other hand, introduce the necessity for having two or three values for every data point. In a Scatter chart, each data point has an *X value* and a *Y value,* the combination of which defines an (X,Y) point in two-dimensional, Cartesian space. A Bubble chart adds a third value: a *bubble size value* that determines the radius of the bubble centered at the (X,Y) point. Optionally, the bubble size value can be set to represent the area of the bubble instead of the radius.

Things get a little more complicated when using a *High-Low-Close (HLC) chart* because again three values make up each data point, except that they are now called the *high value, low value,* and *close value.* An *Open-High-Low-Close (OHLC) chart* has four values associated with each data point, and the extra value is called, not surprisingly, the *open value*. (These types of charts are often called *Stock charts* because they are most commonly used to display such data.)

When dealing with a Polar chart, you need to provide another set of values: *R values* and *Theta values*. The R value defines the distance of the data point from the center of the chart, and the Theta value represents the angle away from a horizontal line passing through origin.

Axes

The term "axes" is probably more familiar to you. In the Chart component, axes have essentially the same meaning that they do in the world of geometry. However, the Chart control adds another layer of meaning to an axis by referring to it either as a *category axis* or a *value axis*. In Figure 3-4, the category and value axes are labeled.

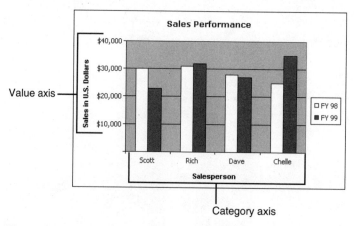

Figure 3-4. *Category and value axes in a Column chart.*

A category axis is subdivided into equal segments—one for each distinct category, and data points are plotted in the middle of each category. No notion of a minimum or maximum exists for a category axis. A value axis, on the other hand, is a continuous axis that has a minimum and a maximum. Along a value axis, data points are plotted where they would fall between the minimum and maximum points.

Since the placement of the category and value axes depends on the chart type, "category" and "value" are logical names that do not directly map to X and Y. For example, a Column chart has the category axis extending horizontally along the bottom (X) and the value axis rising vertically on the left (Y). But in a Bar chart, the placements are reversed, with the category axis on the left and the value axis along the bottom. For more on the various chart types, see the "Supported Chart Types" section on page 61.

Scaling

Although you have certainly heard the term "axis," you might not have heard the term "scaling" before. Every axis has a scaling, though you commonly use a scaling with a value axis. A scaling defines a measurement scale for its axis, determining the minimum and maximum values for the axis. The scaling also determines whether the intervals along the axis are *linear* or *logarithmic*. A linear scale subdivides the axis into even segments that increase linearly from the minimum value to the maximum value (for instance, 20, 40, 60, 80, 100). A logarithmic scale also divides the axis into even segments; however, the increment from one segment to the next is logarithmic instead of linear (for example, 1, 10, 100).

We will discuss axis scaling in more detail later in the chapter when we talk about split axes, as well as in Chapter 6, where we will see how to "zoom in" to show a portion of your data in more detail.

Trendlines

The Chart component supports the creation of one trendline for each series in your chart. As in Excel, a *trendline* is used to show the trend of data in a series. Trendlines are commonly used in trend analysis and forecasting when you want to predict what a certain value will be in the future if it keeps increasing or decreasing at the historical rate. Like Excel, the Chart control offers a few different trendline calculations, including linear, logarithmic, polynomial, exponential, and power. However, the Chart control does not offer the moving average trendline type found in Excel. Figure 3-5 shows an example of a trendline.

Error Bars

Error bars, shown in Figure 3-6, are short line segments extending from the data points that indicate some uncertainty about your data, known as the *error amount*. Each data point can display an error bar, which indicates that the data point's true value can be anywhere within the error range.

WHY A SEPARATE SCALING OBJECT?

You might be wondering why the concept of scaling is not just part of an axis. After all, it seems that the scaling determines the minimum and maximum values of an axis. However, the scaling's minimum and maximum values determine the dimensions of the viewable region called the *plot area*. An axis displays tick marks and labels, but it is the scaling that determines the exact pixel/value ratio for that dimension of the plot area. By separating the scaling from the axis, the Chart control can support charts that have no visible axes.

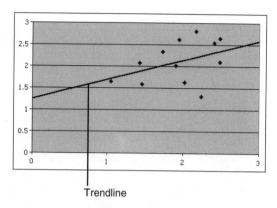

Figure 3-5. *A trendline in a Scatter chart.*

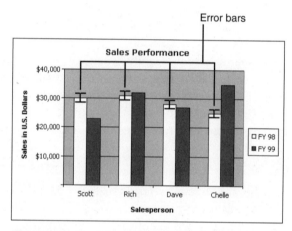

Figure 3-6. *Error bars in a Column chart.*

Like trendlines, error bars are attached to a series. An error bar is displayed for each data point in the series, and the collection of error bars for that series can be set to show a positive error amount, a negative error amount, or both. The error amount can be expressed as a percentage (such as +10%, −10%, or +/−10%), a relative value (such as +2, −2, or +/−2), or a custom amount (for example, an upper bound of 12 and a lower bound of 8 for a data point of 10). Error bars can also be data-bound, in which case the Chart control treats the values in the result columns as custom error values for each data point. Although Excel charting also provides Standard Error and Standard Deviation options for the error amounts, the Chart control does not yet natively support these. Of course, you could calculate these values yourself and use custom error amounts to display them in the chart.

Data Labels

A *data label* is a small piece of text placed next to a data point that you can set to display the data point's value, percentage in the series, category name, series name, or bubble size. (See Figure 3-7 for an example.) You can display any combinations of these pieces of information in a data label. Plus, you can control the font, color, and border formatting attributes—even which separator character string to use between each piece of information.

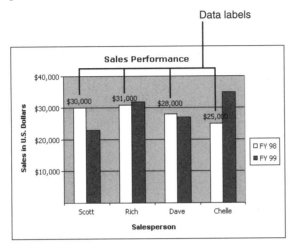

Figure 3-7. *Data labels in a Column chart.*

Data labels are obviously useful when you want to show numbers next to your data points, especially for comparing data points that might be very close to each other. The percentage contribution is of course useful any time you want to show the percent a data point contributes to the overall series, such as in a Pie chart. Showing the category name is a nice way to display extra categorical information in chart types that do not have category axes, such as Scatter and Bubble charts.

Like trendlines and error bars, data labels are attached to a series. You cannot format, hide, or show a data label for an individual data point. All manipulations to data labels affect all data points in the series.

Supported Chart Types

The first question I usually hear from a developer's mouth when I speak about the Chart component is, "What chart types are supported?" Chart types are the bread and butter of charting, so the more types the merrier. I have a reference book on my shelf that contains almost 450 pages of different chart types, chart elements, and information graphics techniques! (This book, *Information Graphics: A Comprehensive Illustrated Reference* [Management Graphics, 1997], is an excellent resource for anyone involved in information graphics, as are any of Edward Tufte's books.)

The first version of the Chart component includes the full set of two-dimensional chart types found in Excel 2000 (except for the Contour type), with the addition of Polar, Stacked Pie, and Filled Scatter chart types. The Chart control does not have any three-dimensional chart types or effects in this version, nor does it support the fancy fill effects offered in Excel.

Let's look at several examples of the supported chart types and discuss what kind of data they are useful for displaying.

Column and Bar Charts

The most typical chart types used in business, Column and Bar charts, show a filled bar for each data point, extending from the zero point on the value axis to the data point.

Most people don't make much of a distinction between Column and Bar charts—after all, they are essentially the same, they just extend in different directions. The Chart component uses the term "Column" to refer to a vertical column that extends up and down the screen and the term "Bar" for a horizontal bar that extends across the screen. Figure 3-8 shows an example of a Column chart and a Bar chart.

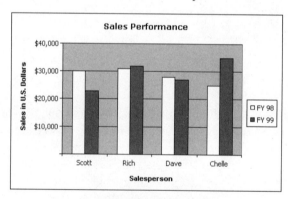

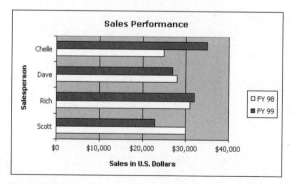

Figure 3-8. *A Column chart (top) and a Bar chart.*

These chart types typically are useful for data containing categories that do not need to appear in any particular order. Unlike Line charts, Column and Bar charts don't portray a sense of order or progression.

As with many of the chart types, there are a few Column and Bar chart sub-types. The default subtype, called *Clustered* Column or Bar, plots bars from different series adjacent to each other within each category. (Figure 3-8 shows a Clustered Column chart and a Clustered Bar chart.) The Clustered subtype is the most useful subtype when the different series are fairly unrelated or when they should not be aggregated visually. For example, if you plot a budget in one series and the actual amount spent in the other, you do not want to aggregate those values. Instead, you would want to compare the bars or columns side by side.

Stacked Column and Bar charts display the different series as stacked upon one another. In such charts, the length of the column or the bar represents the sum of the data points for the category. Figure 3-9 shows an example of a Stacked Column chart.

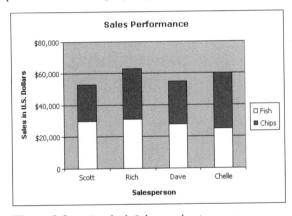

Figure 3-9. *A Stacked Column chart.*

Stacked Column and Bar charts are useful for displaying data in which the series' values can and should be aggregated to depict a visual total for each category. For example, if you plot sales information by country and by product, you might want to use a Stacked Column chart to show the total sales for each country (the category) across all products. The bar is still segmented by the exact value each product contributes—meaning top-selling products will have longer segments, while products that do not sell well will have shorter segments. Stacked charts are useful when it is not as necessary to assess the relative contribution as it is to assess the total for each category.

Finally, the *100% Stacked* subtype is a bit like a Pie chart: it draws a bar or column all the way across the plot area and then subdivides the bar or column into segments representing the percent contribution of each series' data point. The key difference between this subtype and the Stacked subtype is that the length of each segment is the *percentage* of the data point's contribution to the total of the data points in that category, not the literal value. Since all the bars are the same length (100%), such a chart is not useful for comparing one category's total to another. However, this type of chart is useful for viewing the same type of information a pie chart shows, but for many categories and series at once.

Most of the other chart types described here have the same set of subtypes—Clustered, Stacked, and 100% Stacked. I will not redefine each of these three subtypes in the descriptions that follow, but I will indicate when they are available. Refer back to this section for a description of the subtypes and which types of data are appropriate to display using them.

Pie, Stacked Pie, and Doughnut Charts

Pie charts are also common in business charting, which is almost a shame since they provide the least dense (and the least efficient) display of information available. However, their simplicity also makes them very understandable, and often, very persuasive. For example, when showing a breakdown of market share information, the effect of an extremely large or small slice is indeed powerful. Figure 3-10 shows a typical Pie chart.

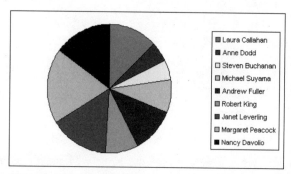

Figure 3-10. *A Pie chart.*

The important quirk of Pie charts is that the legend shows the category values instead of the series values. Most charts show the various series in the legend, but since a Pie chart shows only one series, the legend is used to show the category labels that correspond to the colored pie "slices."

A Pie chart is obviously useful for showing the percentage contribution or breakdown of a total. A Pie chart shows only one dimension of data because, as stated a moment ago, it can display only one series of data points.

The Stacked Pie and Doughnut chart types, however, can show multiple series at once, much like the 100% Stacked Column chart can display data for many series and categories at once. The only real difference between the Stacked Pie chart and the Doughnut chart is that the Doughnut chart has a hole in the middle (the "doughnut hole" if you will). Figure 3-11 depicts the same information in first a Stacked Pie chart and then a Doughnut chart.

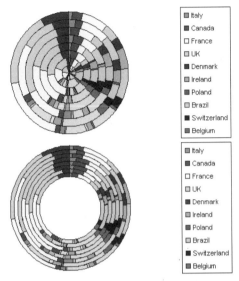

Figure 3-11. *A Stacked Pie chart and a Doughnut chart.*

I admit that these are somewhat bizarre chart types; in fact, I recommend using them only in those unique circumstances under which no other chart type will suffice (for example, displaying the percentage chemical makeup of soil in concentric rings around a bomb explosion site). The concentric circles can be misleading for abstract data because their relative size and order are not based on any numeric value.

Line, Smooth Line, and Area Charts

Line charts and Area charts fall within the group of simpler chart types but unfortunately are not used as often as they should be. Figure 3-12 shows what a typical Line chart and Area chart look like.

Line and Area charts are useful for displaying data in which the categories actually have a meaningful order, such as a series of dates or times. For example, plotting sales over a series of dates or plotting stock prices over a series of hours is more effectively displayed in a Line chart than in a Column chart. This is because it is easier to tell whether there's a trend up or down when lines are drawn between the data points in a chart.

The only real difference between a Line chart and an Area chart is that in the Area chart, the section between the category axis and the line is filled with the series color. The occlusion that occurs when one series' values are higher than another's can make Area charts somewhat difficult to work with—unless you are using the

Stacked subtype we discussed earlier. Since the series are drawn over each other in order, the last series drawn will cover any series previously drawn. Use nonstacked Area charts only when you know that a series has consistently higher values than all the series that follow it.

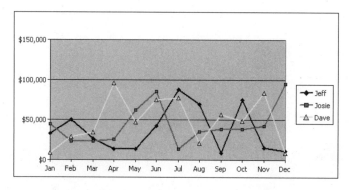

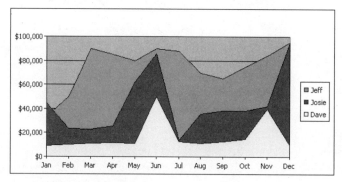

Figure 3-12. *A Line chart and an Area chart.*

As in the Column and Bar chart cases, Line charts and Area charts have the Clustered, Stacked, and 100% Stacked subtypes. However, the term "Clustered" is not commonly used to describe the default subtypes, and these defaults are simply called Line chart and Area chart without any special distinction.

Line charts have one other subtype that Column and Bar charts do not. Lines in a chart can be drawn either "straight" or "smoothed." It should come as no surprise that charts drawn with smoothed lines are called *Smooth Line charts*. Instead of drawing the line straight from one data point to another, the Chart component draws the line on a curve so that there are no jagged peaks or valleys.

Scatter and Bubble Charts

Scatter charts are used less often in business presentations, which is unfortunate considering that they can be a more powerful analysis tool than the simpler chart types described earlier. Although a Scatter chart has series and categories, it also has two values (rather than one) that determine the location of a data point. Each data point in a Scatter chart has an X value and a Y value, and the combination of the two determines its placement on the plot area.

The key difference between a Scatter chart and a Bubble chart is that the data points in a Bubble chart are circles that have dynamic size. A data point in a Bubble chart contains a third value called *bubble size,* which determines either the radius or the area of the bubble. Figure 3-13 shows typical Scatter and Bubble charts.

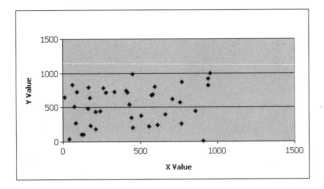

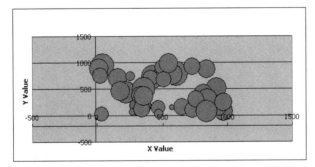

Figure 3-13. *A Scatter chart and a Bubble chart.*

Scatter charts and Bubble charts are useful for comparing two different values to discover a correlation or distribution pattern. For example, using a Scatter chart to plot a department's morale budget allocation against its revenue might reveal a strong correlation, showing that a high morale budget commonly increases revenue. (At least, most employees would like to think this is true!)

Scatter charts have a few unique subtypes. The default subtype is simply called *Scatter Markers* and uses *markers* (small geometric shapes such as diamonds or squares) to indicate the data points. Different shapes are used to indicate the different series. You can choose to connect the markers of each series with a smoothed or straight line. Furthermore, you can choose to have lines without any markers at all. The Chart component includes a final subtype that is not included in Excel. It allows you to fill in the polygon made from the data points and connecting lines, creating a *Filled Scatter chart.*

FUN WITH FILLED SCATTER CHARTS

You can try a rather creative Filled Scatter chart demo on the companion CD. Open the DrawWithChart.htm file in the Chap03 folder, and click the chart surface to create points of a filled polygon. Double-click the mouse to end the shape. This demo was written by Jeff Couckuyt, one of the extremely talented Chart component developers, and was created using only the Chart control and a Filled Scatter chart type.

Keep in mind that Bubble charts have the same problem of occlusion as Area charts. A large bubble will hide any data points underneath it, so only use Bubble charts when you know the chance of occlusion is low; otherwise, consider setting the bubble fill to transparent.

Radar Charts

Radar charts do not seem to be typically used in the United States, but I understand that they are much more common in Asian countries for portraying data such as nutritional information about food products. Figure 3-14 shows what this interesting and useful chart type looks like.

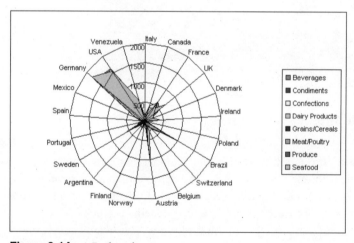

Figure 3-14. *A Radar chart.*

A Radar chart has categories, series, and values like the other simple chart types; however, Radar charts plot the category labels in a circle surrounding the chart and contain spokes extending from the center of the chart out to each category label. Each spoke is a value axis. The data points for each category are plotted on the corresponding spoke's scale at the appropriate point and in the appropriate series color. The chart then joins the data points of each series with a line and optionally fills the series color from the line toward the origin. Filled Radar charts have the same old problem of occlusion that Area and Bubble charts have, so beware of using the Filled subtype unless you know that your data will not cause occlusion (or unless you are not concerned about it).

Radar charts also support the Smooth Line subtype we discussed earlier. Plus, you have the option of plotting data point markers in both the Smooth Line and Straight Line subtypes.

High-Low-Close and Open-High-Low-Close Charts

Anyone displaying information about stocks or financial securities will be interested in these two chart types. The High-Low-Close chart type (or HLC chart) displays a line segment for each category. Each line segment extends from the low to the high value and features a small tick mark that denotes the close value. Figure 3-15 shows an example of an HLC chart.

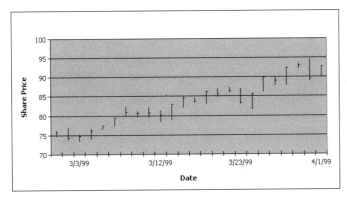

Figure 3-15. *A High-Low-Close chart.*

You should consider using this chart type any time you have data containing a range of values for a given period and a special value that needs to be marked within the range. For example, you could use an HLC chart to display temperature readings over an extended period of time.

An Open-High-Low-Close chart (or OHLC chart) adds one extra piece of information to the data of an HLC chart: *the open value*. The chart indicates the open value by displaying a filled rectangle between the open value and the close value, as Figure 3-16 shows.

The filled rectangle either will be the series color or it will be black, depending on whether the difference between the close value and the open value is positive or negative. Positive differences get the normal series color, while negative differences are shown as black. This shows the viewer whether the values increased or decreased during the specified period so that he or she can ascertain whether the value improved or worsened and by how much.

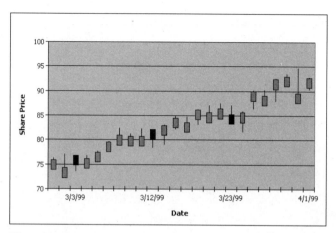

Figure 3-16. *An Open-High-Low-Close chart.*

Both the HLC and the OHLC chart types still maintain the notion of series. However, in an HLC chart type, the Chart component places different series in the same horizontal position. In other words, the control will draw multiple series over one another. Generally, this chart type is most useful with only one series of data points. OHLC charts, on the other hand, can manage multiple series and draw the bars of multiple series next to one another.

Polar Charts

The Polar chart type is the one new chart type that appears in the Chart component but not in Excel charting. Polar charts, which Microsoft Office users have been requesting for some time, are useful for displaying relationships between angles and distances. Polar charts are commonly used in the audio and radio fields, for example, to show the power and direction of a microphone's pickup. Figure 3-17 depicts a typical Polar chart.

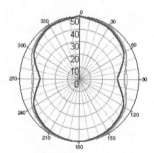

Figure 3-17. *A Polar chart.*

The Polar chart includes the Smooth Line subtype, and you can choose whether to display data point markers with the lines.

Combination Charts

As mentioned at the beginning of the chapter, one of the great secrets of charting is that a chart does not really have a chart type. Instead, each individual series has a type, and if all series in a chart happen to have the same type, the Chart object's Type property returns that type. However, you can use this distinction to create more complex combination charts, in which you plot some series as columns or bars while plotting others as lines.

Not all chart types can be combined, and in this version of Office the Chart component allows you to combine only the Column, Line, and Area chart types. The most common combination chart used for business data is a mixture of the Column and Line chart types.

Loading Data

Now that you know what the various chart elements are called and what chart types the Chart control can display, you need to learn how to load a chart with data. Like most of the Office Web Components, the Chart control can load data from a variety of sources, and the loading can be performed by using the Chart Wizard in a design environment or by writing code. The Chart component binds to all the other Office Web Components—the Spreadsheet, PivotTable, and Data Source components—as well as to all other controls that implement the IDataSource interface (the standard interface for a data source control in Microsoft Internet Explorer or Microsoft Visual Basic, documented in the Microsoft Developer Network Libraries and the OLE DB SDK), ADO Recordset objects, and even literal arrays or delimited strings of data.

The general approach to loading data into the Chart control is to tell the chart where it should retrieve data from and what "parts" of the data source should be used for the series, categories, and values the current chart type requires. In the programming model, the Chart control refers to these chart elements as *dimensions* that you can bind to some part of the data source. When binding to a spreadsheet, the "part" of the data source you specify is a range reference, such as A1:C1. For an OLE DB data source, you specify what column name or ordinal index of the resultset to use. For the PivotTable control, you specify which pivot axis to use. (We will discuss this further in Chapter 4.) In literal data, only one "part" exists: the array or delimited string itself.

The Chart Wizard performs much of the binding for you, presenting you with a simple user interface for specifying this information. However, the Chart Wizard merely calls the public programming model of the Chart control, so by writing your own code you can do anything the Chart Wizard does—and more. The Chart Wizard is fairly self-explanatory, and its online help covers much of its use. Since this book focuses on developing custom solutions with the Office Web Components, I will not detail using the Chart Wizard here. Instead, I'll dive into the code you need to write when programmatically filling the chart with data.

Loading the Chart with Literal Data

The following subroutine, taken from the LoadFromLiteral.htm file in the Chap03 folder on your companion CD, shows how to load the Chart control with literal data:

```
'-------------------------------------------------------------------------
' LoadChartWithLiteral()
' Purpose: Loads the chart with literal data
' In:        cspace        reference to the ChartSpace object
'            vSeries       variant array or
'                          tab-delimited string of series names
'            vCategories   variant array or
'                          tab-delimited string of category names
'            avValues      array of variant array or
'                          tab-delimited string of values;
'                          one entry in the outer array per series
'
Sub LoadChartWithLiteral(cspace, vSeries, vCategories, avValues)
    ' Local variables
    Dim cht    ' Chart object we'll create in the chart space
    Dim ser    ' Temporary series

    ' Grab the Constants object so that we can use constant names in
    ' the script. Note: This is needed only in VBScript -- do not include
    ' this in VBA code.
    Set c = cspace.Constants

    ' Clear out anything that is in the chart space
    cspace.Clear

    ' Create a chart in the chart space
    Set cht = cspace.Charts.Add()
    cht.HasLegend = True

    ' Now call SetData to bind the various dimensions
    ' Second parameter is c.chDataLiteral, meaning the last parameter
    ' is a variant array or a tab-delimited string
    cht.SetData c.chDimSeriesNames, c.chDataLiteral, vSeries
    cht.SetData c.chDimCategories, c.chDataLiteral, vCategories

    ' When loading the chart with literal data, you must
    ' load each series with values individually
    For each ser In cht.SeriesCollection
        ser.SetData c.chDimValues, c.chDataLiteral, avValues(ser.Index)
    Next 'ser

End Sub 'LoadChartWithLiteral()
```

When loading the chart with literal data, the data can be contained either in an array of variants or in a tab-delimited string, each element or token representing a different value. In the file on your companion CD, I pass the literal data as an array using the Array function that is supported in Microsoft VBScript as well as in Microsoft VBA.

The SetData method is used to pass the literal data, but note that the second argument (normally the data source index) is the constant chDataLiteral. This constant, which is equal to −1, tells the chart that the next argument is literal data and not part of a data source.

Also note that you must use the SetData method of the WCSeries object (the object representing a series) when passing literal values to the chart. Since the Chart control itself can accept only a one-dimensional array of values, if it allowed you to pass literal values to the SetData method of the WCChart object (the object representing a chart), it would have no way of knowing which values belong to which series. The previous procedure handles this by simply looping through the series collection and passing the appropriate array of values to the current series' SetData method.

Binding to the Spreadsheet Component

The following subroutine, taken from the LoadFromSpreadsheet.htm file in the Chap03 folder on your companion CD, shows how to bind a Chart component to ranges in the Spreadsheet component:

```
'---------------------------------------------------------------------
' BindChartToSpreadsheet()
'
' Purpose: Binds a chart to specified ranges in the source spreadsheet
' In:      cspace          reference to the ChartSpace object
'          sheet           reference to the Spreadsheet object
'          srngSeries      string-based range reference to where the
'                          series names come from
'          srngCategories  string-based range reference to where the
'                          category names come from
'          srngValues      string-based range reference to where the
'                          values are
'
Sub BindChartToSpreadsheet(cspace, sheet, srngSeries, srngCategories, _
                    srngValues, fSeriesInCols)
    ' Local variables
    Dim cht         ' Chart object that we'll create in the chart space
    Dim ser         ' Temporary series
    Dim rngValues   ' Range object of values

    ' Grab the Constants object so that we can use constant names in
    ' the script. Note: This is needed only in VBScript -- do not include
    ' this in VBA code.
    Set c = cspace.Constants
```

(continued)

```
' Clear out anything that is in the chart space
cspace.Clear

' First tell the chart that its data is coming from the spreadsheet
Set cspace.DataSource = sheet

' Create a chart in the chart space
Set cht = cspace.Charts.Add()
cht.HasLegend = True

' Now call SetData to bind the various dimensions
' Second parameter is zero, meaning the first data source should be
' used if there are multiple data sources
cht.SetData c.chDimSeriesNames, 0, srngSeries
cht.SetData c.chDimCategories, 0, srngCategories

' The spreadsheet can bind to one-dimensional ranges only,
' so loop through the series collection and set the values
' for each series individually
Set rngValues = sheet.Range(srngValues)

For Each ser In cht.SeriesCollection
    If fSeriesInCols Then
        ser.SetData c.chDimValues, 0, _
            rngValues.Columns(ser.Index + 1).Address
    Else
        ser.SetData c.chDimValues, 0, _
            rngValues.Rows(ser.Index + 1).Address
    End If
Next 'ser

End Sub 'BindChartToSpreadsheet()
```

I would like to point out a few things about this example. First, to bind the Chart and Spreadsheet controls, I set the Chart control's DataSource property to the instance of the Spreadsheet control. By receiving the pointer to the Spreadsheet control instance, the Chart control can now ask the Spreadsheet control for cell values in the specified ranges.

Second, the SetData method is used to bind first the Series Names dimension and then the Categories dimension. You must bind the chart dimensions in this order: series names first, then categories, then values. In the rare case in which you have only one series of information, you can skip the Series Names dimension and just bind categories and values. Doing so will create one series for you with the default name Series, which you can change by setting the Name or Caption property of the WCSeries object.

My last point is that when binding to the Spreadsheet component, the Chart component needs to receive explicit range references for the values in each series. Unfortunately, you cannot just hand the chart a two-dimensional range of values and let it automatically figure out which series and categories the values belong to. Instead, you must pass a one-dimensional range reference to the last parameter in the SetData method for each WCSeries object. The previous example does this in a generic fashion by using the Spreadsheet component's Range object to yield a range reference for each column or row in the two-dimensional range, which in turn gets passed to the series' SetData method. The fSeriesInCols flag indicates whether the values for a given series are arranged down a column or across a row in the spreadsheet. If the flag is True, the Columns collection is used; if False, the Rows collection is used.

Also note that this example adds 1 to the series' index value. This is because the Columns and Rows collections are 1-based for compatibility with Excel's programming model, while the Chart component's series index is 0-based. Adding 1 to the series index yields the corresponding column or row in the range.

Binding to the Data Source Component

The following method, taken from the LoadFromDSC.htm file in the Chap03 folder on the companion CD, shows how to bind a Chart component to a Recordset returned from the Data Source component (DSC). (We'll discuss the DSC more thoroughly in Chapter 5.)

```
'-------------------------------------------------------------------
' BindChartToDSC()
'
' Purpose: Binds a chart to a Recordset in the Data Source component.
'          (This example creates a Pie chart.)
' In:      cspace        reference to the ChartSpace object
'          dsc           reference to the Data Source control
'          sRSName       name of Recordset to bind to in the
'                        Data Source control
'          sCategories   name of the result column containing categories
'          sValues       name of the result column containing values
'
Sub BindChartToDSC(cspace, dsc, sRSName, sCategories, sValues)
    ' Local variables
    Dim cht    ' Chart object that we'll create in the chart space
    Dim ser    ' Temporary series

    ' Grab the Constants object so that we can use constant names in
    ' the script. Note: This is needed only in VBScript -- do not include
    ' this in VBA code.
    Set c = cspace.Constants
```

(continued)

```
' Clear out anything that is in the chart space
cspace.Clear

' First tell the chart that its data is coming from
' the Data Source control
Set cspace.DataSource = dsc

' Next tell it what Recordset within the Data Source control
' it will bind to
cspace.DataMember = sRSName

' Create a Pie chart in the chart space
Set cht = cspace.Charts.Add()
cht.HasLegend = True
cht.Type = c.chChartTypePie

' Now call SetData to bind the various dimensions
' Second parameter is zero, meaning the first data source should be
' used if there are multiple data sources

' In this example of a Pie chart, we will add one
' series manually and use the SetData method there
Set ser = cht.SeriesCollection.Add()
ser.SetData c.chDimCategories, 0, sCategories
ser.SetData c.chDimValues, 0, sValues

' Finally, for this example, add some
' data labels since it's a Pie chart
Set dls = ser.DataLabelsCollection.Add()
dls.HasPercentage = True
dls.HasValue = False

End Sub 'BindChartToDSC()
```

The DSC can retrieve data from and provide data to both the Chart component and the PivotTable component. It also implements the same data source COM interface (IDataSource) that Visual Basic and Internet Explorer data source controls implement, so this code can be used for any other valid data source control used in those environments.

The DataSource and DataMember properties of the ChartSpace object are fundamental to this example. Since they are part of the data-binding standards established by Visual Basic and Internet Explorer, you will commonly see them on other data-bound controls in those environments. The DataSource property is set to point at the control providing the data (in this case the DSC), and the DataMember property is set to a string value naming the specific data set desired. Because a DSC can expose many data sets at once, the DataMember property is used to tell the Chart control which data set to request. If you leave the DataMember property blank, the Chart control will ask for the default data set, the identity of which is determined by the DSC.

The SetData method is used in this example much the same way it was used in the BindChartToSpreadsheet method, except that the "data part" (the last parameter to SetData) is now the name of a column in the Recordset returned from the DSC. Alternatively, this data part can be the ordinal index of the column (0, 1, 2, and so on). The Chart control will pass this to the ADO Fields collection object's Item method, so any value that is valid for that method can be used as the last parameter to the SetData method. Typically, you use column names if you don't expect them to change over time but do expect the ordinal positions to change; you use ordinal indexes if you don't expect them to change but do expect the column names to change.

As stated earlier, an interesting twist of Pie charts is that the entries in the legend are categories, not series. Therefore, when binding a Pie chart, you should bind the column you want to appear in the legend to the Categories dimension rather than the Series dimension. This also applies to Stacked Pie charts and Doughnut charts.

The last code block in this example creates some data labels (which we just discussed) to show the percentage each data point contributes to the whole. The Chart control can show a number of values for each data point, and by default the actual number value is displayed. Since I wanted to show only the percentage contribution of each slice, I set the HasPercentage property to True and HasValue to False.

Although this particular example creates a Pie chart, you can use any of the supported chart types when binding to the DSC. I chose to create a Pie chart in this example only to show how binding is performed using the Pie chart type.

Binding to a Recordset

The following function, taken from the LoadFromRecordset.htm file in the Chap03 folder on the companion CD, shows how to bind a Chart control to an ADO Recordset object:

```
'- - - - - - - - - - - - - - - - - - - - - - - - - - - - - - - - - - - - - - - - - - - - - - - - - -
' BindChartToRecordset()
'
' Purpose: Binds a chart to a Recordset. (This example creates a
'          Scatter chart.)
' In:      cspace      reference to the ChartSpace object
'          rst         reference to Recordset object to bind to
'          sfldSeries  name of the series field
'          sfldXValues name of the field containing the X values
'          sfldYValues name of the field containing the Y values
'
Sub BindChartToRecordset(cspace, rst, sfldSeries, sfldXValues, _
    sfldYValues)
```

(continued)

```
' Local variables
Dim cht     ' Chart object that we'll create in the chart space
Dim ser     ' Temporary series pointer
Dim ax      ' Temporary axis pointer

' Grab the Constants object so that we can use constant names in
' the script. Note: This is needed only in VBScript -- do not include
' this in VBA code.
Set c = cspace.Constants

' Clear out anything that is in the chart space
cspace.Clear

' First tell the chart that its data is coming from the Recordset
Set cspace.DataSource = rst

' Create a Scatter chart in the chart space
Set cht = cspace.Charts.Add()
cht.HasLegend = True
cht.Type = c.chChartTypeScatterMarkers

' Now call SetData to bind the various dimensions
' Second parameter is zero, meaning the first data source should be
' used if there are multiple data sources

' In this example of a Scatter chart, we will bind
' two value dimensions: X and Y
cht.SetData c.chDimSeriesNames, 0, sfldSeries
cht.SetData c.chDimXValues, 0, sfldXValues
cht.SetData c.chDimYValues, 0, sfldYValues

' Finally, let's add some axis labels using
' the column names as the axis captions
Set ax = cht.Axes(c.chAxisPositionBottom)
ax.HasTitle = True
ax.Title.Caption = sfldXValues
ax.Title.Font.Name = "Tahoma"
ax.Title.Font.Size = 8
ax.Title.Font.Bold = True
ax.NumberFormat = "#,##0"

Set ax = cht.Axes(c.chAxisPositionLeft)
ax.HasTitle = True
ax.Title.Caption = sfldYValues
ax.Title.Font.Name = "Tahoma"
ax.Title.Font.Size = 8
```

```
    ax.Title.Font.Bold = True
    ax.NumberFormat = "$#,##0"

    ' Let's also set the marker size a bit smaller than normal
    For Each ser In cht.SeriesCollection
        ser.Marker.Size = 5
    Next 'ser

End Sub 'BindChartToRecordset()
```

You will no doubt quickly notice that this example is similar to the previous example involving the DSC, except that this example uses a Scatter chart. This is because the ADO Recordset object is itself a valid data source in Visual Basic and Internet Explorer, and it implements the same data source interface as the DSC. This makes it possible to set the Chart control's DataSource property to point to the Recordset object just as you would set it when using the DSC. However, the Recordset object by definition has only one data set to expose, so the DataMember property does not need to be set when binding to it.

Because the chart type used in this example is a Scatter chart, the code sets two value dimensions: X Values and Y Values. As described earlier in the section on supported chart types, a Scatter chart uses two values for each data point, so we need to bind the X Values dimension to one column in the Recordset and the Y Values dimension to another column. (You could bind them to the same column, but that would make for a highly correlated Scatter chart!)

AN ACCIDENT OF GOOD ARCHITECTURE

When I sent this chapter to the Chart component developers for review, one of them commented that the component does not actually "support" loading from a Recordset and that the OWC team had not officially tested this scenario. However, almost all the demos and real pages we wrote internally use this method, so in actuality, this scenario was quite well tested.

The reason that loading the Chart component from a Recordset works is an accident of good architecture. When the Visual Basic and Internet Explorer development teams selected the standard data source interface (IDataSource), the ADO team decided that it made sense for the Recordset object to implement this interface since it could easily return the underlying IRowset interface from the GetDataMember method. Because the Chart control uses IDataSource when loading data from a DSC, it all just worked. To the Chart control, the Recordset object looks like any other data source control.

When binding to a Recordset object, you must ensure that the Recordset is using the Microsoft Windows Cursor Engine (WCE) or is capable of being sorted and scrolled. The WCE is an ADO component that provides scrolling, sorting, filtering, and more on any OLE DB Rowset regardless of the Rowset's source or native capabilities. To use this engine, set the CursorLocation property of your ADO Connection or Recordset object to adUseClient, which has a value of 3 if you are in an environment that does not recognize constants. To ensure that the Chart control can scroll around the Recordset, you can use the adOpenStatic cursor type, which also has a value of 3. Use adOpenStatic or 3 for the CursorType parameter of the Recordset's Open method or for the CursorType property of the Recordset object. (Chapter 4 will discuss the WCE in more detail.)

For an example of setting the necessary Recordset properties, see the full source listing in the LoadFromRecordset.htm file on the companion CD. When viewing this file, note the use of the column names for the axis captions. Scatter charts have two value axes (X and Y), so you should give those axes titles and explain what values you are showing on them. Using the column names in the Recordset can be an easy way to label these axes; of course, you can set your own captions if the column names in the Recordset are not intelligible.

Binding to the PivotTable Component

The last possible source of data for the Chart component is the PivotTable component. (We will talk more about this component in the next chapter.) As you might expect, this component also implements the same data source interface that all valid data sources expose in Visual Basic and Internet Explorer, so the following example, taken from the LoadFromPivot.htm file in the Chap03 folder on the companion CD, looks similar to the DSC example we discussed earlier but has a few important differences:

```
'--------------------------------------------------------------------
' BindChartToPivot()
'
' Purpose: Binds a chart to a PivotTable component
' In:      cspace         reference to the ChartSpace object
'          ptable         reference to the PivotTable object
'          fSeriesInCols  Boolean flag indicating whether the series
'                         of the chart should come from the column
'                         axis or the row axis of the PivotTable control
'
Sub BindChartToPivot(cspace, ptable, fSeriesInCols)
    ' Local variables
    Dim cht    ' Chart object that we'll create in the chart space
    Dim ax     ' Temporary axis reference
    Dim fnt    ' Temporary font reference
```

```
' Grab the Constants object so that we can use constant names in
' the script. Note: This is needed only in VBScript -- do not include
' this in VBA code.
Set c = cspace.Constants

' Clear out anything that is in the chart space
cspace.Clear

' First tell the chart that its data is coming from the
' PivotTable component
Set cspace.DataSource = ptable

' Create a chart in the chart space
Set cht = cspace.Charts.Add()
cht.HasLegend = True
cht.Type = c.chChartTypeBarClustered

' Now call SetData to bind the various dimensions
' Second parameter is zero, meaning the first data source should be
' used if there are multiple data sources
If fSeriesInCols Then
    cht.SetData c.chDimSeriesNames, 0, c.chPivotColumns
    cht.SetData c.chDimCategories, 0, c.chPivotRows
Else
    cht.SetData c.chDimSeriesNames, 0, c.chPivotRows
    cht.SetData c.chDimCategories, 0, c.chPivotColumns
End If 'fSeriesInCols

' Set the values dimension. The value
' you pass for the data reference (the last parameter)
' is the index of the total you want to use.
' Since there is only one total in this example,
' we pass zero, indicating the first one.
cht.SetData c.chDimValues, 0, 0

' Finally, let's add an axis title to the value
' axis, using the label on the pivot total
' as the caption, and set the number format
Set ax = cht.Axes(c.chAxisPositionBottom)
ax.HasTitle = True
ax.Title.Caption = ptable.ActiveView.DataAxis.Totals(0).Caption
Set fnt = ax.Title.Font
fnt.Name = "Tahoma"
fnt.Size = 8
fnt.Bold = True

ax.NumberFormat = ptable.ActiveView.DataAxis.Totals(0).NumberFormat

End Sub 'BindChartToPivot()
```

As in the earlier Recordset and DSC examples, to bind the Chart control to the PivotTable control, you start by setting the Chart control's DataSource property to point to an instance of the PivotTable control. As in the Recordset example, the PivotTable control has only one data set to expose, so you do not need to change the DataMember property from its default setting.

The critical difference between this example and the DSC example is the use of special constant values for the last parameter to the SetData method. As you will remember, this last parameter specifies which part of the data you want to bind to the specified chart dimension. In a PivotTable control, the logical parts available are the row and column pivot axes and all the totals in the view. In a PivotTable control, the row axis refers to all the labels displayed down the left side of the table, and the column axis refers to all the labels displayed across the top of the table (more on these axes in the next chapter). All the Chart control needs to know is which axis you want to bind to the Series Names dimension and which axis you want to bind to the Categories dimension.

Binding the various values dimensions of the Chart control is slightly different. Since a PivotTable report can display many totals at once, the Chart control needs to know which total you want to use for the specified values dimension. You indicate this by passing the ordinal index of the total as the last parameter to the SetData method. In the BindChartToPivot example, we use a Clustered Bar chart so that each data point has only one value. We tell the Chart control to use the total at index zero (the first one, since this is 0-based) for the data point values. Note that this is the ordinal index of the available totals shown in the PivotTable control's current view—not all the possible totals in the data source.

While the PivotTable control does implement the standard COM interface for a data source control, it does not know how to return ADO Recordsets or OLE DB Rowsets. The Chart control has special code for knowing how to read the PivotTable control's crosstab data display and properly ignore subtotals and grand totals, which if used, would skew the chart's scale. Therefore, even though the Chart control can consume data from the PivotTable control, not all data-bound controls will be able to use the PivotTable control as their data source.

Chart and Axis Titles

Charts can be effective mechanisms for displaying large quantities of information in a quick-to-assimilate visual manner. However, the data plotted in charts is rarely self-explanatory; often you will want to add a descriptive title to your chart or to the axes displayed within it.

USING MULTIPLE TOTALS FOR MULTIVALUED CHARTS

The Scatter, Bubble, Polar, and OHLC chart types all have something in common: they need more than one value to determine a data point on the chart. A Scatter chart requires both an X value and a Y value, a Bubble chart needs both those values as well as a bubble size value, a Polar chart needs Theta and R values, and an OHLC chart needs the four values its name suggests. Since PivotTable reports can show more than one total at a time, it's often desirable to map those totals to the different chart values to make a single data point.

You can do this by specifying the index of the total in the PivotTable view as the last parameter to the SetData method. For example, to bind the first total to X and the second total to Y in a Scatter chart, you would write this code:

```
cht.SetData c.chDimXValues, 0, 0    ' First total
cht.SetData c.chDimYValues, 0, 1    ' Second total
```

Sometimes you want to use those multiple totals with a chart type that uses only one value per data point, such as a Stacked Column chart. In this case, you might want the caption of the total to appear as a nested category or a nested series label. To do this, you use a special constant:

```
cht.SetData c.chDimCategories, 0, c.chPivotRowAggregates
```

This setting would use any total captions appearing on the row axis as nested category names on a hierarchical category axis. To get the results you want, you also should set the TotalsOrientation property of the PivotView object to the plTotalOrientationRow constant so that the total captions are displayed on each row.

Perhaps you want to display multiple totals as different series in the chart. To do this, leave the column axis on the PivotTable report empty, add the totals you want to appear as different series, and then write the following code:

```
cht.SetData c.chDimSeriesNames, 0, c.chPivotColAggregates
```

This code will create a series in the chart for each total in the PivotTable report. Refer to the sample file PivotTotalsAsSeries.htm in the Chap03 folder on your companion CD to see what this looks like.

If you add more than one chart to the Chart control (detailed on page 86 in the section "Multiple Charts in 'Chart Space'"), you can give each chart its own title. In fact, you can give the Chart control itself a global title that will be displayed above all the individual charts. Chart titles can be formatted with all the basic font attributes (name, size, bold, italic, underline, and color). You can also set their backgrounds to a specific color or leave them transparent. The same is true for axis titles.

By default, newly created charts will have neither a chart title nor axis titles. You can add chart and axis titles either at design time using the Property Toolbox or at runtime using code. The following method, taken from the AddTitles.htm file in the Chap03 folder on the companion CD, shows how to add a chart title:

```
'-----------------------------------------------------------------
' SetChartTitle()
'
' Purpose: Sets the chart's title
' In:      cht       reference to a chart
'          sTitle    new title caption
'
Sub SetChartTitle(cht, sTitle)
    Dim fnt     ' Temporary font reference

    ' If the title is nonblank
    If Len(sTitle) > 0 Then
        ' Add a title if necessary
        cht.HasTitle = True

        ' Set the caption and its font formatting
        cht.Title.Caption = sTitle
        Set fnt = cht.Title.Font
        fnt.Name = "Tahoma"
        fnt.Size = 10
        fnt.Bold = True
    Else
        ' Title is blank. Remove it.
        cht.HasTitle = False
    End if
End Sub 'SetChartTitle()
```

You add an axis title the same way you add a chart title, except that the first parameter of the method accepts an Axis object reference instead of a Chart object reference.

Also note that you can set the Color property for the title's font or background to either an RGB color value or to one of the Internet Explorer color names—for instance, "FireBrick" or "PapayaWhip". This also applies to any use of color in the Chart control, such as the chart's background color, plot area color, series color, and so on.

Axis Labels

By default, the Chart control will include labels on all your axes to show where a data point lies on the scale (for value axes) or which category a data point belongs to (for category axes). You might want to adjust a few aspects of these labels using either code at runtime or the Property Toolbox at design time.

For value axes, the labels show numeric points on the overall value scale of the axis. These numbers initially have no formatting unless the source is a spreadsheet with cells containing explicit numeric formatting. To change the default number formatting, set the axis's NumberFormat property to a new number format name or string. The list of named formats you can use appears in the Spreadsheet control's help file (opened by clicking the Help button on the spreadsheet) under the topic, "Number formats in a spreadsheet." You can also build a custom format string just like you can in Excel, and the symbols used in custom number formats are documented in the Excel 2000 help files starting with the overview topic titled, "Create a custom number format."

For both value and category axes, you can choose to drop some of the labels— for example, showing only every fifth label. This is useful only for axes that have too many labels to show without overlapping and for which the dropped labels can be inferred from visible labels such as a series of dates. Category axes will not drop labels by default. But suppose you have a large set of dates on a category axis. You can choose to drop some of them by setting the TickLabelSpacing property of the appropriate WCAxis object, either by selecting the axis and using the Property Toolbox at design time or in code at runtime. The setting for this property determines how many labels to skip between the labels that appear. Note that this property affects only labels, meaning the axis will still show tick marks where each label would have appeared. However, you can drop some of these tick marks as well by adjusting the TickMark-Spacing property to the same value as TickLabelSpacing.

The Chart Legend

By default, newly created charts do not have a legend. If you plan on showing more than one series of data points, you might want to add a legend to your chart to explain which color maps to which series. To add a legend, either select the chart and use the Property Toolbox at design time, or set the HasLegend property of the WCChart object to True in code at runtime.

Initially, the legend will contain one entry per series by default, but you can adjust that. To hide a legend entry, use the LegendEntries collection of the WCLegend object to retrieve the legend entry you want to hide, and then set the returned object's Visible property to False. At design time, you can simply select the legend entry itself and press the Delete key.

If you have more than one chart in the Chart control, you can create a legend for each individual chart or you can create one for the control as a whole. If you are showing multiple Pie charts, for example, it probably makes the most sense to show only one legend for all the pies since the color/category mapping will be same for each chart. Other chart types that show the series in the legend can benefit from individual legends if the set of series displayed differs among charts.

One rather annoying aspect of using a single legend for multiple charts that show series in the legend (charts other than Pie, Stacked Pie, and Doughnut) is that the Chart control will initially add an entry to the legend for each occurrence of each series in each chart. If you are showing two series on five charts, the chart space legend will contain ten legend entries, the same two entries repeated five times. To eliminate the extra legend entries, select and delete them at design time or use the WCLegendEntry object's Visible property in code as described earlier.

ADVANCED FUNCTIONALITY OF THE CHART COMPONENT

Now that we've covered all the basics of charting, let's explore a few of the more advanced features of the Chart component, especially those not found in traditional Excel charting. You will see many of these features put to use in the solutions presented in Part II of this book. When we get to those solutions, if you need to refresh your memory on the basics of any particular feature, simply refer back to this section for a more general explanation.

Multiple Charts in "Chart Space"

As noted earlier, the Chart control can display more than one chart at a time in what is known as a chart space. The top-level programming interface for the Chart control is actually called ChartSpace, and when you insert a new Chart control into a container, the default name given the control is usually ChartSpace1.

Showing multiple charts at once in a control is useful for displaying related plots that you want to compare in one glance. This design, often called *small multiples,* can be a powerful analysis tool. For example, if you need to show sales data across time, salespeople, and geography simultaneously, you might create one chart for each country, each displaying the salespeople as series and the time as categories. Figure 3-18 shows what the resulting charts might look like.

The Chart control can show up to 16 charts in the same chart space, but all the charts must share the same set of categories. If two charts have a different set of categories, the set of categories used for both charts will be the union of the categories from each chart. This is because small-multiple designs rely on the consistency of the categories, series, and axis scalings among the various charts so that you notice large differences and trends easily.

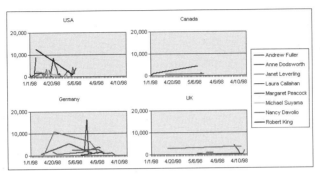

Figure 3-18. *Multiple charts in one chart space.*

That said, the Chart control will not automatically normalize the value axis scales among all the various charts for you, but you can do this quite easily with a little bit of code from the MultipleCharts.htm file in the Chap03 folder on the companion CD:

```
'-----------------------------------------------------------------------
' NormalizeCharts()
'
' Purpose: Makes all value axes of charts in a chart space the same
'          so that you can accurately compare values
' In:      cspace = reference to the ChartSpace object
'          nAxis =  index of the value axis in the WCAxes collection
'
Sub NormalizeCharts(cspace, nAxis)
    ' Local variables
    Dim cht      ' Temporary chart object reference
    Dim ax       ' Temporary axis object reference
    Dim nMax     ' Maximum value across the axes

    nMax = 0

    ' Loop through all the charts once to determine the overall maximum
    For Each cht In cspace.Charts
        Set ax = cht.Axes(nAxis)
        If ax.Scaling.Maximum > nMax Then
            nMax = ax.Scaling.Maximum
        End If
    Next 'cht
```

(continued)

```
' Loop again to set the maximum
For Each cht In cspace.Charts
    Set ax = cht.Axes(nAxis)
    ax.Scaling.Maximum = nMax
Next 'cht

End Sub 'NormalizeCharts()
```

The code here performs two loops over all the Chart objects in the chart space. The first determines the maximum value across all the value axes, and the second sets the Scaling.Maximum property to the maximum value so that all charts have the same maximum on their value axis. Note that this kind of method is necessary only when your chart has a value axis—so it does not apply to multiple Pie, multiple Stacked Pie, or multiple Doughnut charts.

You can also control the layout of multiple charts within the chart space by adjusting the ChartLayout and ChartWrapCount properties of the top-level ChartSpace object. You can set the ChartLayout property to make the charts lay out horizontally or vertically. ChartWrapCount controls how many charts appear in each row or in each column before wrapping to the next. You can also adjust the HeightRatio and WidthRatio properties of each WCChart object to allow more or less room for specific charts.

Server-Side Use

Each of the Office Web Components can be used as a nonvisible, in-memory object in addition to a COM control hosted on a form. But when it comes to running on a web server, the Chart component is probably the most desirable of the Office Web Components. When the OWC team first started releasing beta builds internally at Microsoft, we immediately began to receive e-mail from other groups in the company that wanted to know how to use the Chart control on the server to generate charts of live data (in most cases, to report bug statistics). Many businesses have a set of metrics they use to measure a production or operational process; it's a manager's dream to simply open his or her web browser and see a chart with up-to-the-minute data. Since the Chart control can be used on the server and can emit a GIF image of itself, many developers find utilizing the Chart control on the server a compelling way to generate charts of live data that can be used across the Internet or in enterprises where the client desktop is heterogeneous.

You will find this type of solution implemented in Chapter 6, where we will examine it in much greater detail. For now, I will familiarize you with what the Chart control can do when running on the server and show you the basics of saving the Chart control's contents as a GIF image.

You can employ all the normal features of the Chart control when using it on the server. Also, all the code we discussed earlier that is used to load the chart with different data is applicable in that environment. Typically, you load the Chart control from an ADO Recordset object obtained from either a server-side object or another script on the server. You can refer to all the elements of the chart as if they were on the screen, and when you are finished creating the chart, you can use the ChartSpace object's ExportPicture method to write the GIF image to a file. The Chart control supports exporting to only the GIF image format in this release, but you can specify any width and height you want in pixels.

The last point I want to make about server-side usage is that you should check the license agreement that comes with your copy of Office 2000 and ask a Microsoft Application Developer Customer Unit (ADCU) representative for more information on distributing a solution that uses the Office Web Components on a web server. At the time of this writing, the Office marketing group was putting together a special server-side usage license for the Office Web Components. Although the details had not been finalized, this fee was intended to cover an unlimited number of clients so that you could use these components on an Internet site.

Split Axes

Another commonly requested charting feature is the ability to split a value axis at a certain point so that you can portray small and large numbers on the same value axis and still show the local variation. Figure 3-19 depicts a common Split-Axis chart.

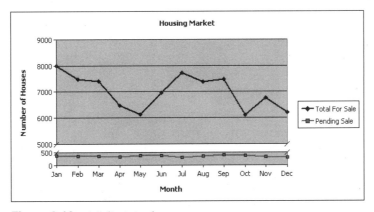

Figure 3-19. *A Split-Axis chart.*

Charts can have one split per value axis, and you can specify the exact values where the value axis's split starts and ends. You can do this in the Property Toolbox at design time by selecting the value axis and using the Split Axis section of the Property Toolbox to set the start and end split values. You can also do this with code at runtime by setting the HasSplit property of the axis's Scaling object to True and then setting the SplitMinimum and SplitMaximum properties.

Adjusting an Axis's Scaling

The Chart control by default will choose an automatic minimum and maximum for a value axis that will make all the data points visible and leave a little bit of margin around the plot area. However, sometimes you will want to override these defaults and manually adjust an axis's scaling attributes to get precisely the minimum and maximum you want.

Every WCAxis object has a Scaling property that returns a WCScaling object. The WCScaling object has properties called Minimum and Maximum for setting an explicit minimum and an explicit maximum or for reading the current values. You can also set the HasAutoMinimum and HasAutoMaximum properties to True to force the axis to return to automatic scaling behavior.

The WCScaling object also lets you tell the axis to use a logarithmic scale instead of a linear one. Set the Type property of WCScaling to the chScaleTypeLogarithmic constant to make the scale logarithmic, or restore it to the chScaleTypeLinear constant to make it linear again. You can also adjust the LogBase property to set the base of the logarithmic scale.

Another interesting setting you can adjust is the Orientation property, which makes a scale display backwards, from minimum to maximum, rather than vice versa. This might or might not be useful for a value axis, but it is the easiest way to make a category axis show the categories in reverse order.

Probably the most interesting use of the Scaling object is to simulate zooming and panning on an axis. If your chart is densely packed with data points, it is useful to allow an analyst to zoom into a specific section of the axis and then pan across the axis to see various sections. You can do this by simply manipulating the Minimum and Maximum properties of the Scaling object, which has the effect of zooming and panning in the chart because the chart shows less numerical distance in the same visual distance on the screen.

Homemade Chart Tips

The Chart component does not yet have the chart tips feature that you have no doubt seen in Excel. Chart tips are the larger ScreenTips that show up when you hover the mouse over a data point or chart element. Chart tips show the data point's value, category, series, and other useful information. The bad news is that these chart tips are not a native feature of the Chart control; the good news is that you can add them yourself by catching a few events raised by the Chart control. In Part II of the book, I will explain how you can create these homemade chart tips. For now, I will just give you the basics of how they work.

The Chart control raises the MouseMove event whenever the mouse is moved over the control. During this event, you can ask for the mouse's current X and Y coordinates with respect to the control's top-left pixel. These X and Y coordinates not only help you position other elements where the mouse is, but you can also feed them to the ChartSpace object's RangeFromPoint method to get the chart object that is currently under the mouse. For example, if your mouse is positioned over a data point, this method will return a WCPoint object, with which you can determine the parent series, the category, and the exact value of the point using the GetValue method. You can also adjust the formatting for that specific data point using the WCPoint object, which means you can, for instance, change the border color to highlight the value or change the interior color to a slightly darker or lighter shade of the current fill color. If the mouse is positioned over a chart element such as the legend, you will get a WCLegend object back from this method. Use the TypeName method in VBScript and VBA to determine what kind of object you get back from the Range-FromPoint method. You can also use the ChartSpace object's SelectionType property to determine the type of object returned from the Selection property.

For an example of using the Chart component's events and reacting to the mouse, see the file ReactingToMouse.htm in the Chap03 folder on the companion CD.

WHY IS IT CALLED RANGEFROMPOINT?

When I first started looking into the nooks and crannies of the Chart component's programming model, I asked Jason Cahill, the Chart component's program manager, why this method was called RangeFromPoint when it clearly had nothing to do with ranges and instead returned chart objects. "Shouldn't this be called ObjectFromPoint?" I asked.

Jason explained that when Microsoft's accessibility group first decided to build screen readers for the blind, they wanted a method in Excel that would return the current range underneath the mouse so that they could read the values in the cells over the computer's audio system. (In case you were wondering, the accessibility group makes computers accessible to people with disabilities. Screen readers use audio to "read" onscreen text aloud for blind users.) Excel correctly named the method RangeFromPoint since it returned a range from an (X,Y) point. However, the accessibility group coded that method name into their application, and now anyone who wants accessibility to the screen reader must implement the RangeFromPoint method even though his or her application might not have anything to do with spreadsheet ranges.

KEY ELEMENTS OF THE PROGRAMMING MODEL

As in the previous chapter, I want to finish by highlighting the key elements of the Chart component's programming model. The properties, methods, and events listed in this section are the subset that you will likely want to use often and are organized according to the tasks you will typically want to perform.

I will not repeat the parts of the Spreadsheet component's programming model that I noted in the previous chapter as applying to all the controls in the Office Web Components library—you can refer back to Chapter 2 for a list and explanation of those properties.

Creating Charts in the Chart Space

When you create a new ChartSpace object, it initially does not contain any charts. To add a chart to the ChartSpace object, use the Add method of the WCCharts collection. Table 3-1 lists the properties and methods you will use to add and remove charts from the chart space.

Property or Method	Description
ChartSpace.Charts	This property returns the WCCharts collection of all the WCChart objects in the Chart control.
WCCharts.Add	Use this method to add a new chart to the chart space.
ChartSpace.Clear	This method clears all content from the Chart control. Use it to quickly remove all charts, data sources, and any other elements created within the chart space.

Table 3-1. *Properties and methods for adding and removing charts from the chart space.*

Changing Chart or Series Types

As you will recall, we discussed the various chart types much earlier in the chapter. Changing from one chart type to another is as simple as setting one property, as Table 3-2 shows.

Property or Enum	Description
WCChart.Type	This property sets or returns the type for all series in a chart.

Table 3-2. *Properties and constants for changing chart or series types.*

Property or Enum	Description
WCSeries.Type	This property sets or returns the type for a single series in a chart. Multiple series can each have their own type, but not all types can be combined in one chart (as discussed earlier in the chapter in the "Combination Charts" section).
ChartChartTypeEnum	This enumeration contains all the constants you can use with the two Type properties just described.

Loading the Chart with Data

Table 3-3 lists the methods you will use to load the Chart component with data. For more detailed explanations and example code, see the section "Loading Data" that appears earlier in the chapter.

Method	Description
WCChart.SetData	This method can be used to load data into the entire chart at once, including the series names.
WCSeries.SetData	This method loads data into a given series.

Table 3-3. *Methods for loading data into a chart.*

Exporting a GIF Image

You can export the Chart control's current contents to a GIF image on disk at any time. Use the ExportPicture method, which is described in Table 3-4.

Method	Description
ChartSpace.ExportPicture	This method exports the Chart control's current contents to a GIF image file. You can specify the filename, width, and height. If you specify the optional FilterName parameter, it must be "GIF" since the only format implemented in this version of the control is GIF.

Table 3-4. *Method for creating a GIF image of the chart space.*

Working with Axes

Often you will want to adjust the look of the various axes in your chart. Use the properties outlined in Table 3-5 to accomplish this.

Property	Description
WCChart.Axes	This property returns the WCAxes collection, from which you can obtain a specific axis. To ask for an axis by its location, use the appropriate constant from ChartAxisPositionEnum. To retrieve the axes in order, use their index values.
WCAxis.NumberFormat	This property sets or returns the number format used for value axis labels. You can specify any number format that the Spreadsheet control supports, including the named formats and the custom formats.
WCAxis.Font	This property returns the OWCFont object for the axis. You can use the properties of this object to adjust the name, size, and other font attributes of the axis labels.
WCAxis.HasTitle	This property sets or returns whether the axis has a title. If this property is False, no title exists; the space it would have used is reclaimed for the chart. If this property is set to True, the axis will have a title; you can use the WCAxis.Title property to get at the WCTitle object and set its caption. Note that accessing the Title property while WCAxis.HasTitle is False results in a run-time error.
WCAxis.Title	This property returns the WCTitle object for the axis, with which you can set the title's caption, font, and color settings.
WCAxis.TickLabelSpacing	This property sets or returns the tick label spacing used for the axis. The tick label spacing determines how many labels are dropped from the axis between those that are displayed. This technique is useful for dropping date values when you have too many to show. The dropped labels can be assumed based on the surrounding labels.
WCAxis.TickMarkSpacing	This property sets or returns the spacing between tick marks on an axis. Like the TickLabelSpacing property, this property determines how many tick marks should be dropped between those that are shown.

Table 3-5. *Properties for formatting the chart axes.*

Manipulating the Legend

You might want to hide or show the legend of a chart or hide individual legend entries. To do so, use the properties discussed in Table 3-6.

Property	Description
ChartSpace.HasChartSpaceLegend, WCChart.HasLegend	Like the WCAxis.HasTitle property described in Table 3-5, the HasChart-SpaceLegend and HasLegend properties determine whether the chart space and individual chart will show and reserve space for a legend. To use the Chart-SpaceLegend or Legend property described below, first set the HasChart-SpaceLegend or HasLegend property to True.
ChartSpace.ChartSpaceLegend, WCChart.Legend	The ChartSpaceLegend and Legend properties return WCLegend objects that represent the legends for the entire chart space and the individual chart, respectively.
WCLegend.LegendEntries	This property returns the WCLegend-Entries collection of all entries in the legend. The collection has a Count property that tells you how many entries appear in the legend and an Item property that lets you retrieve each one.
WCLegendEntry.Visible	This property determines whether a legend entry appears in the legend. Setting this to False will hide the legend entry.
WCLegend.Position	This property determines where the legend is placed in the chart. It can be placed on the top, bottom, left side, or right side (the default) of the chart.

Table 3-6. *Properties for manipulating legend display.*

Useful Events

The Chart control exposes a few interesting events that you might want to catch. All events are raised from the top-level ChartSpace object. Table 3-7 lists the most interesting events.

Event	Description
Click, DblClick	Raised whenever the user clicks or double-clicks anywhere on the Chart control. Use the WCChartEventInfo object passed to these events to determine the current X and Y coordinates of the mouse within the Chart control, and pass those to the RangeFromPoint method to retrieve the chart object at that (X,Y) point.
MouseMove	Raised whenever the user moves the mouse over the Chart control. The WCChartEventInfo object is also passed to this event.
DataSetChange	Raised whenever a bound data source notifies the chart that the data has changed. The Chart control will automatically update to show the new data; however, you should use this event to reformat the chart in case new series were added. Beware of putting too much code in this event: since any change to the source data will raise the event, it can fire quite often.

Table 3-7. *Useful ChartSpace events.*

SUMMARY

Although the Chart component might look rather simple on the surface, there is quite a bit of complexity hiding in it. We've covered much of the functionality of the Chart control in this chapter. However, you'll find more information on using the Chart component in Part II of this book where I discuss several solutions you can build using it. Also, spend some time looking at this chapter's example files on the companion CD as they will help you get started writing code against the Chart control.

Chapter 4

The PivotTable Component

During the last few years, OLAP and data warehousing technology have exploded in popularity and practicality. OLAP has been around for quite some time, but it did not achieve a critical mass in the business world until recently. Today, you can hardly pick up a computer or information systems trade journal that does not mention OLAP or data warehousing. (For those of you not familiar with OLAP, I will provide a brief overview on page 107.)

In many ways, the OLAP explosion is not a surprise. During the last four decades, corporations have become extremely adept at capturing large amounts of transactional and research data in order to run their core business systems and develop new products. Once that information has been captured, it's a valuable resource just waiting to be tapped—most businesspeople want to see summaries to help them make decisions about marketing campaigns, sales efforts, production processes, and so on. Unfortunately for the business decision makers in these corporations, this resource often is locked safely in that impenetrable vault known as the centralized IT department. The IT employees have their hands full keeping the core business systems running and usually do not have the time to generate the myriad desired reports, the requests for which are often vaguely phrased and poorly defined. If and when the IT department *does* produce these reports, the reports tend to be inflexible. In fact, requesting a simple change such as grouping data by a different field might require the IT department to generate a new report—unfortunately, with a painfully slow turnaround.

OLAP and data warehousing promise to alleviate some of these problems by letting IT groups concentrate on what they do best and by putting simple yet powerful tools in the hands of those with questions about the data, enabling them to generate any slice of data needed. The IT group can spend its time extracting, consolidating, and cleaning the data; designing a cube structure that matches the business's mental model; and developing batch programs to load daily transactional data into the OLAP servers. Users can "slice and dice" to find answers to their particular questions—for instance, "How much did we sell per capita for each state in my region?" or, "How much have the sales of my product increased or decreased compared to this time last year?"

The PivotTable component is one of those simple yet powerful client tools often categorized as "business intelligence" tools. While those who read the comic strip Dilbert on a regular basis might consider "business intelligence" an oxymoron, it's a good description of what these tools aim to deliver. The mass of data stored in an OLAP system is useless until it is translated into information presented in a report, which hopefully becomes useful knowledge to someone making a business decision. You can use the PivotTable component to build powerful, web-based data analysis systems that allow your users to sort, filter, and regroup data within the web browser. Many corporations are discovering that web browsers and intranet sites provide an easy way to convey information to employees. However, static representations of data are as limiting as those obsolete printed reports. Not only does the PivotTable control deliver interactive data analysis, but it also offers easy installation and upgrading. Much of the ease of deployment can be attributed to Microsoft Internet Explorer's automatic code download mechanism, which is used for all COM components on a web page. (We'll discuss deployment in greater detail in Chapter 12.)

> **NOTE** Despite all this talk of HTML and web pages, you should realize that the PivotTable control runs in Microsoft Visual Basic forms and the other control containers listed in Chapter 1 as well as it runs in web pages. However, most of the discussions in this chapter focus on using the PivotTable control on a web page simply because many developers find this immensely appealing.

This chapter will discuss the conceptual details of the PivotTable component, starting with an explanation of why a PivotTable report is useful. Next, you will see the various types of data that the PivotTable control can consume. Plus, you'll get a brief overview of OLAP technology, one of the key data sources for the PivotTable component. After that, you will learn about the terminology of the elements in the PivotTable control and see how they map to the underlying elements in each type of data source. Finally, you'll discover how to use the PivotTable control to add analysis features to your solution.

This chapter will not explicitly cover creating a PivotTable interactively in a designer. The PivotTable control's help file covers this topic quite thoroughly; you can view it by clicking the control's Help toolbar button. For information on publishing

Microsoft Excel 2000 PivotTable reports to the PivotTable control, see the Excel help topic entitled, "About displaying Microsoft Excel PivotTable reports on the Web."

OVERVIEW

Combining the PivotTable dynamic report and external data range (which is also known as *query table*) features in Excel, the PivotTable component provides interactive data analysis of both tabular and OLAP data sources. The output of the control is commonly referred to as a *cross tabulation* because it shows summary (aggregated) values for an intersection of categories. For example, you can display sales information grouped by product line within years down the rows, intersected with customer gender across the columns. When using a tabular data source, the PivotTable control can also show detail data rows for any aggregate value in addition to the summarized aggregates, or it can simply display all the tabular data in a flat list.

Whenever I talk about the PivotTable control, I usually jump right into a demonstration. Trying to explain what it does is infinitely harder than simply showing it in action. The technology behind the control is incredibly abstract, but its use is actually quite natural and intuitive. Many business analysts can use the control quite effectively but cannot describe what it does with any degree of accuracy. They know only that it can help them obtain answers to their questions. For that reason, I encourage you to open the file PivotTableIntro.htm from the Chap04 folder on the companion CD and experiment with it as I describe what this control can do. When opened, the sample page looks like Figure 4-1.

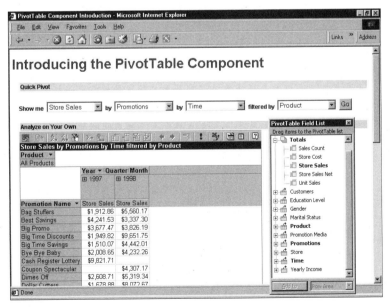

Figure 4-1. *A sample PivotTable report.*

The data source for this report is a sample cube that comes with Microsoft SQL Server OLAP Services. It contains sales information for a fictitious grocery chain named Foodmart. I have exported this cube to the Data\Sales.cub file on your companion CD so that you can use it without needing an OLAP server on your machine; however, this cube file is naturally slower than a server-based cube.

The sample page initially configures the PivotTable control to display a report of the sales amounts attributed to various promotions offered in 1997 and 1998. Using this report, you can answer questions such as, "What was the most successful promotion in 1997?" or, "Which promotions helped to sell the most product in the Drink product family?" To answer the first question, right-click any number in the 1997 column and choose the Sort Descending command, or select any number in the 1997 column and click the Sort Descending toolbar button. The report immediately re-sorts to show the promotions with the highest sales first, as shown in Figure 4-2.

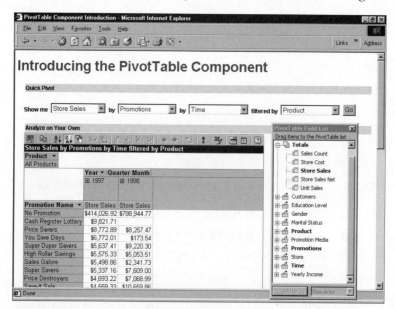

Figure 4-2. *A sorted PivotTable report.*

The No Promotion item is first in the list, meaning that more products are bought in response to no promotion than any particular promotion. The Cash Register Lottery promotion is next, but notice that it was not run in 1998. This discovery might lead a marketing manager to investigate why it was not continued, since it was the most successful promotion in 1997.

One of the most typical analysis techniques is to ask for more detail about an interesting piece of data. In OLAP terminology, this is often called *drilling down*. In fact, the PivotTable control lets you easily perform this technique. For example, suppose that a report displays the sales attributed to the Cash Register Lottery promotion in 1997 and you want to know whether that promotion was more effective during a particular season. In other words, you want to know how the sales attributed to that promotion break down into the four quarters of 1997. To show the detail, double-click the 1997 column label or click the plus sign (+) to the left of the label. The report expands to show the four quarters of 1997 and the sales amounts attributed to each, as Figure 4-3 illustrates.

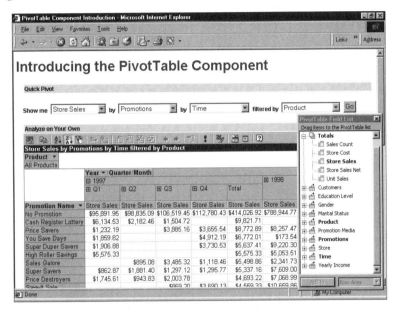

Figure 4-3. *A drilled-down PivotTable report.*

You can see that almost all the sales occurred in the first quarter, indicating that the promotion was popular when first introduced but waned over time, probably explaining why it was not run in 1998.

You can use the Quick Pivot interface on the page to quickly generate different cuts of the data, but to view more complex reports, drag items from the floating window called the PivotTable Field List (shown in Figure 4-4) to the report.

The field list displays all the totals and fields available in the data source. You can use this list to nest fields within each other, add more totals to the report, or put more fields in the filter area to restrict the data shown. For example, drag the Store field and drop it to the right of the list of promotion names to see how the promotion fared by country, state, and city. Next, drag the Sales Count total to the center of the report (where all the numbers are) to see the quantity sold in addition to the dollar amount. Finally, drag the Gender field to the right of the Product field at the top of the report. Once you have dropped it, click the small drop-down button at the right of the field label, choose "M" to show only the sales attributed to men, and click the OK button. The final report should look like Figure 4-5.

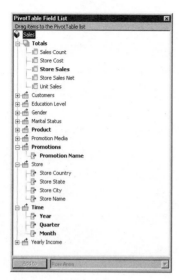

Figure 4-4. *The PivotTable Field List.*

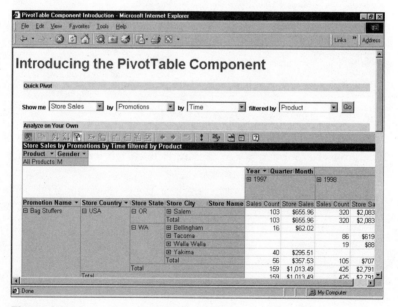

Figure 4-5. *A complex PivotTable report.*

The PivotTable component is obviously useful for sales analysis, but you can also use it to summarize any type of numeric data across many categories. When combined with the Chart component described in the previous chapter, it can be quite a powerful analysis tool. We will see a real-world example of this in Chapter 7.

HOW THE PIVOTTABLE COMPONENT WORKS WITH DATA

One of the most important and complicated aspects of the PivotTable component is how it interacts with various data sources and how it manages that data during a session. This section will explain how the PivotTable control communicates with data sources, as well as how data is transferred and manipulated during a session.

The PivotTable control is a bit schizophrenic—much of its capabilities depend on the kind of data source to which it is connected. Essentially, the PivotTable control can use only two kinds of data sources: tabular and multidimensional. (Multidimensional data sources can also be called *OLAP data sources;* I will use these two terms interchangeably in this book.) We'll also discuss using XML data as a data source. Although XML data looks like any other tabular data source to the PivotTable control, it has a few requirements that warrant special discussion.

Tabular Data Sources

Tabular databases include any existing OLE DB data sources that expose tables of data. Traditionally, these are the relational database engines of the world. However, this category can also include nonrelational data providers—as long as they have some form of textual command syntax or named tables.

Figure 4-6 shows how a report initially looks when the PivotTable component is loaded with data returned from a tabular data source. (You can also see this report by running the PivotTableList.htm file from the Chap04 folder on the companion CD.)

The report is similar to that produced by using an external data range in an Excel spreadsheet. However, since the PivotTable control combines the functionality of external data ranges and PivotTable reports, you can now group the data by any field and create a new total for any field. For example, using the Move To Row Area, Move To Column Area, and AutoCalc toolbar buttons, you can transform this flat list of data into the PivotTable report shown in Figure 4-7.

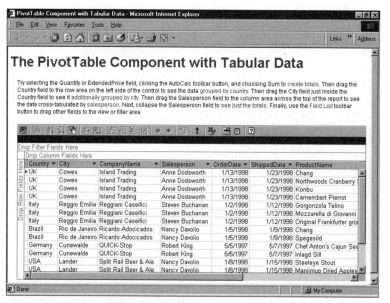

Figure 4-6. *A PivotTable report filled with data from a tabular data source.*

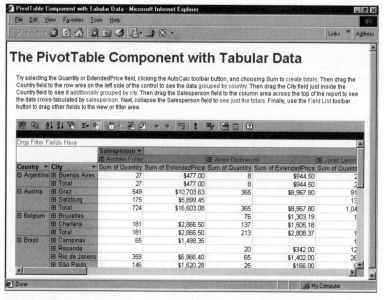

Figure 4-7. *A PivotTable report created from a flat list of data.*

Because the data source is tabular, the PivotTable control can show the details behind any total—meaning you can expand any number and see the rows that contributed to it right in place. Figure 4-8 shows the general architecture for accessing tabular data sources.

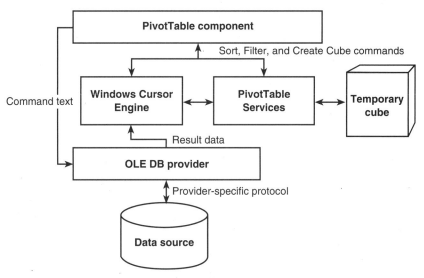

Figure 4-8. *Accessing tabular data sources.*

When retrieving data, the PivotTable control first connects to the OLE DB provider named in the provider attribute of the connection string. When building a report in a designer, you typically will choose this provider from a list in the Data Link Properties dialog box. The provider is an in-process COM component that resides on the client machine and typically communicates to the data server (if it is an actual server machine) through a private protocol. For example, the provider for SQL Server communicates to the server using a variety of protocols, the most common being named pipes. However, the provider for Microsoft Jet databases requires file access to the MDB file because the Jet database engine is not a client-server system.

After the PivotTable control connects to the data source, it passes the contents of its CommandText property to the provider for execution. You can set the Command-Text property at design time using the Data Source section of the Property Toolbox, or you can set it in code at runtime. The PivotTable control uses the ADO Recordset object to execute the command text, so any value that can be passed to the Recordset's Open method can be used in the CommandText property. These values typically include SQL statements or the name of a table, view, or stored procedure. The provider then returns an OLE DB IRowset interface that allows access to data returned from the command.

When working with a tabular data source, the PivotTable control uses ADO to immediately load the returned data into a component known as the Windows Cursor Engine (WCE). The WCE is a component provided in the Microsoft Data Access Components (MDAC), offering advanced scrolling, sorting, and filtering functionality over any data provider. The WCE loads the data from the source provider into its own memory cache, which will eventually page to disk if it contains more data than its memory threshold will allow. (This keeps the WCE from using all your available system memory.) After the data is loaded into the WCE, the PivotTable control communicates with it to filter, sort, and scroll around the data set.

The magic begins when you start to group the resultset by a field or when you create a total using steps similar to those described earlier. To perform the cross tabulations, the PivotTable control employs another piece of data plumbing known as the *PivotTable Services component*. This component is actually the client-side provider for OLAP Services, but it also can provide temporary cube creation on the client regardless of the data source. When you group fields or create a total, the PivotTable control hands the PivotTable Services component a reference to the data set and describes what dimensions and totals it needs in the temporary cube. This engine will create a temporary file in the folder that serves as the temporary folder for Microsoft Windows, so beware of this requirement if your company's policy is to not allow controls in a web browser to create temporary files.

NAMING THE TEMPORARY CUBE

When implementing this feature, one of the star data developers of the PivotTable component, David Wortendyke, had to devise a scheme for naming the temporary cube so that it would not overwrite any existing file or interfere with PivotTable controls running in other applications. His eventual scheme was to construct the name of the file using the current process and thread ID and the traditional CUB extension.

So when grouping and creating totals in a PivotTable control using a tabular source, if you see some crazily named file in your temporary folder, remember that it is a temporary cube file being created by the PivotTable control. Don't worry—these files will be deleted automatically when the control is destroyed.

When working with tabular data, the PivotTable control also will automatically generate two time hierarchies for each date or date/time field in the detail data. One hierarchy contains the grouping intervals Year, Quarter, Month, and Day; the other contains the intervals Year, Week, and Day. (Both hierarchies are necessary because weeks do not neatly roll up into months.) These automatic hierarchies make it easier to analyze data that has a time dimension, allowing you to see summary values for each of the intervals.

If you plan to use the PivotTable control on a web page, you might also want to investigate using Remote Data Services (RDS). This is another piece of data access plumbing provided in MDAC, which accesses data sources over HTTP. When using RDS, the only provider needed on the client machine is the RDS provider, which is installed with the Office Web Components. The RDS provider then communicates with the real data provider—for example, SQL Server—through a web server, allowing the native data source provider to exist only on the server. For more information on RDS, consult the data access portion of the Microsoft web site at http://www.microsoft.com/data.

Multidimensional (OLAP) Data Sources

While you are most likely familiar with tabular or relational data sources, you might not be as familiar with multidimensional (or OLAP) data sources. Before I describe how the different elements of the PivotTable component map to the structures of a multidimensional database, let me give you a brief introduction to multidimensional database concepts.

A Brief Overview of OLAP

In a relational database, tables and relationships are the primary data structures and concepts. You construct databases by defining tables that contain one or more columns, a primary key, rules, and so on. Then you relate those tables to each other by specifying the foreign keys that match primary keys in other tables. Once this is done, you can execute a SQL statement against the database engine and it will join, sort, restrict, and group data as needed to fulfill the request.

In a multidimensional database, the primary data structure is a *cube,* or more precisely, a *hypercube.* This structure is an N-dimensional matrix, which is a bit hard to visualize. The items contained in each dimension are called *members,* and the intersection of N members produces a number. Looking at an example will help make this much less abstract.

Imagine that we are modeling sales data for a company in this hypercube. In our example, we will start with two dimensions: Products and Customers. A two-dimensional structure is fairly easy to visualize because it looks like a matrix you might see for comparing two dimensions of information, such as a crosstab report. Figure 4-9 shows how this matrix might look.

	Customers				
Products	Jeff	Dave	Jon	Gina	All
Widgets	$10,000.00	$12,000.00	$15,000.00	$17,000.00	$54,000.00
Gears	$12,000.00	$11,500.00	$12,000.00	$15,000.00	$50,500.00
Levers	$8,000.00	$10,000.00	$14,500.00	$16,000.00	$48,500.00
Bolts	$9,000.00	$10,500.00	$10,000.00	$18,500.00	$48,000.00
All	$39,000.00	$44,000.00	$51,500.00	$66,500.00	$201,000.00

Figure 4-9. *A two-dimensional database.*

Note that customer names appear in one dimension, product names appear in the other, and the numbers in the center are sales. For any combination of product and customer, a value is stored representing the amount of money the customer spent on the product. Also note that one extra member, named All, appears in each dimension. This member represents the total for all members in that dimension (often a sum of all the members). So the intersection of Customers.All and a specific product represents the total sales for that product. Similarly, the intersection of Products.All and a specific customer represents the total sales made to that customer. The intersection of the two All members is the grand sales total of all products to all customers.

Now imagine adding to this matrix a third dimension that contains salesperson names. The structure becomes a three-dimensional cube and conceptually looks like Figure 4-10.

Three coordinates—a customer, a product, and a salesperson—now determine each intersection or cell in the cube. Again a member named All appears in the Salesperson dimension and symbolizes the total sales for all salespeople. This structure can help you answer a variety of questions by allowing you to view the data from a number of perspectives. Since these numbers are stored in the structure, the multidimensional database can return any set of these cells quickly.

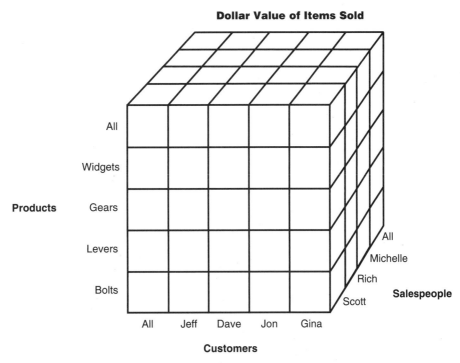

Figure 4-10. *A three-dimensional database.*

It is harder to visualize four dimensions, but suppose you want to summarize additional data values. For example, you might want to track quantity sold as well as the dollar value of items sold. These multiple values create a fourth dimension that has two members (Quantity Sold and Dollar Value of Items Sold). These data values are called *measures* in the multidimensional database; however, most data sources treat measures like any other dimension. Figure 4-11 shows one way of visualizing four dimensions of data.

Internally, the multidimensional database will still store all the data in one, four-dimensional hypercube. But you can conceptualize a four-dimensional data structure by thinking of the fourth dimension as multiple three-dimensional cubes. If you want to see the dollar value of items sold for a given customer, product, and salesperson intersection, you would look at the first cube. If you want to know the quantity sold for the same intersection, you would look at the second cube. You could of course expand this example to show tables of cubes and cubes of cubes—but I will stop before your mind explodes from visualizing 16-dimensional space.

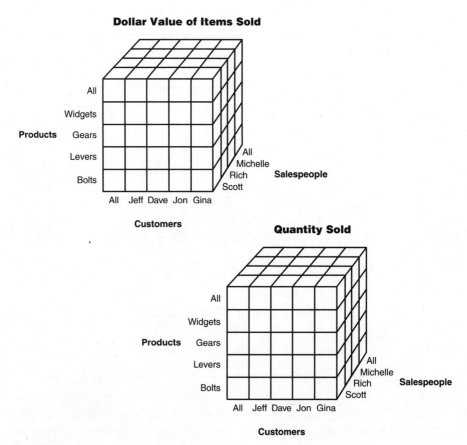

Figure 4-11. *A four-dimensional database.*

Most multidimensional databases also let you group the members contained in a dimension, potentially specifying a parent and set of children for each member. In fact, dimensions have one or more *hierarchies* defined within them, and each hierarchy has one or more *levels*, each of which has a set of members. This mimics the natural structure of most categorical data—products typically fall into groups of related products, customers live in cities within states within countries, and salespeople belong to certain districts that belong to certain regions and so on. For example, the Customers dimension might have the levels All, Country, State, City, and Customer Name. The set of members at the Country level might be USA, Canada, and Mexico, while the set of members for the State level might be Washington, Oregon, British Columbia, Alberta, Jalisco, Veracruz, and so on.

It is possible to have multiple hierarchies within a single dimension. For example, if you have an Employees dimension, you might want to calculate travel expenses along organizational lines to see totals for each manager and department head, or you might want to see the totals for all employees that perform a certain job function, such as marketing, sales, product development, or executive staff. The members of the dimension remain the same (the individual employees), but they are organized into different hierarchies and therefore create different totals.

A number of books, journals, reports, and pieces of documentation describe multidimensional databases in depth. If you have purchased a multidimensional database, chances are the documentation that came with your database explains these concepts in much more detail than I have time to do here.

How the PivotTable Component
Interacts with OLAP Data Sources

The PivotTable component communicates and interacts with OLAP data sources using a similar approach to tabular data sources. Figure 4-12 provides a general picture of the architecture.

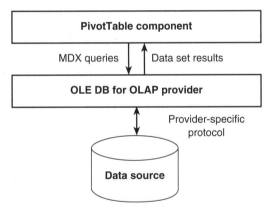

Figure 4-12. *The interaction between the PivotTable component and an OLAP data source.*

The PivotTable control uses the OLE DB for OLAP standard defined by Microsoft and supported by many multidimensional databases. This model is an extension of the OLE DB standard, so much of the PivotTable control's interaction with the OLAP data provider naturally is similar to how it interacts with tabular data providers. The control begins by connecting to the data provider, which again is an in-process COM component that resides on the client machine. The provider determines how it will communicate with the multidimensional database. For example, OLAP Services uses a TCP/IP socket connection between the client and the server.

After the PivotTable component is connected to the OLAP data source, it can display all the hierarchies and measures in the specified hypercube through the PivotTable Field List window. As the user drags and drops hierarchies and measures to the PivotTable control, or as the developer inserts hierarchies and measures programmatically, the PivotTable control generates the necessary queries in MDX (Multidimensional Expressions, which is the query language defined by the OLE DB for OLAP specification) and executes them against the data source. The data provider returns the results, and the PivotTable control displays them onscreen.

When working with an OLAP data source, the amount of data transmitted across the network is quite small. The OLAP provider typically sends only the MDX query string to the server, and the server returns only the cells and member names that you see onscreen. The server sends only the aggregate values back to the client, rather than all the underlying detail data that was necessary to create those aggregate values. This makes the PivotTable control very responsive and allows the system to scale to support a large number of simultaneous clients.

SHOULD I MAKE A CUBE OR JUST GROUP TABULAR DATA?

When I show people that the PivotTable component can group and total tabular data so that it looks like a report from an OLAP cube, they often ask, "So why should I make a cube?"

The answer is twofold. First, using a precreated, server-based hypercube often yields drastic improvements in performance over using the PivotTable control to create temporary cubes of tabular data. Every time you group a new field in the tabular data, the PivotTable control must re-create the cube and reprocess all the aggregates. A server-based cube processes the aggregates only once and shares them with all the clients accessing the cube.

Second, a precreated cube can define hierarchies with multiple levels that establish a clear drill-down path through the data. When the PivotTable control groups relational data, it creates hierarchies for date fields only; it cannot know that fields such as Country, State, and City are actually three levels of the same hierarchy. In a precreated cube, you can define these hierarchies and make it easier for users of the data to find the information they seek.

XML

One special data source for the PivotTable component is a URL that returns XML data in a specific format. In the ADO 2.1 release, the Data Access Group at Microsoft (the group that makes MDAC) defined an XML format for persisting an OLE DB Rowset. They also built a piece of data access plumbing called the *persistence provider,* which can save and load an OLE DB Rowset by writing and reading XML data in this format. The PivotTable control is capable of using this provider to load the Windows Cursor Engine with XML data returned from a specified URL. Figure 4-13 depicts the architecture for this scenario.

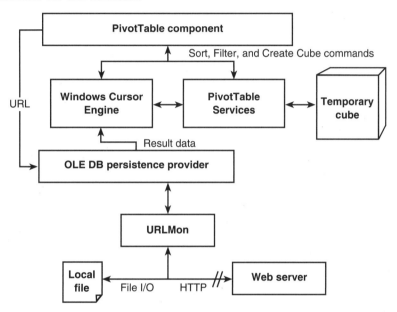

Figure 4-13. *Using the persistence provider to load the WCE with XML data.*

In a moment, I will explain what type of connection string you must pass to the PivotTable control to use this approach. However, for purposes of the discussion at hand, the important piece of information the PivotTable control needs is the URL from which it should retrieve the XML data stream. The PivotTable control hands this URL to the persistence provider, which in turn uses the Internet services of Windows to request the results of that URL. The results are parsed and loaded into the WCE, and the PivotTable control continues on—just as it would when working with tabular data.

The format for this XML data is specific and unfortunately is not well documented. However, the easiest way to see what it looks like is to use the ADO Recordset object's Save method with the adPersistXML format to save the contents of a Recordset to a file. If you want to generate XML data in this format dynamically—for example, in a Microsoft Active Server Pages page—use the Recordset's Open method to test your output. If you can load your XML data into an ADO Recordset object, it will load into the PivotTable control because the control uses the same mechanism. For an example of generating XML data from an ASP page, see the source code for the solution discussed in Chapter 6.

PivotTable Component Terminology

One of our goals while designing the PivotTable component was to make the user interface and programming model consistent between tabular and multidimensional data sources. Although each type of data source has special requirements, we wanted the aspects of the two that overlapped to look and feel the same.

At the same time, we thought that the terminology commonly used in the OLAP world was less than intuitive for businesspeople who simply want to retrieve the data they need to perform their jobs. Fortunately, the Excel PivotTable report feature has established a set of standard terminology with which many users are already familiar. We followed the terminology established by Excel, but changed just a few names where there was a better term to express the concept in the worlds of both tabular and multidimensional data.

The terminology presented here is the terminology I will use throughout the rest of the book, and it is the terminology used in the programming model of the PivotTable control. I will explain what each of these terms represents in the control and what the term maps to in both the tabular and multidimensional data source terminology.

Figure 4-14 shows a typical PivotTable report and highlights various elements defined in the following sections. Refer to this diagram to see where the PivotTable control displays a particular element.

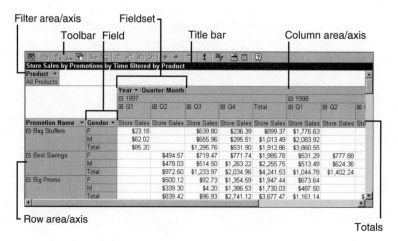

Figure 4-14. *Various elements of a PivotTable report.*

Totals

For a tabular data source, a *total* is an aggregation (sum, count, minimum, or maximum) of the detail values in a field. Totals are created using the AutoCalc toolbar button or the programming model. By default, a tabular data source has no totals since the source data is merely a set of rows. You can create multiple totals for any field using the Sum, Count, Min, or Max summary functions. (Text-based fields can only be counted.) You also can delete any totals you create by using either the context menu in the PivotTable Field List or the programming model.

For an OLAP data source, a total is a collection of values and aggregates that represent a measure in the hypercube. All measures exposed from the OLAP provider will be available to the PivotTable report, and you can include any set of them. Unlike using the tabular data source, you cannot create additional totals when connected to an OLAP data source. If you want a calculated total (such as Store Sales Net = Store Sales − Store Cost), you must create a calculated measure in the hypercube. This measure will be exposed as a total in the PivotTable control.

You can place totals only in the data area (the center) of the PivotTable control, and they typically generate all the numbers in a PivotTable report. The totals available to view are displayed separately in the PivotTable Field List, with a unique icon denoting that they are indeed totals.

Fieldsets and Fields

The term "field" is often used to describe a column in a tabular data resultset, and it seems to be the predominant term used in Microsoft products. Although I prefer the term "column," Microsoft Access and Excel have too much history using "field." For this reason, the Office Web Components use *field* and *fieldset* to describe a result column for a tabular data source. For an OLAP data source, field is used to describe a level and fieldset is used to describe a hierarchy. A fieldset is a collection of related fields that belong together in a hierarchy—for example, the Geography fieldset might contain the fields Country, State, and City.

A tabular data source returns a resultset containing a set of completely unrelated fields. In other words, you cannot know universally that any particular field belongs with any other field in a hierarchy. For example, if you have both a Country and a State field in a resultset, there is no metadata indicating that the two fields are levels of a single hierarchy. For this reason, when using a tabular data source, every result field is independent in the PivotTable control and is therefore a fieldset with just one field. The exceptions to this rule are date fields and date/time fields. When the PivotTable control encounters a date field in the resultset, it automatically generates two additional fieldsets that provide a calendar-based time hierarchy for the field. One fieldset contains the fields Year, Quarter, Month, and Day while the other contains the fields Year, Week, and Day. The PivotTable control creates these two extra fieldsets for each date or date/time field in your tabular resultset. Unfortunately, you cannot create your own fieldset hierarchies from a set of result fields in this version of the control.

When using an OLAP data source, the PivotTable control creates a fieldset for each hierarchy in the hypercube. Some OLAP databases allow you to define multiple hierarchies for a single dimension. The PivotTable control will expose each hierarchy as a separate fieldset. Each fieldset contains one field for each level in the OLAP hierarchy, skipping the All level if it exists.

Members

A fieldset in the PivotTable control contains a set of *members,* one for each distinct category in each of its fields. Members are displayed as row or column headings in a crosstab report and are frozen to scrolling so that they are always visible.

When using a tabular data source, the PivotTable component creates a member for each distinct value in each result field. It also creates a member called (Blank) if it finds any Null or blank values in a given field.

When using an OLAP data source, the PivotTable control creates a member for each element in each hierarchy, including the All member if it exists.

Row, Column, Filter, and Data Areas (Axes)

The PivotTable control has a few *areas* that you can use to construct your report. Areas often are called *axes* in the programming model. OLAP databases also use the term "axis" to describe part of a query result. The *row area* is the region to the left of the control where the row headings are displayed and on which you can drop a field to group your data by rows. The *column area* is the region across the top of the control where the column headings are displayed and on which you can drop a field to group your data by columns. You can place as many fields in these two areas as you want, limited of course by your available system resources.

The *filter area* is the strip across the top of the control. This area is where you place fields that you want to filter by, choosing one value at a time. For example, you might want to see sales information for one product line, one country, or one salesperson. The data in the report is filtered to show the totals attributed to only the selected member. You can place as many fields in the filter area as you want, and if you want the totals for all members in the field, select the "(All)" member. When using a tabular data source, the selection you make in a filter field is used as a local filter on the client, meaning that the PivotTable control still has all the detail data on the client and is simply filtering the data locally. If you want to filter the data at the server, you must use a WHERE clause in the command text used to populate the Pivot-Table report.

The *data area* is the region in the center of the report where the PivotTable control displays totals. Totals placed in this area will cause the PivotTable control to display numbers for the intersections of row and column members. You can add as many totals to the report as you want. The numerical values are displayed in separate columns by default.

The data area also is capable of showing any detail rows that are available for a given total. This capability is of course available only when the data source is tabular because OLE DB for OLAP data sources return only aggregates, not the detail source data behind those aggregates. When working with a tabular data source, the PivotTable control can display the detail data behind any aggregate by expanding the aggregate cell and showing the detail rows in place. This allows the user to simply double-click a number about which he or she wants to see more detail, causing the PivotTable to expand the cell occupied by that number and show the detail data rows contributing to that aggregate.

UniqueName, Name, and Caption

When you start writing code using the PivotTable component's programming model, you will notice that many objects have three properties related to their identity. Each of these properties does in fact represent something different.

The UniqueName property of an object returns its unique name as reported by the data source. Many OLAP data sources have a method for creating unique names for members, levels, dimensions, and so on, and these names are hardly fit for any-one to see. Unique names are intended to be opaque strings that you retrieve and use without trying to understand their internal format; however, they are guaranteed to uniquely identify the object. An example of a unique name from OLAP Services is "[Time].[All].[1997].[Q1]". You can use the unique name of an object when looking it up in a collection or when setting a filter. Often it's safest to do so because this dis-ambiguates cases in which you might have the same member name at two different levels in a single hierarchy or at the same level, as with Portland, Maine and Portland, Oregon. Both of these members have the same name ("Portland"), but their unique names are different ("[USA].[Maine].[Portland]" vs. "[USA].[Oregon].[Portland]").

The Name property of an object is friendlier than the UniqueName property, but it is still intended to identify an object in a collection. The Name property is initial-ized to the value of the object's Caption property, but the Name property will not change if you change the Caption property for display purposes. The Name property also can be used to look up an object in a collection or when setting a filter, but you should use it only if you know that you do not have multiple members with the same name in a hierarchy.

You use an object's Caption property when displaying the object in the report. You should not use it to look up an object in a collection or when setting a filter. For instance, if your report has a total named Sum of ExtendedPrice, you might want to adjust it to Sales in the report since that name is easier to read. Changing the Caption property has no effect on the internal names of objects, but it will change what is displayed in the report.

BASIC PROGRAMMING OF THE PIVOTTABLE COMPONENT

Now that you have a conceptual overview of the PivotTable component, let's discuss how you manipulate it to produce a desired report. As with the other Office Web Components, you can insert the PivotTable component through a designer such as Microsoft FrontPage 2000, Access 2000, Visual Basic, and so on. You can then activate it and manipulate the user interface the same way you would at runtime. (See Chapter 1 for a refresher on the containers that OWC supports and information on how to activate the controls.) The report is saved when you save the containing object (such as the web page or Visual Basic form), but in the case of the PivotTable component, only the view definition is saved. The view definition describes which fields appear on which axes, how the report is filtered and sorted, and any formatting you have applied. The control will always connect to the data source and retrieve up-to-date data when it runs.

Since this book focuses on building solutions with the Office Web Components, I will not go into building reports interactively in a designer. If you want more information on this topic, see the help file displayed when you click the PivotTable control's Help toolbar button, which explains how to do this in detail. In the sections that follow, I will describe how to build reports programmatically and how to use code to adjust many other visual aspects of the report.

Getting Data into the PivotTable Component

The PivotTable component is a fabulous piece of technology—but only if it contains data. The first thing you must do is tell the PivotTable control from where you want it to get data: a tabular data source, an OLAP (multidimensional) data source, or an XML stream.

Binding to the Data Source Component

In addition to the three sources of data mentioned above, the PivotTable component offers one more choice for retrieving data. You can use the Data Source component (DSC), the fourth member of the Office Web Components, in one of two ways:

by using the built-in properties of the PivotTable component to specify a connection string and command text or cube name, or by creating the DSC directly. (Chapter 5 will discuss the DSC in much greater detail.)

The built-in properties are actually just a front for the DSC. When you set them, the PivotTable component creates a DSC internally. So in reality, you are always using the DSC, but the built-in properties save you from having to put an extra <object> tag in your HTML page or having to put an extra control on your form. Since there are no appreciable performance differences between the two options, it is purely a choice of convenience.

Whether you are using the built-in properties or the DSC, your code generally will be the same. I will note any differences between the two approaches in the discussion that follows. After this section, however, I will use only the built-in properties in the example code because it typically is easier to read.

Tabular Data Sources

To load the PivotTable component with data from a tabular data source, you would write the following code, taken from the PivotTableList.htm sample file in the Chap04 folder on the companion CD:

```
Sub ConnectToTabular(ptable, sConnString, sSQL)
    ptable.ConnectionString = sConnString
    ptable.CommandText = sSQL
End Sub 'ConnectToTabular()
```

This example uses the built-in properties for data binding. If you have ever written ADO code to open a connection and execute a command, you will recognize the names of these properties. The ConnectionString property can accept any connection string that you can use with the ADO Connection object's Open method. The ADO documentation and help file provide examples and lists of all the accepted attributes for a large set of providers. (See the "Using providers with ADO" section of the ADO help file.)

A typical connection string for a Jet database looks like this:

```
provider=microsoft.jet.oledb.4.0;data source=PathToMDBfile
```

And a typical connection string for SQL Server looks like this:

```
provider=sqloledb;data source=NameOfServer;
    initial catalog=NameOfDatabase;integrated security=SSPI
```

Note that this connection string indicates that the PivotTable control should use integrated security with SQL Server, which means it will use the client's Windows NT credentials when connecting to the server running SQL Server. If you simply want to use SQL Server's standard security, use the user id and password attributes instead.

After setting the connection string, you should set the CommandText property of the PivotTable component to your SQL statement or whatever command text the provider supports. (Some providers, such as the OLE DB provider for the Microsoft Active Directory services, support special command text that looks nothing like SQL but still returns a resultset.) The PivotTable component will execute this command text and process the results as described earlier in the "How the PivotTable Component Works with Data" section.

To use the DSC directly instead of via the built-in properties, you would write the following code:

```
Sub ConnectToDSC(ptable, DSC, sDataMemberName)
    Set ptable.DataSource = DSC
    ptable.DataMember = sDataMemberName
End Sub 'ConnectToDSC()
```

We'll discuss how to initialize the DSC in the next chapter, but right now, let's look at how the PivotTable component is bound to it. As with the Chart component, you first set the DataSource property of the PivotTable component to an instance of the DSC. Then you set the DataMember property to the name of a data set exposed from the DSC. As in the case of the Chart component, the PivotTable component will ask the DSC for the data set by name and will then display any fields you want to include in the view (more on this in a moment).

To get started, you'll also want to use the ActiveView.AutoLayout method of the PivotTable object to quickly add all the fields in the data set to the detail area. The code you execute is just one line long:

```
PivotTable1.ActiveView.AutoLayout
```

OLAP Data Sources

Connecting to an OLAP data source is also easy. A typical function to connect the PivotTable component to an OLAP cube looks like this code snippet, taken from the PivotTableIntro.htm file in the Chap04 folder of your companion CD:

```
Sub ConnectToCube(ptable, sConn, sCube)
    ' Set the PivotTable component's ConnectionString property
    ptable.ConnectionString = sConn

    ' Set the DataMember property to the cube name
    ptable.DataMember = sCube

End Sub 'ConnectToCube()
```

The ConnectionString property is set just as it is in the previous tabular data source example, but this time the connection string looks slightly different. A typical connection string for a server running OLAP Services looks like this:

```
provider=msolap;data source=NameOfServer;initial catalog=NameOfDatabase
```

Because OLAP Services always uses integrated security, you don't need to specify that attribute in the connection string. The above connection string will get you connected to a server cube, but to connect to a cube file on disk, you need a connection string like this:

```
provider=msolap;data source=PathToCubeFile
```

After setting the ConnectionString property, you set the DataMember property of the PivotTable object to the name of the cube with which you want to work. As you adjust the report view, either through the user interface or through the programming model, the PivotTable control will generate the appropriate MDX query, execute it against the OLAP data source, and display the results in the view.

Strangely enough, the AutoLayout method has the opposite effect on the PivotTable report when using an OLAP data source instead of a tabular data source. When using a tabular data source, this method adds all fields to the detail area, showing all the data in a flat list. When using an OLAP data source, however, AutoLayout completely clears the view. Semantically, it performs the same task in both cases, but since an OLAP data source has no detail data to expose (it only exposes aggregates), the view is empty. This effect might not be exactly what you expect, but it's useful nonetheless.

XML Data Sources

As noted earlier, an XML stream (or file) is essentially the same as any other tabular data source as far as the PivotTable component is concerned. However, the way that you tell the PivotTable control to use the XML stream is slightly different. To load XML data returned from a URL into the PivotTable control, use the following code, taken from the PivotTableXML.htm file in the Chap04 folder on your companion CD:

```
Sub ConnectToXML(ptable, sURL)
    ptable.ConnectionString = "provider=mspersist"
    ptable.CommandText = sURL
End Sub 'ConnectToXML()
```

This is the easiest code of all. The ConnectionString property should always be set to "provider=mspersist" when loading XML data, and the CommandText property is simply set to a URL that will return data in the specific XML format defined by ADO. Note that this URL could point to an ASP page or a CGI program that dynamically generates this XML data, providing a simple way to transmit data to the PivotTable control over HTTP.

Adjusting the View Layout

After you have connected the PivotTable component to a data source, you probably will want to add fieldsets and totals to the view, include and exclude fields in a fieldset from the view, and expand or collapse members or fields.

Immediately after connecting to the data source, the PivotTable control populates the PivotFieldSets and PivotTotals collections with all the fieldsets and totals exposed by the data source. (As you'll recall, we discussed what constitutes a fieldset and a total when using different data source types.) These two collections are returned by the FieldSets and Totals properties, which are available from the ActiveView property of the PivotTable object, and they define what is available to add to the view.

To add a fieldset or total to the view, you must first decide to which axis you want to add the element and then insert the fieldset or total into that axis. (See page 116 for a review of the various axes in the view.) When you insert the fieldset or total into that axis, you can specify whether you want it to fall before any other fieldset on the axis. By default, the PivotTable component will append the new element as the innermost field on the axis.

Following is an example taken from the PivotTableIntro.htm file on the companion CD that shows how to configure a simple report for an OLAP data source:

```
Sub QuickPivot(ptable, ptotal, fsRows, fsCols, fsFilter)
    ' Local variables
    Dim pview     ' Reference to the view

    ' Grab a reference to the view
    Set pview = ptable.ActiveView

    ' Clear the view
    pview.AutoLayout()

    ' Put the fsRows dimension on the row axis
    pview.RowAxis.InsertFieldSet pview.FieldSets(fsRows)

    ' Put the fsCols dimension on the column axis
    pview.ColumnAxis.InsertFieldSet pview.FieldSets(fsCols)

    ' Put the fsFilter dimension on the filter axis
    pview.FilterAxis.InsertFieldSet pview.FieldSets(fsFilter)

    ' Finally, put ptotal in the data area
    pview.DataAxis.InsertTotal pview.Totals(ptotal)

    ' Synchronize the drop-down lists in the Quick Pivot interface
    If vartype(fsRows) = vbObject Then
        cbxRow.value = fsRows.Caption
        cbxCol.value = fsCols.Caption
```

```
        cbxFilter.value = fsFilter.Caption
        cbxTotal.value = ptotal.Caption
    Else
        cbxRow.value = pview.FieldSets(fsRows).Caption
        cbxCol.value = pview.FieldSets(fsCols).Caption
        cbxFilter.value = pview.FieldSets(fsFilter).Caption
        cbxTotal.value = pview.Totals(ptotal).Caption
    End If

    pview.TitleBar.Caption = cbxTotal.value & " by " & _
        cbxRow.value & " by " & _
        cbxCol.value & " filtered by " & _
        cbxFilter.value

End Sub 'QuickPivot()
```

You pass the names of fieldsets or totals available in the PivotFieldSets collection or PivotTotals collection to the method in the parameters ptotal, fsRows, fsCols, and fsFilter. For example, you could pass "Store Sales", "Promotion", "Time", and "Gender" as arguments, and the method will place the Promotion fieldset along the rows, the Time fieldset across the columns, the Store Sales total in the center as the numbers of the report, and the Gender fieldset on the filter axis for filtering.

Although this method places only one fieldset on each axis, you can easily nest many fieldsets on a single axis. For example, the following code builds a report showing customer locations inside customer genders on the row axis:

```
pview.RowAxis.InsertFieldSet pview.FieldSets("Gender")
pview.RowAxis.InsertFieldSet pview.FieldSets("Customer")
```

You also can add multiple fieldsets to the column and filter axes and multiple totals to the data axis.

To insert a fieldset before an existing fieldset in the view without adding it as the innermost fieldset on the axis, use the optional *Before* parameter on the InsertField-Set method:

```
pview.RowAxis.InsertFieldSet pview.FieldSets("Gender")
pview.RowAxis.InsertFieldSet pview.FieldSets("Customer"), 0
```

This code adds the Customer fieldset to the left (or outer) side of the Gender fieldset. The last argument is the zero-based index of the fieldset on the axis that the new fieldset should be inserted before. Since this argument is 0 in the above code, the Customer fieldset is inserted as the outermost fieldset. You should always check whether the axis contains a fieldset before using this argument because passing an invalid index generates a runtime error.

Although you might be tempted to fiddle with that last optional parameter of the InsertFieldSet method, don't do it! The *Remove* parameter is reserved for future use and must remain set to its default value of True.

Besides adding entire fieldsets to an axis, you might also need to show a few fields of the fieldset while hiding the others. For example, if you have a fairly deep hierarchy (fieldset), such as the Product hierarchy in the sample cube, you might want to initially put only three levels (fields) of that hierarchy on the report to avoid cluttering the report with all those field buttons. To do so, set the IsIncluded property of the PivotField objects you want to hide to False. For example, to show only the first three levels of the Product hierarchy, use the following code:

```
Set pview = PivotTable1.ActiveView
Set fsProd = pview.FieldSets("Product")

pview.RowAxis.InsertFieldSet fsProd
For nField = 3 To fsProd.Fields.Count - 1
    pview.FieldSets("Product").Fields(nField).IsIncluded = False
Next
```

To add or remove fields of a fieldset, simply set the IsIncluded property of the respective field to True or False.

You might also want to set the Expanded property for outer fields on an axis so that they automatically expand to show the child members. You can adjust the Expanded property of the entire field and of each individual member within the fieldset. For example, to expand the first level of the Product fieldset to show the children beneath each top-level item, use the following code:

```
Set fsProd = pview.FieldSets("Product")
fsProd.Fields(0).Expanded = True
```

If you add fieldsets to an axis, you probably will also want to remove them at some point. Removing a fieldset from an axis is fairly simple and, not surprisingly, involves the RemoveFieldSet method:

```
PivotTable1.ActiveView.RowAxis.RemoveFieldSet FieldSet
```

The *FieldSet* parameter is actually quite lenient—you can specify the name of the fieldset, a reference to a PivotFieldSet object, or the index of the fieldset on the axis.

If you want to clear everything from the view of an OLAP data source, you can use the AutoLayout method as described earlier. If you are working with a tabular data source and want to completely remove all detail fields, use the following code:

```
For Each fs In PivotTable1.ActiveView.DataAxis.FieldSets
    PivotTable1.ActiveView.DataAxis.RemoveFieldSet fs.Name
Next
```

To manipulate both the detail fieldsets and the totals on the data axis of the PivotTable component, use the ActiveView.DataAxis property. The PivotDataAxis object returned by the DataAxis property has both InsertFieldSet and InsertTotal methods—along with their "Remove" counterparts. Use the *FieldSet flavor when working with detail fieldsets and the *Total flavor when working with totals.

Creating New Totals for Tabular Sources

If your data source is tabular, the PivotTable component will not have any totals available for the report by default. To see subtotal and grand total values, you must create new totals for fieldsets that *do* exist in the returned data. In an OLAP data source, an existing set of defined measures can be exposed as totals; however, no such set exists for tabular data.

The following code, taken from the PivotTableList.htm file on the companion CD, shows how to create a new total:

```
Set c = PivotTable1.Constants
Set pview = PivotTable1.ActiveView

On Error Resume Next
pview.DataAxis.InsertTotal _
pView.AddTotal("Sales", pview.FieldSets("ExtendedPrice").Fields(0), _
    c.plFunctionSum)
pview.DataAxis.InsertTotal _
pView.AddTotal("Total Qty", pview.FieldSets("Quantity").Fields(0), _
    c.plFunctionSum)
```

This code snippet creates two totals, one for the ExtendedPrice fieldset and one for the Quantity fieldset. The code also adds those new totals to the data axis so that they are displayed in the report. The AddTotal method creates a new total for a given fieldset, but you also must add it to the data axis before it will appear in the report. This code uses the summary function plFunctionSum—just one of the summary functions available. The other functions supported are plFunctionMin, plFunctionMax, and plFunctionCount, which are PivotTotalFunctionEnum constants. The first release of the Office Web Components does not contain an average function and does not support custom summary functions.

Deleting totals is as simple as removing fieldsets from an axis. To do so, simply use the DeleteTotal method of the PivotView object and pass the total's name, index, or object reference.

Sorting

Now that you know how to load data into the PivotTable component and lay out the view to produce a simple report, you might want to set an initial sorting order or adjust the sorting of the report in response to a specialized user interface you have supplied.

The PivotTable control allows users to perform all the sorting operations through default user interface mechanisms, such as toolbar buttons and context menus. However, you can do anything in code that the user can do in the default user interface.

There are two areas of the report that you might want to sort. When working with a tabular data source, you can sort the detail data. When working with either type of data source, you can sort the members of a grouped field by their captions or by a total—for example, sorting product promotions by the sales they generated. You can even sort members in a particular scope instead of sorting by the grand totals. Let's look at the simpler scenarios first.

The following code, taken from the SortingDetails.htm file on your companion CD, shows you how to sort the detail data in your report. You might want to run the file right now to see what this code does:

```
Sub btnSort_onClick()
    ' Local variables
    Dim pview      ' Active view
    Dim c          ' Constants

    ' Grab the active view and the Constants object
    Set pview = PivotTable1.ActiveView
    Set c = PivotTable1.Constants

    ' Set the SortDirection property for the fields to be sorted
    pview.Fieldsets(cbxSort1.value).Fields(0).SortDirection = _
        c.plSortDirectionAscending
    pview.Fieldsets(cbxSort2.value).Fields(0).SortDirection = _
        c.plSortDirectionAscending
    pview.Fieldsets(cbxSort3.value).Fields(0).SortDirection = _
        c.plSortDirectionAscending

    ' Set the DetailSortOrder property to our array
    PivotTable1.ActiveView.DetailSortOrder = Array(cbxSort1.value, _
        cbxSort2.value, cbxSort3.value)

End Sub 'btnSort_onClick()
```

Two elements determine sorting of the detail data: the SortDirection properties of the individual fields and the DetailSortOrder array of the active view. To sort the detail data by a field or set of fields, first set the SortDirection property of each field you want to sort. The SortDirection property takes a constant that can mean ascending, descending, or ordered naturally (which is the default). The example above sorts all the fields in ascending order, but you can use any combination of ascending and descending orders for the fields. This example also supports only three levels of sorting, but of course, you can sort every field in the report if you want.

REMEMBER TO SET THE SORTDIRECTION PROPERTY!

If you fail to set the SortDirection property to a value other than the default (plSortDirectionDefault) for any field indicated in the DetailSortOrder array, the PivotTable component will not generate an error—it simply will not sort the field. I found this out the hard way when building the SortingDetails.htm sample and was thoroughly confused about why the component wasn't sorting the report even though the code seemed to run without error. The programming model help file (Msowcvba.chm) actually notes this, but of course, I didn't read the file because I thought I already knew how to do it!

If you are sorting by multiple columns at once, the second piece of information the PivotTable component needs is the order it should sort the columns in. This allows you to display the fields in one order but sort by a different order. To specify the order, you build an array of field names and hand it to the DetailSortOrder property of the active view. The preceding example uses the handy Array function in Microsoft VBScript to build a temporary array.

You also might want to sort the members of a grouped field, either by caption or by a total value. The following code, taken from the SortingMembers.htm sample file on the companion CD, shows how to do this. This technique can be somewhat confusing because you have two axes of information, so you might want to run and experiment with this file while looking at the code:

```
Sub btnSort_onClick()
    ' Local variables
    Dim pview      ' Active view
    Dim c          ' Constants
    Dim fs         ' Temporary fieldset pointer

    ' Grab the active view and the Constants object
    Set pview = PivotTable1.ActiveView
    Set c = PivotTable1.Constants

    ' Get the fieldset the user wants to sort
    Set fs = pview.Fieldsets(cbxDim.value)

    ' Since this report has only one field per fieldset on an
    ' axis, we can grab the first field and sort by it
    ' If you have a hierarchy and want to sort a particular level,
    ' use the corresponding field object
    If cbxDir.value = "A" Then
        fs.Fields(0).SortDirection = c.plSortDirectionAscending
```

(continued)

```
    Else
        fs.Fields(0).SortDirection = c.plSortDirectionDescending
    End If

    ' If the cbxBy select's value is something other than
    ' an empty string, get the total of that name and tell
    ' the PivotTable control to sort by that total instead of
    ' sorting by the member caption
    If Len(cbxBy.value) > 0 Then
        Set fs.Fields(0).SortOn = pview.Totals(cbxBy.value)
    Else
        ' To sort by the member caption, set SortOn to Nothing
        Set fs.Fields(0).SortOn = Nothing
    End If

    ' Set the SortOnScope property to the cbxScope value
    fs.Fields(0).SortOnScope = Array(cbxScope.value)

End Sub 'btnSort_onClick()
```

As in detail data sorting, the first step in sorting members in a grouped field is to set the field's SortDirection property to ascending or descending. Again, setting this property to the default will return the field to its natural order. If you stop after setting the SortDirection property, the PivotTable component will sort the members alphabetically, by their captions. To sort the members by a total—for example, sorting product promotions by the amount of sales they generated—set the SortOn property. Setting this property to a PivotTotal reference causes the PivotTable component to sort the field's members by their respective values for the specified total. You must set this property to a PivotTotal object (rather than the total's name or its unique name), so you will need to look it up in the PivotTotals collection (which is returned by the Totals property) as the above code does.

By default, sorting by a total will sort the members by the grand total for the members' grid row or column. Sometimes you might want to sort the members by a total but only within a certain scope. For example, you might want the report to show the product promotions sorted by sales to men only rather than by the grand total of sales to men and women. To do this, set the SortOnScope property, which takes an array of unique member names from a field on the other axis. For instance, if you want to sort the product promotions by the sales generated from men, set the SortOnScope property to "[Gender].[All Gender].[M]", which is the unique name for the male member in the Gender fieldset. (Remember, you can retrieve this unique name from the PivotMembers collection dynamically.) If you want to sort the genders by sales made because of a particular product promotion, set the SortOnScope property of the Gender field to be the unique member name of the specified product promotion.

This concept will be clearer once you see an example of it in action. To do so, run the SortingMembers.htm sample file on the companion CD and adjust the last two drop-down lists to see the difference in results. You also can explore what the SortOnScope property does by using the built-in user interface of the control to perform complex sorting and then breaking into your debugger to see the values for the SortDirection, SortOn, and SortOnScope properties for each field in the view.

Filtering

After setting the sort order for your report, you might want to set some initial filtering for it so that only a subset of data is displayed. You can perform two types of filtering in a report: including or excluding a set of members for a field on the row or column axis, and filtering for a single member in a field on the filter axis. The first approach limits what appears down the rows or across the columns in your report; the second approach slices the data by a certain value and shows data only for that member.

For example, suppose you want to show a small subset of the product promotions in your report. If your Promotions dimension has numerous members, you might need to check that the dimension is filtered before the PivotTable component executes a query and retrieves results. The following code, taken from the FilteringMembers.htm sample file on the companion CD, shows how to set an initial filter for use when the PivotTable control queries the database:

```
' Grab references to the active view and to the Constants object
Set pview = PivotTable1.ActiveView
Set c = PivotTable1.Constants

' Include only the following four members in the Promotions field
Set fld = pview.FieldSets("Promotions").Fields(0)
fld.FilterFunction = c.plFilterFunctionInclude
fld.FilterMembers = Array("Cash Register Lottery", _
                    "Free For All", _
                    "Price Savers", _
                    "Two for One")
```

Filtering in the PivotTable component is conceptually similar to filtering in the Spreadsheet component (discussed in Chapter 2); however, the way you specify which items to include or exclude differs slightly. First, set the FilterFunction property to one of the filter function constants: plFilterFunctionInclude or plFilterFunctionExclude. Second, set the FilterMembers property to an array of member names, unique names, or PivotMember object references. The code above uses member names, but as discussed earlier, you should do this only when certain that the friendlier name is unique across the field.

To set the initial value for a fieldset on the filter axis, write the following code:

```
' Set the initial Product filter field selection to
' "Dairy", which is contained within "Drink". The first member
' of this fieldset is the All member, so look in its
' ChildMembers collection to find the "Drink" member.
' Then look in its ChildMembers collection to find the
' "Dairy" member.
Set mems = pview.FilterAxis.Fieldsets(0).Members
pview.FilterAxis.Fieldsets(0).FilterMember = _
    mems(0).ChildMembers("Drink").ChildMembers("Dairy")
```

This code, also taken from the FilteringMembers.htm sample file on the companion CD, sets the FilterMember property for the entire fieldset. When filtering on a set of members within a field, use the field's FilterMembers property; when setting the selected member for a fieldset on the filter axis, set the fieldset's FilterMember property.

This example uses the Members collection of the fieldset to get a reference to the desired PivotMember object. Although you can use the unique name here as well, I want to show you how to dynamically locate a member using the Members collection. This collection is available for every fieldset and returns a hierarchical collection of PivotMember objects. If the fieldset has an All member, representing the total for all members (most do), the top level of the PivotMembers collection will have one item representing the All member. Each member has a ChildMembers collection and a ParentMember property, allowing you to navigate up and down the member hierarchy. You can retrieve child members either by name or by index.

Although the PivotTable component does not yet support top or bottom N filtering, you can simulate these techniques by retrieving the top or bottom N member names and using the FilterMembers property to show only those members. If you already have retrieved all members from the server, you can use the top and bottom N filtering techniques described in Chapter 2. However, if you want to include only the top or bottom N items (and not retrieve the rest), consider using MDX or ADO MD (the multidimensional extensions to ADO) to execute a top or bottom N MDX query to get the member names. Then set the FilterMembers property to include only those members. For an example of this technique, see Chapter 7.

Customizing the View

We have not discussed a few elements of the PivotTable component yet—specifically the *toolbar* and the *title bar*. As you know, the toolbar is the row of command buttons across the top of the control, and the title bar is the strip of text beneath the toolbar that gives you a title for your report.

The toolbar can be either visible or hidden; by default, it is visible. Although the toolbar offers many useful commands, you might want to hide it and show your own user interface for manipulating the control. To do so, simply set the DisplayToolbar property at the top-level interface of the control to False.

The title bar can also be visible or hidden. You can customize the text in it, the background and text colors, and the font settings (font name, font size, and the bold, underline, and italic settings). Typically, you will want to set the caption of the title bar to an appropriate title for your report. To do so, you need only one line of code:

```
PivotTable1.ActiveView.Titlebar.Caption = "My Report"
```

The Titlebar property returns a PivotLabel object, with which you can adjust all the other font and color settings just mentioned.

A few other properties control the overall look of the report. The DisplayExpand-Indicator property toggles on and off the small plus (+) and minus (–) signs next to the member labels. These expand indicators offer a one-click method for expanding and collapsing a member to show or hide its child members. If you turn the expand indicators off, the user can still double-click the member or use the Expand toolbar button to expand and collapse.

Two modeless windows can be displayed floating above the PivotTable component: the PivotTable Field List and the Property Toolbox that was first mentioned in Chapter 2. Both of these windows can also be displayed or hidden programmatically by toggling the DisplayFieldList and DisplayPropertyToolbox properties. Since these are Boolean properties, you can also use them to discover whether the two windows are being displayed. Automatically displaying the field list is useful when a user first opens a report that does not yet have any fields or totals in the view.

Applying Formatting Programmatically

You can format a number of the elements in a PivotTable report differently than their default appearance. However, the PivotTable component does not yet support per-cell formatting in the report. You can set the number format for totals shown in the report, make the subtotal numbers look different than the other numbers, adjust the formatting of the member labels, change the appearance of the field buttons, and change the formatting of the various drop areas. Chapter 7 will explain how to automatically apply formatting based on your web page's current style sheet. For now, let's take a look at some of the simpler formatting tasks.

Most likely, you first will want to format the numbers in your report. By default, the numeric values appear without any number formatting, but you can apply any of the number formats supported in the Spreadsheet component. (See Chapter 2 for more information on this.) For example, if you are analyzing sales data, you generally want to format the numbers in a specific currency format. To do this, you would write code like so:

```
PivotTable1.ActiveView.Totals("Store Sales").NumberFormat = "$#,##0.00"
```

Although you specify the number format for the PivotTotal object, the font and color settings for the totals in your report are not exposed by this object. Instead, you must set them using the active view properties named TotalBackColor and TotalFont.

You'll probably want to make your grand totals stand out in the report—for example, by making the background color something other than white and making the numbers bold. To do so, you would write code like this:

```
Set pfld = pt.ActiveView.RowAxis.FieldSets(0).Fields(0)
pfld.SubtotalBackColor = "Wheat"
pfld.SubtotalFont.Bold = True

Set pfld = pt.ActiveView.ColumnAxis.FieldSets(0).Fields(0)
pfld.SubtotalBackColor = "Wheat"
pfld.SubtotalFont.Bold = True
```

The grand total of the row or column axis is actually a subtotal of the very first included field of the very first fieldset on the particular axis. To adjust its formatting, you establish a reference to this field and then modify the SubtotalBackColor and SubtotalFont properties.

You can use this same technique to format the subtotals at any inner level so that they are different than the numbers contributing to them. To adjust the subtotal formatting, first establish a reference to the field to which the subtotal belongs and adjust the SubtotalBackColor and SubtotalFont properties.

Keep in mind that these properties are carried with the field as the user or your code moves it around the report. If your intention is merely to format the grand totals to look a certain way regardless of what fields are placed on the row or column axis, you need to reapply formatting during the QueryComplete event, which is raised whenever the report's layout is changed.

HOW DO I SELECT THE
ENTIRE COMPONENT TO FORMAT IT?

When applying formatting using the Property Toolbox, you might not be sure how to select the entire control to set control-level formatting such as the text in the title bar or various display settings for the entire view. To select the whole control, click the title bar. To make the title bar visible, use the Show/Hide section of the Property Toolbox.

Using AutoFit

You might notice in all the samples in this chapter that the PivotTable component seems to automatically grow and shrink when you change the view. This behavior, which is called *AutoFit,* is on by default. When AutoFit is on, the PivotTable control will resize itself to show all data in the report without internal scroll bars. This is especially useful in web pages since they already contain scroll bars. The PivotTable control will resize until it reaches the MaxHeight and MaxWidth property settings and then will show internal scroll bars again.

If you are working in a fixed forms environment such as Visual Basic, you likely will want to turn this behavior off so that the control stays the desired size and does not extend outside the form. (The form will crop the control when it extends past the form's edge.) To do so, set the AutoFit property at the control's top-level interface to False.

The PivotTable component has another level of AutoFit; by default, this control resizes the column widths of the detail grid so that no numbers get truncated. Again, each column will grow until it reaches the limits imposed by the DetailMaxWidth and DetailMaxHeight properties. You can disable the AutoFit behavior of the detail grid by setting the ActiveView's DetailAutoFit property to False.

WHAT DO YOU MEAN YOU WANT TO RESIZE YOURSELF DURING SCROLLING?

The Internet Explorer developers found the PivotTable component's AutoFit behavior nothing less than bizarre. They had never seen a control that automatically resized itself *and* did so while you scrolled the document, making more of the report visible. Mike Coulson, the extraordinary developer who programmed the user interface portion of the PivotTable component, spent quite a long time optimizing this control so that it retrieves only the data currently shown onscreen. This allows the control to display data quickly even if it still has to read 10,000 more rows in the background. To keep the AutoFit feature from slowing this process down, Mike dynamically adjusted the control's size as new data scrolled into view (if the data was larger than that shown previously).

Since the Internet Explorer team never thought that a control might resize itself while scrolling in the document, this behavior exposed quite a few bugs in the Internet Explorer code base. Thankfully, the Internet Explorer team was responsive to fixing those bugs for us. However, I think the PivotTable control still qualifies as one of the most complex controls a container can hold, especially when using the AutoFit feature.

ADVANCED PROGRAMMING TECHNIQUES

Now that you know how to perform some of the basic programmatic operations, let's discuss a few of the more advanced techniques you can use with the PivotTable component. Many of these are implemented in the Sales Analysis and Reporting solution covered in Chapter 7, so I will briefly discuss these techniques here and refer you to that chapter for a more detailed explanation of the code involved.

Saving and Restoring Views

Anyone using the PivotTable component for a reporting system will at some point want to enable users to save a report view they have constructed and recall that report later—but with current data. The PivotTable control makes this quite easy to do. In fact, the solution in Chapter 7 illustrates this technique.

The basic approach to saving and restoring a view is to use the XMLData property at the top-level interface of the control. This property is read/write and returns a large string in an XML format. Don't confuse this with using an XML stream as a data source—the XMLData property returns a definition of the current view's layout, formatting, filters, sorts, and so on. The string completely describes the view but does not contain any data values.

If you want to save the current view definition, get this property's value and save it where you can retrieve it later. A typical approach is to post this string to an ASP page or a CGI program, which would in turn write the string to a file or database associated with the current user. When the user wants to view that report again, your code retrieves this string from the persistent storage and sets the XMLData property to the retrieved string. When you set this property, the PivotTable control throws away any data it is currently showing, connects to the original data source (if it's not connected already), and executes the appropriate query to re-create the report. The user will see any new data that appears in the data source, but the report layout will be the same as it was when the user saved it.

The PivotTable control silently discards parts of the view that are no longer valid. For example, if the user had a fieldset in the view that was removed from the data source after the view was saved, the PivotTable control will ignore any information saved with that fieldset and will not attempt to restore it in the view. The same is true for totals or members no longer contained in the data set.

To experiment with the XMLData property, run the XMLDataProperty.htm file on your companion CD. The buttons at the top of the page allow you to get the XMLData property and set it back. Plus, they let you clear the PivotTable report. Try getting the property, clearing the PivotTable report, and resetting the property.

Note that the connection information (connection string and name of the cube or command text) is also included in the string returned by the XMLData property. If the location of the data source changes between the user saving the report and reopening it, the PivotTable will fail to connect and will generate an error. If this is a possibility, you should include error-handling code to catch this and to adjust the connection information in the string before handing it to the PivotTable control. The connection string is stored in the <x:ConnectionString> tag, the data member (cube name for an OLAP source) is stored in the <x:DataMember> tag, and the command text (used for a tabular source) is stored in the <x:CommandText> tag. You can use the InStr and Replace functions in VBScript or Microsoft VBA to easily find and replace the contents of these tags. See Chapter 7 for more information on the XMLData property and changing data sources.

Locking Down a View

Reporting systems often present two types of reports: standard reports that everyone will probably want to see and ad hoc reports that users can construct themselves and save. You might want to configure those standard reports so that users cannot remove or add fields to the reports, but they can still drill down and filter. You might also want to disallow filtering, allowing only expanding and collapsing within the view. The PivotTable component offers a few settings to help you lock down the view. It also raises some events that you can use to monitor what users are doing; however, no general mechanism for denying those actions exists.

ADVENTURES IN XML

All this wonderful XML stuff only works because another of OWC's star developers, Kevin Grealish, spent many a late night wrestling with the XML parser, namespaces, and seemingly daily changes in formats and standards. While we were in the middle of developing the PivotTable component, the XML standards for namespaces were fluctuating quite a bit. Since we had to read in XML data that Excel 2000 published, it was a continual dance to keep Excel and our code bases in sync. When the source of the PivotTable report was on-sheet data, we also had to stay in sync with the MDAC persistence provider used to load the XML-Data streams saved by Excel. This discrepancy eventually worked itself out—so the next time you use the XMLData property or use XML as a data source, thank Kevin.

To prohibit users from adding or removing fields from the row and column axes, set the AllowGrouping property of the PivotTable control to False. When this property is False, the PivotTable control prohibits the user from inserting or removing fields from the row or column axis. Users can still add fieldsets to the filter axis and add new totals to the view.

To prohibit users from changing any of the filter settings, set the AllowFiltering property to False. When this property is false, the PivotTable component will let users open the filtering drop-down lists but prohibit them from changing the current filter settings—in other words, they can view the current filters, but they can't change them. The control also prevents the user from adding more fieldsets to the filter axis.

To make sure the user cannot change formatting applied to the report, set the AllowPropertyToolbox property to False. This will disable the Property Toolbox button on the toolbar and the corresponding context menu item, prohibiting the user from even opening the Property Toolbox. However, users can still use the keyboard formatting commands, such as Ctrl-B, Ctrl-I, and Ctrl-U. To experiment with these various properties, see the LockDownView.htm sample file on your companion CD.

Determining Selection for Drill Through

Like the Chart component, the PivotTable component has a Selection property at the top level that returns the currently selected object. As with the Chart component, the type of object returned by this property varies, so use the TypeName function in VBScript and VBA to determine the object type. To see the different kinds of objects the PivotTable control can return from this property, run the sample file DeterminingSelection.htm on your companion CD.

You can emulate several interesting features if you know what is currently selected. I will discuss one of these features here: drilling through to details.

OLAP systems are good at showing users a high-level data summary and letting them *drill down* to deeper and deeper levels of detail. However, a user will eventually reach the lowest level of the hierarchies in the hypercube and often will want the ability to *drill through* to the underlying details that make up that lowest-level aggregate. In the case of a tabular data source, the PivotTable control can do this automatically because the detail data is readily available. However, there is not yet a general way in OLE DB for OLAP to retrieve the set of details behind an aggregate. Despite this fact, vertical solutions often have enough domain knowledge to pinpoint which tabular data source contains the detail data and to determine how to construct a SQL statement to get the detail rows given all the members that intersect to produce that aggregate.

The following code, taken from the DeterminingSelection.htm sample file on the companion CD, shows how to get all the information from a selected aggregate to formulate a SQL statement that gets the details:

```
Sub PivotTable1_SelectionChange()
    ' Local variables
    Dim sel         ' Temporary selection object
    Dim sFilters    ' Current filter strings
    Dim fSet        ' Temporary fieldset reference

    ' Grab the current selection
    Set sel = PivotTable1.Selection

    ' There are many types of objects that the selection
    ' could be, depending on what was selected
    ' Examples include PivotAggregates, PivotTotals,
    ' PivotMembers, PivotFields, and PivotView
    ' You can use the TypeName function to determine the type
    ' of the object
    '
    ' If the user selected an aggregate number,
    ' the TypeName function will return "PivotAggregates"

    ' Set the type name label
    lblType.innerText = TypeName(sel)

    ' If the type is "PivotAggregates", show how to get
    ' the row and column members that define that aggregate
    ' You could of course make this a Select Case statement
    ' and handle other selection types
    If TypeName(sel) = "PivotAggregates" Then
        ' PivotAggregates could contain many items, but since
        ' this is a sample, I will just work with the first item
        Set pivotagg = sel.Item(0)

        ' Set the value label
        lblVal.innerText = pivotagg.Value

        ' Get the total caption, the row and column members,
        ' and the current filters
        lblTotal.innerText = pivotagg.Total.Caption
        lblColMems.innerText = BuildFullName(pivotagg.Cell.ColumnMember)
        lblRowMems.innerText = BuildFullName(pivotagg.Cell.RowMember)
```

(continued)

```
        For Each fset In PivotTable1.ActiveView.FilterAxis.FieldSets
            sFilters = sFilters & fset.Caption & "=" & _
                fset.FilterMember.Caption & ", "
        Next
        lblFilters.innerText = sFilters

    Else
        ' Selection was something other than a PivotAggregates
        ' object. Clear the labels.
        lblVal.innerText = ""
        lblTotal.innerText = ""
        lblRowMems.innerText = ""
        lblColMems.innerText = ""
        lblFilters.innerText = ""

    End If 'typename(sel) = "PivotAggregates"

End Sub 'PivotTable1_SelectionChange()
```

This code first uses the TypeName function to determine the type of selection; if that type is PivotAggregates, you know that the user has selected an aggregate number. The code then retrieves the value of the aggregate and the total to which the aggregate belongs. (An aggregate by definition belongs to just one total.) Next, the code uses a helper function, BuildFullName, to build a single string representing all members up the hierarchy on the axis. The code for BuildFullName follows:

```
Function BuildFullName(PivotMem)
    ' Local variables
    Dim pmTemp     ' Temporary PivotMember reference

    ' Start by getting the current member's name
    sFullName = PivotMem.Caption

    ' Set the temporary reference to the current member
    Set pmTemp = PivotMem

    ' Navigate up the parent hierarchy until you hit nothing
    While Not(pmTemp.ParentMember Is Nothing)
        Set pmTemp = pmTemp.ParentMember
        sFullName = pmTemp.Caption & "-" & sFullName
    Wend

    ' Return sFullName
    BuildFullName = sFullName

End Function 'BuildFullName()
```

The key part of this code is the While loop in the center. As mentioned earlier, every member has a ParentMember property that returns the parent for the member if one exists. If it does not, the property returns Nothing, which is a Null object pointer in other languages. The loop builds a single string using the Caption property of each member as it walks up the hierarchy. Of course, you might want to use the Name property or even the UniqueName property (instead of the Caption property) to retrieve values needed in a SQL WHERE clause.

Showing Empty Members

By default, the PivotTable component will not display any report row or column that has no data values in any of its cells. However, sometimes the fact that a row or column has no data is meaningful, and you want to display it anyway. To do so, write the following code:

```
PivotTable1.ActiveView.RowAxis.DisplayEmptyMembers = True
PivotTable1.ActiveView.ColumnAxis.DisplayEmptyMembers = True
```

DisplayEmptyMembers is a property of the row or column axis, and by default, its value is False. For an OLAP source, this setting affects the MDX query the PivotTable component sends to the data source, so more data is downloaded when this property is set to True. For a tabular data source, this also affects the MDX used to query the temporary cube. But since all the data is on the client by that time, it hardly affects performance—unless the cube is exceedingly sparse.

Displaying Visual Totals

By default, the PivotTable component displays what are known as *visual totals*. Displaying visual totals means that the subtotals and grand totals in the report are the totals of the data currently displayed in the report. If a member is filtered out, the subtotals and grand totals above that member do not include that member's value. This way, all the data shown in the report adds up, even if you filter out some members.

Suppose you have a geographical hierarchy on the row axis with two levels: State and City. The subtotal for each state reflects the total of all cities in it. Now suppose you filter out the cities Seattle and Redmond. Should the total for Washington state be the same number as before, or should it be the total of all cities still shown in the report? This is actually a hotly debated issue. Fortunately, the PivotTable control supports both modes.

The PivotTable component shows visual totals by default. If you want this control to show totals for all members regardless of their visibility, use this code:

```
PivotTable1.ActiveView.TotalAllMembers = True
```

The PivotTable control will place small asterisks next to the subtotals and grand totals when TotalAllMembers is True to indicate that the values are not reflecting the visibility of members. The asterisks are shown to match Excel 2000's OLAP PivotTable reports feature behavior. Ideally, you should put an explanation of the asterisk in HTML below the PivotTable control.

Showing Total Captions as Rows

By default, the PivotTable component displays total captions as the innermost column headings on the report. Occasionally, it is desirable to show those total captions as the innermost row headings instead. You can easily accomplish this with the following line of code:

```
PivotTable1.ActiveView.TotalOrientation = plTotalOrientationRow
```

The TotalOrientation property is set to one of the PivotViewTotalOrientationEnum constants, which include values for row or column orientation. The PivotTable control does not yet support placing the total caption anywhere but the innermost level of the row or column axis.

Expanding Automatically

By default, the PivotTable component will leave all fields and members collapsed when they are added to the view. Users can then expand any path along the axis about which they want to see more detail. You might want to configure your report to automatically expand all fields and members as soon as they are added to the view. Since this can result in a large and unwieldy display, you should do this only if auto-expansion will generate a reasonably sized report.

To turn the auto-expansion behavior on, write the following line of code:

```
PivotTable1.MemberExpand = plMemberExpandAlways
```

The value of this property is taken from the PivotTableMemberExpandEnum enumeration, with the other possible values of plMemberExpandNever and plMember-ExpandAutomatic (which is the default).

This property also comes in handy when using the PivotTable control on a web server to generate a GIF image of your report, which we'll discuss in the next section. Setting this property so that the members always expand ensures that all information in the report is exposed when the image is written—which is important, considering that the user will get only a static image of the report and will not be able to expand members.

Using the PivotTable Component on a Web Server

Just as the other Office Web Components can be used without a user interface, you can create the PivotTable component as an in-memory object, connect to a data source, construct a report programmatically, and generate a GIF image of the current report or build your own HTML representation by walking the elements of the view. Using the PivotTable control on a web server might be a more compelling option than writing MDX queries, using ADO MD, and handcrafting a formatted result.

All the programmatic manipulation discussed so far can apply to using the PivotTable control on a server. The only new coding element you need to learn about is the ExportPicture method. This method is almost identical to the Chart component's ExportPicture method discussed in Chapter 3. To export the current report to a GIF image file, write the following code:

```
Set fsoTemp = CreateObject("Scripting.FileSystemObject")
strFilename = fsoTemp.GetTempName
PivotTable.ExportPicture Session("strTempFilePath") & strFilename, _
    "gif", PivotTable.MaxHeight, PivotTable.MaxWidth
Response.Write "<IMG SRC='" & Session("strTempURLPath") & _
    strFilename & "'>"
Session("Pivot" & Session("cntPivotImages")) = strFilename
Session("cntPivotImages") = Session("cntPivotImages") + 1
```

The key line in this code block is the call to the ExportPicture method. An instance of FileSystemObject (a class from the Microsoft Scripting Runtime library) retrieves a temporary filename for the new GIF image, and then the code hands that filename plus a root path to the ExportPicture method as the first parameter. As with the Chart component, the second parameter must be "gif". The last two parameters indicate the height and width, but unlike programming the Chart component (which can scale its content to any size), you must use the PivotTable component's MaxHeight and MaxWidth properties to avoid cropping the report image.

Generating a report image on the server creates the most extreme version of a locked-down report. Users can view such an image on any platform and in any browser that can display a GIF image, but the report will not be interactive.

KEY ELEMENTS OF THE PROGRAMMING MODEL

The tables in this section provide a quick synopsis of the key elements in the PivotTable component's programming model. When you sit down to write a new program using the PivotTable control, refer to this section for a reminder of what properties, methods, and events to use.

Property	Description
PivotTable.ConnectionString	Set this to a valid connection string to hook up the Pivot-Table control to the data source.
PivotTable.CommandText	Set this to a SQL statement or whatever command text the provider will accept. CommandText is used only for tabular data sources.
PivotTable.DataMember	Set this to the name of the OLAP cube you want to use or the name of the data set in the DSC referred to by the DataSource property.
PivotTable.DataSource	Set this to an instance of the DSC to use it as the data source. DataSource also will return the DSC even when you use the built-in ConnectionString property.

Table 4-1. *Binding to data.*

Property or Method	Description
PivotView.Fieldsets	This property contains all available fieldsets that you can use in the report.
PivotView.Totals	This property contains all available totals that you can use in the report.
InsertFieldset	Use this method on the row, column, or filter axis to insert a fieldset on the axis.
PivotDataAxis.InsertTotal	Use this method on the data axis to insert a total into the report.
PivotField.IsIncluded	Set this property to False to leave a field of a fieldset out of the report. Use IsIncluded to determine whether the field is in the report.
Expanded	Set this property to True to expand a field or member and show its children. Retrieve the value of Expanded to determine whether a field or member is currently expanded.
PivotView.AutoLayout	Use this method to clear the view for an OLAP data source or to put all fields in the detail area for a tabular source.
PivotView.AddTotal	Use this method to create a new total from a detail field.
PivotField.SortDirection	Use this property to set which way a field should be sorted or to get the field's current sort order.

Table 4-2. *Adjusting and saving the view layout.*

Property or Method	Description
PivotField.SortOn	Use this property to make the field's members sort by their total values instead of by their captions.
PivotField.SortOnScope	Use this property to sort a set of members based on a total, but only for a certain scope of members on the other axis.
PivotFieldset.FilterMember	Use this property to get or set the currently selected member of a fieldset on the filter axis.
PivotField.FilterMembers	Use this property to get the current set of filtered members for a given field.
PivotField.FilterFunction	Use this property to set or determine the filter function being used with the FilterMembers property. The filter function can include or exclude members, or there might be no filtering.
PivotTable.XMLData	Use this property to retrieve the definition of the current report as a large string that you can save and later reset.
PivotView.TotalOrientation	Use this property to make the PivotTable control display the total captions as row headings instead of column headings.
PivotGroupAxis.DisplayEmptyMembers	Use this property to force the PivotTable control to display rows or columns that are completely empty.

Property	Description
PivotTable.AutoFit	Use this property to turn off the AutoFit behavior, especially for a form-based environment such as Visual Basic.
PivotView.TitleBar	Use this property to adjust the title bar's caption and formatting.
PivotTable.DisplayToolbar, PivotTable.DisplayFieldList, PivotTable.DisplayPropertyToolbox	Use these properties to control visibility of elements such as the toolbar, field list, and Property Toolbox.
PivotTotal.NumberFormat	Use this property to format the numbers of a total.

Table 4-3. *Customizing and formatting the view.*   *(continued)*

Table 4-3. *continued*

Property	Description
PivotField.SubtotalBackColor	Use this property to make the background color of a subtotal different than that of the numbers that contributed to the subtotal. SubtotalBackColor is useful for making a visual distinction among different levels of totals in a large report.
PivotField.SubtotalFont	Use this property to differentiate the font used for subtotals from the font used for the numbers that contributed to the subtotals.
PivotTable.MemberExpand	Use this property to make the PivotTable control automatically expand all fields and members when added to the view.

Event	Description
QueryComplete	Raised after the PivotTable control has executed a query against the data source, which is commonly a reaction to a change in the report's layout. This is a good time to adjust the report title and any other user interface elements that need to be synchronized with the report.
Click	Fired when a user clicks anywhere on the report. Use the Selection property to determine where.
DblClick	Same as Click, but is fired when the user double-clicks. Useful for triggering a jump to another page to show details behind an aggregate or perhaps to display the Property Toolbox or your own formatting user interface.
SelectionChange	Fired whenever the selection has changed in the report. Mostly useful when you have other elements on your page or form that should change when new values are selected.
PivotTableChange	Fired for various reasons when using a tabular data source. The *Reason* parameter tells you what happened, which includes events such as a new total being created or a total being deleted.
ViewChange	Fired often, so be careful about doing too much in the event handler. Any slight change in the view causes this event to fire; the *Reason* parameter indicates what happened. See PivotViewReason-Enum in the OWC online help file (Msowcvba.chm) for a complete list of reasons.

Table 4-4. *Noteworthy events.*

SUMMARY

This chapter covered many of the questions that developers commonly ask about the PivotTable component, so you should now have a good understanding of the capabilities of this powerful piece of technology. Stay tuned for more about the PivotTable component in Chapter 7, where we will look at the source code for an OLAP sales analysis and reporting system.

Chapter 5

The Data Source Component

The final character in the cast of the Microsoft Office Web Components is the Data Source component (DSC). The DSC does not get much credit because it is largely invisible. However, it has the difficult job of connecting to data sources, building and executing commands, and retrieving results. The DSC is also the workhorse behind Microsoft Access 2000 data access pages.

When building custom solutions with the other Office Web Components, you generally use only a small set of the DSC's functionality—so you do not need to know much about the DSC. However, this chapter will give you a quick overview of what the DSC can do, discuss how it implements security, describe an easy way to make it use the Microsoft Remote Data Services (RDS) provider, and conclude by demonstrating how to perform the most common DSC programming tasks.

The DSC has much more functionality than this chapter can cover. The functionality not discussed here involves supporting Access 2000's data access pages, which is beyond the scope of this book. Instead, this chapter will concentrate on the DSC features you will need when building custom solutions that use the other Office Web Components.

OVERVIEW

As you have learned, the Office Web Components were designed to encapsulate the data analysis and reporting functionality of Microsoft Excel and Access. The other three Office Web Components have fairly direct analogs: the Spreadsheet component encapsulates Excel's basic spreadsheet and recalculation services, the Chart component encapsulates the basics of Excel charting, and the PivotTable component encapsulates both the PivotTable and QueryTable features in Excel. The DSC also has a direct analog, although you might not recognize it immediately.

Behind each bound Access form or report, a fairly large chunk of code performs the rather unglamorous job of retrieving data, synchronizing user interface controls with the data (or *binding* the controls), and maintaining the notion of a current row. Often the form or report has a hierarchical shape. For example, an order entry form collects information for the entire order, and a subform collects one or more detail rows for each order. Another example is a sales report that groups the data by several levels, showing sales broken down first by month, then by customer region, and then by salesperson. Both the order form and the sales report have a hierarchical data structure: the order form has a one-to-many relationship, and the sales report contains detail data grouped by three levels. The order entry form has a set of rows for the order header information, and each row contains a subset of rows for the individual order detail information. The sales report begins with a row for each month. Each month has a subset of rows for each distinct customer region, each customer region has a subset of rows for each distinct salesperson, and each salesperson has the detail data for the sales transactions in that particular time/region/salesperson group.

The DSC encapsulates all the feature sets just described: it retrieves data, binds controls, and manages row currency. It also exposes mechanisms to define a hierarchical data model and generate the appropriate commands to produce a hierarchical Recordset at runtime. The Data Access Page Designer manipulates the DSC extensively at design time, defining the hierarchical data model based on the placement of fields on the design surface. At runtime, the DSC generates a command grammar known as the *shape syntax,* which gets interpreted by the *Data Shape Provider,* an OLE DB service provider that builds hierarchical Rowsets from related Rowsets returned by the actual data provider. Figure 5-1 shows the data access architecture used by the DSC.

The DSC encapsulates one additional service provided by the code behind Access reports and continuous forms. When designing an Access report, you place fields and other unbound elements into sections known as *bands* to define the visual template for a row in a particular section. A continuous form is like a report with one detail section. At runtime, the code behind the report or continuous form replicates an instance of the visual template for each row in the section, binding the controls in each instance to their corresponding data row. The DSC provides this same functionality to the world of HTML pages in Microsoft Internet Explorer. By employing services in Internet Explorer, the DSC can use a visual template defined in the Data Access Page Designer to replicate an instance of the template for each data row.

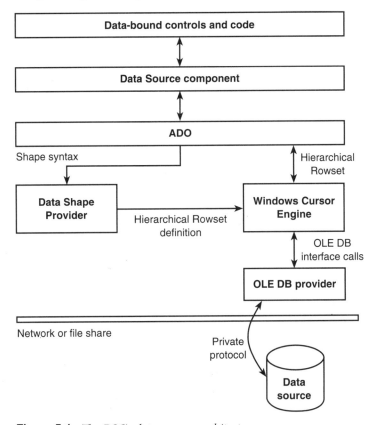

Figure 5-1. *The DSC's data access architecture.*

Since the DSC is a data source for other controls, it implements the standard COM interface for data source controls, known as IDataSource. This interface is recognized in Microsoft Visual Basic as well as in Internet Explorer, enabling the DSC to automatically participate in those environments' standard data-binding mechanisms. For example, if you place the DSC on a Visual Basic form, the form will recognize that the DSC is a potential data source and display it in the DataSource property drop-down list of each data-consuming control.

The DSC is invisible at runtime, meaning that it does not display a user interface at runtime. At design time, it appears as a small square image that looks—not surprisingly—like the Access key icon with a database icon behind it. This design-time display allows you to select the control, set its top-level properties, or delete it. The control's placement is not important because it does not take up any room at runtime.

SECURITY

As soon as I start describing how the Office Web Components access databases directly from a client's web browser, developers start asking tough questions about how the DSC enforces security and protects clients from malicious page developers.

The DSC's security model is largely dependent on the data components and providers below the DSC. However, this component does add some interesting twists to the security model that are unique to the world of web pages. This section will discuss how the DSC works with the data source's security and how it works with Internet Explorer's security mechanism to block malicious page developers.

Database Security

As shown in Figure 5-1, the DSC communicates with an in-memory OLE DB provider, which in turn communicates with the data source by a private protocol. The OLE DB provider is on the client machine and acts as the gateway to the data source, either enforcing security itself or delegating security enforcement to the data source. Therefore, the DSC is subject to all existing security mechanisms enforced by the data source; only authorized users can access the data or make changes to the data source.

PUT THE DSC IN THE <HEAD> SECTION IN HTML PAGES

If you look at the HTML source generated by the Data Access Page Designer, you will see that the designer places the DSC's <object> tag inside the <head> section of the document instead of inside the <body> section. This is legal in HTML, and it is an easy way to ensure that the browser doesn't take the DSC into account when dynamically laying out the document. Although the control is invisible at runtime, you will notice that if you include the DSC in the <body> section, Internet Explorer will initially display a small square where the DSC's <object> tag resides, reserving room in the document's layout. A second later, Internet Explorer realizes that the control is invisible at runtime and removes the square, laying out the document accordingly. You can avoid this rather annoying behavior by putting the DSC's <object> tag in the <head> section instead of in the <body> section.

An alternative to this approach is to use the style attribute in the DSC's <object> tag. If you add style="display:none" in the DSC's <object> tag, Internet Explorer will not include the DSC in the layout calculations, and it will not show the square icon when it initially loads your document.

The key DSC property for specifying the database connection is the Connection-String property. The connection string you pass to this property is like the connection strings discussed in Chapter 4 and is identical to the connection string used in the ADO Connection object's Open method. A connection string consists of a set of attribute/value pairs specifying various pieces of connection information, such as the name of the data source, the initial catalog (database) to use, and the authentication information. This last piece is what concerns us here.

Different data providers use different security schemes, but these providers essentially fall into two categories: those that use an integrated security scheme and those that require specific user names and passwords. Integrated security schemes combine database security with network security, using the client's network credentials for authentication within the database. This approach obviously works only when the client and data source exist on the same network domain, or when there are mechanisms for sharing authentication information between domains. The second type of provider requires an explicit user name and password in the connection string or in response to a prompt dialog box, often shown by the provider itself. The DSC can use either type of provider, but for providers that require a user name and password in the connection string, the DSC will supply the prompt dialog box itself when these values are not present in the connection string. Many providers' prompt dialog boxes allow you to do much more than simply specify a user name and password. In fact, they are often complex and visually unappealing. For these reasons, the DSC displays its own simple dialog box for specifying a user name and password.

Most providers support only one type of security scheme, which makes your choice rather simple. However, some providers (such as the one for Microsoft SQL Server) support both types of security scheme, so you can choose which approach to use. To use integrated security, include "Integrated Security=SSPI" in your connection string. To use an explicit user name and password (called *standard security* in SQL Server), include "User ID=*user name*;Password=*password*" in your connection string. Typically, you should use integrated security when you know that the client and server exist in the same domain and when you do not want to require users to log on to your application in addition to logging on to the network. You should use standard security when you know that the client and server are not on the same domain or when you want the user to have a different password for your application than his or her network password. Standard security is also the correct scheme to use when accessing your database from code executing on a web server, as the following sidebar discusses.

USE STANDARD SECURITY FOR CODE RUNNING ON A WEB SERVER

I have spent many a stressful day preparing for a demo, wondering why code that worked fine in a web page on my machine no longer worked when run in a Microsoft Active Server Pages script. The answer makes perfect sense if you understand how Microsoft Internet Information Server works, but for most developers, this gets quite confusing.

The web server and the code executing your ASP page are running as a Microsoft Windows NT service. Each Windows NT service can run as a local system account or can log on to a domain as a specific user account. Depending on how the service is configured, it can have radically different permissions. By default, IIS is set up to run as a local system account, with few to no privileges on other network resources. This means any code attempting to connect to a SQL Server database generally will not have permissions to access SQL Server itself—much less, the data within it. It also doesn't help that the account is a local system account on the web server, which is not an account in the Windows NT domain. Therefore, you cannot grant the account access to SQL Server via integrated security.

You might think that if you used the Windows NT Challenge/Response security mechanism on your web site, you could work around this. Think again. If you disallow anonymous access to your web site and allow only clients that can get past the Windows NT Challenge/Response security mechanism, your ASP code will run using the client's security credentials. This process—called *impersonation*—applies only to resources on the current machine, which in this case, is the web server. As soon as you try to connect to a network resource on a different machine, the impersonation stops and you again begin running under the IIS service's credentials. This behavior is intentional; otherwise, a serious breach in security would be allowed, permitting people to "spoof" a client and perform tasks on other network resources using the client's security credentials. Windows 2000 promises to allow cross-machine impersonation in a secure manner, but until that release, the preceding information is correct.

Using SQL Server's standard security avoids this whole mess. You create a special user logon to your instance of SQL Server that represents a "web user" and grants permissions to that account accordingly. However, make sure that web clients cannot obtain the source code for your ASP scripts because that would reveal the password and user ID for the account.

You might also consider configuring the IIS service to log on using a domain user account. IIS will use this account when accessing any resource. However, this approach has one land mine. When you configure IIS to use a domain account, you must also enter the domain password for that account so that IIS can log on to the domain without prompting. The domain password is stored on the web server but does not automatically reset when that account's password is changed. I did this once with a web server I had in my office, and one day the entire web server stopped working. It took me a while to realize that I had changed my domain password that morning because it had expired, but the IIS service was still trying to log on to the domain using my old password.

Cross-Domain Data Access

All the information I have covered so far is applicable to any OLE DB client application and has nothing to do with the DSC or the rather unique environment of the Web. However, because our team designed the DSC to operate in a web browser as a signed control that is "safe" for initialization and scripting, we had to add functionality prohibiting malicious page developers from doing damage by using the client's security credentials.

There are primarily two features of the Web and data access that, when combined, offer a frightening potential for mischief. The first is that web pages raise an event when initially loaded (the Window object's onLoad event) in which a developer can execute any script he or she wants. The code is run without asking the browsing user, and without warning, this code can call any method or property of any object that is marked as safe for scripting. We already discussed the second feature: integrated security. When connecting to a data source using integrated security (which for some providers is the only way you can connect), all access to database objects is tied to the client's user credentials. If the client has access to a table, view, or stored procedure, any code running on the client's behalf can access these objects without showing the user any warning.

To illustrate the problem, let's put these two features into a hypothetical situation. Suppose Celeste is an employee in the HR department of your company. She has access to the HR database that contains your salary information and has the permission to change data when necessary (for example, when you get a raise). Now suppose that Brent, an employee you just fired and gave the afternoon to clear out his workspace, is quite disgruntled. Brent develops interactive pages using the Office Web Components. He knows that he can write script in the Window object's onLoad event handler to connect to and access a database, because he typically does this when building reports or data entry forms. Brent decides to get even with you by writing a page that will attempt to access the HR database using integrated security and delete your salary information. He can't run this page because he has no access to the HR database, so the code will generate an error when it attempts to connect using the DSC. But Brent knows that Celeste has access. So Brent sends the page to Celeste as an HTML e-mail message with an enticing title that tempts her to open it. The page opens, the onLoad event fires, and the code connects using Celeste's credentials, deleting your salary information. Celeste doesn't even know what happened until later when you've complained and her boss asks her why she deleted the salary information.

The good news is that this scenario cannot occur; we specifically designed the DSC to warn the user when the page attempts to access a data source that is not in the same domain as the one from which the page originates. In this case, the word "domain" refers to an Internet or intranet domain rather than a Windows NT domain. (A single Windows NT domain might contain many Internet or intranet domains.) So if our fictitious Brent tried to perform the sabotage just described, Celeste would see the warning message shown in Figure 5-2.

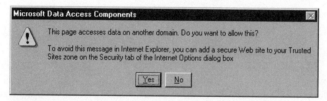

Figure 5-2. *The cross-domain data access warning.*

To understand how the cross-domain data access warning feature works, you need to understand the following:

- What defines an Internet or intranet domain.
- How to control this option so that the user can suppress the warning if he or she trusts the site from which the page originates.

An Internet or intranet domain is essentially the first part of a URL. For example, the domain for http://www.microsoft.com/office is www.microsoft.com, and the domain for http://MyServer/folder/page.htm is MyServer. In the latter case, any URL that starts with http://MyServer is considered to be in the same Internet or intranet domain. However, an instance of SQL Server running on the same machine as the web server is still considered to be in a different domain, as are any file shares exposed from the server. For this reason, most direct data access is inherently cross-domain unless you use RDS, as described in the next section.

So now you know why you must warn users before code in a page accesses data sources on a different domain than where the page originated. But what about when the user knows that the page came from a trusted source and wants to suppress this warning? For example, suppose Celeste regularly works with another web-based tool to view and manipulate employees' records. The easiest way for her to suppress this warning is to add the site from which this page originates to her *trusted sites list* in Internet Explorer. By doing so, Celeste declares that she trusts the site from which this page comes. This causes Internet Explorer to run the page in the *trusted sites zone,* which has lower security settings than the browser's Internet or local intranet zones. To add the site to her trusted sites list, Celeste uses Internet Explorer's Trusted Sites dialog box, shown in Figure 5-3.

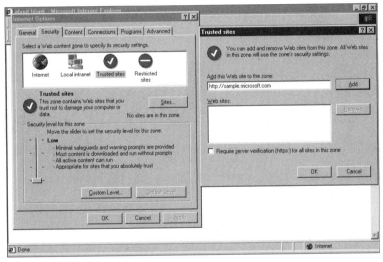

Figure 5-3. *Adding a site to the trusted sites list.*

The trusted sites zone in Internet Explorer defaults the Access Data Sources Across Domains security setting to Enable. This security setting controls whether the current user sees the cross-domain data access warning. The user can set this option explicitly for a specific zone by clicking the Custom Level button on the Security tab of Internet Explorer's Internet Options dialog box and using the Security Settings dialog box that appears.

NOTE   If you are running Internet Explorer 4.01, you will not see this security setting in the Security Settings dialog box. Microsoft added this option to Internet Explorer 5.0 to make this security setting easier to set. In Internet Explorer 4.01, the DSC uses the setting titled Script ActiveX Controls Marked Safe For Scripting instead.

Since using the trusted sites zone works the same for versions 4.01 and 5.0, it is a better choice than adjusting the individual security settings.

Be aware that you can add a portion of a web site to the trusted sites list. For example, if you add http://MyServer to your trusted sites list, Internet Explorer will trust all pages from this site. If you add http://MyServer/MyFolder to the trusted sites list, Internet Explorer will trust all pages starting with this URL. However, Internet Explorer will not trust pages from http://MyServer/MyOtherFolder, and pages from this site will fall into the local intranet zone.

You might be wondering why we did not just mark the DSC as "unsafe" for initialization and scripting. The answer, I hope, is obvious. If we had done that, any page including the DSC would generate warning messages both when the control was initialized and when any code used its methods or properties. There would be no way to suppress the warnings and no way to build applications (that would automatically suppress warning messages) that users could trust. We designed the DSC so that you can create complex custom solutions that run in a web environment and produce no warnings when trusted by the user. However, the DSC also ensures that users are protected from malicious developers.

IN WHAT ZONE DOES HTML E-MAIL RUN?

When the Microsoft Access team first designed the data access pages feature, they were excited about the potential for sending one of these pages via HTML e-mail. Instead of e-mailing a routine report as an attachment, the report itself would *be* the message. Then our team hooked up the cross-domain warning. To our dismay, the warning displayed every time we opened an e-mailed report, and there seemed to be no way to suppress it. Microsoft Outlook always considers HTML e-mail to be from the Internet zone, even if it comes from within your organization; therefore, it is always suspect. You cannot add HTML e-mail to your trusted sites list because it isn't an actual site that has a URL. If you plan to send pages containing the DSC, they will always generate the cross-domain data access warning unless your users enable the security setting noted earlier for the Internet zone. (This is a bit risky though.) However, if you send a link to a page from a site on the user's trusted sites list, you will avert the warning.

CAN I ADD MY SITE TO THE
TRUSTED SITES LIST AUTOMATICALLY?

A few developers have asked me whether any way exists to programmatically add their web site to a user's trusted sites list. To my knowledge, this is impossible—and for good reason. Such a capability would create a gaping security hole because it would enable a developer to add his or her site to the list and redirect the client's browser to a malicious page. However, the Internet Explorer Administrator's Kit does allow a corporation to prepopulate the trusted sites list in a network install setup. When a user installs from such a setup, his or her trusted sites list will automatically contain the sites from the prepopulated list.

USING REMOTE DATA SERVICES

I briefly mentioned RDS in Chapter 4 as a mechanism for retrieving data by routing a command through a web server. I also alluded to it earlier in this chapter as a way to avoid the cross-domain data access warning. Although I will not describe the operational details of RDS here, I will discuss the features of the DSC that make using RDS easier. For more general information on RDS, see the RDS documentation in the OLE DB SDK (which is quite detailed) and the various white papers available at http://www.microsoft.com/data.

The DSC exposes a property at its top-level interface named UseRemoteProvider. By default, this property is set to False and the DSC uses whatever OLE DB provider you specify in the provider attribute of your connection string. However, if you set this property to True, the DSC alters the connection string you specify so that it uses the RDS provider. If you are already familiar with RDS, you know that the RDS provider needs two pieces of information to retrieve data:

- The name of a web server on which the RDS server components reside.

- The name of the real data provider that RDS will use on the web server.

When the DSC alters your connection string, it uses the name of the web server from which the page originates for the first setting and uses the value you indicate in the provider attribute as the name for the real data provider on the server. The DSC also alters your connection string to use the Data Shape Provider (mentioned earlier) whether or not you use RDS.

For example, suppose you use the following connection string:

```
Provider=sqloledb;Data Source=MySQLServer;
Initial Catalog=Northwind;User Id=sa;Password=;
```

After you set the UseRemoteProvider property to True, the DSC changes your connection string to this:

```
Provider=MSDataShape.1;Extended Properties="REMOTE PROVIDER=sqloledb;
REMOTE SERVER=http://web server;EXTENDED PROPERTIES='INITIAL
CATALOG=Northwind;'";Persist Security Info=True;Connect Timeout=15;
Data Source=MySQLServer;User ID=sa;Data Provider=MS Remote
```

Because RDS is set to use the same web server from which the page originated, the data access is considered to be in the same domain. Therefore, you will not see any cross-domain data access warnings, regardless of the zone in which the page runs. RDS is useful for avoiding these warnings, but it does require extra setup and configuration on the web server. Since the RDS client provider is included with the Office Web Components setup, no extra setup steps are needed on the client machine.

PROGRAMMING THE DATA SOURCE COMPONENT

Now that you know what the DSC was designed to do, let's discuss how you accomplish some common programming tasks with it. The following sections describe how to perform tasks using the DSC with the other Office Web Components. These sections do not discuss tasks that involve using hierarchical data access pages. For more information on that subject, see the Access 2000 documentation.

Setting Connection Information

The first step in using the DSC is to configure its connection information. You can do this either at design time by using the container's property editor or at runtime by using code. You already saw how to do this in Chapters 3 and 4, but here is a quick recap of the process.

The following code, taken from the DSCSample.htm file in the Chap05 folder on the companion CD, shows how to set the DSC's connection information:

```
' Set the DSC's ConnectionString property
' Note: Change this line if you move the MDB file or want to connect to
' a different MDB file
sDBPath = "..\Data\Northwind.mdb"
DSC.ConnectionString = "provider=microsoft.jet.oledb.4.0;data source=" & _
                       sDBPath
```

This code simply sets the DSC's ConnectionString property to a valid connection string—in this case, using the Microsoft Jet OLE DB provider and a local MDB file. To connect to a SQL Server data source using integrated security, the code would look like this:

```
DSC.ConnectionString = "PROVIDER=sqloledb;DATA SOURCE=SQLserverName;" & _
                       "INITIAL CATALOG=DatabaseName;" & _
                       "INTEGRATED SECURITY=SSPI"
```

These two connection strings use a direct (also called *two-tier*) connection. To use RDS, which will remote your data requests over HTTP to a web server, you can use your normal connection string and set the UseRemoteProvider property to True:

```
DSC.ConnectionString = "PROVIDER=sqloledb;DATA SOURCE=SQLserverName;" & _
                       "INITIAL CATALOG=DatabaseName;" & _
                       "INTEGRATED SECURITY=SSPI"
DSC.UseRemoteProvider = True
```

Note that the DSC will not immediately connect to the data source when you set the ConnectionString property. Instead, it will wait until your code or a bound control requests data from the data source. It will also attempt to connect if your code requests the DSC's Connection property, which returns an opened ADO Connection object. (More on the Connection property later.) This delayed connection scheme allows you to adjust the ConnectionString property in a <script> block before any controls have asked for data.

Adding a New RecordsetDef

The DSC has a RecordsetDefs collection of RecordsetDef objects, so named because they represent definitions of ADO Recordset objects that the DSC can materialize at runtime. Any RecordsetDef object defined in the DSC's RecordsetDefs collection is a valid data member that a data-bound control can request. (If you need a refresher on data sources and data members, see Chapter 2.) When using the DSC to retrieve data for another Office Web Component, you must add a RecordsetDef object to the DSC to define the table, view, stored procedure, or command text that the DSC should use to get the data.

A page designed in Access 2000's Data Access Page Designer already has a number of RecordsetDef objects defined in the page's DSC. However, you can add more at runtime and use them as data members for bound controls. The following code, also taken from the DSCSample.htm file in the Chap05 folder on the companion CD, shows how to add a RecordsetDef object at runtime:

```
Set rsdef = DSC.RecordsetDefs.AddNew("SELECT Country, " & _
    "Shippers.CompanyName AS Shipper, " & _
    "Count(*) AS Shipments, " & _
```

(continued)

```
"Sum(Quantity) AS Quantity " & _
"FROM Invoices " & _
"WHERE OrderDate Between #1/1/98# " & _
"and #12/31/98# " & _
"GROUP BY Country, Shippers.CompanyName", _
DSC.Constants.dscCommandText, "ChartData")
```

This example adds a new RecordsetDef object using a SQL statement for the first parameter to the AddNew method. You can also use the name of a table, view, stored query, or stored procedure in this first parameter. The second parameter tells the DSC what kind of expression you used in the first parameter, and the valid values you can pass for this argument are listed in the DscRowsourceTypeEnum enumeration. The last parameter is the name you want to assign the new RecordsetDef object; if not specified here, the DSC will assign it a new unique name. The AddNew method returns the new RecordsetDef object, so if you want to perform a task with it right away, you can set a variable to the return value and further modify the new object.

Adding Calculated Fields

Occasionally, you will need to use a calculated field in your solution. Usually, you will want to use a calculated field expression in the SQL statement for your Recordset-Def object, using the database engine's capabilities to calculate a new field value for each returned row. However, you cannot always do this, either because the database engine does not support calculated columns or because you want to use a different expression service to resolve the calculation.

ADDING A RECORDSETDEF OBJECT BASED ON XML DATA

Chapter 4 described how to load the PivotTable component with XML data (in a specific format) returned from a URL. When you set the PivotTable control's ConnectionString and CommandText properties, the control creates a DSC in memory and adds a RecordsetDef object programmatically, just as you saw in the previous code snippet. To add a RecordsetDef based on XML returned from a URL, use the following code:

```
DSC.RecordsetDefs.AddNew sURL, DSC.Constants.dscCommandFile
```

This should look a lot like the example in Chapter 4 because the PivotTable control acts as a front for the DSC. Note that you pass the constant dscCommand-File as the second argument. This tells the DSC the first argument is a URL that will return XML data in the specific format that ADO Recordset objects know how to load. For an example of this technique, see the sample file LoadingXML.htm from the companion CD.

The DSC exposes the Data Shape Provider's ability to create calculated fields in your Recordset object. The Data Shape Provider evaluates the calculation expression at the client using the Jet expression service. The Jet expression service exposes all the "safe" VBA runtime functions, allowing you to build some complex expressions.

The following code, taken from the DSCSample.htm file, shows how to add a calculated field to a RecordsetDef object:

```
' Add a calculated field to the RecordsetDef object
rsdef.PageFields.Add "[Quantity]/[Shipments]", _
    DSC.Constants.dscCalculated, "AvgQtyPerShipment"
```

To add a calculated field, use the Add method of the PageFields collection. Every RecordsetDef object has a PageFields collection that contains definitions for all the fields in the RecordsetDef object. To add a new calculated field to this collection, specify the calculation expression as the first parameter, the dscCalculated constant as the second parameter, and the name for your new calculated field as the last parameter.

The previous calculation expression is quite trivial. You would probably just include it in your SQL statement, letting the database engine perform the calculation. However, the Jet expression service and VBA runtime functions allow you to use more complicated expressions than most database engines allow. For example, you can use all the VBA string manipulation functions—such as InStr, Left, Mid, Right, and Format—to massage text values in your database. Another example is using the Left function to extract an alpha-grouping value to group names by their first letter.

Although the Jet expression service in Access allows you to reference the Microsoft VBA functions you defined in the current database, they are not available to the data shape engine's expression service. The OLE DB provider for Jet databases does not permit use of your custom functions, even in stored queries.

WHICH VBA FUNCTIONS ARE NOT CONSIDERED SAFE?

VBA exposes a few runtime functions that are not considered safe and therefore are not available in the Jet expression service for calculated fields. For example, VBA exposes a function named Kill that deletes files on your hard drive. If this function were permitted, a malicious developer could use it in a field expression and delete critical files on the client's machine. For this reason, none of the VBA functions that access the hard drive or interact with the system settings are allowed in calculated field expressions.

WARNING   Although you might be tempted, do not use calculated fields with the PivotTable component. When I started playing with client-side calculated fields in the DSC, I tried using the Left function to create a new column with only the first letter of a customer's last name. I thought I could use this technique with the PivotTable component to perform an alpha-grouping of customer data. I tried running the page, and it immediately caused a general protection fault and disappeared.

The PivotTable control does not support using client-side calculated fields in this version of the Office Web Components; however, it will support them in future releases. For the Office 2000 release, you should include expressions in your SQL statements to create calculated fields for the PivotTable control. For example, the task I just described could also be performed using the Left function in Transact SQL or in Jet SQL.

Adding Server Filters

When you add a RecordsetDef object, you can simply use the name of a table or view, instead of a full SQL statement. If you do so, you can use the ServerFilter property of the RecordsetDef object to specify a WHERE clause that the DSC will include in the command text sent to the data source. This limits the amount of data returned from the data source, which is much faster than retrieving all data and then filtering locally.

To set the ServerFilter property, use the following code (from DSCSample.htm):

```
Set rsdef = DSC.RecordsetDefs.AddNew("Invoices", _
    DSC.Constants.dscView, "ChartData2")

rsdef.ServerFilter = "OrderDate Between #1/1/98# and #1/31/98#"
```

The DSC will use the value of the ServerFilter property as a WHERE clause when fetching data from the table or view. If you use command text as the source for your RecordsetDef object, add the WHERE clause as part of your command text.

Using Parameters

The DSC also supports using parameterized commands and using parameters with stored procedures. Each RecordsetDef object has a ParameterValues collection. The collection holds a set of ParameterValue objects, one for each parameter in the source command.

When code or a bound control asks the DSC for the results of a RecordsetDef object, the DSC checks whether any parameter values (represented by ParameterValue objects) are needed for the command. If values are needed and the Value properties of the ParameterValue objects are not set, the DSC will display a parameter prompt dialog box that allows the user to specify parameter values. Typically, a custom solution displays its own user interface for collecting these parameter values and then programmatically sets the Value properties of the ParameterValue objects.

The following code shows how to add a RecordsetDef object based on a stored procedure and how to add parameter values for execution:

```
Set rsdef = DSC.RecordsetDefs.AddNew("Employee Sales by Country", _
    DSC.Constants.dscProcedure)

rsdef.ParameterValues.Add "[Beginning Date]", "1/1/98"
rsdef.ParameterValues.Add "[Ending Date]", "1/31/98"
```

This example adds a RecordsetDef object that uses the stored procedure Employee Sales by Country as its source. This stored procedure has two parameters, and the code adds ParameterValue objects for each. This code was written to use the Jet database engine version of the Northwind database, so the parameter names have square brackets around them. However, if you are using SQL Server, you must omit the square brackets and use an at sign (@) in front of each parameter name.

Getting Recordset Objects from the Data Source Component

Once you add a RecordsetDef object to the DSC, you can retrieve the resulting ADO Recordset object in code by using the DSC's Execute method. The first time your code or a bound control requests a certain RecordsetDef object, the DSC will execute the source command to get the ADO Recordset object. Successive requests for the same RecordsetDef object will return the ADO Recordset object that the DSC already retrieved—meaning multiple controls bound to the same RecordsetDef object will display the same data and will have the same current row.

Having multiple controls bound to the same RecordsetDef object has an interesting effect when you set a local filter on the object. For example, if you bind the Chart component to a RecordsetDef object in the DSC, you can use the DSC's Execute method to retrieve a reference to the source Recordset, and you can then apply a local filter. The Recordset object notifies all controls to which it is bound that its contents have changed and that they should refresh themselves. The Chart component, therefore, updates itself so that it shows the current data.

The following code, taken from the DSCSample.htm file on the companion CD, shows how to accomplish this:

```
Sub btnFilter_onClick()
    ' Local variables
    Dim rs                ' Recordset object
    Dim asCountries       ' String array of country names
    Dim sFilter           ' Filter expression
    Dim ct                ' Counter

    ' Get the Recordset object the chart is bound to
    Set rs = DSC.Execute(ChartSpace1.DataMember)
```

(continued)

```
    ' Get the set of country names to filter on
    asCountries = Split(txtCountries.value,",")

    ' Build the filter expression
    On Error Resume Next
    sFilter = "Country='" & Trim(asCountries(0)) & "'"
    If err.Number = 0 Then
        For ct = 1 To Ubound(asCountries)
            sFilter = sFilter & " OR Country='" & _
                Trim(asCountries(ct)) & "'"
        Next 'ct
    Else
        sFilter = ""
    End If

    ' Now set the filter expression
    ' The chart will automatically update
    rs.Filter = sFilter
End Sub 'btnfilter_onClick()
```

This example uses the DataMember property of the Chart control to retrieve the name of the RecordsetDef object to which the Chart control is bound. It uses the DSC's Execute method to obtain a reference to the same Recordset object the Chart control is using to load the chart. It then builds a filter expression based on the country names typed into the text box and sets the Recordset object's Filter property to this filter expression.

Executing Ad Hoc Statements and Manipulating the Connection

The DSC exposes a property named Connection at its top-level interface. This property returns the ADO Connection object the DSC is currently using to communicate with the database. You can use this ADO Connection object reference to execute ad hoc statements that access the data source, such as a stored procedure call to retrieve certain lookup values or to ensure that the version of the database schema is what the client solution expects. You can also use the properties and methods of the ADO Connection object to perform tasks such as beginning and ending a transaction, determining or setting the database isolation level, or setting a new command timeout value.

For example, to retrieve the version of the SQL Server database engine to which your DSC is connected, you can use the following code:

```
Set rsVerInfo = DSC.Connection.Execute("Select @@Version")
```

The ADO Connection object's Execute method takes a command to execute and returns a forward-only, read-only Recordset with the results of the command. You can use this method to execute stored procedures in the data source or to execute any command text accepted by the data source.

Catching Data Access Errors

The DSC raises an important event related to data access errors. If the DSC encounters a data access error while connecting or fetching data for a bound control, it will raise its DataError event, passing a DSCEventInfo object to the event handler. This object has a property named Error, which returns the ADO Error object that the DSC obtains when the data access error occurs. To catch this error and display your own message, use the following code:

```
Sub MSODSC_DataError(einfo)
    MsgBox "Data Error!" & vbCrLf & einfo.Error.Description, vbCritical
End Sub
```

Make sure you set the DSC's DisplayAlerts property to False to suppress the message boxes the DSC itself displays when it encounters an error.

You can obviously perform other tasks in this event handler besides displaying the error. For example, you might use this event to catch conditions in which a certain data source is no longer available and to automatically switch to a backup data source. The ADO Error object exposes the data source's native error number to help you detect certain types of errors from which you might try to recover.

SUMMARY

When building custom solutions with the Office Web Components, you typically do not need to write code that directly uses the DSC. However, the DSC offers a number of useful techniques that you can use to enhance your solutions.

This is the last chapter in Part I of the book, the conceptual overview of the Office Web Components. Part II contains a number of useful and exciting solutions you can build with the Office Web Components and explains the various techniques used to build them. Now that you know how to perform the basic programming tasks with each of the controls, it's time to start putting them together and integrating them with other technologies to build real-world business solutions.

Building Solutions with the Office Web Components

Chapter 6

Dynamic and Real-Time Charting

Most businesses have some set of metrics that they monitor on a fairly regular basis, often judging the overall health of a project or company based on their current values or trends. This chapter shows you how to use the Chart component to deliver dynamic and real-time visualizations of these business metrics.

ABOUT THE SOLUTION

At Microsoft, our most important project metrics center around bugs: the number of bugs opened today; the number of bugs resolved today; the number of bugs assigned to different subgroups; and the number of bugs per area, per severity, and per priority. We use these metrics to measure the overall health of the project, to determine whether it is still on schedule, and to project when we think the product will be ready for a beta or final release.

These metrics come from our bug tracking system—an internal tool that stores information in a Microsoft SQL Server database. Every week, our test leads prepare detailed reports with charts showing the bug count activity during the previous week. These reports are extremely useful; however, when we approached critical points in the Microsoft Office 2000 cycle, the program managers wanted to see some of these metrics daily. We decided to put the Office Web Components to the test and develop a solution that produced charts of these important metrics on a daily basis. We offered several on-demand charts that displayed the metrics' values the moment a client requested them. This solution was so successful that we began getting requests from many other product groups within Microsoft for early builds of the components as well as for instructions on how we generated the charts.

In this chapter, I will describe exactly how we built this solution, and I will describe some more advanced techniques. However, I will present this solution in a slightly different context. Because bug tracking is relevant primarily to software companies, I decided to develop a solution around a similar process that most large companies have: tracking helpdesk logs. A *helpdesk* is a group of employees or contractors who help others in the company solve their technical problems, which are often related to software or hardware. Any time a new problem is reported, a new log is generated (some companies refer to this as a *ticket*) and the log progresses through a series of states until it is closed. The manager of a helpdesk needs to monitor a number of metrics on a daily basis to measure how successful the helpdesk is. For example, the manager often wants to see the number of new logs opened that day and the number of logs currently active, broken down by technician or type of technology. The manager might also want to watch the current call volume to determine whether there are enough technicians to handle the incoming calls. This chapter's solution, the Helpdesk Reporting solution, shows how to implement the presentation of a set of metrics in a variety of ways: as a server-generated chart, as a client-side interactive chart, and as a real-time updating chart.

TECHNIQUES ILLUSTRATED IN THIS SOLUTION

Table 6-1 lists the various techniques illustrated in the Helpdesk Reporting solution. You can use this table as a quick reference for locating the techniques in which you are interested. I will not discuss all of these techniques in this chapter; however, you can refer to the Chapter 6 source files on the companion CD to learn more about the techniques not covered here.

Technique	Source File
Using the Chart component in a Microsoft Active Server Pages page to create a GIF.	GetChart.asp
Managing temporary files produced by the Chart component.	GetChart.asp
Producing an XML-Data stream from an ASP page.	GetData.asp
Using the Data Source component (DSC) with an XML-Data stream.	HistoricalCharts.htm
Binding the Chart component to the DSC.	HistoricalCharts.htm

Table 6-1. *Techniques demonstrated by the Helpdesk Reporting solution.*

Technique	Source File
Loading a Chart component with literal data.	RealTimeChart.htm
Updating a Chart component with real-time data.	RealTimeChart.htm
Formatting a Chart component using styles from the parent page.	HistoricalCharts.htm, RealTimeChart.htm
Including common script routines using an src attribute in a <script> tag.	HistoricalCharts.htm, RealTimeChart.htm
Implementing chart tips using a scriptlet.	HistoricalCharts.htm, RealTimeChart.htm, ChartTips.scp
Adjusting category tick label spacing dynamically to show only a certain number of category labels regardless of density.	HistoricalCharts.htm

RUNNING THE SOLUTION

The Helpdesk Reporting solution is a mixture of HTML and ASP pages. To run this solution, you must open the Default.htm page using an http:// URL, meaning that you cannot simply double-click the files on the companion CD. The easiest way to set up the solution is to follow these steps:

1. If you are using a Microsoft Windows NT Server machine with Microsoft Internet Information Server, use the IIS manager to add a virtual directory to your root web. Copy the Chap06 and Scripts directories on the companion CD to your machine's hard drive and specify these directories as the sources for peer virtual directories. Make sure you enable scripting support, and make sure you have designated the Chap06 folder as an application by choosing the Create button in the Application Settings section of the Folder Properties dialog box.

2. If you are running Personal Web Server (say on Windows 98 or Windows NT Workstation), use the Personal Web Manager to add a virtual directory as described in Step 1, but make sure that you check the Execute option in the Access section of the Add Directory dialog box.

3. Type the URL for the directory into your browser—for example, *http://MyServer/Chap06*. The Default.htm page should load unless you have configured your web site to use another default filename. If you have, simply type */Default.htm* at the end of the URL.

Note that this solution does have a Global.asa file. If you do not set up the directory as a web application, the Global.asa file will never be invoked. If you forget to designate the directory as an application, you'll notice a large number of temporary files generated in the directory. That's because the Global.asa file is set up to delete the temporary GIF images produced by the server-side chart example when the session times out. If no application is defined, no session timeout occurs and the Global.asa file is never called.

CREATING SERVER-SIDE CHARTS ON DEMAND

Many users ask me how to use the Chart component to generate charts as GIF images on demand and return them to the client. They find this scenario attractive, as it requires no client installation and will render and function in many browsers on many platforms. I implemented this technique in the GetChart.asp file; let's take a look at it now.

Using the Chart Component on the Server

When using the Chart component on the server, you must remember to create it, use it, and destroy it all within the same client request. You might be tempted to create an instance of the Chart component and put it into the Session or Application state objects, thinking you are saving resources or optimizing your object usage. But you should not do this. If you do, your web application might not function properly, will not scale well, and will perform poorly under moderate to heavy loads.

ADDING VIRTUAL DIRECTORIES USING PERSONAL WEB SERVER

When I first tested installing this solution, it was trivial to add it to an IIS installation. Then I tried adding it to a Personal Web Server installation on Windows 98. I could not figure out why it wouldn't work. After some searching on MSDN, I found an article saying that you must set the Execute access permission on a directory that you want to declare as a web application. On IIS, execute access allows for server-side execution of binary code, not scripts, so I never would have thought to enable that permission.

I also tried to add the entire CD tree as a virtual directory, figuring that Personal Web Server would add directories for the subdirectories automatically. It did allow access to them, but it still would not run my Global.asa file in the Chap06 directory. I then found another note in MSDN that reminded me to manually add any subdirectories as virtual directories if they are applications unto themselves. After I did that, everything worked fine.

Why, you ask? Because the Chart component, like all the Office Web Components, uses the *apartment threading model*. The apartment threading model stipulates that all calls to an object must be routed through the thread that created the object. This ensures synchronization, keeping multiple threads that are using the same object from causing each other grief. To illustrate what can go wrong in the absence of the apartment threading model, suppose you have two independent threads of execution that are both trying to create different charts in the same Chart component instance at the same time. Imagine that the first thread starts creating its chart but is then interrupted by the second thread, which clears the Chart component and starts creating a different chart. The result would be chaos. Since client requests in ASP pages run concurrently on different threads, developers using the Chart component on a web server would commonly find themselves in this chaotic environment.

Instead of forcing developers to code synchronization primitives (which are not available in Microsoft VBScript or Microsoft JScript anyway) around the components, our team chose to develop the components using the apartment threading model—which is the same model used for objects created in Microsoft Visual Basic. The apartment threading model forces all calls to an object to use the same thread on which the object was initially created. This ensures that two threads don't call the same object at the same time, but it still does not prohibit two different threads from using the same object instance at different times. Although the apartment threading model guarantees that another thread can't enter the object's code while your thread is executing a method, it does not prevent that other thread from marshaling a request to your thread and executing a method while your thread is not actively executing other code and checking for new messages. Therefore, if you share a Chart component instance using the Session or Application state object, you can still encounter the situation in which two threads try to use the same object instance to create a chart and can interfere with each other. This is because creating a chart involves many method calls, each of which affects the object's global state.

Sharing an apartment threading model object creates an enormous overhead in the server, causing lots of cross-thread marshaling and thread context switching. Since all calls have to route through a single thread (the thread that originally created the object instance), your massively multithreaded server turns into a single thread of execution with all other threads waiting in line to execute. Your web application will never scale to support hundreds or thousands of concurrent users if you attempt to share an apartment threading model object in the Session or Application state.

To avoid this mess, create the Chart component instance, load it with data, export it to a temporary GIF file, and destroy it in the same client request. Our team designed the Chart component to initialize quickly, so all this creation and destruction occurs rather rapidly. To see how it runs, click the Current Logs link in the Helpdesk Reporting solution. Use the drop-down list to select different charts, and click the button next to the drop-down list to submit the form and run the ASP page. Each time you click the Go button next to the drop-down list, the ASP page creates a Chart component instance, loads it with data, formats the chart, exports the chart to a GIF, and destroys the component instance. On my rather wimpy Pentium laptop, this takes less than a second.

Generating a Server-Side Chart

Now that we have established how to use the Chart component on the server, let's look at some of the GetChart.asp file's source code. This file creates a new GIF image each time it is called, returning the GIF to the client browser. Let's start by creating an instance of the Chart component as an in-memory object:

```
Dim m_cspace          ' OWC ChartSpace object reference
Dim m_cht             ' WCChart object reference
Dim m_ser             ' WCSeries object reference
Dim c                 ' Constants object reference

' Create the Chart object in the server context
Set m_cspace = server.CreateObject("OWC.Chart")
Set m_cht = m_cspace.Charts.Add()
Set c = m_cspace.Constants
:
```

You create an instance of the Chart component using the standard CreateObject method exposed from the Server object of ASP. The parameter passed here is "OWC.Chart", which is the ProgID for the Chart component. A ProgID is a string-based name for a COM object. The Spreadsheet and PivotTable components use the ProgIDs "OWC.Spreadsheet" and "OWC.PivotTable", respectively.

Note that these are *version-independent* ProgIDs, meaning the system will create the most current registered version of the object rather than a specific version. Although this ensures that you will always get the most current version of a component, it might be a curse rather than a blessing. If the new version does not operate how you expect it to, it could cause your script to fail. However, if you think this is a concern, use the "OWC.Chart.9" ProgID instead. This is the *version-dependent* ProgID, and if you use it, COM will always attempt to create the Office 2000 version of the Chart component.

After creating an instance of the Chart component, this code adds a new chart to the chart space and sets a variable to the Constants object so that constants can be used in an untyped language. Note that when developing ASP scripts, you can add a reference to the Office Web Components type library in the Global.asa file. Doing so allows you to use type names explicitly in your ASP scripts, as well as the enumeration constants, just as you would in Visual Basic. For more information on this, see the ASP help topic "TypeLibrary declarations," available in the IIS product documentation.

From this point on, the code should look familiar. Programming the Chart component in an ASP page is exactly like programming the Chart control on a web page. The code continues by adding some series and data values to the chart:

```
⋮
' Set the chart type to Clustered Bar, and give it a legend
m_cht.Type = c.chChartTypeBarClustered
m_cht.HasLegend = True

' Add two series to the chart
Dim asPri(1)
asPri(0) = "Normal Priority"
asPri(1) = "High Priority"

For m_ct = 0 To 1
    Set m_ser = m_cht.SeriesCollection.Add()
    m_ser.Caption = asPri(m_ct)

    m_ser.SetData c.chDimCategories, c.chDataLiteral, _
        Array("Jeff", "Laura", "Kevin", "Elaine", "Rico", "Hannah")

    m_ser.SetData c.chDimValues, c.chDataLiteral, _
        GenRandomValues(6, 5, 15)
Next 'm_ct

' Add a chart title, some axis titles, and so on
FormatChart m_cht, "Active Logs by Priority", "Number of Logs", _
    "Technician", "#,##0"
⋮
```

This code (taken from Case 1 of the GetChart.asp script) sets the chart's type to Clustered Bar, adds a legend, and adds two series filled with literal data. The data in this example is randomly generated, but you would of course use the appropriate mechanism for obtaining your metrics. For example, if the metrics you want to chart are in a database, you would use an ADO Recordset object to get the data and bind the Chart component to the Recordset (as Chapter 3 demonstrated). However, some business metrics come from sources that are not databases, such as machines on a manufacturing floor or sensors monitoring an aspect of a system. In those cases, loading literal data is the best approach.

The FormatChart function called at the end of this code block is a simple function on the same ASP page that formats the chart elements, adding chart and axis titles. The code for the FormatChart function looks like this:

```
Sub FormatChart(cht, sTitle, sValTitle, sCatTitle, sValNumFmt)
    ' Local variables
    Dim ax              ' Temporary WCAxis object
```

(continued)

175

```
        Dim fnt          ' Temporary OWCFont object
        Dim c            ' Constants object

        Set c = cht.Parent.Constants

        cht.HasTitle = True
        cht.Title.Caption = sTitle
        set fnt = cht.Title.Font
        fnt.Name = "Tahoma"
        fnt.Size = 10
        fnt.Bold = True

        For Each ax In cht.Axes
            If ax.Type = c.chValueAxis Then
                ax.HasTitle = True
                ax.Title.Caption = sValTitle
                set fnt = ax.Title.Font
                fnt.Name = "Tahoma"
                fnt.Size = 8
                fnt.Bold = True
                ax.NumberFormat = sValNumFmt

            Else
                ax.HasTitle = True
                ax.Title.Caption = sCatTitle
                set fnt = ax.Title.Font
                fnt.Name = "Tahoma"
                fnt.Size = 8
                fnt.Bold = True

            End If
        Next 'ax

End Sub 'FormatChart()
```

This code should also look similar to code you saw in Chapter 3. You format a chart on the server exactly the same way as you do on the client. The only difference is that the chart is not actually visible on the screen. Since I want this code to work for many chart types, I loop over all the chart's axes using the For Each construct and use the Type property of the axis to determine whether it is a value axis or a category axis so that I can format the axes differently. This works for most of the common chart types. However, because a Scatter chart has two value axes and no category axis, this code would add the same title to both the X and Y value axes of a Scatter chart—which is probably not what you would want.

The last line of the main script follows:

```
' Export the chart to a GIF, and emit the rest of the HTML
m_sFilePath = ExportChartToGIF(m_cspace)
```

The ExportChartToGIF function is another function on the same ASP page. It returns the new GIF filename (as a relative path), which I then use in the returned HTML fragment as the src attribute of the <img> tag:

```
<img src=<%= m_sFilePath %>>
```

For example, the HTML fragment returned to the client browser might look like this:

```
<img src=radDD604.tmp>
```

When the browser sees this tag, it returns to the web server to get this file and display it in the page.

The ExportChartToGIF function is where most of the complicated stuff happens. Let's take a look at it:

```
Function ExportChartToGIF(cspace)
    ' Local variables
    Dim fso              ' FileSystemObject
    Dim sFilePath        ' Root file path for GIF
    Dim sFileName        ' Filename for GIF

    ' Now save the current chart to a GIF file
    ' Build a temporary filename that is unique
    Set fso = CreateObject("Scripting.FileSystemObject")

    sFilePath = Request.ServerVariables("PATH_TRANSLATED")
    sFilePath = Left(sFilePath, InStrRev(sFilePath, "\"))
    sFileName = fso.GetTempName()

    ' Call ExportPicture to generate the chart
    ' The last two arguments are width and height, respectively
    m_cspace.ExportPicture sFilePath & sFileName, "gif", 600, 350

    ' Add this new file to Session state so that we can delete
    ' it later
    Session("TC:" & sFilePath & sFileName) = sFilePath & sFileName
    ExportChartToGIF = sFileName
End Function 'ExportChartToGIF()
```

THE CASE OF THE MYSTERIOUS, UNDELETABLE FILE

When I first started working on a server-side chart example, I thought I would make it simple by overwriting a single temporary GIF file each time the client requested an ASP page. I thought I could use FileSystemObject to delete the existing file and use the Chart component to write a new file with the same name.

Interestingly enough, the DeleteFile method of FileSystemObject ran without error. However, the ExportPicture method on the next line failed, saying the file was in use. But how could the file be in use if I had just deleted it? I looked in the directory where the temporary file lay and sure enough, it was still there. The DeleteFile method returned no error, but it did not delete the file.

I don't know why this is the case. Several people I've spoken to think that IIS is somehow caching the file and that although FileSystemObject thinks it deleted the file, it did not. So keep in mind that even though the DeleteFile method runs without error, the file might still exist.

The only complicated part of this function is coming up with the name and file path for the temporary GIF the code creates and keeping track of it so that you can delete the file later. This code uses Scripting.FileSystemObject (from the Microsoft Scripting Runtime library) to generate a temporary filename using the GetTempName method. This method returns a temporary name that you can later pass to the Chart component's ExportPicture method. You can of course generate a name using your own scheme, but be aware that the Chart component will generate an error if you pass the name of a file in use. Plus, IIS will mark files requested by clients as "in use" for a longer period of time than you might expect.

When you generate a temporary GIF, you will likely want to put it in the same directory as your ASP page or in some subdirectory underneath it. To get your ASP page's current directory in the server's file system, use the PATH_TRANSLATED server variable. This returns the entire path and filename of your ASP page, so the previous code looks for the last backslash (\) and takes everything before it in order to get only the directory path in which the current ASP page resides. It then appends the temporary name returned from the GetTempName method and passes that as the first parameter to the ExportPicture method. You can also specify a width and height for the new GIF in pixels. This code uses the hard-coded values of 600x350, but you might consider letting the client pass those dimensions to your ASP page as query string parameters so that you generate an appropriate size image based on the client's display resolution.

The last technique to note in this function is the next to last line. Let's look at it again:

```
' Add this new file to the Session state so that we can delete it later
Session("TC:" & sFilePath & sFileName) = sFilePath & sFileName
```

We just generated a new temporary file on the server's file system, but IIS does not automatically clean up this file after the client browser requests it. If you do not delete such files, the file system on the server machine will fill up rather quickly. We need to ensure that we clean up temporary files created within the session. The Session object and Session_OnEnd event in the Global.asa file provide us with a mechanism to accomplish this task.

The previous code adds the full file path for the temporary GIF to the Session object, giving it a name starting with TC: (meaning *temporary chart*). Using the temporary file's name in the Session variable name keeps the name unique in the Session namespace. The TC: prefix lets us know later that this is indeed a temporary chart that needs to be deleted, as opposed to another session variable that is not a file path to a temporary chart. You can use other naming schemes here, such as appending an integer until you get a unique index number in the Session variable's Contents collection. The previous code adds the file to the Session state, and the Session_OnEnd event in the Global.asa file does the cleanup:

```
Sub Session_OnEnd
    ' Clean up any temporary image files created during the session
    Set fsoTemp = CreateObject("Scripting.FileSystemObject")

    For Each imagefile In Session.Contents
        If Left(imagefile,3) = "TC:" Then
            fsoTemp.DeleteFile Mid(imagefile,4), True
        End If
    Next
End Sub
```

IIS executes this subroutine whenever a session has timed out, meaning that the client has not requested a page in the current application within the session timeout duration (set to 1 minute in the Session_OnStart event). This is our clue that it is safe to delete any temporary GIFs created for this session because the client browser certainly has already downloaded them. The code here creates a FileSystemObject again and loops through the Session variable's Contents collection looking for variables whose names start with TC:. If it finds one, it uses the DeleteFile method to delete the temporary GIF file. We can be sure that the DeleteFile method will work because IIS should have released the file lock by this time for files requested by the client whose session is ending.

Other Approaches to Managing Temporary Files

The code we just discussed demonstrates one way to manage temporary files created by the Chart component. This approach works well because it automatically deletes temporary files when a session ends. However, the shortest timeout you can set for a session is 1 minute. If your server is destined to have an incredibly heavy and constant load, you might run into file space problems because of your application producing large numbers of charts per session and having to wait a full minute before the session ends.

The browser typically retrieves the temporary GIF right after your ASP page returns the HTML fragment containing the <img> tag. If the browser is using HTTP 1.1, it might do this within the same socket connection, meaning it will download the GIF long before your 1-minute timeout value. If the client returns for another chart, the timeout clock is reset and your Session_OnEnd might not fire for quite a while.

If you expect this to be the case in your application, you might consider another approach to managing the temporary files. Instead of relying on session timeouts, use a server-side daemon process that deletes temporary files that are older than a specified time duration, such as 30 seconds. This process could periodically check a specific directory in which you create temporary GIF files and delete any files with a timestamp older than your threshold.

Another approach is to use a file naming scheme that rotates through a set of filenames and eventually loops around to reuse the same filenames for successive groups of charts. IIS will mark a file as "in use" for a period of time after a client requests it. While that file is in use, you cannot write over it using the ExportPicture method. However, if you have a large enough set of filenames, IIS will probably have released the file lock by the time you loop back to the same filename. For example, you could start generating images named TC000.GIF and keep track of the current index number in an Application state variable. The next time the page generated a temporary GIF, it would first increment the current index value (so that other threads don't have a chance to use your thread's index) and then generate the file TC001.GIF. When you reach TC999.GIF, your page will reset the current index to 0, causing other calls to overwrite previously generated files that now should be unlocked. This strategy ensures that you will have at most only 1000 temporary GIF files, but it is of course highly dependent on timing. If your application starts to receive errors from the ExportPicture method, you will have to increase the number of digits used in your filenames to ensure a longer time between loops. There is also a minute chance that you might encounter a problem if your thread is interrupted just after updating the current index but before reading the current index value. Without using a transaction, it's impossible to guarantee that both operations are isolated. However, if you require transaction isolation, you can use a database table instead of the Application state to store your current index.

The last approach is to produce your GIFs either by using a batch process or by intelligently sharing GIFs that have already been produced with clients requesting the same chart and data. If your metric is not that dynamic—for instance, some metrics change only once per hour or day—you might consider using a batch process to generate all the interesting charts in one shot. The pages you then put on your web site simply reference existing GIF files that your batch program updates every hour or night. If you think that clients might request these files while you are generating new ones, put the new files in a directory name that is keyed to your update interval and code your ASP pages to use a directory name based on the current time. For example, if you update the charts nightly, put the new GIFs into a subdirectory named with the next day's date (such as 19990423). Your ASP page should use the current system date to determine which subdirectory to pull the image from. Your batch program could safely delete the directory from the previous day, because it knows that no clients will access the files in that directory.

Our team used this last approach with many of our daily bug statistic charts. We used a Visual Basic program to produce the charts, typically generating 50 chart images in 30 to 40 seconds.

FORMATTING THE CONTROLS FROM PAGE STYLES

If you run the solution shown in this chapter, you will notice that the Chart controls on the pages entitled Historical Charts and Current Call Levels blend in well with the colors and fonts used on the rest of the page. You might think that this was just custom formatting implemented in code, but actually it was done in a much more generic way (described momentarily) that you can use to format any Chart control to match the containing page's style information.

Linked and embedded style sheets allow web developers to separate formatting information from their content and layout information in a web page. Keeping colors and fonts consistent throughout a site is often difficult when you embed formatting information into the HTML document using <font> tags. However, you can use style sheets to define what formatting the browser should use when rendering specified HTML elements. This feature is known as *cascading style sheets* (CSS) and is documented in the MSDN libraries. I use linked style sheets (meaning the style sheet exists as a separate file and is linked into each page) in all this book's examples and solutions so that the pages look consistent.

Style sheets allow you to specify formatting for any HTML element, but unfortunately they have no control over the content displayed within a COM control on a web page. Because the Office Web Components support all the HTML color and font names Microsoft Internet Explorer supports, you can write code to automatically format your components (in this case the Chart component) to match the styles in your page. Let's take a look at how I did this in the Helpdesk Reporting solution.

I implemented the control formatting code as a generic set of functions that you can include in any HTML page. It resides in a file called FormatControls.scp in the Scripts directory on the companion CD. To include this in the HistoricalCharts.htm page, I inserted the following HTML fragment:

```
<!-- Common routines for formatting the Office Web Components
based on styles -->
<script language=vbscript src="../Scripts/FormatControls.scp">
</script>
```

In the HTML <script> tag, you can add an optional src attribute. The value for this attribute is the URL of another file containing the contents for the script block. In this case, I've used a relative URL to the FormatControls.scp file in the Scripts directory. This script file implements a number of functions, but the only one needed in this example is the FormatChartFromStyles function, used in the BindChart function:

```
' Format the chart
FormatChartFromStyles cspace
```

This function takes a reference to the entire Chart control, and it performs the rest of the formatting work inside the function.

Implementing Functions in the FormatControls.scp File

Let's look at the beginning of the FormatChartFromStyles function:

```
Sub FormatChartFromStyles(cspace)
    ' Local variables
    Dim cht              ' Temporary WCChart object reference
    Dim ax               ' Temporary WCAxis object reference
    Dim ser              ' Temporary WCSeries object reference
    Dim dls              ' Temporary WCDataLabels object reference
    Dim vStyleVal        ' Temporary style value
    Dim ct               ' Loop counter

    ' Format the various elements of the ChartSpace
    ' ChartSpace background
```

```
vStyleVal = FindStyleValue(Array("ChartSpace","TH"), _
    "background-color")
If Not(IsEmpty(vStyleVal)) Then cspace.Interior.Color = vStyleVal

' ChartSpace title
If cspace.HasChartspaceTitle Then
    vStyleVal = FindStyleValue(Array("ChartspaceTitle","H2","H1"), _
        "background-color")
    If Not(IsEmpty(vStyleVal)) Then _
        cspace.ChartspaceTitle.Interior.Color = vStyleVal

    SetFontInfo cspace.ChartspaceTitle, _
        Array("ChartspaceTitle","H2","H1")
End If 'Has a title

' ChartSpace legend
If cspace.HasChartspaceLegend Then
    vStyleVal = FindStyleValue(Array("Legend","Body"), _
        "background-color")
    If Not(IsEmpty(vStyleVal)) Then _
        cspace.ChartspaceLegend.Interior.Color = vStyleVal

    SetFontInfo cspace.ChartspaceLegend, Array("Legend", "P")
End If 'Has a legend
    ⋮
```

This function cycles through all those elements in the Chart control that can be formatted with color or fonts. Then it cycles through each chart, each series of each chart, and each axis of each chart, formatting each of those elements using the page's style information. This function uses two helper functions in the same script file: FindStyleValue and SetFontInfo. The FindStyleValue function finds style values for the requested selector and style attribute; SetFontInfo is a wrapper function that sets a number of font properties based on the specified selector.

Before I describe how to obtain style information, I want to define a few terms used in style sheets. To help define these terms, let's look at part of the style sheet used for this chapter's code (from Styles.css on the companion CD):

```
body
{
    background-color: Whitesmoke;
    font-family: Tahoma;
    color: Black;}
```

(continued)

```
p
{
    color: Black;
    font-family: Verdana;
    font-size: 10pt;
}

h1
{
    font-family: Tahoma;
    font-size: 24pt;
    font-weight: bold;
    color: Indigo;
}

Legend
{
    font-family: Tahoma;
    font-size: 8pt;
}

Axis
{
    font-family: Tahoma;
    font-size: 8pt;
    color: Black;
}

PlotArea
{
    background-color: Whitesmoke;
}

ValueAxis
{
    font-family: Tahoma;
    font-size: 8pt;
    number-format: #,##0;
    color: Maroon;
}
```

A style sheet is essentially a listing of formatting *rules*. Each rule starts with a logical element name called a *selector,* and within each rule, you can define a set of *style attributes*. A selector is often an HTML tag name such as <p> or <h1> or a class name such as td.button. However, you can also include additional names that are not known tags—for example, Legend. Internet Explorer will retain these selectors and expose them in the Document Object Model (DOM), but it will not know how to apply them automatically since it has no idea what Legend is. Style attributes are formatting definitions such as color: Indigo, which states that any element matching the selector should have the color indigo.

All the information from the style sheet is parsed and loaded into objects that you can use from scripts in the page. Given the name of a selector, you can find its style rule and ask for any of its style attributes such as color, background-color, or font-family. The FindStyleValue and GetStyleValue functions use these objects to extract the style value and return it, enabling the FormatChartFromStyles function to apply the same formatting value to the particular chart element. Since the Office Web Components support the same named colors as Internet Explorer, you can assign color values directly from the returned style attribute value to the chart element. Let's look at the GetStyleValue function first:

```
Function GetStyleValue(sSelector, sAttributeName)
    ' Local variables
    Dim ctStyleSheet        ' Style sheet loop counter
    Dim ctRule              ' Rule loop counter
    Dim ssCur               ' Current styleSheet object reference

    ' Check to see that we have at least one styleSheet
    If document.styleSheets.length = 0 Then Exit Function

    ' Loop over all styleSheets backward
    ' (to get the ones with highest precedence first)
    For ctStyleSheet = (document.styleSheets.length - 1) To 0 Step -1

        ' Grab a reference to the current style sheet
        Set ssCur = document.styleSheets(ctStyleSheet)

        ' Make sure the style sheet is enabled
        If Not(ssCur.disabled) Then

            ' Loop over all rules in the style sheet
            For ctRule = 0 To ssCur.Rules.Length - 1

                ' If the selectorText = the selector we're looking for,
                ' get the value for the specified attribute
                If LCase(ssCur.Rules(ctRule).selectorText) = _
                    LCase(sSelector) Then
                    GetStyleValue = GetAttributeValue( _
                            ssCur.Rules(ctRule), _
                            sAttributeName)
```

(continued)

```
              ' Since we found the selector and
              ' GetAttributeValue will get the attribute
              ' if it exists, it's OK to exit the function
              ' now and return what we have
              Exit Function

            End If 'Element we're looking for
          Next 'ctRule
        End If 'styleSheet is not disabled
    Next 'ctStylesheet
End Function 'GetStyleValue()
```

GetStyleValue takes parameters indicating what selector and attribute name you want to get. The function loops over all style sheets in the current document in reverse order. (You might have both a linked style sheet and an embedded style block.) This ensures that you get the last style definition for the given selector because that will usually be the one that overrides all previous definitions. The code also checks that the style sheet is enabled before attempting to find a selector within it.

Unfortunately, this code must loop over the style rules in the style sheet, looking for one that has a selector property value equal to the requested value. You can define multiple rules that use the same selector, defining some style attributes in one rule and others in different rules. This code does not catch this condition and will simply attempt to use the first rule it finds involving the desired selector. This makes the function a bit faster because I can short-circuit the loop when I find the selector instead of always looping over all rules. Note that I use the LCase function from VBScript to make sure I compare the selector text in a case-insensitive way. You can also use StrComp to perform a case-insensitive comparison.

Once I find a rule involving the desired selector, I use another helper function called GetAttributeValue. This function contains a simple Select Case block that uses the appropriate style object property based on the desired attribute name:

```
Function GetAttributeValue(rule, sAttributeName)
    ' Local variables
    Dim sCssText            ' Holder for CSS text
    Dim nPosStart           ' Temporary start position pointer
    Dim nPosEnd             ' Temporary end position pointer

    ' Switch on the desired attribute name
    Select Case LCase(sAttributeName)
        Case "backgroundcolor", "background-color"
            GetAttributeValue = rule.style.backgroundcolor

        Case "color"
            GetAttributeValue = rule.style.color
```

```
        Case "fontfamily", "font-family"
            GetAttributeValue = rule.style.fontFamily

        Case "fontsize", "font-size"
            GetAttributeValue = rule.style.fontSize

        Case "fontweight", "font-weight"
            GetAttributeValue = rule.style.fontWeight

        Case Else
            ' Custom style attribute
            ' See whether we can find it in the cssText property
            sCssText = rule.style.cssText
            nPosStart = InStr(sCssText, sAttributeName)
            If nPosStart > 0 Then
                ' Found it; now extract it
                nPosStart = nPosStart + Len(sAttributeName) + 1
                nPosEnd = InStr(nPosStart, sCssText, ";")
                If nPosEnd <= 0 Then nPosEnd = Len(sCssText) + 1
                GetAttributeValue = Trim(Mid(sCssText, nPosStart, _
                    nPosEnd - nPosStart))
            End If 'Found attribute in cssText

    End Select 'sAttributeName

End Function 'GetAttributeValue()
```

Because no method for looking up a style value by string name exists, this function determines the appropriate property of the style object based on the specified style attribute name. It also has a long Case Else block that attempts to find attributes that are not part of the CSS standard but might be in the style sheet. A great example of this is the style information for the ValueAxis selector I showed you earlier. I defined an attribute called number-format, which is not part of the CSS standard but should be defined for a chart's value axis. The GetAttributeValue code parses the value for non-CSS attributes from the style object's cssText property. This property returns the original text from the section of the style sheet in which the current rule exists.

Now that you have a way to get any style attribute value for any selector and attribute name, you need a way to find values given an escalating list of selectors. Suppose you want to allow developers to specify a rule in the style sheet for the chart title. However, if they do not make this specification, you want to use the rule defined for H3. If H3 is not defined, you might want to use the rule for H2 instead. This escalation is done using the FindStyleValue function.

```
Function FindStyleValue(asSelectors, sAttributeName)
    ' Local variables
    Dim ct           ' Loop counter

    ' Loop over all the selectors until GetStyleValue returns
    ' something other than Empty
    For ct = LBound(asSelectors) To UBound(asSelectors)
        FindStyleValue = GetStyleValue(asSelectors(ct), sAttributeName)
        If Not(IsEmpty(FindStyleValue)) Then Exit Function
    Next 'ct

End Function 'FindStyleValue
```

This method simply loops over the array of selector names passed in the asSelectors argument, handing each one to the GetStyleValue function and determining whether it found a value. If it did, the function short-circuits and returns. If it did not, it continues with the next selector. If no value is found, the function simply returns Empty and the FormatChartFromStyles function skips formatting the chart element, leaving it set to its default values.

The last routine that I want to mention is the SetFontInfo function. Because the Chart control uses the same programming interface for any font information on any chart element, you can encapsulate the setting of font formatting information on a chart element in one function and reuse it. Here is what the function looks like:

```
Sub SetFontInfo(obj, asSelectors)
    ' Local variables
    Dim vStyleVal            ' Temporary style value

    vStyleVal = FindStyleValue(asSelectors, "font-family")
    If Not(IsEmpty(vStyleVal)) Then obj.Font.Name = vStyleVal

    vStyleVal = FindStyleValue(asSelectors, "font-size")
    If Not(IsEmpty(vStyleVal)) Then obj.Font.Size = _
        Left(vStyleVal, Len(vStyleVal) - 2)

    vStyleVal = FindStyleValue(asSelectors, "font-weight")
    If Not(IsEmpty(vStyleVal)) Then obj.Font.Bold = _
        (LCase(vStyleVal) = "bold")

    vStyleVal = FindStyleValue(asSelectors, "color")
    If Not(IsEmpty(vStyleVal)) Then obj.Font.Color = vStyleVal

    vStyleVal = FindStyleValue(asSelectors, "number-format")
    If Not(IsEmpty(vStyleVal)) Then obj.NumberFormat = vStyleVal

End Sub 'SetFontInfo()
```

This code is just like the code in FormatChartFromStyles, but it operates on a generic object that has a Font property that exposes the Name, Size, Bold, and Color properties. It also applies the NumberFormat information if found.

Reusing the FormatChartFromStyles Function

You can reuse this code in your own solutions and modify it to include any additional functionality you need. To reuse this code in your solution, simply perform the following steps:

1. Add the following script block to your HTML page, changing the URL of the src attribute to point to wherever you place the FormatControl.scp file:

   ```
   <!--Common routines for formatting the Office Web Components
   based on styles -->
   <script language=vbscript
   src="../Scripts/FormatControls.scp">
   </script>
   ```

2. Whenever you want to format a chart control using the current style information, execute this line of script:

   ```
   FormatChartFromStyles MyChartSpace
   ```

   In the above fragment, *MyChartSpace* is the name of your Chart control.

BUILDING AN INTERACTIVE CHART ANALYSIS PAGE

The Historical Charts page in this chapter's sample solution illustrates a few ways you can add some useful analysis features by writing code that interacts with the Chart control. This section will discuss the two most prominent techniques: displaying information about points on the chart with chart tips and using a Range Slider control to zoom in on a large axis.

Implementing Chart Tips

In Microsoft Excel charting, when you position your mouse cursor over a data point, a small, tooltip-like window appears that shows you the series, category, and data point value. Although the Chart control does not yet implement this feature, you can add it using a scriptlet developed by Jason Cahill, the ever-talented program manager for the Chart control. The source for the scriptlet (Charttips.scp) is included in the Scripts directory on the companion CD, so you can modify it to include any information you want.

A *scriptlet* is a small piece of reusable HTML and script that you can include in a web page much like you do a COM control. Scriptlets are documented in the MSDN libraries and work in Internet Explorer version 4.0 and higher. Although I will not describe in detail how to create a scriptlet in this book, I will show you some of the important parts of the chart tips scriptlet. First, let's look at how to use the scriptlet in an HTML page:

```
<!------------------------------------- BEGIN CHART TIPS ---------------->
<!-- TODO: Add one handler, below, for each Chart control --------------->
<script language=vbscript for=csHistorical event="MouseMove(e)">
ChartTips.HandleChartTips ChartTips, csHistorical, e.x, e.y
</script>

<!-- Generic chart tip code (do not modify) ----------------------------->
<object  id=ChartTips width=0 height=0
style="position:absolute;display:none" type="text/x-scriptlet"
data="../Scripts/Charttips.scp">
</object>
<script language=vbscript for=document event="onmouseover()">
ChartTips.ClearChartTips ChartTips
</script>
<script language=vbscript for=document event="onmouseout()">
ChartTips.ClearChartTips ChartTips
</script>
<!------------------------------------- END CHART TIPS ----------------->
```

This HTML fragment adds the <object> tag for the scriptlet itself, specifying that its code (the less-than-intuitively-named "data" attribute) is in the Charttips.scp file in the Scripts directory. It also sets the object's position style to "absolute," meaning that it can be positioned using two-dimensional coordinates and can lay on top of another element (in this case, the Chart control). It then sets up a couple of event handlers to clear (hide) the chart tip when the mouse pointer is no longer over the Chart control. You must add a handler for the Chart control's MouseMove event, calling the HandleChartTips method. This allows the chart tip scriptlet to determine what chart element the mouse pointer is over and to display the appropriate content. Note that you can write your own additional code in the MouseMove event if you want. Just remember to call the HandleChartTips method in your handler at some point.

To see this chart tip in action, click the Historical Charts link on the left frame of the solution and move your mouse pointer over a data point. Figure 6-1 depicts what you will see.

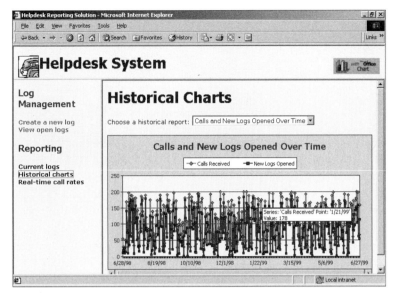

Figure 6-1. *Chart tips.*

Now let's look at how Jason implemented the chart tips scriptlet. The scriptlet file contains this HTML fragment at the top:

```
<body leftmargin=0px topmargin=0px>
<table border=0 cellspacing=0 cellpadding=0>
    <tr>
        <!-- Style info removed for readability -->
        <td id=tdTip nowrap bgcolor=infobackground style=... ></td>
    </tr>
</table>
```

This is the viewable portion of the scriptlet, and it is a simple table cell formatted using a style attribute so that it looks like the chart tips in Excel. Since the scriptlet is just HTML, you can change this formatting to anything you want. Immediately following the HTML, you will see two public methods:

```
Sub public_HandleChartTips(tip, csChart, x, y)
    Set hTip = tip
    ClearChartTips
    tdTip.InnerText = GetTipText(csChart, x, y)
    tip.Style.Left = (x + 10 + csChart.OffsetLeft) & "px"
    tip.Style.Top = (y + 20 + csChart.OffsetTop) & "px"
    tip.Width  = tdTip.offsetWidth & "px"
```

(continued)

```
        tip.Height = tdTip.offsetHeight & "px"
        hChartTipTimer = SetTimeout("ShowChartTip", 500, "vbs")
End Sub

Sub public_ClearChartTips(tip)
        Set hTip = tip
        ClearChartTips
End Sub
```

We called these methods from the event handlers back in our HTML page. The first one sets up the tip to show the appropriate content (returned from the GetTipText method) and sizes the tip so that it is only big enough to display its content. HTML table cells provide an easy way to determine how big a tip must be because table cells automatically size to fit their content if you do not specify a particular width or height value. Jason also uses a timer to delay showing the tip for half a second (500 milliseconds), which is commonly done when implementing tip windows.

The second method hides the chart tip by calling ClearChartTips, which simply sets the tip's display attribute to "none." If an element's display attribute is set to "none," Internet Explorer will not display the element and will not reserve room for it when laying out the page.

The GetTipText method uses the Chart control's RangeFromPoint method to get the charting element at the specified X and Y coordinates and uses the TypeName function to determine what kind of object the method returned. This should sound familiar—we discussed this technique in Chapter 3. You can modify this function to return alternate text for the tip. For example, you might want to include other calculated values in the tip, such as the average for all points in the series or the current point's percentage contribution to the entire series or to all data points in the chart.

Zooming with a Range Slider Control

When plotting historical data, you can run into a situation in which you have many time values to display on the category axis but not enough room to display the data clearly. Instead of summarizing the data values to a higher level of aggregation or including only part of the data, you can provide a simple mechanism for a user to zoom in on an axis and show only part of the more granular data at a time. The user can still scroll left and right to see other time periods or can zoom out slightly to see more data at once.

I implemented this technique in the Historical Charts page. To follow the discussion in this section, it is best if you run the page and try using the Range Slider control to zoom in on part of the data. When you first load the page, the chart will look fairly crowded, as it does in Figure 6-2.

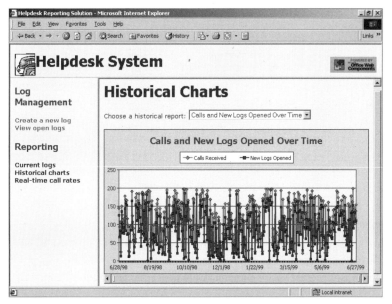

Figure 6-2. *The Historical Charts page when first opened.*

When you zoom in using the Range Slider control, the chart should be more readable as it is in Figure 6-3.

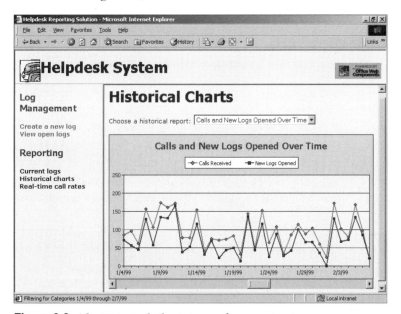

Figure 6-3. *The Historical Charts page after zooming in.*

The Range Slider control was also implemented by Jason and was developed using Visual Basic 6. I will not detail how Jason constructed this control because it has no direct relation to the Chart control. It simply takes a minimum and maximum value and returns the current scroll thumb minimum and maximum set by the user. The source code for this control is included on the companion CD in the SliderSource directory under the Chap06 directory. To include the Range Slider control in the HTML page, I used the following HTML fragment:

```
<!-- Range Slider control -->
<object classid="clsid:4A3C4CD7-F6AB-11D2-82A2-00A0C90565FE" id=RngSldr
style="width:100%;height:20px"
codebase="RangeSliders.CAB#version=1,0,0,20">
</object>
```

You can add the Range Slider control just as you would add one of the Office Web Components. You include an <object> tag in your HTML page indicating the COM class ID for the control. (Many HTML editors, including Microsoft FrontPage 2000 and Microsoft Visual InterDev, insert this for you.) This fragment also includes a codebase attribute in the <object> tag, referring to a CAB file in the Chap06 directory. The first time you run this page, Internet Explorer will detect that the Range Slider control is not yet installed on your system and will automatically download the CAB file and install it (after asking you if it's all right to do so).

BEWARE OF USING SCALING.MAXIMUM DURING WINDOW_ONLOAD

When I first tried to implement this example, I attempted to use the category axis's Scaling.Maximum property to get the number of categories in the chart. This seems like a logical technique, and it does work most of the time. However, if you ask for this property during the Window_onLoad event (or any code called from that event handler), you might get back 0 or an uninitialized value. Sometimes it will work—typically when the page is first loaded. However, upon returning to the page later, you will get 0 or an uninitialized value and your code will fail.

This occurs because the container (in this case, Internet Explorer) might not have created a window for the Chart control yet. Until it does, the Chart control does not know what the scaling maximum and minimum should be because it doesn't know what size window the container will create. (Containers can give the control any size window they please.) However, the control does know how many points exist per series, and from there, you can determine the number of categories.

To initialize the Range Slider control, set its FilterMax and ThumbMax properties to match the number of categories in the chart. The following code, called from the BindChart function, accomplishes this:

```
Sub InitRangeSlider(cht)
    ' Local variables
    Dim c          ' Constants object

    m_fIgnoreSliderChange = True

    ' Initialize the Range Slider control
    RngSldr.FilterMax = cht.SeriesCollection(0).Points.Count
    RngSldr.ThumbMax = RngSldr.FilterMax
    RngSldr.FilterMin = 1
    RngSldr.ThumbMin = 1

    m_fIgnoreSliderChange = False

End Sub 'InitRangeSlider()
```

This code asks the first series for the number of data points it has, which naturally returns the number of categories, as each series has a point for each category. Even if the first series did not have a value for certain categories, the Chart control still reports the total number of points, including the empty ones—so you can use this to determine how many categories your chart has.

All that's left to do is catch the Change event raised from the Range Slider control and adjust the category axis scaling to show only part of the axis. This has the visual effect of zooming in as the chart redraws, showing a smaller segment of data in the same physical space. Let's look at the code in the Range Slider control's Change event handler:

```
Sub RngSldr_Change
    ' Local variables
    Dim ax         ' Temporary WCAxis object
    Dim scl        ' Temporary WCScaling object
    Dim ser        ' Temporary WCSeries object
    Dim c          ' Constants object

    If not m_fIgnoreSliderChange Then
        Set c = csHistorical.Constants

        ' Get the scaling for the category axis
        Set ax = csHistorical.Charts(0). _
            Axes(csHistorical.Constants.chAxisPositionBottom)
        Set scl = ax.Scaling
```

(continued)

```
      Set ser = ax.Parent.SeriesCollection(0)

      ' Adjust it based on the Range Slider control's current settings
      scl.Minimum = RngSldr.ThumbMin
      scl.Maximum = RngSldr.ThumbMax
      window.status = "Filtering for Categories " & _
      ser.Points(RngSldr.ThumbMin - 1).GetValue(c.chDimCategories) & _
      " through " & _
      ser.Points(RngSldr.ThumbMax - 1).GetValue(c.chDimCategories)

      SetTickLabelSpacing ax
    End If 'm_fIgnoreSliderChange

End Sub 'RngSldr_Change()
```

USE THE CACHESIZE PROPERTY WHEN BINDING TO DATA AND ZOOMING

If you look closely at the HistoricalCharts.htm file, you'll see the use of a property in the LoadChartDataSources function called CacheSize:

```
Set cds = cspace.ChartDataSources.Add()
Set cds.DataSource = dsc
cds.DataMember = "ChartData" & ct
cds.CacheSize = 400
```

You can use the CacheSize property to tell the Chart control to cache a certain number of data rows in its own internal structures. Doing so will increase the chart rendering speed quite a bit. So any time you perform effects such as zooming in, animating, or requiring the Chart control to redraw frequently, set this property to a number equal to or greater than the number of data rows in your resultset. Although it creates an extra copy of data in memory, the performance gain can be worthwhile if you need the chart to render quickly.

If you look in the object browser or the programming help for the Chart control, you will not see this property by default. This is because it is a hidden property. You can see hidden properties by checking the Show Hidden Members item on the Visual Basic or Visual InterDev object browser's context menu. Periodically, the OWC developers implement properties or methods we feel are stable and functional, but our testing team doesn't have time to fully test them. If we think a property or method will be genuinely useful, we will mark it as hidden—developers are free to use it at their own risk. So far, I have not had any problems using the CacheSize property, but it is not an "officially" supported feature.

This code gets a reference to the category axis (on the bottom for a line chart) and sets the axis's Scaling.Maximum and Scaling.Minimum properties to match the ThumbMin and ThumbMax properties of the Range Slider control. These properties return the current minimum and maximum values for the filtered range on the Range Slider control. Every time the user drags an edge of the control's thumb or the thumb itself, this event fires many times, updating the filter values accordingly.

To inform the user of what date range the chart is currently showing, I use the window.Status property to update Internet Explorer's status bar text. To get the actual category names (in this case, the date values) for the minimum and maximum categories, I use the Points collection of the first series to get the minimum and maximum data points. I then use the GetValue method of these objects to get the category name for the data point.

CHARTING REAL-TIME DATA

The last major technique used in the Helpdesk Reporting solution that I will describe is feeding real-time data into the Chart control. There is no great trick to doing this; however, a few aspects might not be initially obvious.

The general approach to feeding real-time data is to allocate arrays into which you will place new values as they become available and to set those arrays into the chart as literal data. Although you cannot dynamically add only one point to the chart, you can reset the entire array into the Chart control so that it will reload the data and refresh its display. The Chart control can keep up amazingly well, and in my personal tests, it loaded and displayed new data as fast as three times a second.

The scripts in the RealTimeChart.htm file start by declaring three page-level arrays to hold the categories (time values) and two series worth of values. This file also declares a variable to hold the position in the array that should be filled next:

```
Dim m_avOnHold(59)        ' Array of values representing people on hold
Dim m_avBeingHelped(59)   ' Array of values representing people being helped
Dim m_avTime(59)          ' Array of time readings
Dim m_nCurSlot            ' Current slot in the array to fill
```

I give each of these arrays 60 elements (indexes 0 to 59) because I will show the last 60 real-time values in the chart. In the Window_onLoad event, I initialize these page-level variables by setting the first element of each array and setting the current slot index to 1:

```
' Set the first value for each of the arrays
m_avTime(0) = Time()
m_avOnHold(0) = GenRandomValue(0, 10)
m_avBeingHelped(0) = GenRandomValue(0, 20)
```

(continued)

```
' Initialize the current slot variable
m_nCurSlot = 1

' Start the timer
window.setInterval "OnTimer", 1000, "vbscript"
```

The last line of the script uses the setInterval method to start a timer that will fire every second (1000 milliseconds). When the timer fires, it will call the OnTimer method in my script, which I tell Internet Explorer is a VBScript function. On each timer interval, the OnTimer method will add another value to the page-level arrays and call the SetData method on the chart's series to reload the chart with new data. If you were using another COM control on the page to get your real-time data, you could code that control to raise an event whenever new data arrived, and your script to reload the chart with new data would be in that event's handler:

```
Sub OnTimer()
    ' Local variables
    Dim ser         ' Temporary WCSeries reference
    Dim c           ' Constants object
    Dim ct          ' Loop counter

    If m_nCurSlot > UBound(m_avTime) Then
        ' Shift the array values down one position
        For ct = (LBound(m_avTime) + 1) To UBound(m_avTime)
            m_avTime(ct - 1) = m_avTime(ct)
            m_avOnHold(ct - 1) = m_avOnHold(ct)
            m_avBeingHelped(ct - 1) = m_avBeingHelped(ct)
        Next 'ct

        m_nCurSlot = UBound(m_avTime)
    End If 'At the end

    ' Set the next value for each of the arrays
    m_avTime(m_nCurSlot) = Time()
    m_avOnHold(m_nCurSlot) = Abs(m_avOnHold(m_nCurSlot - 1) + _
        GenRandomValue(-2, 2))

    m_avBeingHelped(m_nCurSlot) = Abs(m_avBeingHelped(m_nCurSlot - 1) + _
        GenRandomValue(-2, 2))

    ' Increment the current slot variable
    m_nCurSlot = m_nCurSlot + 1

    ' Now set the chart series with the new data
    Set c = csRealTime.Constants
    Set ser = csRealTime.Charts(0).SeriesCollection(0)
```

```
ser.SetData c.chDimCategories, c.chDataLiteral, m_avTime
ser.SetData c.chDimValues, c.chDataLiteral, m_avBeingHelped

set ser = csRealTime.Charts(0).SeriesCollection(1)
ser.SetData c.chDimCategories, c.chDataLiteral, m_avTime
ser.SetData c.chDimValues, c.chDataLiteral, m_avOnHold
```

End Sub 'OnTimer()

The first part of the OnTimer method is fairly straightforward. If the current slot index is at the end of the array, the code quickly shifts the existing values down one position so that the chart appears to scroll backward as new data points appear at the end of the line. The code then adds the new data point, using the VBScript Time function to get the current system time and a random data generator to get the delta values for the two series. In a real system, you would obviously use a COM object or another mechanism to get the new values.

The second part of the OnTimer method should look similar to the script we discussed in Chapter 3. The code uses the SetData method on each series to pass the Chart control new literal data, and the Chart control automatically refreshes itself, showing the new data values.

The only trick to this page is how I made the lines appear to grow from left to right, instead of the category axis seeming to compress as it would appear to do by default. I also fix the value axis so that it does not continually change its minimum and maximum as new data points appear. These effects are again done using the axes' Scaling object properties. In the CreateChart method (called from Window_onLoad), I use the following code to accomplish these effects:

```
Set ax = cht.Axes(c.chAxisPositionBottom)
ax.Scaling.Maximum = 60
ax.TickLabelSpacing = 10

Set ax = cht.Axes(c.chAxisPositionLeft)
ax.Scaling.Maximum = 50
ax.Scaling.Minimum = 0
```

By setting the Maximum property of the category axis's Scaling object to 60, I force the chart to reserve room on the category axis for 60 categories, even though the data I pass to the chart might not yet have 60 distinct categories. I also set the TickLabelSpacing property to 10 so that the Chart control displays only every tenth time value, which is about every 10 seconds because the timer fires every second. The code also sets a manual minimum and maximum value for the value axis scaling so that the value axis does not automatically adjust as new data points arrive or existing data points fall off the left edge when scrolling. Note that if my real-time feed produced a value greater than the maximum I set here, it would not display on the chart. If you do not know the upper limit of your real-time data in advance, you might need to check new values as they arrive and increase the Scaling object's Maximum property to accommodate the new values.

SUMMARY

This chapter showed you how to build a solution that displays business metrics using server-generated charts, interactive client-side charts, and real-time data charts. The basic techniques illustrated in this chapter apply to a vast array of solutions involving the Chart component, and we will see some of these same techniques used in later chapters.

Chapter 7 involves both the Chart control and the PivotTable control. The solution presented in that chapter is a sales analysis and reporting system that uses OLAP (multidimensional) and tabular data sources—which is, along with charting business metrics, one of the main scenarios for using the Office Web Components.

Chapter 7

Sales Analysis and Reporting System

Enabling rich, web-based data analysis and reporting systems was one of our team's key goals when we designed the Microsoft Office Web Components. In this chapter, I will describe my implementation of such a system and show you how to combine a number of the techniques presented in Part I to build a sales analysis and reporting system for your company. Although the solution in this chapter focuses on sales information, the techniques used here are applicable to any type of data.

ABOUT THE SOLUTION

Most businesses sell something, whether it is a physical product or a service. Information about these sales is commonly captured in a core business system for invoicing and shipping purposes; however, that information also has a critical influence on marketing, sales, and product development decisions. The IT groups in such companies are often called on to provide summary reports of sales information. Typically users want these reports in an electronic format so that they can perform further analysis or reporting. OLAP and web technologies provide an extremely attractive mechanism for responding to these requests.

The solution in this chapter is a preliminary version of a web-based sales analysis and reporting system. I call it a "preliminary" version because you will probably want to enable many other features in your solution. However, the techniques illustrated by this solution are the ones developers commonly ask me about, and they are often the key to knowing how to implement other features as well. This solution allows users to quickly analyze data stored in a multidimensional data source, save reports they create and reload them later, and view their data in either the PivotTable control or the Chart control. Users can choose to use an online OLAP server or an offline cube file, and they can reload reports in either case. This solution also shows how to implement a useful feature not built in to the first release of the PivotTable component: top/bottom *N* filtering.

TECHNIQUES ILLUSTRATED IN THIS SOLUTION

Table 7-1 lists the various techniques the Sales Analysis and Reporting solution demonstrates. Use this table as a quick reference for locating the techniques that interest you. Although this chapter will not cover every technique listed, you can consult the appropriate source files on the companion CD to explore techniques not explicitly discussed here.

Technique	*Source File*
Saving and loading stored reports.	SaveLoad.asp, PivotView.htm
Using a hidden frame to save and load reports with HTTP.	SaveLoad.asp, Default.htm, PivotView.htm
Using the LOGON_USER server variable to automatically obtain the current user's name.	SaveLoad.asp
Emulating top/bottom *N* filtering.	PivotView.htm
Implementing a Quick Pivot user interface.	PivotView.htm
Displaying a chart view of the report and dynamically changing the chart type based on the number of totals in the report.	PivotView.htm
Changing connections between on line and off line.	PivotView.htm
Formatting the PivotTable control based on styles defined for the containing page.	PivotView.htm, FormatControls.scp

Table 7-1. *Techniques demonstrated by the Sales Analysis and Reporting solution.*

RUNNING THE SOLUTION

This solution is a mixture of HTML and Microsoft Active Server Pages. To run this solution, you must open the Default.htm page using an http:// URL, meaning that you cannot simply double-click the files on the companion CD. The easiest way to set up the solution is to follow these steps:

1. If you are using a Microsoft Windows NT Server machine with Microsoft Internet Information Server, use the IIS manager to add a virtual directory to your root web. Copy the Chap07 and Scripts directories on the CD to the machine's hard drive, and specify those directories as the sources for peer virtual directories. Make sure to enable scripting support.

2. If you are running Personal Web Server (say on Windows 98 or Windows NT Workstation), use the Personal Web Manager to add a virtual directory as described in Step 1, but make sure that you select the Execute option in the Access section of the Add Directory dialog box.

3. Type the URL for the directory into your browser—for example, *http:// MyServer/Chap07*. The Default.htm page should load unless you have configured your web site to use another default filename. If you have, just add */Default.htm* to the end of the URL.

For tips on how to create virtual directories for ASP applications using Personal Web Server, see the sidebar on page 172 in Chapter 6.

Note that the ASP page in this solution will use the LOGON_USER server variable for the current user name when saving reports. By default, IIS leaves the Allow Anonymous Access authentication method on, which means that LOGON_USER will return a blank string. If you want to enable the solution to save reports based on actual user names, disable anonymous access by editing the security settings of the virtual directory that contains the ASP page.

SAVING AND RELOADING REPORTS

As I mentioned in Chapter 4, the PivotTable component exposes a property on its top-level programming interface that returns an XML stream representing the current *view definition*. The view definition is essentially the report description, defining the layout of various fields on the report axes; the expanded state of members on those axes; and the current filters, sorts, formatting, and so on. In Chapter 4, I hinted that you could use the view definition to save and reload reports. In this chapter, I will show you the code you need to write to accomplish this.

Saving and reloading reports is actually quite easy. The XMLData property is read/write, and you can use it to get the current view definition or restore a view definition. The general approach to saving reports is to get the XMLData property and save the returned string where you can retrieve it later. Reloading a report is essentially the reverse operation—you fetch the view definition from your storage place and set the XMLData property to the fetched string. When you set the PivotTable control's XMLData property, the control will reorient the view, returning it to the state it was in when you saved the report. Remember that this is only the view definition and not a snapshot of the aggregate values in the report. The control will always query the data source for the current values when you reload a view definition.

A number of options exist for saving the current view definition. For example, you can save it in a text file, a database table, a Microsoft Exchange public folder, or a temporary dictionary object in memory. The Sales Analysis and Reporting solution takes the rather exotic approach of posting the view definition to an ASP page, which in turn writes it to a Microsoft Jet database located on the web server. This approach has a number of advantages: First, the ASP script can quickly be rewritten to save the report definition in another location. Second, users' reports are saved on a server and therefore are available from any physical workstation. Third, reports can easily be shared by modifying the ASP script to include reports marked as public that have been created by several different users.

To keep the user experience smooth and to retain the caching benefit of using a connection to the data source for many different queries, I implemented the report-saving mechanism using a hidden frame. When you run the solution, it appears that only one frame exists, but in reality, a second frame lurks above the main page. I set its size to zero and disabled resizing and scrolling, making it invisible. When I save a report, I push the view definition and report name into form fields in that hidden frame and submit the form. Figure 7-1 illustrates how this architecture works.

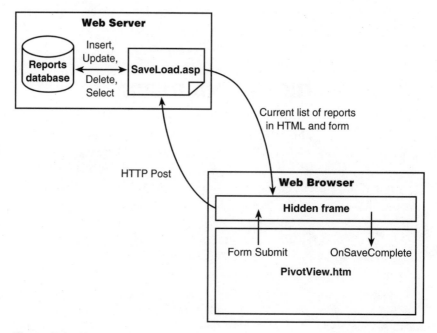

Figure 7-1. *The Sales Analysis and Reporting solution's report-saving architecture.*

The following code, taken from PivotView.htm, shows how to start the process:

```
Sub btnSave_onClick()
    ' Local variables
    Dim nRepID                      ' Report ID if one exists
    Dim sRepName                    ' Report name
    Dim frm                         ' HTML form in hidden frame

    ' Find the form in the hidden frame
    Set frm = window.parent.frames(0).frmSave

    ' Prompt for a report name if new
    If Len(cbxReports.value) > 0 Then
        sRepName = cbxReports.options(cbxReports.selectedIndex).text
    End If

    If Len(sRepName) = 0 Then
        ' New report
        sRepName = InputBox("Enter a name for your report:", _
            "Foodmart Sales Analysis System", _
            ptable.ActiveView.TitleBar.Caption)
    Else
        nRepID = Left(cbxReports.value, _
            InStr(cbxReports.value, "~") - 1)
    End If

    ' If the user supplied a name, save it
    ' If the user pressed Cancel on the input box, the
    ' sRepName variable will be an empty string
    If Len(sRepName) > 0 Then
        SaveReport frm, nRepID, sRepName, ptable.XMLData, IsEmpty(nRepID)
    End If
End Sub 'btnSave_onClick()
```

This code is the Click event handler for the Save Report button. It begins by finding the HTML form in the hidden frame using the parent window's frames collection. It then checks whether you are resaving an existing report or saving a new one. The code determines this by checking the length of the value property of the Reports drop-down list. The option named (Choose A Saved Report) has a value of empty string, so if the value of the drop-down list has length zero, the user has not chosen an existing report; hence, the report must be new.

If the report being saved is a new report, the code prompts for a report name using the InputBox function in Microsoft VBScript. If the user clicks the Cancel button on this input box, the returned value will be an empty string, so the code checks the length of the sRepName variable again and exits if it is zero. If the length is not zero, the code calls the SaveReport method, passing it five arguments: a reference to the HTML form in the hidden frame, an empty report ID, the report name, the PivotTable control's XMLData property, and the value of IsEmpty(nRepID)—TRUE in this case, indicating that the report ID is empty.

If the report being saved is an existing report, the code extracts the report ID from the current value property of the Reports drop-down list. When this list is loaded (which I will demonstrate later), the value property of each new option is set to a compound value consisting of the report ID and the report definition separated by a tilde (~). This makes it easy to retrieve either part later by using the InStr or Split function. This is not the most elegant solution, but it is a convenient way to pack three pieces of information (the report name, ID, and definition) into two properties (the text and value properties). You should probably consider using a Dictionary object instead and looking up the report definition based on the report ID stored in the value property.

Let's move on to the Save Report method:

```
Sub SaveReport(frm, nRepID, sRepName, sRepDef, fNew)
    If fNew Then
        frm.txtAction.value = "insert"
    Else
        frm.txtAction.value = "update"
        frm.txtReportID.value = nRepID
    End If
    frm.txtReportName.value = sRepName
    frm.txtReportDef.value = sRepDef
    frm.submit
End Sub 'SaveReport()
```

The SaveReport method sets the values of the various form elements and submits the form. Submitting the form posts the values to the SaveLoad.asp page, which we will examine shortly. Note that I use a form field called txtAction to indicate what type of action I want the ASP page to take. If the report is new, I set this field to "insert"; if it is not, I set the field to "update". This will cause the ASP page's script to perform either an insert or an update against the database table. If the report is new, it does not have an ID yet, so I leave that form field blank. When the page finishes and returns, you can reload the report list and get the newly assigned report ID (more on that later).

Let's take a quick look at the HTML form in the hidden frame:

```
<form id=frmSave action="SaveLoad.asp" method="Post">
<input type="text" id=txtAction name=Action>
<input type="text" id=txtReportID name=ReportID>
<input type="text" id=txtReportName name=ReportName>
<input type="text" id=txtReportDef name=ReportDef>
<input type="submit" value="Submit" id=submit1 name=submit1>
</form>
```

The SaveLoad.asp page generates this hidden form after it returns the list of available reports, so the form is always available to the other frame for inserting, updating, or deleting reports. Note that the action attribute refers back to the same ASP page and that the method attribute is set to Post. Using Post as the method instead of Get is important here. A form using the Get method appends the various field values to the URL specified in the action attribute. This can produce very long URLs because one of the form fields holds the XMLData property from the PivotTable control. When using the Post method, Microsoft Internet Explorer sends the form field values in the content of the HTTP request instead, allowing you virtually unlimited length.

Note that while this form does contain a Submit button, it is purely for my own debugging purposes. Since the frame in which this form resides is hidden, and since this form is submitted only by the SaveReport method in the main frame, you don't need a Submit button on the form. However, its presence does make it easier to debug the SaveLoad.asp page. You can load the frame directly in your browser and experiment with manually sending insert, update, and delete requests using the form fields and the Submit button.

The final step in saving a view definition is accomplished by the SaveLoad.asp script. Let's take a look at the relevant parts of that ASP page, starting with the module code that executes when the page is called:

```
On Error Resume Next
m_fSuccess = False
m_sErrText = ""

' Get the current user name if known
m_sCurUser = Request.ServerVariables("LOGON_USER")
If Len(m_sCurUser) = 0 Then m_sCurUser = "Anonymous"

' Get a connection to the database
Set m_cn = GetConnection()
If Err.Number = 0 Then
    ' See if there's an action requested
    m_sAction = Request.Form("Action")

    Select Case LCase(m_sAction)
        Case "insert"
            m_fSuccess = InsertReport(m_cn, m_sCurUser, _
                Request.Form("ReportName"), _
                Request.Form("ReportDef"))

            If Not m_fSuccess Then m_sErrText = Err.Description
            ⋮
```

Typically, you will want to save reports under the current user's name so that different users can save different sets of reports. The SaveLoad.asp script first looks at the LOGON_USER server variable, which returns the Windows NT account that the current user has logged on to. By default, new directories in IIS allow anonymous access, meaning this server variable will return an empty string. However, if you disable anonymous access and require authentication, this variable will return the current user's Windows NT logon name. One advantage of utilizing the LOGON_USER server variable is that users can see their reports from any workstation provided that they have been authenticated on the Windows NT domain. In this chapter's solution, I use Anonymous as a default name if anonymous access is still enabled or if this server variable returns an empty string for any other reason.

Next the script connects to the database and determines what to do based on the Action form field. Although this solution uses a Jet database, you can easily retarget the script to use Microsoft SQL Server or another database management system. When saving a new report, you're interested in the insert Case block that calls the InsertReport method, shown here:

```
Function InsertReport(cn, sUser, sRepName, sRepDef)
    Dim cmd

    Set cmd = Server.CreateObject("ADODB.Command")
    Set cmd.ActiveConnection = cn
    cmd.CommandText = "InsertReport"
    cmd.CommandType = 4
    cmd.Parameters.Append cmd.CreateParameter("RepName", 202, 1, 255)
    cmd.Parameters.Append cmd.CreateParameter("RepUser", 202, 1, 255)
    cmd.Parameters.Append cmd.CreateParameter("RepDef", 8, 1)
    cmd.Parameters(0) = sRepName
    cmd.Parameters(1) = sUser
    cmd.Parameters(2) = sRepDef
    cmd.Execute

    InsertReport = True
End Function 'InsertReport()
```

The InsertReport function is a fairly straightforward use of ADO to call a stored procedure, passing the new report name, user name, and report definition (the XMLData property from the PivotTable control) as parameters. Since this is a Jet database, this code uses a stored append query called InsertReport. If you wanted to use SQL Server, you would typically define a stored procedure for inserting a new report row. This code creates the ADO Command object, sets up the parameter list, fills the parameter values, and executes the command. If no error occurs, the code returns True.

I use a stored append query here for two reasons:

■ Stored queries and procedures are generally faster and definitely more encapsulated.

■ Large string values containing embedded single and double quotes are typically hard to embed in an INSERT SQL statement because the SQL parser often treats the embedded single or double quote as the end of a value. Also, many database management systems impose a maximum length on SQL statements that are submitted. Embedding a long XMLData property in an INSERT statement could exceed this limit.

Once this method is finished executing, it means that the new report has been inserted into the database, and execution in the main script continues:

```
  ⋮
' Get the list of reports saved by the current user
Set m_rs = m_cn.Execute("select ReportID, Name, ReportDef " & _
                        "from Reports where User='" & m_sCurUser & _
                        "'")

If Err.Number = 0 Then
    ' Write them in the Reports table
    Response.Write "<table id=tblReports>"
    While Not m_rs.EOF
        Response.Write "<tr>"
        For Each fld In m_rs.Fields
            Response.Write "<td>" & _
                Server.HTMLEncode(fld.Value) & "</td>"
        Next
        Response.Write "</tr>"
        m_rs.MoveNext
    Wend
    Response.Write "</table>"
    m_fSuccess = True
Else
    ' Error getting reports
    m_sErrText = Err.Description
End If 'Got the reports recordset OK
Else
    ' Error connecting
    m_sErrText = Err.Description
End If 'Connected OK
%>
  ⋮
```

The script continues by selecting all the reports saved by the current user. It then writes the results as an HTML table with an ID of tblReports. This ID is used by code in the main PivotView.htm page when loading the Reports drop-down list, as you will see shortly. Using the HTMLEncode function while writing the Recordset values is important. Since the XMLData property returns a string full of XML, you must not send it back to the browser without encoding. If you do, the browser will interpret it as XML. Instead, you want to simply write the XML into the table cell as text so that your code on the main page can hand it to the XMLData property when reloading a view. The HTMLEncode function encodes characters such as less than (<) and greater than (>) into their respective HTML symbols, &lt and &gt. The browser will display them as < and > and will return these characters when you retrieve the table cell value in script but will know not to interpret them as XML.

The last part of the SaveLoad.asp page tells the main page that the save is complete and that it should reload the list of reports:

```
    ⋮
<% If Len(m_sAction) > 0 Then %>
<script language=vbscript>
Sub window_onLoad()
    window.parent.frames(1).OnSaveComplete <%= m_fSuccess %>, _
        "<%= m_sErrText %>"
End Sub
</script>
<% End If %>
```

This is one of the trickiest parts of this solution, and it took me many hours to figure out. Remember that when the script on the main page prepares to save a report, it fills out an HTML form in the hidden frame and submits the form. That submission is executed asynchronously, so the main page has no way of knowing when it is done. Therefore, it is the hidden frame's job to notify the main page when it returns, passing a success or failure state so that the main page knows whether the save action was successful. The SaveLoad.asp writes a small script block into the returned page that executes during the hidden frame's onLoad event. This code finds the main frame and calls the OnSaveComplete method defined in that page's script. The code passes an argument indicating success or failure, as well as some error text in the event of failure. Let's take a look at the OnSaveComplete function:

```
Sub OnSaveComplete(fSuccess, sErrText)
    If fSuccess Then
        ' Reload the reports list
        LoadReports
    Else
        ' Display the error
        MsgBox "Error saving or deleting report!" & String(2, vbCrLf) & _
            sErrText, vbCritical
    End If
End Sub 'OnSaveComplete()
```

This fairly simple routine checks the success flag and either reloads the list of reports or displays the error text.

DON'T TRY TO CALL FUNCTIONS
ACROSS FRAMES OUTSIDE AN EVENT

When I first started working on this solution, I tried using the following script block in the hidden frame's returned page instead of the one just shown:

```
<script language=vbscript>
window.parent.frames(1).OnSaveComplete <%= m_fSuccess %>, _
    "<%= m_sErrText %>"
</script>
```

Since the code is at module scope and not in an event handler, Internet Explorer and the Active Scripting Engine attempt to execute the code when the page is parsed. However, this attempt will always fail, stating that the object does not support the OnSaveComplete method. I ran this script under the debugger, looked at the target frame, looked in the Scripts collection, saw my function, and even saw the function text. However, I could not call the function. I finally tried putting it in the Window object's onLoad event handler, and it worked like a charm. Apparently, you cannot call methods in other frames from script executed at parse time.

The final step in this process—and the code that loads the list of stored reports when the solution first runs—is the LoadReports function:

```
Sub LoadReports()
    Dim tblReports
    Dim tr
    Dim opt
    ' Clear the existing Reports list except for the blank report
    While cbxReports.options.length > 1
        cbxReports.options.remove cbxReports.options.length - 1
    Wend

    If window.parent.frames.length > 0 Then
        Set tblReports = window.parent.frames(0).tblReports
        For Each tr In tblReports.rows
            Set opt = document.createElement("OPTION")
            opt.text = tr.cells(1).innerText
            opt.value = tr.cells(0).innerText & "~" & tr.cells(2).innerText
            cbxReports.options.add opt
        Next 'tr
    End If
End Sub 'LoadReports()
```

This function is also fairly simple. It starts by clearing all the items in the drop-down list except for the (Choose A Saved Report) item. Next it checks that the hidden frame is present, and it sets a reference to the tblReports HTML table, which was generated near the end of the SaveLoad.asp script. The code then loops over all rows in the table, loading a new item into the Reports drop-down list for each row in the table. As noted earlier, I encoded a compound value into the new option's value, consisting of the report ID and report definition separated by a tilde (~).

Updating and deleting reports happens in much the same way as saving reports. The code on the main page uses the form in the hidden frame, specifying "update" or "delete" as the Action field and specifying the appropriate values for this action. The main page submits the form in the hidden frame and the returned page calls the OnSaveComplete method in the main page, indicating success or failure.

This use of a hidden frame enables you to provide a consistent and smooth user experience, but it is rather difficult to debug. You might instead consider using a Data Source control (DSC) to connect to the database and execute stored procedures directly. However, using hidden frames and posting to an ASP page is very flexible because you can program the page to do anything you want with the input, including storing it in an Exchange mailbox, mailing it to another location, saving it to a file on the server, and so on. This approach also avoids the cross-domain data access warnings that you get when using a DSC to call your stored procedures directly.

IMPLEMENTING A QUICK PIVOT USER INTERFACE

This solution offers what I call the *Quick Pivot user interface,* which helps novice users quickly produce a report. The PivotTable Field List (described in Chapter 4) exposes all totals, fieldsets, and fields defined in the cube; however, this can be quite daunting to someone who has no idea how to begin. Because you can perform all user interface operations through the programming model, you can offer a simpler interface to your users—one that provides them with more direction. The Quick Pivot user interface in this solution enables novice users to quickly begin analyzing data by giving them a sentence-building user interface. When our team talks to customers, many of them say, "I want to see *some value* by *some dimension* by *some other dimension.*" The Quick Pivot user interface capitalizes on that natural expression by helping the user construct that sentence. Figure 7-2 shows the Quick Pivot user interface in action.

Note that once the user configures a report using the Quick Pivot user interface, the report is still fully functional, as if the user dragged the various totals, fieldsets, and fields to it. The user can still sort, filter, and rearrange the report as he or she wants. However, the simpler user interface helps get novice users over the blank report hurdle.

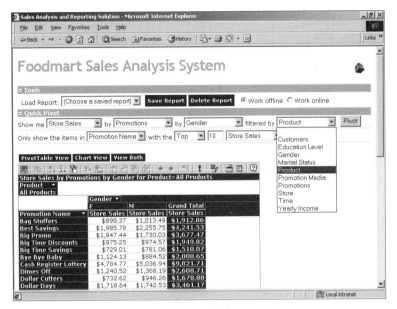

Figure 7-2. *The Quick Pivot user interface.*

Building this user interface in HTML is actually quite easy. Let's start by looking at the code used to fill the various drop-down lists:

```
Sub LoadQuickPivotLists(ptable, cbxTotal, cbxRow, cbxCol, cbxFilter)
    Dim opt         ' Temporary HTML <option> element
    Dim fs          ' Temporary PivotFieldSet reference
    Dim ttl         ' Temporary PivotTotal reference

    ' Clear the lists of any options besides the
    ' blank ones
    While cbxTotal.options.length > 1
        cbxTotal.options.remove cbxTotal.options.length - 1
    Wend

    While cbxRow.options.length > 1
        cbxRow.options.remove cbxRow.options.length - 1
    Wend

    While cbxCol.options.length > 1
        cbxCol.options.remove cbxCol.options.length - 1
    Wend

    While cbxFilter.options.length > 1
        cbxFilter.options.remove cbxFilter.options.length - 1
    Wend
```

(continued)

```
' Load the Totals list
For Each ttl In ptable.ActiveView.Totals
    Set opt = document.createElement("OPTION")
    opt.text = ttl.Caption
    opt.value = ttl.Name
    cbxTotal.options.add opt
Next

' Load the other lists with all the available fieldsets
For Each fs In ptable.ActiveView.FieldSets
    Set opt = document.createElement("OPTION")
    opt.text = fs.Caption
    opt.value = fs.Name
    cbxRow.options.add opt

    Set opt = document.createElement("OPTION")
    opt.text = fs.Caption
    opt.value = fs.Name
    cbxCol.options.add opt

    Set opt = document.createElement("OPTION")
    opt.text = fs.Caption
    opt.value = fs.Name
    cbxFilter.options.add opt
Next

End Sub 'LoadQuickPivotLists()
```

This function starts by clearing the various drop-down lists of all items except the blank one at the top, which is used to indicate that the user wants nothing on that particular axis. The function then loads the Totals drop-down list with the names of the totals exposed through the Totals collection of the ActiveView property. The code ends by loading each of the other three drop-down lists (Rows, Columns, and Filters) with all the available fieldsets, which you can get through the ActiveView property's Fieldsets collection.

This function is called whenever the connection context changes. So when you elect to use an offline cube, the function reloads the available totals and fieldsets because they might be different. (We'll discuss using offline cubes in more detail later in the chapter.) In fact, the cube file on your companion CD has fewer totals and dimensions than the server-based cube that comes with SQL Server OLAP Services. That's because OLAP Services does not download calculated measures or virtual dimensions to cube files. Both calculated measures and virtual dimensions are described in detail in the OLAP Services product documentation.

The real work begins when the user chooses items from the drop-down lists that are now filled and clicks the Pivot button:

```
Sub QuickPivot(ptable, ptotal, fsRows, fsCols, fsFilter)
    ' Local variables
    Dim pview        ' Reference to the view

    ' Grab a reference to the view
    Set pview = ptable.ActiveView

    ' Clear the view
    pview.AutoLayout()

    ' Put the fsRows dimension on the Row axis
    If Len(fsRows) > 0 Then
        pview.RowAxis.InsertFieldSet pview.FieldSets(fsRows)
    End If

    ' Put the fsCols dimension on the Column axis
    If Len(fsCols) > 0 Then
        pview.ColumnAxis.InsertFieldSet pview.FieldSets(fsCols)
    End If

    ' Put the fsFilter dimension on the Filter axis
    If Len(fsFilter) > 0 Then
        pview.FilterAxis.InsertFieldSet pview.FieldSets(fsFilter)
    End If

    ' Finally, put ptotal in the data area
    If Len(ptotal) > 0 Then
        pview.DataAxis.InsertTotal pview.Totals(ptotal)
    End If

    ' Give the PivotTable control an appropriate title
    AutoTitlePivot ptable

End Sub 'QuickPivot()
```

The Pivot button's Click event handler calls the QuickPivot function, passing the values from the various drop-down lists. The function first clears the current view by calling the AutoLayout method and then adds the specified totals and fieldsets to the appropriate axes. Finally, it calls a method to automatically set the PivotTable control's title based on what is in the view. We'll take a look at that method (AutoTitlePivot) in the next section.

AUTOMATICALLY GENERATING A TITLE

The PivotTable control offers a title bar at the top of the view, enabling you or the user to specify a meaningful title for the report. However, while users browse the data, it is often helpful to generate an automatic title based on what the user has included in the report. This title then can be suggested as the title of the report when saved, which is what occurs in the Save Report button's Click event handler described earlier.

Generating an automatic title is easy. The following code shows one method for doing so:

```
Sub AutoTitlePivot(ptable)
    Dim sTitle
    Dim sSep
    Dim sBy
    Dim sFor
    Dim sAnd
    Dim ttl
    Dim fset
    Dim pview

    sTitle = ""

    ' Constant string tokens used to build the title
    sSep = ", "
    sBy = " by "
    sFor = " for "
    sAnd = " and "

    ' Grab the active view
    Set pview = ptable.ActiveView

    ' Start by including the names of the totals used
    If pview.DataAxis.Totals.Count > 0 Then
        For Each ttl In pview.DataAxis.Totals
            sTitle = sTitle & ttl.Caption & sSep
        Next
        sTitle = Left(sTitle, Len(sTitle) - Len(sSep))
    Else
        sTitle = "(No Totals)"
    End If 'Some totals in the report

    ' Next put " by <row fieldsets>"
    If pview.RowAxis.FieldSets.Count > 0 Then
        sTitle = sTitle & sBy
        For Each fset In pview.RowAxis.FieldSets
            sTitle = sTitle & fset.Caption & sSep
        Next
        sTitle = Left(sTitle, Len(sTitle) - Len(sSep))
    End If 'Fieldset(s) on row axis

    ' Next put " by <col fieldsets>"
    If pview.ColumnAxis.FieldSets.Count > 0 Then
        sTitle = sTitle & sBy
```

```
        For Each fset In pview.ColumnAxis.FieldSets
            sTitle = sTitle & fset.Caption & sSep
        Next
        sTitle = Left(sTitle, Len(sTitle) - Len(sSep))
    End If 'Fieldset(s) on column axis

    ' Finally, include any filters
    If pview.FilterAxis.FieldSets.Count > 0 Then
        sTitle = sTitle & sFor
        For Each fset In pview.FilterAxis.FieldSets
            sTitle = sTitle & fset.Caption & "=" & _
                fset.FilterMember.Caption & sAnd
        Next
        sTitle = Left(sTitle, Len(sTitle) - Len(sAnd))
    End If 'Fieldset(s) on filter axis

    pview.TitleBar.Caption = sTitle

End Sub 'AutoTitlePivot()
```

This method starts by declaring a number of variables and giving them default values. These variables are used as the separator values in the eventual title, and you can change these variables to use different separators. The code begins by concatenating all total captions in the view, separating them using the sSep variable. It then concatenates the fieldset captions on the Row axis if any exist. It continues by concatenating the Column axis fieldset captions and then concatenating any fieldset captions placed on the Filter axis, noting their current filter members. For example, if you use the Quick Pivot user interface to build a report that shows Store Sales by Promotions by Time filtered by Product, the automatic title generated by this method is "Store Sales by Promotions by Time for Product=All Products". If you change the filter field to show only the sales for the Drink product family, the last part of the title changes to "Product=Drink".

EMULATING TOP/BOTTOM *N* FILTERING

Top or bottom *N* filtering is a common analysis feature. Unfortunately, the PivotTable component does not yet implement this feature natively. However, you can still provide this functionality in your solutions because the PivotTable component allows you to specify which members you want to include from a given field. Plus, it is fairly easy to retrieve the top or bottom (according to the total of your choice) *N* members of a field by executing your own MDX query against the OLAP data source. To try this, use the same report you built in the previous section and click the Filter button in the Quick Pivot user interface. Your report should now show only the top 10 promotions according to store sales.

To see how I implemented this, let's start at the Filter button's Click event:

```
Sub btnFilter_onClick()
    ' Local variables
    Dim avFieldInfo           ' String array, 0=fieldset unique name,
                              ' 1=field unique name
    Dim pfld                  ' Temporary PivotField reference

    ' Ensure that N is an OK value
    If txtN.value <= 0 Then
        MsgBox "The number of items value was " & txtN.value & _
            "! This number must be greater than zero.", vbCritical
        Exit Sub
    End If 'N <= 0

    ' Ensure that the cellset has the proper connection
    If (csetOLAP.ActiveConnection Is Nothing) Then
        csetOLAP.ActiveConnection = dsc.ConnectionString
    End If

    ' The Filter Field value is a compound value with
    ' the fieldset unique name as the first part and
    ' the field name as the second part, separated by
    ' a tilde (~)
    avFieldInfo = Split(cbxFilterField.value, "~")

    ' Get the reference to the PivotField object so that
    ' we can tell it what members to include
    Set pfld = ptable.ActiveView.FieldSets(avFieldInfo(0)). _
        Fields(avFieldInfo(1))

    ' Note: The following line builds a level name using the naming
    ' convention of OLAP Services ([hierarchy].[level])
    ' If you are not using OLAP Services, change this to use
    ' whatever convention your provider uses
    pfld.FilterMembers = GetTopBottomMems(csetOLAP, ptable.DataMember, _
        avFieldInfo(0), _
        avFieldInfo(0) & ".[" & avFieldInfo(1) & "]", _
        cbxFilterTotal.value, txtN.value, _
        (cbxTopBottom.value = "Top"))

End Sub 'btnFilter_onClick()
```

The code begins by performing a simple check to ensure that the value entered for *N* is greater than zero. After it has established that, the code accesses an ActiveX Data Objects Multidimensional (ADO MD) Cellset object embedded into the page with an <object> tag. If the Cellset object's Connection property is blank, it is set to the ConnectionString property of the DSC so that it uses the same data source as the PivotTable component.

> **WARNING** You might have to lower your security settings to use ADO MD. If you try to use top/bottom *N* filtering in this solution, you might get a cranky error message from Internet Explorer stating that your current security settings prohibit you from running "unsafe" controls. Since ADO MD accesses multidimensional databases using your security credentials, it is naturally unsafe. To run this solution, you might need to lower your security settings or add the current site to your trusted sites list.

The next part of the code extracts two values from the Filter Field drop-down list. This list is populated with all fields currently on the Row axis, and I encoded two pieces of information into the list's value property, using the tilde (~) character to separate the values. The two values are the unique name of the fieldset to which the field belongs and the name of the field itself. The code uses these two values to build a unique level name, which I will use in the MDX query to find the top 10 members. Although I assume the OLAP Services naming convention in this code, you can use ADO MD to determine the level's unique name, given the fieldset's unique name and the field's name. Unfortunately, the PivotTable control does not expose a UniqueName property on the PivotField object, an oversight that should be corrected in the next version.

The code in the Filter button's Click event handler uses a function called GetTop-BottomMems to retrieve the top or bottom *N* members and copy them to an array, which the handler in turn passes to the field's FilterMembers property. Setting the FilterMembers property causes the PivotTable control to show only the specified members. You can also use the FilterFunction property to exclude these members instead. Let's continue by examining the heart of this feature, the GetTopBottomMems function:

```
Function GetTopBottomMems(cset, sCubeName, sFieldsetName, _
                          sFieldName, sTotalName, N, fTop)
    ' Local variables
    Dim sMDX            ' MDX query
    Dim pos             ' Temporary ADOMD.Position reference

    ' Construct the appropriate MDX statement to
    ' get the top N members based on the specified total
    If fTop Then
        sMDX = "select non empty {TOPCOUNT(" & _
            "Filter(" & sFieldName & _
            ".Members, Not IsEmpty(" & sFieldsetName & _
            ".CurrentMember))" & _
            ", " & N & ", " & sTotalName & ")}" & _
            " on columns" & _
            " from " & sCubeName & _
            " where (" & sTotalName & ")"
```

(continued)

```
    Else
        sMDX = "select non empty {BOTTOMCOUNT(" & _
                "Filter(" & sFieldName & _
                ".Members, Not IsEmpty(" & sFieldsetName & _
                ".CurrentMember))" & _
                ", " & N & ", " & sTotalName & ")}" & _
                " on columns" & _
                " from " & sCubeName & _
                " where (" & sTotalName & ")"
    End If 'Top N

    ' Open the Cellset object using the MDX query string
    ' as the command source
    cset.Open sMDX

    ' Redimension the avMems array to be the size
    ' of the number of returned members in the Cellset object
    ReDim avMems(cset.Axes(0).Positions.Count - 1)

    ' Load the avMems array with the unique member names
    ' returned in the Cellset object
    For Each pos In cset.Axes(0).Positions
        avMems(pos.Ordinal) = pos.Members(0).UniqueName
    Next 'pos

    ' Close the Cellset object so that you can use it again later
    cset.Close

    ' Return the array of members
    GetTopBottomMems = avMems

End Function 'GetTopBottomMems
```

The function begins by constructing the appropriate MDX query to retrieve either the top or bottom N members from the specified field based on the specified total. It uses the TopCount and BottomCount MDX functions, and it uses the Filter function to filter out empty members (the ones without any recorded store sales). I filter out empty members because, by default, the PivotTable control does not show empty members returned from a query. For example, although you might have requested the bottom 10, the report might display only 7 because 3 were empty. By excluding the empty members from the MDX query, the function will return the bottom 10 members that actually contain data. For a full tutorial on the MDX query language, see the OLE DB for OLAP specification (downloadable from http://www.microsoft.com/data/oledb/olap).

After executing the MDX query, I get the list of members returned by walking the positions on the Cellset object's first axis, loading the UniqueName property into the array that will eventually be returned. When I am done loading the unique member names, I close the Cellset object and return the array.

You can use this same sort of technique to expose many other high-end filtering functions permitted in MDX. Because the PivotTable control enables you to specify a set of members to include or exclude, you can emulate advanced filtering functions by obtaining the set of members to include or exclude by executing your own MDX queries. You can also enable users to define sets of members they typically want to include or exclude and reapply those filter definitions at a later time.

IMPLEMENTING A DYNAMIC CHART VIEW

Now that you know how to adjust the PivotTable control to display different slices of information, you will probably want to let users view that data in a chart as well as in a table full of numbers. This is fairly easy to implement: you bind the Chart control to the PivotTable control, and the Chart control graphically displays the contents of the PivotTable control's report, adjusting automatically when the report's layout changes. For an overview of this topic, refer to Chapter 3.

In the Sales Analysis and Reporting solution, you can click the Chart View button to view the data as a chart or click the View Both button to see both the Chart control and PivotTable control at the same time. The code behind these buttons simply sets the Style.Display property of the control (Chart or PivotTable) to "none" to hide the control or to an empty string to show the control.

Binding the Chart control to the PivotTable control is simple:

```
Sub BindChart(ptable, cspace)
    Set cspace.DataSource = ptable
    cspace.Charts.Add
End Sub 'BindChart()
```

Setting the Chart control's DataSource property to the PivotTable control tells the Chart control that it should retrieve its data values from the PivotTable control's report. I also add a Chart object to the chart space here but wait until another event to call the Chart object's SetData method. I use the PivotTable control's QueryComplete event, which fires after the PivotTable control has executed a query against the data source. This event provides a good opportunity to perform any task that might depend on the contents of the PivotTable control because it fires whenever the report's layout changes or when the report is filtered or sorted. The code in this event handler calls the LoadChart method, the first half of which is listed here:

```
Sub LoadChart(ptable, cspace)
    ' Local variables
    Dim c            ' Constants object
    Dim cht          ' Temporary WCChart reference
    Dim ctTotals     ' Count of totals in the PivotTable view
    Dim pview        ' Temporary PivotView reference
```

(continued)

```
Dim ax          ' Temporary WCAxis reference
Dim ttl         ' Temporary PivotTotal reference

Set c = cspace.Constants

' Bind the chart to the PivotTable if necessary
If cspace.ChartDataSources.Count = 0 Then
    cspace.DataSource = ptable
End If

' Get the chart or create one if needed
If cspace.Charts.Count = 0 Then
    Set cht = cspace.Charts.Add()
Else
    Set cht = cspace.Charts(0)
End If

' Make sure the chart has a legend
cht.HasLegend = True

' Get the PivotTable's active view
Set pview = ptable.ActiveView

' Set the Chart title to the PivotTable title
cht.HasTitle = True
cht.Title.Caption = pview.TitleBar.Caption

' First bind the series and categories dimensions
' as you would do for any chart type
cht.SetData c.chDimSeriesNames, 0, c.chPivotColumns
cht.SetData c.chDimCategories, 0, c.chPivotRows

' Get the current number of totals on the data axis
ctTotals = pview.DataAxis.Totals.Count
    ⋮
```

The code begins by ensuring that a Chart object has been created in the Chart control, that the Chart object has a legend, and that its title is set to match the PivotTable control's title (which we automatically set earlier). The code then uses the SetData method to bind the chart's series to the column members in the PivotTable control's report and the chart's categories to the row members in the report. This tells the chart to create a series for each member displayed across the columns of the report and a category for each member displayed down the rows of the report.

Next, the code determines how many totals are included in the current report. This is significant because different chart types are designed to show different types of data sets. A Column, Bar, Line, Area, or Pie chart is good for displaying data that has one value per intersection of category and series. But if there are two data values for each intersection of category and series, a Scatter chart is a more effective visualization. Similarly, if three values make up an intersection of category and series, a Bubble chart or High-Low-Close chart is the appropriate chart type to use. The remainder of the LoadChart function uses this count of totals to dynamically adjust the chart type and bind the appropriate chart dimensions based on the type:

```
         :
' Reset the chart type if necessary, and use SetData to
' bind the appropriate value dimensions
Select Case ctTotals
    Case 0
        ' No totals--no change

    Case 1
        ' Use a Bar chart if there is one total
        If cht.Type <> c.chChartTypeBarClustered Then
            cht.Type = c.chChartTypeBarClustered
        End If

        ' Use the first (and only) total for values
        cht.SetData c.chDimValues, 0, 0

        ' Label the axes, and set the value axis number format
        ' to match the number format of the total
        Set ax = cht.Axes(c.chAxisPositionBottom)
        Set ttl = pview.DataAxis.Totals(0)
        ax.NumberFormat = ttl.NumberFormat
        ax.HasTitle = True
        ax.Title.Caption = ttl.Caption

        ' Set the category axis to list categories
        ' in the reverse order so that it matches the
        ' way the PivotTable control is showing them
        Set ax = cht.Axes(c.chAxisPositionLeft)
        ax.Scaling.Orientation = c.chScaleOrientationMaxMin

    Case 2
        ' Use a Scatter chart if there are two totals
        If cht.Type <> c.chChartTypeScatterMarkers Then
            cht.Type = c.chChartTypeScatterMarkers
        End If
```

(continued)

```
                    ' Use the first total for Y values and
                    ' the second for X values
                    cht.SetData c.chDimYValues, 0, 0
                    cht.SetData c.chDimXValues, 0, 1

                    ' Set the label and number format for the Y axis
                    Set ax = cht.Axes(c.chAxisPositionLeft)
                    Set ttl = pview.DataAxis.Totals(0)
                    ax.NumberFormat = ttl.NumberFormat
                    ax.HasTitle = True
                    ax.Title.Caption = ttl.Caption
                    ax.Scaling.Orientation = c.chScaleOrientationMinMax

                    ' Set the label and number format for the X axis
                    Set ax = cht.Axes(c.chAxisPositionBottom)
                    Set ttl = pview.DataAxis.Totals(1)
                    ax.NumberFormat = ttl.NumberFormat
                    ax.HasTitle = True
                    ax.Title.Caption = ttl.Caption
                    ax.Scaling.Orientation = c.chScaleOrientationMinMax

            Case Else
                    ' Use a Bubble chart if there are three or more totals
                    If cht.Type <> c.chChartTypeBubble Then
                        cht.Type = c.chChartTypeBubble
                    End If

                    ' Use the first total for Y values,
                    ' second for X values, and third
                    ' for bubble size values
                    cht.SetData c.chDimYValues, 0, 0
                    cht.SetData c.chDimXValues, 0, 1
                    cht.SetData c.chDimBubbleValues, 0, 2

                    ' Set the label and number format for the Y axis
                    Set ax = cht.Axes(c.chAxisPositionLeft)
                    Set ttl = pview.DataAxis.Totals(0)
                    ax.NumberFormat = ttl.NumberFormat
                    ax.HasTitle = True
                    ax.Title.Caption = ttl.Caption
                    ax.Scaling.Orientation = c.chScaleOrientationMinMax

                    ' Set the label and number format for the X axis
                    Set ax = cht.Axes(c.chAxisPositionBottom)
                    Set ttl = pview.DataAxis.Totals(1)
                    ax.NumberFormat = ttl.NumberFormat
                    ax.HasTitle = True
                    ax.Title.Caption = ttl.Caption
                    ax.Scaling.Orientation = c.chScaleOrientationMinMax
```

```
                    ' Add the bubble size total caption to the chart title
                    Set ttl = pview.DataAxis.Totals(2)
                    cht.Title.Caption = cht.Title.Caption & _
                        " (Bubble Size Represents " & _
                        ttl.Caption & ")"

        End Select 'ctTotals

        FormatChartFromStyles cspace

End Sub 'LoadChart()
```

If the report has no totals, I leave the chart alone since there is no data to plot anyway. If one total exists, I change the chart type to Clustered Bar (though you can use many other types depending on the nature of the data). For example, a Line chart is most appropriate when time values are displayed down the rows of the report. A Pie chart might be more appropriate when no column fields exist because there is only one data dimension to plot. Note that I used the category axis's Scaling.Orientation property to reverse the order of the categories. By default, the Chart control displays categories in a Bar chart starting at the bottom of the Y axis and moving to the top. The PivotTable control naturally displays row members starting at the top row and heading down. To make the Chart control draw the categories in the reverse order, set the Orientation property to chScaleOrientationMaxMin.

If the PivotTable report has two totals, I switch the chart's type to Scatter and bind the first total to the Y values and the second to the X values. For three totals, I use the Bubble chart type and bind the third total to the bubble size values. The only chart type that can depict four values at once is the Open-High-Low-Close chart, but that obviously is only appropriate for certain kinds of data.

In all cases, I use the total's caption as the chart axis label and use the total's number format as the axis number format. This is an easy way to automatically title your chart elements and format numbers consistently among the different views. Finally, I call the FormatChartFromStyles function (detailed in Chapter 6) to format the chart based on the style sheet of the containing page.

SWITCHING CONNECTION CONTEXT

In Chapter 4, I told you that the PivotTable component embeds connection information into the XMLData property when you use its built-in ConnectionString and CommandText properties. This is true, but it does not embed this information if you use a DSC and bind the PivotTable component to it. This chapter's solution does just that, and it uses this technique to allow you to switch between an online OLAP server and an offline cube file. You can open the same reports while connected to either source because the connection information is not embedded in the XMLData property.

By default, this solution attempts to connect to an online server when you first load the page. If you have an OLAP Services server, you can enter the name of it in the input box and the solution will use that server as its data source. You can later click the Work Offline radio button, and the solution will prompt you for the location of the Sales.cub file included in the Data directory on your companion CD. The code that resets the connection is the SetConnection method, shown here:

```
Function SetConnection(dsc, fOffline)
    If fOffline Then
        ' If no offline cube file path exists yet, prompt
        ' for the location of the offline cube file
        If Len(m_sOfflinePath) = 0 Then
            ' Show the FindCubeFile.htm dialog box. This lets the user
            ' specify a file path or browse for the cube file.
            m_sOfflinePath = window.showModalDialog("FindCubeFile.htm",, _
                "dialogHeight:160px;dialogWidth:400px")

            ' Check whether the user entered something
            If Len(m_sOfflinePath) = 0 Then
                SetConnection = False
                Exit Function
            End If 'User cancelled
        End If 'No offline cube path yet

        ' Set the connection string to use the cube file
        dsc.ConnectionString = "provider=msolap;" & _
            "data source=" & m_sOfflinePath

    Else
        ' Prompt for the name of the online server if needed
        If Len(m_sOnlineServer) = 0 Then
            m_sOnlineServer = InputBox( _
                "Enter the name of your online server:" & _
                String(2, vbcrlf) & _
                "(Must be an OLAP Services server with a Foodmart" & _
                " sample cube)", "Foodmart Sales Analysis System", _
                "(Foodmart Server)")

            ' Check whether the user entered something
            If Len(m_sOnlineServer) = 0 Then
                SetConnection = False
                Exit Function
            End If 'User cancelled
        End If 'No online server yet

        ' Set the connection string to indicate an OLAP Services server
        dsc.ConnectionString = "provider=msolap;" & _
            "data source=" & m_sOnlineServer & _
            ";initial catalog=foodmart"
    End If
```

```
    ' Return success
    SetConnection = True
End Function 'SetConnection()
```

The only difference between the connection string for an online server and the connection string for an offline cube file is that the data source attribute names a server in the online case and a path to a cube file in the offline case. This code prompts the user for a server name or a cube file location if not already specified and sets the DSC's ConnectionString property to the appropriate value.

When loading a report that uses totals, fieldsets, or fields that no longer exist in the current data source, the PivotTable control silently ignores those parts and drops them from the report. Therefore, if you build a report using a fieldset not available in your offline cube, the PivotTable control will display the portions of the report that it can and ignore the rest. But if you then save the report, the PivotTable control will return information for the parts of the report definition it was able to reload and will not return the information that is no longer valid for the current source.

FORMATTING THE REPORT
BASED ON PAGE STYLES

In the previous chapter, I showed you how to format the Chart control based on the formatting encoded into the containing page's style sheet. This solution uses that same code for the chart and uses the sister function FormatPivotFromStyles to format the PivotTable control with the style sheet information. I will not discuss this function in detail because it is similar to the FormatChartFromStyles function covered in Chapter 6.

Note that the FormatPivotFromStyles function will look for a few extra selectors and attributes in the style sheet that you might want set. For example, it is often useful to format total values with a nice number format. You can apply these number formats in code, or you can use the FormatPivotFromStyles function and encode them in your style sheet like so:

```
Store Sales
{
    number-format: $#,##0.00
}

Unit Sales
{
    number-format: $#,##0.00
}

Sales Count
{
    number-format: #,##0
}
```

The function will look for selectors of the same name or unique name as the total. You can also use selectors such as PivotTable, PivotTitlebar, PivotFields, and PivotMembers to format the various PivotTable control elements. For more details on which selectors are supported, see the FormatPivotFromStyles function in the FormatControls.scp file in the Scripts directory on the companion CD.

The other interesting formatting function is FormatPivotSubtotalsFromStyles, also in the FormatControls.scp file on the CD. This function runs through the various fields on the Row and Column axes and sets the SubtotalBackColor and SubtotalFont properties based on the GrandTotals and SubtotalsLevel$N$ selectors in the style sheet. N is the subtotal level in your report starting at 1. For example, suppose you have the following code in your style sheet:

```
GrandTotals
{
    color: White;
    background-color: #9faccb;
    font-family: Verdana;

    font-size: 9pt;
    font-weight: bold;
}


SubtotalsLevel1
{
    color: Black;
    background-color: White;
    font-family: Verdana;

    font-size: 9pt;
    font-weight: bold;
}

SubtotalsLevel2
{
    color: Black;
    background-color: White;
    font-family: Verdana;

    font-size: 8pt;
    font-weight: bold;
}
```

In this example, the FormatPivotSubtotalsFromStyles function would set the background color of the report's grand totals to #9faccb (a pleasant baby blue) and the font to bold, white, 9-point Verdana. The function would format the subtotals in the next level as bold, black, 9-point Verdana and the subtotals in the following level as bold, black, 8-point Verdana. If you call this function from the PivotTable component's QueryComplete event handler, you can emulate automatic formatting so that the grand total and each level of subtotals appears in a particular way, regardless of which fields are located on which axes.

SUMMARY

Although the source code in this solution is quite long, it merely scratches the surface of what you can do in a sales analysis and reporting system. The combination of the Chart and PivotTable components provides a powerful analysis surface, and the ability to save and reload reports gives the user the power to create custom slices of data and recall them later.

You can implement a number of other ideas in this kind of system. For example, you can offer standard reports that are built on the server and returned as GIF images. You can also use more advanced MDX functions to filter for members with sales that were 10 percent greater than or less than they were during the same period the year before. And you can enable users to double-click an aggregate value and drill through to a transactional system, viewing the detailed invoices that comprise the aggregate.

This chapter focused on decision support systems and OLAP data sources. Chapter 8 will show you how to use the Office Web Components in a ubiquitous transactional system: timesheet tracking.

Chapter 8

Timesheet System

In Chapter 6, I showed you how to use the Chart component to build dynamic chart-based reporting solutions. In Chapter 7, I showed you how to use both the PivotTable component and the Chart component to build rich, interactive data analysis and reporting systems. In this chapter, I will show you how to combine three components—Chart, PivotTable, and Spreadsheet—to build a common business system: one that tracks the time that employees spend working on their projects.

ABOUT THE SOLUTION

When I worked in the IT group at Microsoft, we were not initially required to keep track of the time we spent working on various projects. Then the IT group consolidated itself and became much more organized. Soon we were required to keep track of all our time, recording how many hours we spent working on each project daily. At the end of each week, I and the other developers spent a few minutes filling out and submitting our timesheets. The theory was that project managers and resource planners would use this data to more accurately plan future projects. The IT group would use the data to "charge back" other departments for the amount of time we had spent working on their projects.

The system we used was a custom Microsoft Windows application purchased by the IT group. Each developer had to install this client program on his or her computer, and when we periodically upgraded machines or reinstalled operating systems for debugging, we had to reinstall this application before submitting our timesheets.

The application was rather large because it emulated much of the functionality found in a spreadsheet program—for example, recalculating, inserting and removing rows, editing in place, and so on. I have seen other timesheet systems implemented in Microsoft Excel, but these systems often must turn off Excel's entire user interface to make the program look and behave like a custom application.

Such universal, simple transactional and reporting systems are perfect candidates for web-based implementation. A web-based application requires no explicit setup and allows developers to easily control all aspects of the user interface. However, developers often want the rich interactivity that a product such as Excel or a custom-written application provides. Developers want to create a product that will automatically total the hours worked per day and per project, enabling the user to see his or her running total for the week. What developers need is a smaller, embeddable spreadsheet control, such as the Spreadsheet component.

In this chapter, I will describe how to build such a timesheet system. The Timesheet solution uses a Spreadsheet control for the entering of work hours, saves timesheets to a database on the web server, and uses the PivotTable component to analyze hours worked by employee, by date, and by project. The Timesheet solution focuses on how to use the spreadsheet as a data entry form and how to move data between the spreadsheet and a database. I will also briefly discuss how to track the use of this solution for logging purposes and how to view a usage report in the PivotTable control.

The Timesheet solution is similar to an expense reporting system, in which users fill out expense report templates (often implemented as Excel spreadsheets) and submit them for processing. The only additional feature required for an expense reporting system is the capability of being used off line. You will learn more about this in Chapter 10 when I discuss the Real-Time Stock Portfolio solution.

TECHNIQUES ILLUSTRATED IN THIS SOLUTION

Like the solutions presented in the previous two chapters, the Timesheet solution illustrates many techniques. Table 8-1 lists these various techniques and gives the source file in which each technique is implemented. Although I might not discuss each technique listed here, you can use this table to find the appropriate source file on the companion CD and examine the implementation on your own. You also can refer back to this table later if you need a quick reminder of the techniques implemented by the Timesheet solution.

Technique	*Source File*
Hiding the Spreadsheet component's user interface elements.	Timesheet.asp
Protecting the spreadsheet and locking cells.	Timesheet.asp
Binding a Chart component to the Spreadsheet component.	Timesheet.asp
Inserting and removing spreadsheet rows.	Timesheet.asp
Validating data entry in a spreadsheet.	Timesheet.asp
Saving and reloading the Spreadsheet component's contents.	Timesheet.asp
Using a hidden frame to post content to a Microsoft Active Server Pages script.	Timesheet.asp, SaveSubmit.asp
Using the Spreadsheet component in an ASP script.	SaveSubmit.asp
Using the PivotTable component to analyze tabular data.	Analyze.asp
Tracking the use of your web site.	Visitors.htm
Playing sounds in reaction to events.	Timesheet.asp
Using the LOGON_USER server variable to determine the Windows NT name of the current user.	Timesheet.asp, SaveSubmit.asp.
Implementing buttons with hover effects and tips in HTML.	Timesheet.asp

Table 8-1. *Techniques demonstrated by the Timesheet solution.*

RUNNING THE SOLUTION

The Timesheet solution is a mixture of HTML and ASP. To run this solution, you must open the Default.htm page using an http:// URL, meaning that you cannot simply double-click the files on the companion CD. The easiest way to set up this solution is to follow these steps:

1. If you are using a Windows NT Server machine with Microsoft Internet Information Server, use the IIS manager to add a virtual directory to your root web. Copy the Chap08 directory on the companion CD to your machine's hard drive, and specify that directory as the source for a virtual directory. Make sure to enable scripting support.

2. If you are running Personal Web Server (say on Windows 98 or Windows NT Workstation), use the Personal Web Manager to add a virtual directory as described in Step 1.

3.   Type the URL for the directory into your browser (for example, *http://MyServer/Chap08*). The Default.asp page should load unless you have configured your web site to use some other default filename. If you have, simply add */Default.asp* to the end of the URL.

For tips on how to create virtual directories for ASP applications under Personal Web Server, see the sidebar on page 172 in Chapter 6. Note that this solution does not use a Global.asa file and therefore does not need to be set up as an application.

The ASP scripts in this solution will use the LOGON_USER server variable for the current user name when saving reports. By default, IIS leaves the "Allow Anonymous Access" authentication method on and when it is enabled, LOGON_USER returns a blank string. If you want to enable the solution to save reports based on the actual user name, disable anonymous access by editing the virtual directory's security settings.

THE TIMESHEET PAGE

Although this solution comprises a few frames and many pages, the Timesheet.asp page is by far the most interesting and important. Furthermore, it is where all the scripting action happens. Before I discuss how I saved and loaded spreadsheets, performed validations, and added and removed projects, I want to describe how I constructed the HTML part of the page and made the Spreadsheet control look built in.

Configuring the Spreadsheet as a Data Entry Form

When you first run the Timesheet solution, you will see a page that looks like Figure 8-1. This page is a mixture of HTML, a Spreadsheet control, and two Chart controls. Notice that the spreadsheet looks built into the page and does not look much like Excel at all. There are no column and row headers, no toolbars, no blank cells to the right or below, and no scroll bars, plus the control seems to automatically resize as you add projects. The charts also have no borders, and the chart backgrounds match the background of the page itself.

Although you can use code to hide row and column headings, hide the toolbar, set the viewable range, and enable AutoFit, I chose to simply set these properties using the Property Toolbox while designing the page in Microsoft FrontPage 2000. These changes are persisted by the Spreadsheet control as parameters, and in HTML, these parameters are written as <param> tags. The parameters are then reloaded by the Spreadsheet control at runtime or during another design session, setting the initial state of the Spreadsheet control. The following HTML fragment comes from Template.htm and shows the control's <object> tag and the <param> tags just mentioned:

```
<object classid="clsid:0002E510-0000-0000-C000-000000000046"
id=ssTimesheet style="width=600px">
    <param name="HTMLData" value="...(omitted)...">
    <param name="DataType" value="HTMLDATA">
    <param name="AutoFit" value="-1">
    <param name="DisplayColHeaders" value="0">
    <param name="DisplayGridlines" value="-1">
    <param name="DisplayHorizontalScrollBar" value="-1">
    <param name="DisplayRowHeaders" value="0">
    <param name="DisplayTitleBar" value="-1">
    <param name="DisplayToolbar" value="0">
    <param name="DisplayVerticalScrollBar" value="-1">
    <param name="EnableAutoCalculate" value="-1">
    <param name="EnableEvents" value="-1">
    <param name="MoveAfterReturn" value="-1">
    <param name="MoveAfterReturnDirection" value="0">
    <param name="RightToLeft" value="0">
    <param name="ViewableRange" value="A1:J4">
</object>
```

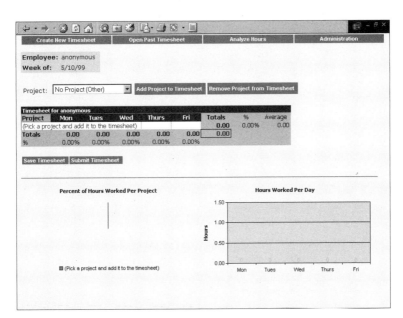

Figure 8-1. *A blank timesheet.*

As you can see, the names of these parameters match the names of their respective properties in the Spreadsheet control's programming model. For example, the third parameter, AutoFit, sets the Spreadsheet control's AutoFit property to the value specified in the value attribute. A value of 0 indicates False, and a value of nonzero (here −1) indicates True. Therefore, the third parameter sets the AutoFit property to True when the Spreadsheet control loads its parameters. To hide row and column headers as well as the toolbar, I set the DisplayRowHeaders, DisplayColHeaders, and DisplayToolbar parameters to 0.

As you will remember from Chapter 2, the ViewableRange property determines how much of the spreadsheet is viewable and accessible to the user. Although the spreadsheet might contain many cells, the ViewableRange property can restrict the user to seeing only those cells in the viewable range. Additionally, if the AutoFit property is set to True, the Spreadsheet control will automatically resize itself so that it is exactly the size of the viewable range and has no internal scroll bars. In this case, I set the viewable range to A1:J4, which encompasses the content of the timesheet template.

While designing the timesheet page in FrontPage 2000, I enabled protection for the spreadsheet. Enabling protection locks all cells, so the Spreadsheet control prohibits the user from editing those cells or viewing their formulas. After protecting the spreadsheet, I unlocked only the cells in which a user types his or her work hours. This information is saved in the rather long text in the value attribute of the HTMLData parameter tag. (I omitted this tag from the previous example for clarity, but you can see it in its entirety in the Template.htm file.)

I entered all other content in the timesheet template—such as the calculations for the average time spent on a project during the week, the total hours worked on a certain day, the percentage contribution to the total hours for the week, and so on—directly into the Spreadsheet control while I was working in FrontPage. The Spreadsheet component also saves this content in the HTMLData parameter and reloads it into the spreadsheet at runtime.

You can also approach initialization by using the HTMLURL property to load a template spreadsheet from another HTML file. Because Excel 2000 can save a spreadsheet in an HTML file, and because the Spreadsheet control and Excel share the same format for saved HTML, you can edit and maintain your timesheet template in Excel 2000 and load the content into the Spreadsheet control using the HTMLURL property. In the next chapter, I will demonstrate this and discuss the technique in more detail.

Binding and Formatting the Charts

As you will remember, we discussed in Chapter 3 how to bind the Chart control to the Spreadsheet control. As you would expect, the Timesheet solution uses extremely similar code to do the job. I chose to bind the charts using code instead of using the Chart Wizard in FrontPage because I knew that I would have to modify the charts' bound ranges when the user added or removed projects from the timesheet, so it was easier to perform all binding through code. The following method is called from the Window object's onLoad event handler to bind the charts to the spreadsheet:

```
Sub BindCharts(csPerProj, csPerDay, ss)
    ' Local variables
    Dim c               ' Constants object
    Dim cds             ' WCChartDataSource reference
    Dim cht             ' Temporary WCChart reference
    Dim rngVisible      ' Spreadsheet's viewable range
    Dim ser             ' Temporary WCSeries reference

    Set c = csPerProj.Constants

    ' Set the spreadsheet as the data source
    Set csPerProj.DataSource = ss
    Set csPerDay.DataSource = ss

    ' Make PerProj a pie chart for total hours on projects
    Set cht = csPerProj.Charts.Add()
    cht.Type = c.chChartTypePie

    ' Get the viewable range of the spreadsheet
    Set rngVisible = ss.Range(ss.ViewableRange)

    ' Add a series, and bind it to the spreadsheet
    Set ser = cht.SeriesCollection.Add()
    ser.SetData c.chDimCategories, 0, "a2:a" & rngVisible.Rows.Count - 2
    ser.SetData c.chDimValues, 0, "h2:h" & rngVisible.Rows.Count - 2

    ' Make PerDay a second column/bar chart showing hours worked each day
    Set cht = csPerDay.Charts.Add()
    cht.Type = c.chChartTypeColumnClustered

    ' Add a series, and bind to the spreadsheet
    Set ser = cht.SeriesCollection.Add()
    ser.SetData c.chDimCategories, 0, "c1:g1"
    ser.SetData c.chDimValues, 0, "c" & rngVisible.Rows.Count - 1 & _
        ":g" & rngVisible.Rows.Count - 1

End Sub 'BindCharts()
```

This code starts by setting the DataSource property of each Chart control to the Spreadsheet control. This tells the Chart controls where they should get their data when the SetData method is called later. It is not necessary to use the ChartDataSources collection if you have only one data source for the chart. (For a refresher on the DataSource and DataMember properties, see Chapter 2.)

Next the code creates a chart in the Chart control representing the total hours per project and sets the chart type to Pie. The code then gets the viewable range from the spreadsheet and uses it as the mechanism for knowing what range references encompass the Project Name column and the Percentage Contribution column. Since the project names and percentage contribution values extend from the second row to the second-to-last row, you can calculate range references that encompass all the project names and all the percentage contribution values. The code continues by binding the chart's categories and values based on these calculated ranges.

Finally this code creates a chart in the second Chart control, setting its type to Clustered Column. The code uses the same technique to calculate the ranges for the chart's categories (days of the week) and values (total hours worked each day) and binds the chart dimensions to those ranges.

The Window object's onLoad event handler calls one other method to format the charts, which is shown here:

```
Sub FormatCharts(csPerProj, csPerDay)
    ' Local variables
    Dim c          ' Constants object
    Dim cht        ' Temporary WCChart reference
    Dim ax         ' Temporary WCAxis reference
    Dim dl         ' Temporary WCDataLabels reference

    Set c = csPerProj.Constants

    csPerProj.Border.Color = document.bgColor
    csPerProj.Interior.Color = document.bgColor

    csPerDay.Border.Color = document.bgColor
    csPerDay.Interior.Color = document.bgColor

    ' Format the per-project chart
    Set cht = csPerProj.Charts(0)
    cht.HasTitle = True
    cht.Title.Caption = "Percent of Hours Worked Per Project"
    cht.Title.Font.Name = "Tahoma"
    cht.Title.Font.Size = 8
    cht.Title.Font.Bold = True
    cht.HasLegend = True
    cht.Legend.Position = c.chLegendPositionBottom
    cht.Legend.Interior.Color = document.bgColor
    cht.Legend.Border.Color = document.bgColor

    ' Format the per-day chart
    Set cht = csPerDay.Charts(0)
    cht.HasTitle = True
    cht.Title.Caption = "Hours Worked Per Day"
```

```
cht.Title.Font.Name = "Tahoma"
cht.Title.Font.Size = 8
cht.Title.Font.Bold = True
cht.PlotArea.Interior.Color = "wheat"

' Set and format the value axis title
Set ax = cht.Axes(c.chAxisPositionLeft)
ax.HasTitle = True
ax.Title.Font.Name = "Tahoma"
ax.Title.Font.Size = 8
ax.Title.Caption = "Hours"
ax.Title.Font.Bold = True

' Set the series color
cht.SeriesCollection(0).Interior.Color = "darkred"

' Add data labels, and show the values only
Set dl = cht.SeriesCollection(0).DataLabelsCollection.Add()
dl.Font.Name = "Tahoma"
dl.Font.Size = 8
dl.Font.Color = "silver"
dl.Position = c.chLabelPositionInsideEnd
```

```
End Sub 'FormatCharts()
```

Chart-formatting code should be quite familiar to you now; however, one point is worth noting in this example. To make the charts appear built into the page, I set each Chart control's border and interior color to the same color as the surrounding page. I did this by passing the value returned from the document.bgColor property to the Color property of the Chart control's Border and Interior objects. Because the Office Web Components accept any color name, or any hexadecimal or RGB value you might use in HTML, you can directly assign colors from the surrounding HTML document to make the element's color match. As you will remember from Chapter 6, you also can use the common script routine FormatChartFromStyles. In this case, however, I wanted to show you how to manually perform this technique.

The rest of the code in this method creates titles and applies formatting. Note that I also set the legend's interior color and border to the same color as the document. This again creates the effect of the legend being built into the page rather than being separate from it. I also placed the legend at the bottom of the pie chart so that it leaves more room for the actual pie. Since users commonly have up to three projects in their timesheet, this arrangement is much more space efficient.

You might be wondering why I did not use only one Chart control and create two charts in the chart space. Remember that charts within the same chart space share a master set of categories. Since the charts in the Timesheet solution do not have the same set of categories (project names vs. days of the week), you cannot put them in the same chart space and keep each chart's categories separate. If you do put them in the same chart space, both charts' categories set will be the union of all categories. Conveniently, Microsoft Internet Explorer allows you to size controls to a percentage of the containing element (in this case, the entire page), so you can easily keep the Chart controls equally spaced on the same horizontal line by setting their width attributes to a percentage value:

```
<object classid="clsid:0002E500-0000-0000-C000-000000000046"
id=csPerProj width="49%" height="200">
</object>
<object classid="clsid:0002E500-0000-0000-C000-000000000046"
id=csPerDay width="50%" height="200">
</object>
```

ADDING AND REMOVING PROJECTS IN THE TIMESHEET

The first task a user must perform when starting a new timesheet is to add one or more projects. The Timesheet solution allows the user to add any number of projects to the timesheet but allows the user to add a particular project only once because there is no need to have two different entries for the same project on the same day. This solution dynamically generates the list of projects based on the contents of the Projects table in the database, and you can enable additional projects by simply adding rows to that table.

THE MYSTERIOUS MISSING PERCENT

When I first wrote this example, I used "50%" as the width value for each of the Chart controls. I expected this to keep both Chart controls on the same horizontal line, sizing their width to half the width of the document. I noticed however that at certain window sizes, Internet Explorer wrapped the second chart to the next line of the document, even though the charts' sizes should have been exactly half the width.

I surmised that this mysterious behavior was the result of rounding errors that occurred when the document size was not an even number. However, I could not confirm this and eventually found that setting the first Chart control's width to "49%" seemed to fix the problem.

Let's first look at how I populate that drop-down list of projects. The following HTML and ASP script fragment is taken from the Timesheet.asp file:

```
<td>Project: 
    <select id=cbxProject>
<%
Set m_rs = m_cn.Execute("select ProjectID, ProjectName from Projects" & _
    " where Active = True")

    While Not m_rs.EOF
        Response.Write "<option value=" & m_rs("ProjectID") & ">" & _
            m_rs("ProjectName") & "</option>"
        m_rs.MoveNext
    Wend

    m_rs.Close
    Set m_rs = nothing
%>
    </select>
</td>
```

The code starts by emitting some HTML for the table in which the project's drop-down list and the Add Project To Timesheet and Remove Project From Timesheet buttons reside. It also emits the beginning of the <select> tag, giving it an ID of cbxProject, which I will use later in the client-side script.

Next, the code jumps back into ASP script and executes a query to retrieve the list of active projects. (As any ASP programmer knows, the <% and %> symbols demarcate ASP script.) The code then loops through the Recordset and emits an <option> tag for each project. After the last project, the code closes and releases the Recordset and emits the closing </select> tag.

My use of *where Active = True* in the SQL statement is worth noting. I designed the timesheet database so that it has referential integrity between the Projects table and the WorkHours table—meaning you cannot delete a project from the Projects table if any work hours are associated with that project. For reporting reasons, you would want to keep records of hours worked on projects that are no longer active, but you would not want those projects to appear in the list of available projects in the timesheet system. By setting the project's Active column to False (0), you can hide a project from the user while keeping it for reporting and analysis purposes.

Now that the Project drop-down list is loaded with all the active projects, let's turn our attention to what happens when the user clicks the Add Project To Timesheet button. The click is caught in the button's onClick event handler as shown on the next page.

```
Sub btnAddProj_onClick()
    Dim rng              ' Temporary Range reference
    Dim sProj            ' Project name

    ' Get the name of the selected project
    sProj = cbxProject.children(cbxProject.selectedIndex).Text

    ' Check whether the project ID is already in the timesheet
    ' The project ID is in the hidden B column
    Set rng = ssTimesheet.Range("B2")
    While Len(Trim(rng.Text)) > 0
        If rng.Text = cbxProject.value Then
            MsgBbox "The project '" & sProj & _
                "' is already in your timesheet!", _
                vbCritical, "Timesheet Demo"
            Exit Sub
        End If
        Set rng = rng.Offset(1)
    Wend

    ' Turn off screen updating to avoid flashing
    ssTimesheet.ScreenUpdating = False

    ' We either hit a blank row, or we went into the Totals row
    ' (which is one less than number of visible rows)
    If rng.Row >= _
        (ssTimesheet.Range(ssTimesheet.ViewableRange).Rows.Count - 1) then
            ' Not within viewable range
            ' Need to add a row and fix up the summary functions
            Set rng = ssTimesheet.Range("A" & _
                ssTimesheet.Range(ssTimesheet.ViewableRange).Rows.Count - 1)

            ' Turn off the Allow Inserting Rows protection option
            ' while we insert a row programmatically
            ssTimesheet.ActiveSheet.Protection.Enabled = False
            rng.InsertRows(1)
            ssTimesheet.ActiveSheet.Protection.Enabled = True

            ' Move back to the newly inserted row,
            ' and move to the Project ID column
            Set rng = rng.Offset(-1,1)

            ' Fix up formulas
            FixupFormulas ssTimesheet
    End If
```

```
' Set the current cell to the project ID and
' one cell left to the project name
rng.Locked = False
rng.Value = cbxProject.value
rng.Locked = True

Set rng = rng.Offset(0,-1)
rng.Locked = False
rng.Font.Color = "Black"
rng.Value = sProj
rng.Locked = True

' Do autofit on the first column to make sure
' the project name is fully visible
ssTimesheet.Range("a1:a" & _
    ssTimesheet.ActiveSheet.UsedRange.Rows.Count).AutofitColumns

' Turn the screen updating back on to force a redraw
ssTimesheet.ScreenUpdating = True
End Sub 'btnAddProj_onClick()
```

This event handler begins by getting the name of the project selected in the drop-down list. It then scans through the list of projects in the timesheet to see whether the project has already been added. If it finds the project in the timesheet, it displays an error message and exits the handler. If it does not find the project in the timesheet, it continues executing the code to insert the project.

Before performing any row insertions, I set the ScreenUpdating property to False. The Spreadsheet control will redraw itself by default when you make changes to its content. If you plan on making a few changes at once, it's often beneficial to turn ScreenUpdating off while doing so and then turn it back on when you are done. The spreadsheet will wait to redraw itself until you turn ScreenUpdating back on, preventing the flashing that can occur when you make many changes at once. Just be sure you remember to turn ScreenUpdating back on—if you do not, the spreadsheet will appear frozen and unresponsive.

The code continues by checking whether it encountered a blank row (which happens when you have no projects in the timesheet) or the Totals row on its journey through the timesheet's current projects. If it encountered the Totals row, I need to insert a new row in the spreadsheet and fix up the summary formulas at the bottom and on the right side of the timesheet so that they include the newly inserted row. Because the spreadsheet is protected, I must disable protection by setting the Protection object's Enabled property to False before I can insert the new row. I then immediately turn protection back on so that the user cannot modify the spreadsheet.

The code continues by calling the FixupFormulas method. This method adjusts the formulas in the bottom two rows and right three columns so that they include the newly inserted row. In the case of the column summary formulas, I need to add them to the newly inserted rows so that the spreadsheet calculates the same totals for the new row as it does for other rows. Let's take a look at the FixupFormulas method:

```
Sub FixupFormulas(ss)
    Dim rng           ' Temporary Range reference
    Dim nRows         ' Number of rows in the timesheet
    Dim col           ' Temporary column counter
    Dim sColLetter    ' Column letter

    ' Go to the first column before the first day in the Totals row
    Set rng = ss.Range("b" & ss.ActiveSheet.UsedRange.Rows.Count - 1)

    ' Turn protection off temporarily
    ss.ActiveSheet.Protection.Enabled = False

    ' Fix up the column sum formulas
    For col = 1 To 6          ' Days of the week + Totals column
        Set rng = rng.Offset(0,1)
        sColLetter = left(rng.Address,1)
        rng.Formula = "=sum(" & sColLetter & "2:" & _
            sColLetter & rng.Row - 1 & ")"
    Next

    ' Go up one to do the row total
    Set rng = rng.Offset(-1)
    rng.Formula = "=sum(c" & rng.Row & ":g" & rng.Row & ")"

    ' Go over one to do the row percentage of total
    Set rng = rng.Offset(0,1)
    rng.Formula = "=if(h" & rng.Row & "=0, 0, h" & rng.Row & _
        "/h" & rng.Row + 1 & ")"

    ' Go over one to do the row average
    Set rng = rng.Offset(0,1)
    rng.Formula = "=if(h" & rng.Row & _
        "=0, 0, average(c" & rng.Row & ":g" & rng.Row & ")"

    ' Finally, adjust the data references for the first chart
    nRows = ss.ActiveSheet.UsedRange.Rows.Count - 2
    csPerProj.Charts.Item(0).SeriesCollection.Item(0).SetData _
        csPerProj.constants.chDimCategories, 0, "a2:a" & nRows
    csPerProj.Charts.Item(0).SeriesCollection.Item(0).SetData _
        csPerProj.constants.chDimValues, 0, "h2:h" & nRows
```

```
' Turn protection back on
ss.ActiveSheet.Protection.Enabled = True
```

End Sub 'FixupFormulas()

This code begins by disabling protection because it will update formulas in locked cells. It loops over the various cells in the Totals row (second from the bottom), updating the sum formulas to include the newly inserted row. This also updates the grand total cell formula to include the per-project total for the new project row. The Percent Of Total row (the bottom row) is derived from the per-day totals and the grand total, so you do not need to update the formulas in that row.

The code then moves the range reference up one cell to add the per-project total formulas in the three rightmost columns of the timesheet. These formulas are the per-project sum, the percent of total, and the average. It has to add these formulas for only the newly inserted row and does not have to modify the formulas for the other existing rows because they are unaffected by the new row.

Finally the code updates the source data references of the per-project chart. Because I just added a new project to the timesheet, I need to extend the existing range reference the chart has for the category names and values. The Chart and Spreadsheet controls normally track the insertions of rows in the middle of a range and automatically extend the range references accordingly. However, when a row is inserted just below an existing range reference, the Spreadsheet control does not consider that newly inserted row to be part of the existing range and therefore does not update it.

USE A HIDDEN ROW TO AVOID
FORMULA AND RANGE FIX UP

Although I wanted to show you how to fix up formulas and range references, I could have avoided some of this code by adding a blank row to the spreadsheet just above the rows of totals and then hiding that row. By doing so, all the formulas and range references would include the blank row, and when I insert a new row just above the hidden blank row, the formulas and range references would automatically adjust. I would have to recode the part of my function that looks for an open spot in the timesheet, but inserting the blank row would eliminate most of this other code.

Let's return to the onClick event handler of the Add Project button and examine the rest of the code after the call to FixupFormulas:

```
' Set the current cell to the project name and
' the next cell over to the project ID
rng.Locked = False
rng.Value = cbxProject.value
rng.Locked = True

Set rng = rng.Offset(0,-1)
rng.Locked = False
rng.Font.Color = "Black"
rng.Value = sProj
rng.Locked = True

' Do autofit on the first column to make sure
' the project name is fully visible
ssTimesheet.Range("a1:a" & _
    ssTimesheet.ActiveSheet.UsedRange.Rows.Count).AutofitColumns

' Turn the screen updating back on to force a redraw
ssTimesheet.ScreenUpdating = True
End Sub 'btnAddProj_onClick()
```

The timesheet has a hidden column immediately after the project name. I use this column to store the project ID value, which I will need when I process a submitted timesheet. (I will explain this later.) The rest of this event handler sets the project name and project ID cells for the newly inserted row and then uses the AutofitColumns method to make sure the new project name is fully visible.

The code for removing a project from the timesheet is far easier than the code for adding a project. Removing a project is literally as easy as removing the row in which the project exists. However, you do have to catch the case in which the user deletes the last project from the timesheet. In this case, you should clear only the row's contents and set the project name cell to the help string "(Use 'Add Project to Timesheet' to add a project)". The code starts in the onClick event handler for the Remove Project From Timesheet button:

```
Sub btnDelProj_onClick()
    ' Local variables
    Dim rng         ' Temporary Range reference

    Set rng = ssTimesheet.Selection

    ' If the user was in column 1 (Project Name column)
    ' and not on a header or total row
```

```
If rng.Column = 1 And (rng.Row > 1 And rng.Row <= _
    ssTimesheet.Range(ssTimesheet.ViewableRange).Rows.Count - 2) Then
        RemoveProj ssTimesheet, rng.Row
End If 'In Project Name column

End Sub 'btnDelProj_onClick()
```

This code simply checks that the current selection is in a project row and in the Project Name column. (Perhaps this is too restrictive, but that's how I wrote it.) If so, the code calls the RemoveProj method passing a reference to the Spreadsheet control and the row to remove. Let's take a look at this method:

```
Sub RemoveProj(ss, row)
    ' Local variables
    Dim rng            ' Temporary Range reference

    Set rng = ss.Range("A" & row & ":G" & row)

    ' Turn off protection while we delete the row
    ssTimesheet.ActiveSheet.Protection.Enabled = False

    If ss.Range(ss.ViewableRange).Rows.Count = 4 Then
        ' Last project--clear the row and set help
        rng.ClearContents
        AddHelpText ss
    Else
        rng.DeleteRows(1)
    End If

    ' Turn protection back on
    ssTimesheet.ActiveSheet.Protection.Enabled = True

End Sub 'RemoveProj()
```

The method first disables protection because deleting rows is not allowed while protection is enabled. It then checks for the case in which this is the last project in the timesheet by determining the number of rows remaining in the viewable range. If there are only four rows, the project being removed is the last project, and the code simply clears the row's contents and adds the help text to the project name cell. If the project being removed is not the last project, the code simply deletes the row. Finally the code reenables protection.

After enabling the Remove Project button, I thought it would be nice to let the user remove a project by selecting a project name and pressing the Delete key. This is also fairly easy to trap, though it has a problem that I will discuss after we look at the code on the next page.

```
Sub ssTimesheet_KeyDown(evt)
    ' If the user was in column 1 (Project Name column)
    ' and not on a header or total row
    If evt.Range.Column = 1 And (evt.Range.Row > 1 And evt.Range.Row <= _
        ssTimesheet.Range(ssTimesheet.ViewableRange).Rows.Count - 2) Then

        ' And the key was the Delete key
        If evt.KeyCode = 46 Then
            RemoveProj ssTimesheet, evt.Range.Row

            ' Cancel standard processing
            evt.ReturnValue = False

        End If 'Delete key
    End If 'In Project Name column
End Sub 'Spreadsheet_KeyDown()
```

The Spreadsheet control raises an event called KeyDown whenever a key is pressed down. This is the event you should use to capture special keys such as Delete, Escape, Return, or Tab. The code in this event handler checks that the selection was on a valid project name and then checks whether the keycode was 46, which is the ASCII value for the Delete key. If both conditions are true, the code calls the RemoveProj method just as the onClick event handler of the Remove Project button did. It also attempts to set the ReturnValue property of the event information object (passed to the handler by the spreadsheet) to False in order to cancel the standard processing of this key. I say "attempts" because this is the unfortunate problem that I alluded to earlier. The Spreadsheet control will always process keystrokes even if you set this ReturnValue property to False. Because the spreadsheet is protected and the project name cell is locked, pressing the Delete key will always generate a warning in the user interface, telling the user that he or she cannot update a locked cell. As far as I know no workaround for this exists, so you might want to avoid using this approach with locked cells.

VALIDATING DATA ENTRY

Typically, a data entry application will implement some measure of data validation to keep bad data values from getting into the program. In a timesheet system, it makes no sense to allow a user to enter a negative number or a nonnumeric value because these will simply produce errors when you submit the timesheet. Fortunately, you can perform data validation in the Spreadsheet control and keep bad data from getting into your spreadsheet.

To try out the validation, type a negative or nonnumeric value into one of the unlocked timesheet cells. The control will reject the value, flashing an error message in the title bar and playing a sound (if your system is capable of this). The code that makes this happen is quite simple and starts in the Spreadsheet control's EndEdit event handler:

```
Sub ssTimesheet_EndEdit(evt)
    ' Since the only cells that are editable are those containing the
    ' hours worked, assume that the current cell is one of those and
    ' therefore should be numeric and greater than zero

    ' If the cell is empty, then exit
    If Len(trim(evt.EditData)) = 0 Then Exit Sub

    ' Check to make sure it's numeric and >= 0
    If IsNumeric(evt.EditData) Then
        If evt.EditData >= 0 Then
            ' Good data--let it go

            ' Trick: Set a <bgsound> tag's src property to the
            ' name of a wav file to make the browser play the sound
            sndBG.src = "cashreg.wav"
        Else
            ' Data less than zero
            displayerror "Hours worked must be greater than zero!"
            evt.ReturnValue = False
        End If 'Edit data >= 0
    Else
        ' Data is nonnumeric
        displayerror "Hours worked must be a number!"
        evt.ReturnValue = False
    End If 'Data is numeric
End Sub 'Spreadsheet_EndEdit()
```

The EndEdit event fires when the user finishes editing a cell, but before that new value is inserted into the spreadsheet and before the spreadsheet has recalculated. The Spreadsheet control passes a few crucial pieces of information in the SpreadsheetEventInfo object passed as the parameter to this event. First, the SpreadsheetEventInfo object exposes a Range property, which during this event specifies the range that the user edited. You can use this to determine which cell was edited, perhaps using a different validation rule for different cell ranges. In this example, the only cells that are unlocked (and therefore editable) are the ones containing the hours worked, so I can assume the edited cell is one of those.

The second crucial piece of information is the EditData property. This property returns the value the user is attempting to enter, and this is the value your code should validate. If your code does not reject EditData, the value in this property will be put into the target cell and the spreadsheet will recalculate based on that new value. In this case, I perform two tests on the value. I first check whether it is numeric, and then I check that it is greater than or equal to 0. If both conditions are true, I accept the data and play the cash register sound. (This always gets a laugh when I am giving a demo.) If either condition fails, I display the appropriate error. The key to denying the edit is to set the ReturnValue property on the SpreadsheetEventInfo object to False. Doing so will cause the spreadsheet to reject the edit and keep the current value in the cell.

SAVING AND RELOADING TIMESHEETS

The Timesheet solution allows users to save the timesheets they are currently working on and reload them later to make changes. The way I implemented timesheet saving is similar to how I saved reports in Chapter 7, so some of the discussion in this section should sound familiar.

Although it looks like the Timesheet solution has only two frames, a hidden frame is sandwiched between the navigation bar area and the main frame. This hidden frame's source is SaveSubmit.asp, which emits a form with a number of hidden fields. When saving a timesheet, the main frame sets the values of these fields in the hidden frame and then submits the form, posting the timesheet data and other

HOW TO PLAY A SOUND IN REACTION TO AN EVENT

When I first decided to play a sound when a user enters a new value into the timesheet, I was perplexed at how to accomplish this. There was no PlaySound method in Microsoft VBScript and nothing comparable in the Document Object Model (DOM). I asked around, and no one seemed to know how to do it. Then a helpful program manager from the Internet Explorer team gave me the clue.

I had seen the <bgsound> tag before, but Internet Explorer seemed to play the sound only when the page was loaded and not when I wanted it to. However, like any other HTML element, the <bgsound> tag can be modified using script. If you set the src property of the <bgsound> tag, Internet Explorer will download the sound file and play it immediately. Sometimes a slight delay occurs the first time you play it (while Internet Explorer downloads the file), but after that, the sound plays precisely when you want it to.

information to the web server. The most important piece of information the main frame passes to the hidden frame is the value returned from the Spreadsheet control's HTMLData property. This property returns a string—an entire HTML document with a table in it—that represents the control's state, including the values contained within the cells of the spreadsheet. The SaveSubmit.asp script saves the timesheet data in a database on the server and then returns another form. Figure 8-2 depicts the save architecture of this solution.

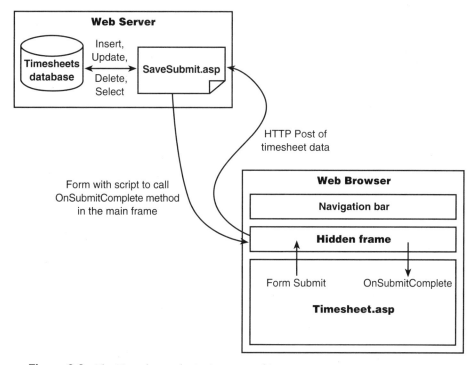

Figure 8-2. *The Timesheet solution's save architecture.*

Let's start by looking at the code in the Save button's onClick event handler:

```
Sub btnSave_onClick()
    ' Post the data as a save
    SubmitForm "Save"
    ssTimesheet.Dirty = False
End Sub 'btnSave_onClick()
```

This fairly simple routine calls the SubmitForm method (which I will describe shortly) and then sets the Spreadsheet control's Dirty property to False. The Dirty property indicates whether any changes have been made to the control, either by the user or by code. You can set this property to False if you want to reset the dirty state, which you would commonly do after saving the timesheet. Later, I'll explain how

I use this property in the Window object's onBeforeUnload event to prompt users to save their timesheets if they forget to do so before attempting to leave the page.

Let's look at the SubmitForm method:

```
Sub SubmitForm(Verb)
    ' Local variables
    Dim frm                 ' Form in hidden frame

    ' Get a reference to the form in the hidden frame
    Set frm = window.parent.frames(1).frmTimesheet

    ' Fill out the form
    frm.TimesheetID.value = frmTimesheet.TimesheetID.value
    frm.Verb.value = Verb
    frm.Employee.value = lblEmployee.innerText
    frm.StartDate.value = lblStartDate.innerText
    frm.Timesheet.value = ssTimesheet.HTMLData

    ' Submit the form
    frm.submit

    If LCase(verb) = "save" Then
        window.parent.status = "Timesheet Saved!"
    End If
End Sub 'SubmitForm()
```

This code is similar to the code from the previous chapter. It first finds the form in the hidden frame; then fills out the various fields on that form, setting the Timesheet field to the value of the HTMLData property; and finally calls the submit method of the form. This function is used for both saving and submitting timesheets, and the Verb parameter distinguishes the action. If the Verb parameter is equal to "Save", the timesheet is simply saved. If it is equal to "Submit", the timesheet is first saved and then processed, which I will describe in the next section.

> **NOTE**   In case you didn't know, you can set the Status property of the Window object to a string that you want to display in the status bar of Internet Explorer. This is a convenient way to provide modeless status information and feedback.

Now that the code in the main frame has submitted the form in the hidden frame, let's look at the form itself and the ASP code that processes its submission. First, the form:

```
<!-- FORM FOR FILE SAVE/SUBMIT -->
<form id=frmTimesheet action=SaveSubmit.asp method=Post>
<input type=hidden name="Verb" id="Verb">
<input type=hidden name="TimesheetID" id="TimesheetID">
<input type=hidden name="Employee" id="Employee">
```

```
<input type=hidden name="StartDate" id="StartDate">
<input type=hidden name="Timesheet" id="Timesheet">
</form>
```

As you will remember from the last chapter, the use of *method=Post* causes Internet Explorer to send the field values in the body of the HTTP request instead of in the URL itself. This is the technique we want to use in this chapter as well because the HTMLData property can be quite long. Also note that the action for this form is to call the SaveSubmit.asp script. Since this happens to be the same file in which this form resides, it is self-referential.

Now let's examine the ASP script that processes this form's submission. It begins by opening a connection to the database and getting the action verb value ("Save" or "Submit"):

```
' Open a connection to the database
Set m_cn = GetConnection()

' Are we saving or submitting?
m_sAction = Request.Form("Verb")
m_sAction = LCase(m_sAction)
```

The GetConnection method comes from an included file called GetConnection.inc. This file uses the page's current path to determine the location of the Timesheets.mdb file on the server. You can reimplement this function quite easily so that it uses Microsoft SQL Server, which I highly recommend doing if you use this solution in your company. I use Microsoft Jet databases in the samples only because of their easy deployment, but the Jet database engine was not designed for a multiuser, high-concurrency environment such as a web server. In your real solutions, I recommend using SQL Server or some other client/server, multiuser, truly transactional database engine.

The code continues by logging the visit to the page. (I will discuss this in more detail later.) After logging the visit, the code continues with the save operation:

```
If Len(m_sAction) > 0 Then
    ' Get the TimesheetID from the form
    m_idTimesheet = Request.Form("TimesheetID")

    ' Save the timesheet stream for both save and submit
    Set m_cmd = server.CreateObject("ADODB.Command")
    Set m_cmd.ActiveConnection = m_cn

    ' If the TimesheetId is valid, then update; otherwise, insert
    If Len(m_idTimesheet) > 0 Then
        m_cmd.CommandText = "UPDATE Timesheets set Timesheet = ? " & _
                            "Where TimesheetID = " & m_idTimesheet
```

(continued)

```
            m_cmd.Parameters.Append m_cmd.CreateParameter("p1", 203, _
                                    1,2000000000)
            m_cmd.Parameters(0).Value = Request.Form("Timesheet")
            m_cmd.Execute
        Else
            m_cmd.CommandText = "InsertTimesheet p1,p2,p3"
            m_cmd.CommandType = 4

            m_cmd.Parameters.Append m_cmd.CreateParameter("p1", 202, 1,70)
            m_cmd.Parameters.Append m_cmd.CreateParameter("p2", 135, 1)
            m_cmd.Parameters.Append m_cmd.CreateParameter("p3", 203, _
                                    1,2000000000)

            m_cmd.Parameters(0).Value = Request.Form("Employee")
            m_cmd.Parameters(1).Value = Request.Form("StartDate")
            m_cmd.Parameters(2).Value = Request.Form("Timesheet")

            m_cmd.Execute

            Dim rs            ' Temporary Recordset
            Set rs = m_cn.Execute("select @@IDENTITY")
            m_idTimesheet = rs(0)
        End If
    End If 'Len(m_sAction) > 0
```

I first check whether the form submitted a timesheet ID along with the timesheet data. If so, I know to perform an update to the database; if not, I know to perform an insert. The code for updating and inserting data into a database is straightforward ADO code, but in this case, I wanted to show you how to use a parameterized SQL query instead of a stored query. In the last chapter, I showed you how to use stored queries or procedures, and I do use a stored query here to insert a new timesheet. However, the code for updating a timesheet shows you how to use parameter markers ("?") in a SQL statement instead of using a stored query.

The last section of this code block illustrates how to get the new primary key for a newly inserted timesheet. Because the Timesheets table uses an AutoNumber field for the primary key, you don't know which number will be assigned to a new row until after you have inserted it. The way you retrieve this new number is by immediately selecting @@IDENTITY after executing the Insert command. Although I don't actually use this value in the ASP script, I wanted to show you how to get the new ID in case you need it for your own solution.

After the ASP script saves the timesheet data to the database, it emits that same form we saw earlier so that the main frame can again save or submit the timesheet. Since the main frame is still in place, you do not need to reload the page.

Let's now look at what happens when an existing timesheet is opened. This occurs when the user clicks the name of a saved timesheet on the Open Past Timesheet page or when the Default.asp page automatically reloads the current week's timesheet. The main timesheet page (Timesheet.asp) is actually an ASP script, so it begins by checking whether it was called to load an existing timesheet or to display a new one:

```
If m_sAction = "load" Then
    ' Get the timesheet stream
    ' Expect Request.QueryString("TimesheetID") to contain the
    ' timesheet ID
    m_idTimesheet = Request.QueryString("TimesheetID")

    If m_idTimesheet >= 0 Then
        Set m_rs = m_cn.Execute("select StartDate, Timesheet from " & _
                                "Timesheets where TimesheetID = " & _
                                m_idTimesheet)

        ' Get the timesheet stream
        m_dtStart = m_rs("StartDate")
        m_sTimesheetStream = m_rs("Timesheet")

        m_rs.Close
        Set m_rs = Nothing
    Else
        ' Invalid timesheet ID
        Response.Write "<h3>" & nTimesheet & _
                        " is not a valid timesheet ID!</h3>"
    End If
End If
```

The m_sAction variable is set earlier in the script and is equal to Request.Query-String("Action"). If it is equal to "load", the code in this script executes a query against the database to retrieve the timesheet identified by the m_idTimesheet variable. This query should return only one row. The code continues by copying the StartDate and Timesheet column values into variables and then closes and releases the Recordset object.

The page continues by emitting the HTML user interface above the Spreadsheet control and eventually comes to this section:

```
<%
' If we are creating a new timesheet, include the template object,
' which has all the formatting and initial settings in it
If m_sAction = "new" Then
%>
<!-- SPREADSHEET COMPONENT WITH SAVED TIMESHEET TEMPLATE -->
<!--#INCLUDE FILE="Template.htm" -->
<%
```

(continued)

255

```
' Otherwise, just include a blank spreadsheet with the same parameter
' settings. We do this because when we load an existing timesheet,
' all the data and formatting will come in with the loaded stream,
' and this keeps the spreadsheet from having to parse the HTML data
' twice (once from the template and once from the loaded stream).
Else
%>
<object classid="clsid:0002E510-0000-0000-C000-000000000046"
id=ssTimesheet style="width=600px">
    <param name="HTMLData" value=" <%= Server.HTMLEncode
    (m_sTimesheetStream) %> ">
    <param name="DataType" value="HTMLDATA">
```

The script checks the m_sAction variable again, and if the variable is equal to "new", the script includes an HTML file that contains the timesheet template. This file contains only an <object> tag and <param> tags for the Spreadsheet control. The HTMLData <param> tag in the template contains the persisted state of the template spreadsheet.

However, if the m_sAction variable is not equal to "new", the page emits an <object> tag and a set of <param> tags for the Spreadsheet control, except that this time it emits the timesheet data as the value for the HTMLData <param> tag. I use the HTMLEncode method to encode the timesheet data so that double quotes are encoded as " and therefore do not confuse Internet Explorer's parser. If I did not use this method, the page would emit a double-quote character, which Internet Explorer would think signified the end of the parameter value.

When Internet Explorer loads the Spreadsheet control on the client, the Spreadsheet control reads this persisted timesheet data from the HTMLData parameter and reloads the spreadsheet exactly as you saved it. Because the Spreadsheet control loads its state from the <param> tags, no extra flashing occurs as a result of loading a default spreadsheet and then reloading the saved timesheet data.

I promised that I would explain how to use the Spreadsheet control's Dirty property to prompt the user before he or she navigates away and loses unsaved changes. Let's look at that technique now:

```
Sub window_onBeforeUnload()
    If ssTimesheet.Dirty Then
        window.event.returnValue = "You have changed your timesheet " & _
            "but have not saved it!"
    End If 'Spreadsheet is dirty
End Sub 'window_onBeforeUnload()
```

The Window object raises an event called onBeforeUnload. From this event, you can request that Internet Explorer prompt the user, giving him or her the option to not leave the page. However, the way you do this is rather odd. You set the event's returnValue property to a string that appears in the middle of a message box displayed by Internet Explorer. The message box allows the user to click OK to leave the page or Cancel to stay. This method also works when the user attempts to close the browser window itself and will stop the window from closing if the user clicks the Cancel button.

SUBMITTING A TIMESHEET

Now that you know how to enable a user to save his or her timesheets, let's look at how to process a submitted timesheet. Submitting a timesheet means that the user has finished entering his or her work hours and wants to commit them to the database. I store work hours in another table and write individual rows for each day/project/employee combination. For example, if an employee entered hours for two projects for all five days of the week, I would write ten rows into the WorkHours table. This enables the user to later analyze his or her work hours across the three different dimensions: Time, Project, and Employee.

Submitting a timesheet follows the same code path as saving a timesheet because saving is part of the submitting process. However, if the user is submitting the timesheet, some extra code in SaveSubmit.asp runs. We will take a look at this on the next page.

WHY DOESN'T INTERNET EXPLORER JUST LET ME CANCEL THE CLOSE?

When I first tried to implement a warning to remind the user to save the spreadsheet, I thought I could simply set the returnValue property to False and stop the page from unloading. Then I saw the dialog box displayed by Internet Explorer and wondered why the Internet Explorer team had designed it to work that way.

I don't know for certain, but my guess is that this was done for security reasons. Imagine a malicious developer enticing you to visit a page that you can never leave. A script developer who can stop a page from unloading can do so under any circumstances, thus preventing you from leaving his or her page.

```
' If the action is submit, add to the WorkHours table
If m_sAction = "submit" Then
    Dim ss          ' Spreadsheet control
    Dim rng         ' Temporary Range object
    Dim dtStart     ' Starting date for timesheet
    Dim idProj      ' Temporary project ID
    Dim nHrs        ' Temporary hours
    Dim iDay        ' Day counter
    Dim sSQL        ' SQL statement buffer

    dtStart = Request.Form("StartDate")

    ' Create a spreadsheet in memory to parse the timesheet
    Set ss = server.CreateObject("OWC.Spreadsheet.9")

    ss.HTMLData = Request.Form("Timesheet")

    ' Begin a transaction
    m_cn.BeginTrans

    ' Delete any existing records for this timesheet
    m_cn.Execute "Delete from WorkHours where TimesheetID = " & _
        m_idTimesheet

    ' Now write the new work hours
    ' Start at the first project row on the Project ID column
    Set rng = ss.Range("b2")

    ' Loop until the project ID is blank
    While Len(trim(rng.Text)) > 0
        ' Get the current project ID
        idProj = trim(rng.Text)

        ' Loop over days
        For iDay = 1 To 5
            ' Check to see whether there were hours for this day
            nHrs = rng.Offset(0,iDay).Text
            If Len(trim(nHrs)) > 0 Then

                sSQL = "INSERT INTO WorkHours " & _
                    "(TimesheetID, Employee, WorkDate, "
                sSQL = sSQL & " ProjectID, WorkHours) Values("
                sSQL = sSQL & m_idTimesheet
                sSQL = sSQL & ", '" & Request.Form("Employee") & "'"
```

```
        sSQL = sSQL & ", #" & CDate(dtStart) + (iDay - 1) & "#"
        sSQL = sSQL & ", " & idProj
        sSQL = sSQL & ", " & nHrs & ")"

        m_cn.Execute sSQL

      End If 'Had some hours
    Next 'iDay

    ' Move down a row
    Set rng = rng.Offset(1)
  Wend 'While project ID is valid

  ' Commit the transaction
  m_cn.CommitTrans
End If 'submit
```

This fairly large block of code is actually quite simple in design. When the user submits his or her timesheet, the data received by the SaveSubmit.asp page is the large text stream of timesheet data along with a few other values, including the start date for the timesheet, the employee name, and the timesheet ID. However, you need to somehow extract the values in the individual cells of the timesheet. The way to do this is by using the Spreadsheet component again, but this time on the web server. Since the timesheet data came from the Spreadsheet control, a server-side Spreadsheet component can reload the data and parse out those individual cell values for you.

I create the Spreadsheet object and set its HTMLData property to the posted timesheet data. The Spreadsheet component immediately parses the string and reloads it into the spreadsheet. I next start a database transaction and delete all previous work hours for this timesheet since the user is submitting it again. I then loop over the project rows in the timesheet until reaching the end (an empty project ID). For each project, I loop over the days—the cells immediately to the right of the Project ID column—and insert a row for each day. For each row, I save the timesheet ID, date, employee name, project ID, and hours worked. When I am all done, I commit the database transaction and exit.

Using the Spreadsheet component on the server is the topic of the next chapter, so I will not discuss it in any more detail here. However, I will say that the Spreadsheet component is a handy mechanism for parsing HTML table data, so if you ever have a need for that, use an in-memory Spreadsheet component and set its HTMLData property to the HTML table data. Then just walk the cells, using the UsedRange property of the Worksheet object to determine how many rows and columns there were.

ANALYZING WORK HOURS

After you have saved all the work hours from all the submitted timesheets, you can let users analyze those work hours across the three dimensions: Time, Employee, and Project. There is naturally one measure or total: Hours Worked. You should not be surprised that the most appropriate control for analyzing this data is the Pivot-Table control.

You will likely want to experiment with using this part of the Timesheet solution, so after you have submitted a few timesheets, click the Analyze Hours button on the navigation bar. You will be prompted to find the Timesheets.mdb file. This is a natural drawback of using the Jet database engine in this solution. The Jet database engine is not a client/server database system. Instead, it requires file share access to the MDB file, and by default, the page cannot know where that file is if the page came from a web server. If you use SQL Server as the database store, the page can directly connect to the instance of SQL Server by name and not require any explicit file share path. Alternatively, you can use RDS as described in Chapter 5, but SQL Server is still a far better engine to use in a real multiuser and highly concurrent system.

After finding the Timesheets.mdb file, I initialize the PivotTable control using the following code from the Window object's onLoad event:

```
' Get the active view
Set view = ptHours.ActiveView
view.AutoLayout
view.DataAxis.InsertTotal _
    view.AddTotal("Total Hours", view.FieldSets("Hours").Fields(0), _
        c.plFunctionSum)

view.TotalBackColor = "Cornsilk"

ptHours.DisplayFieldList = True

' Sort by work date, showing most recent data first
view.Fieldsets("Work Date").Fields(0).SortDirection = _
    c.plSortDirectionDescending

view.DataAxis.RemoveFieldset view.FieldSets("Full Name")

view.Titlebar.Caption = "Work History"
```

Because this is a tabular data source, no predefined totals exist. However, it makes perfect sense for this solution to automatically create a total based on the Hours column in the WorkHours table. The code accomplishes this by using the active view's AddTotal method, passing the name of the new total, the field on which to base the total, and the summary function for the total (in this case, Sum). I also set the total's background color to "Cornsilk" to make it stand out from the detail data.

The code continues by sorting the data in descending order by the Work Date column so that the most recent work hours are shown first. It also removes the Full Name column from the view, leaving the Short Name column. I created these two columns for the case in which you are using Windows NT Challenge/Response Security. In such a case, the user names returned from the LOGON_USER server variable are in the form of *NT Domain Name\NT Logon Name*. This is not the most attractive or easy-to-read name, so I created an additional column that contains only the *NT Logon Name* part. This is the column left in the view by default. To see how I extracted only the second part of the name, see the QueryWorkHours stored query in the Timesheets.mdb file.

After the PivotTable is loaded, the user can filter, sort, and drag fields to the row or column axes to group the data and see subtotals for each group. Any programming technique I described in Chapter 7 (such as saved reports or top *N* filtering) can also be applied here, but for simplicity's sake, I left this page rather meager. To try it out, drag the Project field over the row area and drop it. Then drag the Work Date By Week fieldset from the PivotTable Field List window to the column area to view a cross tabulation of Hours Worked by Project by Week.

THE VISITORS LOG

The last technique I will discuss in this chapter is one that has been occurring without you even realizing it. Every time you run the Timesheet solution and view a page, the page logs this fact in the Visits table in the Timesheets.mdb database. If you have run the solution and saved or submitted a few timesheets, this table will already contain quite a bit of data. To view the data, click the Administration button on the navigation bar, and then click the View The Visitors Log button on the Site Administration page. The resulting page is much like the Hours Worked Analysis page just discussed, but this page shows the records of individual visits instead of the records of hours worked.

This type of logging can be an extremely useful debugging and monitoring tool, and it is actually not that invasive to the normal operation of the system. Most of the ASP pages in this solution have the following block of code near the top:

```
' Log the visit
Dim sPage        ' Name of this page
sPage = Request.ServerVariables("PATH_TRANSLATED")
sPage = Mid(sPage, InStrRev(sPage,"\")+1)
m_cn.Execute "INSERT INTO Visits Values ('" & sPage & "', '" & _
    m_sCurUser & "', #" & Now & "#)"
```

The code quickly determines the name of the current page by using the PATH_TRANSLATED server variable and looking for the last backslash (\) to extract only the page name. It then inserts a row into the database, passing the page name, the current user (obtained from the LOGON_USER server variable), and the current system time. You can encapsulate this into a method and make it even easier to use. You might also want to write more information into the log, such as the query string parameters passed to the page, the values of form fields, the cookie values (CERT_COOKIE), the server IP address on which the request arrived (LOCAL_ADDR), or even the entire set of HTTP headers (ALL_HTTP).

SUMMARY

The Timesheet solution is indicative of the kind of rich, real-world solutions you can build using the Office Web Components. In this chapter, I showed you how to create a grid-based data entry form, complete with interactive charts; how to save that content to a server; how to use the Spreadsheet component on the server to parse out individual cell values; and how to use the PivotTable component to analyze the results.

The next chapter will continue discussing the Spreadsheet component and will demonstrate how you can use this component on the server to perform spreadsheet-type calculations in response to input from a web page.

Chapter 9

Using Spreadsheet Models Programmatically

In Chapter 8, I demonstrated how you can use the Spreadsheet component as a sophisticated data-entry form in the Timesheet solution. In this chapter, I will demonstrate how you can use the Spreadsheet component for its more elemental service: the recalculation engine. The Loan Calculation solution described in this chapter uses the Spreadsheet component in a Microsoft Active Server Pages script to recalculate an existing spreadsheet model based on inputs and then display the results to the client browser as static HTML or an interactive Spreadsheet control.

ABOUT THE SOLUTION

Spreadsheets are probably the most commonly used programming language in existence. This might sound strange to you, since a spreadsheet does not look like any type of programming environment you might know. However, every time you enter a formula into a cell, you actually create a small program or add to the existing program created by all the formulas in the spreadsheet. This program is executed many times during the life of a spreadsheet and usually completes in a few seconds or less.

So, if spreadsheets are really just programs, why do users create spreadsheets instead of small Microsoft Visual Basic or C applications? Is it because you can create programs in a spreadsheet that are impossible to translate into other programming languages? Any talented developer can reimplement the most complex spreadsheet model in Basic or C code, so that can't be the reason. I believe that the real reason users create spreadsheets is threefold.

First, creating certain kinds of models is simply easier in a spreadsheet than in a traditional, procedural programming language. Spreadsheet programs are more *declarative,* meaning you declare your intentions by constructing formulas that reference other cells, and the spreadsheet recalculation engine determines a program's structure from those dependencies. The recalculation engine automatically determines the program's control of flow (which is where the program starts and how it proceeds), and although the flow is derived from your declarative dependencies, you do not explicitly control or dictate it. The recalculation engine's ability to automatically determine control of flow based on dependencies often makes iterative programs, recursive programs, or programs with tricky dependencies easier to express in a spreadsheet model.

Second, the function and cell reference programming model exposed by spreadsheets is much easier to grasp and use, especially for novice programmers. Even those who would never consider themselves programmers can create a SUM formula using Microsoft Excel's AutoSum command bar button. The user thinks of the spreadsheet model much like he or she thinks about a calculator. However, the SUM function creates a small program, equivalent to:

```
Function CellValue(Range)
    For Each cell In Range.Cells
        If IsNumeric(cell.Value) Then
            CellValue = CellValue + cell.Value
        End If
    Next
End Function
```

In fact, the real SUM function is much more complicated than this, handling all kinds of weird cases, such as numbers entered as text (entering a value of '2 into a cell causes the calculation engine to treat it as text, even though it is displayed as a number), error conditions, or Null values. If novice users had to write complex Visual Basic or C code every time they wanted to add up some numbers, they would toss their spreadsheet program and use their trusty solar calculators. Instead, users who are not trained in traditional programming, such as finance analysts, can easily build complex models that equate to hundreds of thousands of lines of procedural code.

Third, spreadsheets allow users to merge their programs with the report presentation they eventually want to see or print. In a more traditional programming language, you must write code (in addition to the code that performs calculations) to display the results in a professional-looking report. Spreadsheets allow users to perform both steps at once because the result of each formula is displayed in the same cell. Spreadsheet programs such as Excel also allow users to heavily format their reports, enabling users to produce any type of output imaginable. This formatting and presentation information is just as critical as the original mathematical model, as is often exemplified by users who spend more time formatting their spreadsheets than verifying the accuracy of their models.

Therefore, if you accept that spreadsheet models can be quite complex programs and that users not formally trained in programming can create and maintain them, it makes sense for you to use these models in business solutions that need them. Furthermore, if you accept that the presentation and formatting in a spreadsheet is just as important as the model itself, it also makes sense for you to use that formatting when displaying the results of the program. The Loan Calculation solution described in this chapter illustrates these two concepts, showing you how to use existing models in your own solutions and how to use the formatting captured in a spreadsheet to drive the presentation of the model's results.

The Loan Calculation solution illustrates a mortgage calculation complete with payment table. I bought my first house about a year ago, and I was surprised to discover just how complicated a mortgage calculation can be. How much could I afford? How much should I include in a down payment? How much difference does it make whether I get a 6.5 percent interest rate or a 7 percent rate? How much could I save in interest if I paid an extra $100 a month toward the principal? I quickly realized that I could model this in Excel, including a full payment table. I could have written a Visual Basic program to calculate all this, but it was much easier to model it in a spreadsheet—plus I could print a nicely formatted report of any calculation result. This solution uses that spreadsheet (enhanced a bit since its original creation), both on the web server and as the model for an interactive Spreadsheet control on the client. I built the model in Excel 2000, saved it in the HTML file format, and used it directly from the Spreadsheet component (more on how that works later). I made all changes to the model using Excel, which allowed me to use all the powerful editing features of that product.

TECHNIQUES ILLUSTRATED IN THIS SOLUTION

Like the previous solutions in this book, the Loan Calculation solution illustrates many techniques. Table 9-1 lists the various techniques and the source file in which each is implemented. Although I might not discuss each technique in this list, you can use it to find the appropriate source file and examine the implementation on your own. Also, you can use this table as a quick reminder of the techniques illustrated in this chapter's solution.

Technique	Source File
Saving an Excel 2000 spreadsheet in HTML file format.	Mortgage.htm
Using a saved spreadsheet in the Spreadsheet component.	Default.asp
Using the Spreadsheet component on the server to recalculate a model based on new inputs.	Default.asp
Generating an appropriate HTML version of the Spreadsheet component for the target browser.	Default.asp
Using the BrowserType object to determine capabilities of the client browser.	Default.asp
Using the table-layout style attribute to help Microsoft Internet Explorer render tables faster.	Default.asp
Translating between RGB color values and HTML color values.	Default.asp

Table 9-1. *Techniques demonstrated by the Loan Calculation solution.*

RUNNING THE SOLUTION

This solution is a mixture of HTML and ASP pages, but it is primarily one ASP page (Default.asp). To run this solution, you must run the Default.asp page using an http:// URL, meaning that you cannot simply double-click the files on the companion CD. The easiest way to set up the solution is to follow these steps:

1. If you are using a Microsoft Windows NT Server machine with Microsoft Internet Information Server, copy the files from the Chap09 directory on the companion CD to a directory under your web site root directory.

2. If you are running Personal Web Server (say on Windows 98 or Windows NT Workstation), copy the files to a directory on your computer and use the Personal Web Manager to add that directory as a virtual directory to your web site.

3. Type the URL for the directory into your browser—for example, *http://MyServer/Chap09*. The Default.asp page should load unless you have configured your web site to use another default filename. If you have, add */Default.asp* to the end of the URL.

THE MORTGAGE SPREADSHEET

I want to begin by familiarizing you with the mortgage spreadsheet model itself. This model drives most of the Loan Calculation solution, so you need to understand how it works before we talk about how the rest of the solution uses it. You can load the

Mortgage.htm file into Excel 2000, or you can load the original Mortgage.xls file. I created the Mortgage.htm file by simply saving the Mortgage.xls file as a web page. Figure 9-1 depicts the spreadsheet loaded into Excel 2000.

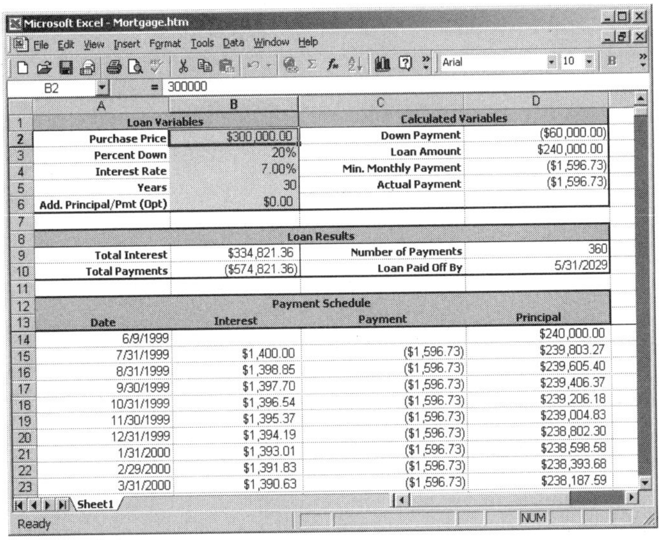

	A	B	C	D
1	Loan Variables		Calculated Variables	
2	Purchase Price	$300,000.00	Down Payment	($60,000.00)
3	Percent Down	20%	Loan Amount	$240,000.00
4	Interest Rate	7.00%	Min. Monthly Payment	($1,596.73)
5	Years	30	Actual Payment	($1,596.73)
6	Add. Principal/Pmt (Opt)	$0.00		
7				
8	Loan Results			
9	Total Interest	$334,821.36	Number of Payments	360
10	Total Payments	($574,821.36)	Loan Paid Off By	5/31/2029
11				
12	Payment Schedule			
13	Date	Interest	Payment	Principal
14	6/9/1999			$240,000.00
15	7/31/1999	$1,400.00	($1,596.73)	$239,803.27
16	8/31/1999	$1,398.85	($1,596.73)	$239,605.40
17	9/30/1999	$1,397.70	($1,596.73)	$239,406.37
18	10/31/1999	$1,396.54	($1,596.73)	$239,206.18
19	11/30/1999	$1,395.37	($1,596.73)	$239,004.83
20	12/31/1999	$1,394.19	($1,596.73)	$238,802.30
21	1/31/2000	$1,393.01	($1,596.73)	$238,598.58
22	2/29/2000	$1,391.83	($1,596.73)	$238,393.68
23	3/31/2000	$1,390.63	($1,596.73)	$238,187.59

Figure 9-1. *The mortgage spreadsheet in Excel 2000.*

The spreadsheet is divided into four sections:

- **The loan variables** Include purchase price, percent down, interest rate, years, and additional principal per payment.
- **The calculated variables** Include down payment, loan amount, minimum monthly payment, and actual payment.
- **The loan results** Include total interest paid, total payments, total number of payments, and date the loan will be paid off.
- **A full payment table** Lists each monthly payment, noting the interest paid, payment, and principal amount remaining.

You can change the values of any of the loan variables and see the entire spreadsheet recalculate to reflect the new values.

Most of the formulas used are fairly simple, with a few exceptions. The minimum monthly payment uses the PMT function, and the number of payments and the date the loan is paid off are complex formulas referencing the payment table. Although this is not an overly complex spreadsheet, the techniques I describe in this chapter work equally well with a wide variety of more complex models. There are certain limits, however, which I will discuss momentarily.

As you will no doubt notice, I have formatted the spreadsheet to make the organization clear and to highlight the portions you enter vs. the portions calculated by Excel or the Spreadsheet component. You might also notice that the spreadsheet is protected and that only the loan variable cells are unlocked. This helps preserve the integrity of the model, by prohibiting users from randomly changing the calculations. Additionally, I have created a frozen pane in the spreadsheet so that the three upper sections are always visible while you scroll the payment table below them. I mention this now so that when I discuss returning this model to an interactive Spreadsheet control later, you will note that these features are preserved.

The ability to open and modify the Mortgage.htm file in Excel is what makes this scenario so interesting. In many cases, one person in your organization knows how to create the spreadsheet model and maintain it, but another person is responsible for building the business solution that might employ the model. For example, a mortgage broker would know how to construct this spreadsheet model (and probably could point out all its inaccuracies), but a software developer writing a web site might not be knowledgeable enough to construct the model, since he or she would know how to write ASP scripts but not how to put together a mortgage. The broker can build and maintain the model in the easy and familiar tool Excel, and the web site developer can simply use that model without needing to know how it was built. This is much like using the Microsoft Scripting Runtime library or the BrowserType object described in the next section.

Note, however, that since the Spreadsheet component has only one sheet, any model you want to use with it must exist on one sheet in Excel. The Spreadsheet component cannot load a multisheet model saved from Excel. If you try to use one sheet from a multisheet model, the Spreadsheet component will just use the last result value from any calculation involving cells on the other sheets.

DETERMINING CLIENT BROWSER CAPABILITIES

In this solution, I want to illustrate how you can determine the browser requesting your ASP page and generate appropriate content based on its capabilities. If the browser supports COM controls, I want to send back an option to view the mortgage calculation in the Spreadsheet control, allowing users to see the content in full fidelity and directly edit the variables to perform a "what if" analysis. If the browser supports cascading style sheets (CSS), I want to use style attributes for formatting static results because style attributes provide more control over the table appearance and layout.

Those of you familiar with ASP programming might already know about the BrowserType object. For those who are not familiar with this object, I will briefly describe what it provides and how it works; for those who are familiar with it, I will show you how I am using it to determine what content to return.

The BrowserType object is supplied with IIS and is implemented in the MSWC library. It uses an INI file called Browscap.ini to determine what functionality a particular browser supports, such as COM controls. The object knows the type of client browser because all browsers by convention pass a string describing themselves when requesting information from a web server. This string contains the browser name, the full version number, and an indication of whether it is a beta or released version. The BrowserType object matches this string to one contained in the Browscap.ini file to determine which capabilities it should indicate the browser supports. Needless to say, the Browscap.ini file is the one that contains all the real information, and it is extremely important to keep this file up to date.

Using the BrowserType object is quite easy. The following code, taken from Default.asp, shows how I use it:

```
' Get information about the client browser
Set m_BrowserInfo = Server.CreateObject("MSWC.BrowserType")
On Error Resume Next
If IsNumeric(m_BrowserInfo.majorver) Then
    m_nMajorVer = CLng(m_BrowserInfo.majorver)
Else
    m_nMajorVer = 0
End If
If IsNumeric(m_BrowserInfo.minorver) Then
    m_nMinorVer = CLng(m_BrowserInfo.minorver)
Else
    m_nMinorVer = 0
End If
m_fCOMCtls = CBool(m_BrowserInfo.ActiveXControls)
m_sBrowserName = m_BrowserInfo.browser
On Error Goto 0


' Determine whether we should use CSS for formatting.
' Note: This assumes that if the browser's major
' version is 4 or greater, it supports CSS. That
' might not be the best test, and it would be better
' to include this in the Browscap.ini file for each browser.
m_fUseCSS = (m_nMajorVer >= 4)
```

As mentioned in the code comment above, there does not seem to be a property for determining whether the client browser supports CSS. In place of an explicit property, I check the major version number of the browser and if it is equal to or greater than 4, I assume that the browser does support CSS. Although Internet Explorer 3 supported some parts of the CSS standard, in this solution I assume that I should use CSS formatting attributes only for version 4 or later.

SO WHERE DO I FIND THE CURRENT BROWSCAP.INI FILE?

When I started to write the code for this chapter, I quickly built a page that would echo back to the client browser a True or False value indicating whether the page thought the browser supported COM controls. I started Internet Explorer version 5.0, hit the page, and promptly got back False. "What do you mean Internet Explorer 5.0 doesn't support COM controls?" I mused.

Of course, my problem was that I had installed IIS 4, which shipped long before Internet Explorer 5 released, and therefore, the Browscap.ini file on my machine had no information for Internet Explorer 5. So I wondered, "How do I get the most current version of this file?" I went to http://www.microsoft.com, went to the search page, and typed *browscap.ini*. Amazingly, the first search result was titled "Where can I find the latest browscap.ini file?" Following the link will eventually lead you to the cyScape.com site, where you can download the latest version of this file for free after viewing lots of advertising for their product that automatically downloads new versions for you.

If you run the Loan Calculation solution using Internet Explorer 5 and you have not downloaded the newest Browscap.ini file, you will notice that you do not have the option to view the results in an interactive Spreadsheet control. Update the file and you will see the option. You can also manually append *Interactive=on* to the end of the URL generated by the form to force the ASP script to return an interactive page.

THE MORTGAGE VARIABLES FORM

When first running this solution, you will see a form presented in your browser asking you for the assorted loan variables mentioned earlier. The page initially looks like Figure 9-2.

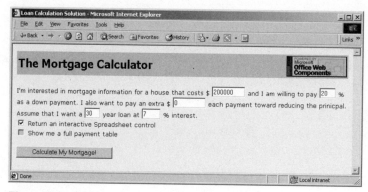

Figure 9-2. *The mortgage calculation input form.*

This form is generated from the ASP script, and certain parts are included only if the browser supports COM controls. Here is the section of the Default.asp page where I generate the form:

```
⋮
' ASP code above
If m_fUseCSS Then
%>
<td valign=middle><p
style="font-family:Tahoma;font-size:18pt;font-weight:bold;">
The Mortgage Calculator</p></td>
<%
Else
%>
<td valign=middle><p><font face=Tahoma size=5><b>
The Mortgage Calculator</b></font></p></td>
<%
End If
%>
<td align=right><img src="PoweredByMSOWC.gif"></td>
</tr></table>

<form action="Default.asp" method=Get>
<p><font face=Verdana size=2>
I'm interested in mortgage information for a house that costs $
<input type="text" name="Price" size=8 value=<%= m_nPrice %>>
and I am willing to pay
<input type="text" name="PctDown" size=2 value=<%= m_nPctDown * 100 %>>
% as a down payment. I also want to pay an extra $
<input type="text" name="AddPayment" size=8 value=<%= m_nAddPayment %>>
each payment toward reducing the principal.
Assume that I want a
<input type="text" name="Years" size=2 value=<%= m_nYears %>>
year loan at
<input type="text" name="Rate" size=3 value=<%= m_nRate * 100 %>>
% interest.

<% If m_BrowserInfo.ActiveXControls Then %>
<br>
<input type="checkbox" name=Interactive id=chkInteractive
<% If m_fInteractive Then %>

  checked
<% End If %>
onclick="chkPayTable.disabled=(chkInteractive.checked);"
>
```

(continued)

```
<label for=chkInteractive>
Return an interactive Spreadsheet control
</label>
<% End If %>

<br>
<input type="checkbox" name=PayTable id=chkPayTable
<% If m_fPayTable Then %>
 checked
<% End If %>
<% If m_fInteractive Then %>
 disabled
<% End If %>
>
<label for=chkPayTable>
Show me a full payment table
</label>

<p>
<input type="submit" value="Calculate My Mortgage!" id=btnSubmit>
</font></p>
</form>
⋮
```

At the beginning of this code and HTML segment, I use the m_fUseCSS flag to determine what kind of formatting I should use for the form header. If the flag is True, I can use more precise formatting of the fonts. The main part of the form is a standard HTML form, but it is arranged in a sentence-building manner. Near the end of the form, I use the ActiveXControls property of the BrowserType object to determine whether the client browser supports COM controls. If it does, I emit a check box (the Interactive check box) that the user can check to get the calculation results in an interactive Spreadsheet control instead of static HTML. If not, I don't emit the check box and the user will never know what he or she is missing. (This is why I'm not in marketing.)

Note that I also include a small in-line onClick event handler for the Interactive check box. It makes no sense to exclude the payment table from the Spreadsheet control, so I disable the PayTable check box if the Interactive check box is currently checked.

RECALCULATING THE MODEL ON THE SERVER

After adjusting the inputs you want, uncheck the Return An Interactive Spreadsheet Control check box and click the Calculate My Mortgage! button to see the results of the calculation. In this section, I will discuss how I perform the calculation on the server, which is what happens when you choose to not return an interactive Spreadsheet control. This is the default and the only choice if the client browser does not support COM controls.

The form in the previous section has an action attribute set to return to the same ASP page (Default.asp). It also contains default values for the various form fields so that you do not have to type them all yourself. When the user clicks the Calculate My Mortgage! button, Internet Explorer submits the form back to the server, appending the assorted loan variables and options to the URL as query strings. Let's look at the code that executes when this form is submitted and see how it processes the request. I first start by extracting the query string values:

```
' Get the query string values
m_nPrice = Request.QueryString("Price")
m_nPctDown = Request.QueryString("PctDown")
m_nRate = Request.QueryString("Rate")
m_nYears = Request.QueryString("Years")
m_nAddPayment = Request.QueryString("AddPayment")
m_fInteractive = (LCase(Request.QueryString("Interactive")) = "on")
m_fPayTable = (LCase(Request.QueryString("PayTable")) = "on")

' Validate the inputs
m_fValidInputs = ValidateInputs(m_nPrice, m_nPctDown, m_nRate, _
                                m_nYears, m_nAddPayment, m_sErrText)
    ⋮
```

Extracting the query string values is quite simple, as you have seen in the other solutions I've described so far. However, one thing that surprised me when I wrote this code was how check box values are sent to the server. I expected that a checked option would appear in the query string as "Interactive=True", "Interactive=1", or something that is coercible to a Boolean variable. However, a checked option is actually passed as "Interactive=on", and nothing is passed if the option is unchecked. Therefore, you must compare a check box option to the string "on" to determine whether the option was checked.

After extracting the inputs, I pass them to a function called ValidateInputs. This is a fairly long but uninteresting function that validates each input according to some business rules I encoded. For example, I enforce that number values are indeed numeric (in other words, the purchase price can't be "hello world"), that they are positive, that the Years value is between 1 and 30, and so on. You can examine this function on your own if you are curious to see how I checked for these conditions. However, do note that the function also converts the string values passed in the URL to real numeric variables (currency, long, and double) so that comparison operations yield the correct results. If you do not convert to numeric form, when you compare the string values "500" and "200000", the script engine will return "500" as greater than "200000" because "500" would sort alphabetically after "200000". I naively assumed that the Greater Than operator would first coerce strings to numbers if it could, but that is not how Microsoft VBScript works.

If the inputs are not valid, I do not load the model or perform any calculations. Instead, I return some nasty error text to the browser and ask the user to correct the bad input. Assuming that the inputs are valid, the code continues:

```
⋮
If m_fValidInputs Then
    If m_fInteractive Then
        ' Omitted for now...
    Else
        ' Write the results header, and flush it so that the user
        ' sees it right away
        If m_fUseCSS Then
            Response.Write "<h3 style=""font-family:Tahoma;" & _
                "font-size:14pt;" & _
                "font-weight:bold;background-color:" & _
                "#B0C4DE"">Your Mortgage Results...</h3>"
        Else
            Response.Write "<h3>Your Mortgage Results...</h3>"
        End If
        Response.Write "<script>"
        Response.Write "window.status = ""Calculating your mortgage" & _
            "...please stand by..."";"
        Response.Write "</script>"
        Response.Flush

        ' Create the Spreadsheet component, and load the mortgage model
        Set m_ssMort = Server.CreateObject("OWC.Spreadsheet.9")
        m_ssMort.HTMLURL = GetCurPath() & "Mortgage.htm"

        ' Push the new inputs into the model
        Dim rngInputs              ' Temporary Range reference
        Set rngInputs = m_ssMort.ActiveSheet.Range("B2:B6")
        rngInputs.Value = Array(m_nPrice, m_nPctDown, m_nRate, _
                            m_nYears, m_nAddPayment)

        ' Let the user know we are finished calculating
        Response.Write "<script>"
        Response.Write "window.status = ""Finished calculation. " & _
            "Displaying Results..."";"
        Response.Write "</script>"
        Response.Flush

        ' Output results
        If m_fPayTable Then
            WriteRange m_ssMort.ActiveSheet.UsedRange, m_fUseCSS
        Else
            WriteRange m_ssMort.ActiveSheet.Range("A1:D10"), m_fUseCSS
        End If
```

```
' Let the user know we are all done
Response.Write "<script>"
Response.Write "window.status = ""All done!"";"
Response.Write "</script>"
Response.Flush

    End If 'm_fInteractive
End If 'm_fValidInputs
```

The code first ensures that the inputs are valid. If the user requested an interactive Spreadsheet control, the code writes the appropriate <object> tag. I purposely omitted that code from this listing because I first want to describe how the server-side calculation and static output work. I will discuss the interactive version later in the chapter.

The code then writes a header with the text "Your Mortgage Results…" and writes a curious script block. As you will remember, any script code not contained in an event handler is executed immediately when it is parsed. After this script block sets the window's status bar text to indicate that the calculation is happening, it flushes the current output to the client. This causes the client browser to parse this script and display the status bar message. If the calculation takes a while, it gives the user some indication of what is happening.

The code then creates a Spreadsheet component as an in-memory object and will release that object when the script ends. (Refer to Chapter 6 for a discussion on why you should not keep an instance of the component in the Session or Application state object.) This code should look similar to the code in Chapter 8, except that this time I use the HTMLURL property to load the Mortgage.htm model. As I described in Chapter 2, the HTMLURL property can reference any URL that returns a document containing an HTML table. If that table has the extra attributes for the cell formula and full precision value written by Excel, the Spreadsheet component will notice them and load the model appropriately. Because the Spreadsheet control and Excel 2000 share the same HTML file format, what one writes, the other can read.

Pushing the inputs into the Spreadsheet component is also relatively simple, though I use a trick here to improve performance. Whenever you set the value of a cell that has dependencies, the Spreadsheet component will recalculate all the dependent cells. This happens both when you set the cell value programmatically and through the user interface. If you need to set five input values (as I do here), it is much more efficient to set them all in one operation and then let the Spreadsheet component recalculate the model once based on all the new values. To accomplish this, set the Range object's Value property to an array of values, one element for each cell. The Spreadsheet component will set all values and then perform one recalculation. In this case, my range is one-dimensional, so it is obvious that each array value maps to the corresponding cell in the range. However, if the range is two-dimensional, the Spreadsheet control expects the array values to be in row/column orientation, meaning the first dimension represents the rows and the second dimension represents the columns.

After setting the values, the results are recalculated and ready for output. I send back another script block that sets the status bar to indicate that I am finished recalculating and now writing back the output. If you run this solution, you will notice that the recalculation takes little time compared to the time it takes for the server to return the results and the browser to load them into view. I will discuss the details of writing the results in the next section, but do note that I use the m_fPayTable flag to determine how much of the spreadsheet to write back. If the user wants the full payment table (360 rows), I write back the entire used range. If the user does not want the full table, I write only the top three sections, which is the range A1:D10.

GENERATING HTML FROM THE SPREADSHEET COMPONENT

On the surface, generating HTML from the Spreadsheet component that you can return to the client browser seems as easy as writing the HTMLData property, just as we did in Chapter 8. However, it is not quite that easy, and there will be many times that you actually will want to send back more basic HTML so that older browsers can display the results.

In Chapter 8, I used the HTMLData property as a way to get the persistence stream for the Spreadsheet control and write that stream to a database table. Later on, I could retrieve that stream and reload the Spreadsheet control by setting the property. In this case, I would want the Spreadsheet component to write a cell value only once instead of writing both a full precision, unformatted version and the formatted display version. By writing the full precision value only, the text stream is smaller; therefore, it transmits over the network more quickly and takes up less space in the database.

In the Loan Calculation solution, I actually want the display value and not the full precision, unformatted version of the value. Unfortunately, we did not have time in this version of the components to implement two properties, one that returns the full precision values and one that returns the display values, so only the former is available. This makes it easy to save and reload the Spreadsheet component but much harder to render its contents as HTML that a browser can display. We hope to offer both properties in the next version.

However, the code to write a range as an HTML table is included in this solution, and I will walk you through it in this section. You can use this code in your own solutions whenever you need to get an HTML representation of a range in the Spreadsheet control. The method, WriteRange in Default.asp, begins like this:

```
Sub WriteRange(rngOut, fUseCSS)
    ' Local variables
    Dim rngRow                  ' Current row
    Dim rngCell                 ' Current cell
    Dim rngMerge                ' Merged cell range
    Dim cxTblWidth              ' Width of the output table


    ' Begin by writing the open table tag
    Response.Write "<table cellspacing=0 cellpadding=2 "

    ' If using CSS formatting, use a fixed table layout
    ' and emit the <col> tags. The fixed table layout
    ' increases perceived rendering speed dramatically since the
    ' browser doesn't have to parse and calculate the entire
    ' table before beginning to render it.
    If fUseCSS Then
        Response.Write " border=0 "
        cxTblWidth = 0
        For Each rngCell In rngOut.Columns
            cxTblWidth = cxTblWidth + rngCell.ColumnWidth
        Next 'rngCell
        Response.Write " style=""table-layout:fixed;width:" & _
                    cxTblWidth & """>"
        For Each rngCell In rngOut.Columns
            Response.Write "<col width=" & rngCell.ColumnWidth & ">"
        Next 'rng
    Else
        ' Not using CSS, so just use a 1-weight border
        Response.Write "border=1>"
    End If

    Response.Flush
    ⋮
```

This method accepts the range to write and a flag indicating whether the function should use CSS attributes for formatting. I start by writing the first part of the <table> tag, specifying a *cellspacing* of 0 and a *cellpadding* of 2. (Cellspacing is the number of pixels between cells, and cellpadding is the number of pixels in the margin between a cell wall and its content.) Then I check the fUseCSS flag and write the rest of the <table> tag accordingly.

If the function is asked to use CSS, it performs a few tasks that dramatically speed up rendering in Internet Explorer. First it sets the borders explicitly to 0. Internet Explorer seems to default the borders to 0, while Netscape Navigator seems to default them to 1—when I explicitly set them to 0, the results look identical in both browsers. Next I quickly calculate the total width of all the columns in the output range and write it as the overall table width. I also use the "table-layout:fixed" style setting, which tells the browser that it should use a fixed width for the table, and I write column width values for each column as <col> tags. If the browser knows that the table will be a certain width and that all columns will have a fixed width, it can begin to display the content as soon as it gets the first row. If the table is not fixed, the browser must first parse the entire table and determine how large to make the table based on all the content. Since a spreadsheet has fixed column widths, you can give the browser a hint that the table will be fixed. This will dramatically increase the speed at which the browser loads and displays the results.

If the function is not supposed to use CSS, I instead set the borders explicitly to 1. When formatting without CSS, you cannot control individual cell borders within a table. Instead, you can control only the size of all cell borders for the entire table. Since the mortgage spreadsheet does use cell borders to denote various sections, I chose to turn borders on for the whole table in the non-CSS case so that there is some semblance of cell borders. If you do not like that, you can change this to read "border=0". After writing the starting <table> tag, I call the Flush method on the Response object to send the start of the table to the client browser.

The WriteRange method continues like this:

```
    ⋮
' Loop over all rows and columns in the range
For Each rngRow In rngOut.Rows
    If fUseCSS Then
        Response.Write "<tr height=" & _
                        rngRow.RowHeight + 2 & ">"
    Else
        Response.Write "<tr>"
    End If
    ⋮
```

The basic plan for writing a range is to walk row-by-row, cell-by-cell and write <tr> and <td> tags for each row and cell, respectively. This block of code is the start of the outer row loop and uses the For Each syntax over the Range object's Rows collection. For each row, it writes a <tr> tag, formatting it with an explicit row height if fUseCSS is True. I add 2 to the row height here because the output looks a little less cramped with an extra 2 pixels per row.

Within each row, the code continues:

```
    ⋮
For Each rngCell In rngRow.Cells
    ' Check whether this cell is in a merged cell range
    ' If so, process it only if it is the upper-left
    ' cell in the range (the owner cell). Otherwise,
    ' ignore the cell and go to the next one.
    If rngCell.HasMergeCells And (rngCell.Address <> _
        rngCell.MergeArea.Cells(1,1).Address) Then
            ' Ignore this cell
    Else
```

```
If rngCell.HasMergeCells Then
    ' Get the merged cell area
    Set rngMerge = rngCell.MergeArea

    ' Write a <td> tag with colspan and rowspan
    ' attributes to emulate the merged cell
    Response.Write "<td colspan=" & _
        rngMerge.Columns.Count & _
        " rowspan=" & _
        rngMerge.Rows.Count
Else
    ' Write the starting <td> tag
    Response.Write "<td"
End If
⋮
```

I use the For Each syntax again to loop over all cells within the current row. For each cell, I first check whether the cell is merged. (A cell is merged if it is anywhere within a merged cell range.) The *owner cell* of a merged range is the upper-left cell, and this is the cell that actually defines the value for the merged range. If the current cell is part of a merged area but not the owner cell, I can ignore it because I would have already written a <td> tag with the appropriate rowspan and colspan attributes to cover this current cell. This is one critical difference between the Spreadsheet control and HTML tables. In the Spreadsheet control, the individual cells in a merged range still exist, though they have no value. In HTML tables, there is only one <td> tag for the merged area, and you indicate how big it should be by specifying the rowspan and colspan attributes.

After dealing with the merged cell case, the code continues as follows:

```
⋮
If fUseCSS Then
    ' Start the style attribute
    Response.Write " style="""

    ' Write the cell's alignment
    Response.Write " text-align:" & _
        SSAlign2HTML(rngCell) & ";"

    ' Write the cell background color
    Response.Write "background-color:" & _
        RGB2HTML(rngCell.Interior.Color) & ";"

    ' Write the font information for the cell
    Response.Write "font-family:" & _
        rngCell.Font.Name & ";"
    Response.Write "font-size:" & _
        rngCell.Font.Size & "pt;"
```

(continued)

```
Response.Write "color:" & _
    RGB2HTML(rngCell.Font.Color) & ";"
If rngCell.Font.Bold Then
    Response.Write "font-weight:bold;"
End If
If rngCell.Font.Italic Then
    Response.Write "font-style:italic;"
End If

' Write the cell border info. (We can do
' this in CSS because it supports per-cell
' borders.) If the cell is merged, write
' the borders for the whole merged area
' and not the cell itself.
If rngCell.HasMergeCells Then
    Response.Write _
        GetBorderStyles(rngMerge, 1, "bottom")
    Response.Write _
        GetBorderStyles(rngMerge, 2, "left")
    Response.Write _
        GetBorderStyles(rngMerge, 3, "right")
    Response.Write _
        GetBorderStyles(rngMerge, 4, "top")
Else
    Response.Write _
        GetBorderStyles(rngCell, 1, "bottom")
    Response.Write _
        GetBorderStyles(rngCell, 2, "left")
    Response.Write _
        GetBorderStyles(rngCell, 3, "right")
    Response.Write _
        GetBorderStyles(rngCell, 4, "top")
End If

' End the style attribute and the <td> tag
Response.Write """>"
    ⋮
```

This code block is executed when fUseCSS is True, and it writes a rather lengthy style attribute for the <td> tag. This code uses a number of helper functions to translate between Spreadsheet control settings or constants and those defined by the CSS standard. I will not describe all these functions in detail here, but I do want to discuss one that is rather tricky.

The Spreadsheet control natively expresses colors as RGB values, just as most other Windows programs do. RGB stands for Red Green Blue, which describes the physical layout of the various bits in the RGB value (red value at the lowest position, then green value, then blue value). For example, the color pure red has the decimal value 255 and the hexadecimal value 0000FF. The color pure blue has the decimal value 16711680 and the hexadecimal value FF0000. However, HTML colors are laid out in exactly the opposite manner (BGR). The color pure red has the hexadecimal value FF0000, and the color pure blue has the hexadecimal value 0000FF. When writing <td> tag background colors, you must write an HTML color value, so you need to translate between the two. Fortunately, the mapping is fairly easy, and the following function, RGB2HTML, converts between the two:

```
Function RGB2HTML(rgb)
    RGB2HTML = Hex(rgb)
    ' Hex returns a single zero for black
    ' Change it to six zeros if it is
    ' just one zero
    If RGB2HTML = "0" Then
        RGB2HTML = "#000000"
    Else
        ' If not zero, we have to convert between RGB values
        ' as hexadecimal strings and the way HTML colors are represented
        ' HTML colors are laid out as BGR instead of RGB, so this
        ' line flips the first two and last two hexadecimal digits
        RGB2HTML = "#" & Mid(RGB2HTML, 5) & Mid(RGB2HTML, 3, 2) & _
            Left(RGB2HTML, 2)
    End If
End Function 'RGB2HTML()
```

This function simply uses the Hex function to convert the RGB value to a hexadecimal string and then uses the Mid and Left functions to swap the first two (red) and last two (blue) characters.

If the method was instructed to not use CSS for formatting, the WriteRange method continues with this block of code:

```
    ⋮
    Else
        ' No CSS formatting (use <font>, <b>, and <i> tags)

        ' Write the cell's alignment
        Response.Write " align=" & SSAlign2HTML(rngCell)

        ' Write the cell background color
        Response.Write " bgcolor=" & _
            RGB2HTML(rngCell.Interior.Color) & _
            ">"
```

(continued)

```
                    ' Write the font information for the cell
                    Response.Write "<font face=" & rngCell.Font.Name & _
                        " size=" & _
                        Points2HTML(rngCell.Font.Size) & _
                        " color=" & _
                        RGB2HTML(rngCell.Font.Color) & _
                        ">"

                    ' If the cell is bold, write a <b> tag
                    If rngCell.Font.Bold Then
                        Response.Write "<b>"
                    End If

                    ' If the cell is italic, write an <i> tag
                    If rngCell.Font.Italic Then
                        Response.Write "<i>"
                    End If
                End If 'fUseCSS
                :
```

This is similar to the previous code, except that it uses <font>, , and <i> tags to encode the cell formatting information. Note that I also have to translate between explicit font point sizes and the HTML font size value, which is on a scale from 1 to 7. This doesn't guarantee a purely accurate rendering at the client, but it is as close as HTML can get.

The WriteRange method continues by writing the current cell's formatted display text:

```
            :
            ' Write the cell's formatted text
            If Len(rngCell.Text) > 0 Then
                Response.Write rngCell.Text
            Else
                Response.Write " "
            End If
            :
```

Note that I write a   symbol if the cell's text is blank. If I do not, Internet Explorer will not draw the cell border properly. The   symbol is decoded by the browser as a nonbreaking space, so the user sees only a space and not the   character string.

The WriteRange method continues by writing the closing and </i> tags if fUseCSS is False and then ends the loops like so:

```
            :
            ' Close the table cell
            Response.Write "</td>"
```

```
        End If 'Ignore nonowning merged cell
    Next 'rngCell

    ' Close the table row
    Response.Write "</tr>"

    ' Flush every 10 rows
    If (rngRow.Row Mod 10) = 0 Then
        Response.Flush
    End If
Next 'rngRow

' End by writing the closing table tag
Response.Write "</table>"

End Sub 'WriteRange()
```

I periodically flush the content I have written back to the client browser. After ending a row, if the row number is evenly divisible by 10 (that is, every 10 rows), I call the Flush method of the Response object. At the end of this method, I write the closing </table> tag and exit the method. The code that calls this method will call the final Flush method to send back the last part of the table.

ANOTHER APPROACH TO GENERATING HTML FOR A RANGE

Although the HTMLData property does not include the display value in between the starting <td> and ending </td> tags, the Spreadsheet control will include the display value in HTML that it generates when you copy a range of cells to the clipboard. It does this so that a user can copy some cells and paste them into an HTML document as a table, but you can also take advantage of this programmatically. The Range object has a Copy method that copies the range's contents to the clipboard in the CF_HTML clipboard format. Although VBScript does not provide a function to read from the clipboard, you can retrieve the generated HTML from the clipboard with the help of a custom-written COM object that accesses the clipboard for you.

However, the HTML generated by the Spreadsheet control relies heavily on CSS formatting, so you might still want to use something like the WriteRange function I just discussed. When you write the range yourself, you have total control over how the content is generated and can add formatting not present in the spreadsheet, such as alternating background colors in a long table of numbers.

RETURNING AN INTERACTIVE SPREADSHEET COMPONENT

If the client browser supports COM controls (indicated by the ActiveXControls property of the BrowserType object), I allow the user to request an interactive Spreadsheet control containing the results of his or her mortgage calculation. The code to output this is amazingly easy:

```
' Write an object tag for the Spreadsheet control
' and a couple parameter tags to tell it where the model is
Response.Write "<object " & _
    "classid=""clsid:0002E510-0000-0000-C000-" & _
    "000000000046"" style=""width:100%;height:75%;""" & _
    "id=ssMort>"
Response.Write "<param name=HTMLURL value=""Mortgage.htm"">"
Response.Write "<param name=DataType value=""HTMLURL"">"
Response.Write "</object>"
Response.Write "<script language=vbscript>"
Response.Write "ssMort.ActiveSheet.Range(""B2:B6"").Value="
Response.Write "Array(" & m_nPrice & "," &  m_nPctDown & "," & _
    m_nRate & "," & m_nYears & "," & _
    m_nAddPayment & ")"
Response.Write "</script>"
```

To cause the browser to load an interactive Spreadsheet control into the page, I simply have to write back an <object> tag with the appropriate COM class ID. To tell the Spreadsheet control from where to load the model, I include two <param> tags, one specifying the relative URL to the Mortgage.htm spreadsheet model and another telling the Spreadsheet to use this instead of expecting an HTMLData <param> tag. Because the HTMLURL property loads via HTTP and a URL, the Spreadsheet control can load the same file I used on the web server.

The only remaining task is pushing the loan variables into the Spreadsheet control so that it will recalculate the mortgage information based on the inputs. I do that by emitting the same code I used to push the values into the Spreadsheet component on the server, and since this script executes as soon as it is parsed, the new values are almost instantly set into the Spreadsheet control.

SUMMARY

This chapter demonstrated how you can use existing spreadsheet models as a part of your solution via the Spreadsheet component. Although the Loan Calculation solution used the model in the context of an ASP script, you can just as easily use models in Visual Basic or C++ applications that utilize the Spreadsheet component. For example, if your product discount model exists in a spreadsheet, you can use that spreadsheet in an order entry application to determine the discount rate for a certain customer ordering a certain quantity of product.

The next chapter will also discuss the Spreadsheet component but will focus on getting real-time data into the component using its property-binding feature.

Chapter 10

Real-Time Stock Portfolio

In Chapter 2, I introduced you to the Spreadsheet component's property-binding feature. In this chapter, I will describe property binding in great detail and show you how to implement a solution involving real-time data and the Spreadsheet component. I will also describe how to enable your users to save the current state of the Spreadsheet control in a local copy of the web page—a new feature of Microsoft Internet Explorer 5.

ABOUT THE SOLUTION

As I discussed in Chapter 6, most businesses have some set of metrics by which they measure the health of a project, a production process, or the entire company. Often those metrics are fairly stable, and a user needs to examine them only once a day, week, or month. However, occasionally those metrics are exceptionally volatile, changing nearly every second, and spreadsheet models that use them as input need to recalculate as they change. Common examples of real-time metrics include current call loads at a call center, production line reject rates, network server statistics, and financial market information.

To illustrate integrating real-time data into the Spreadsheet component, I built a real-time stock portfolio application. Using this application, you can build a custom stock portfolio and watch the net worth change as prices fluctuate throughout the trading day. (Note that values will not change after the market closes at 4:00 P.M. Eastern time.) Since the solution gets its data from the Microsoft Investor web site (http://www.investor.msn.com), the data is actually delayed by 20 minutes. However, the technique would be exactly the same if you purchased a real-time data feed from the market itself. You can also save your current portfolio to a new local file using Internet Explorer's File|Save As menu command. Although you might think saving the current state of the control should require no additional work, it actually does. I will describe the details and hidden traps of this later in the chapter.

Stock prices have a fairly universal appeal, and it is relatively easy to get stock information (delayed 20 minutes) from the Internet, so this type of data makes for an easy example. However, you can use the same techniques I discuss in this chapter to integrate any type of highly dynamic data. The key is to expose that data as properties of a COM object, which is quite simple using Microsoft Visual Basic.

> **WARNING** The Spreadsheet component can handle quite a few property bindings in one spreadsheet, but its performance will degrade proportionally to the number of bindings you create. To test the scalability of this feature, I created a Clock object that exposes a Time property. The clock sends a property change notification every second, causing the Spreadsheet control to get the new time value. To start with, I inserted the formula "=document.Clock.Time" into the first cell and let it run for a while. The cell's value updated every second, and everything seemed to work well. I then entered that same formula into 200 spreadsheet cells and let the sample run for a while. The Spreadsheet control handled it, but it took longer than 1 second to process all the change notifications and get all the new values. Instead of seeing the cells update every second, I saw them update every 2 seconds. You should use this technique only when you have few cells to update or when the properties do not change faster than the Spreadsheet control can process the change notifications.

TECHNIQUES ILLUSTRATED IN THIS SOLUTION

As in the other solutions we have discussed, the Real-Time Stock Portfolio solution illustrates many techniques. Table 10-1 lists the various techniques and the source file in which each technique is illustrated. Although I might not discuss each technique in this list, you can use it to find the appropriate source file and examine the implementation on your own. You also can refer back to this table for a quick reminder of the techniques implemented in this chapter's solution.

Technique	Source File
Creating property bindings in the Spreadsheet control.	Default.htm
Implementing a control in Visual Basic to expose real-time data as properties.	Default.htm
Using the saveSnapshot behavior in Internet Explorer to enable saving the current state to a local file.	Default.htm
Using the Microsoft Internet Transfer control to access a web site programmatically.	StockTicker.ctl
Using the Spreadsheet control to parse an HTML table.	StockTicker.ctl

Table 10-1. *Techniques demonstrated by the Real-Time Stock Portfolio solution.*

RUNNING THE SOLUTION

This solution requires no explicit setup. You can run this solution directly from the companion CD by opening the Default.htm file in the Chap10 folder. To install this solution on a web server, copy the Default.htm and Ticker.cab files from the Chap10 folder to your web site.

The first time you run the solution, you might see a prompt asking you to confirm the installation of the Ticker.cab file, which contains the StockTicker.ocx file. You might also receive a prompt to install the WinInet control, which is used by the Stock Ticker control to access web sites. Both of the controls should automatically install and initialize if you give your approval. If you do not allow the installation, the solution will not function. Note that if you run the files directly from your file system, you will not see a prompt because that scenario is considered safe by Internet Explorer, meaning a page can load and install any content without warning.

THE NUTS AND BOLTS OF PROPERTY BINDING

Before I describe the specifics of the Real-Time Stock Portfolio solution, I want to describe the general property-binding mechanism used by the Spreadsheet component. The Spreadsheet component uses the standard COM mechanism for property binding, known as the IPropertyNotifySink interface. This interface can be implemented by any component that wants to know when a property of a COM object has changed. The COM object calls methods on this interface to let the listening component (in this case, the Spreadsheet component) know when a *bindable* property value has changed. Any time the Spreadsheet component hears that a property value has changed, it asks the COM object for the new value, sets the bound cell's value to the new property value, and recalculates any dependent cells. Figure 10-1 diagrams the whole process.

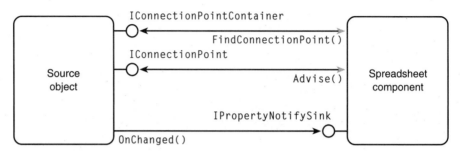

Figure 10-1. *The COM property-binding architecture.*

Technically, the COM standard requires a source object to let a listening object know about changes to properties only if the source object has marked those properties as bindable, though many source objects will notify the listener when any property changes. You can mark object properties as bindable by including the bindable keyword in the property's declaration in your type library. If you build an object in C++, the relevant part of your IDL file will look like this:

```
interface _Class1 : IDispatch {
    [id(0x68030000), propget, bindable]
    HRESULT BindableProp([out, retval] VARIANT* rhs);
};
```

In Visual Basic, you can declare a property bindable by checking an option in the Procedure Attributes dialog box. While your class code module is open, choose the Tools|Procedure Attributes menu item and click the Advanced button to fully expand the dialog box. Select the property using the Name drop-down list at the top of the dialog box, and select the Property Is Data Bound check box. Figure 10-2 shows the Procedure Attributes dialog box and the relevant check box.

When the source object wants to indicate that a property value has changed, it calls the OnChanged method on the listening component's IPropertyNotifySink interface. Visual Basic makes this rather easy by offering the PropertyChanged method on the UserControl object or, as you will see soon, on public classes marked as simple data bound. Any time a source object tells the Spreadsheet component that a bound property has changed, the Spreadsheet component requests the property's new value, sets the new value into the bound cell, and recalculates any dependent cells. All this happens automatically, without requiring any special code.

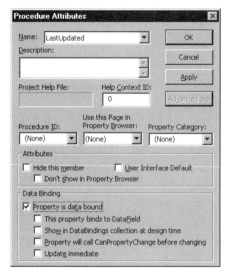

Figure 10-2. *The Procedure Attributes dialog box.*

Ordinarily, the Spreadsheet control is smart enough to request new values for only those properties that have actually changed and update only the cells referencing those changed properties. However, there is one special case in which the Spreadsheet control obtains new values whenever the spreadsheet is recalculated, regardless of whether the source control has raised a property change notification. If you use parentheses anywhere in your property-binding expression, the Spreadsheet control will consider the formula volatile and will put it into a *semi-calc* mode. By convention, the Spreadsheet control evaluates semi-calc cells every time it recalculates any part of the model. The classic example of a semi-calc function is the NOW function, which returns the current system time.

For example, suppose you enter a property binding that looks like this:

```
=document.MyControl.MyMethod(A1).MyProperty
```

The Spreadsheet control will consider this formula volatile and will evaluate the formula (requesting a new property value) whenever the control recalculates any part of the spreadsheet, even if this cell has no dependency on the changed cells. Sometimes this is a desirable behavior because it always ensures that the newest possible value is in the spreadsheet. However, if obtaining the new property value is a time-consuming operation, you will want to avoid this side effect. To circumvent this, make sure you have no parentheses in the property-binding formula. This might be difficult if your real-time source control can take a dynamic parameter, such as a stock symbol. If the possible values the source can return are limited or fixed, make the values individual properties instead of using a single method or an indexed property that requires parentheses in your expression.

Note that the Stock Ticker control in this solution does require that you use parentheses in property-binding formulas. That was somewhat unavoidable, as I wanted to let users enter any stock symbol in the left column and see real-time data to the right of that symbol. I could have designed the Stock Ticker control to fetch data for only one symbol at a time and then used script to set a CurrentSymbol property to the newly entered symbol in the spreadsheet. The downside of that approach is that it requires placing many instances of the Stock Ticker control on the page, each of which would make separate requests against the Microsoft Investor web site. This would decrease the scalability of the control. Because the control gets new values for all symbols at the same time and then caches those values until the next refresh, the semi-calc behavior is not inconvenient in this solution.

The key aspect of the Spreadsheet control's property-binding feature in relation to real-time data is that the control continues to listen for and process property change notifications even while the user edits cell formulas or applies formatting. Users can continue to augment their spreadsheets as new values flow into the model.

Note that the spreadsheet can establish property bindings only when it is hosted in Internet Explorer. You cannot use the property-binding feature in other containers.

THE STOCK PORTFOLIO SPREADSHEET

Now that you know how property binding works, let's examine the specific use of property binding in the Real-Time Stock Portfolio solution. It might be helpful to run the solution as you read the rest of this chapter so that you can follow along and see it in action.

The stock portfolio spreadsheet is logically divided into two sections: The top part is the real-time information and is where the property-binding formulas are located. The bottom section is for building a personal portfolio, and the cells in that section retrieve current prices from the Last Sale cells in the upper section. The Totals row at the bottom of the spreadsheet provides net worth totals for the entire portfolio. You can insert new rows into either section to track more symbols or to add more items to your portfolio—just remember to copy the formulas from the previous row's cells to the new row. Figure 10-3 depicts the stock portfolio spreadsheet model.

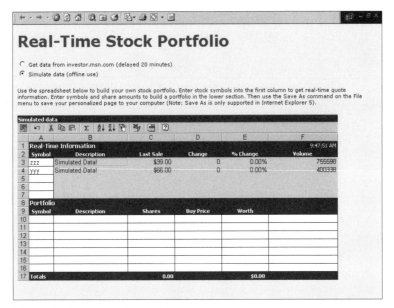

Figure 10-3. *The stock portfolio spreadsheet.*

I used Microsoft FrontPage 2000 to create this page and the spreadsheet model within it. I set the ViewableRange property to A1:F17 and set the AutoFit property to True, causing the Spreadsheet control to automatically resize to the width and height of the viewable range. Because I did not protect the spreadsheet, you can view any of the cell formulas and insert or delete columns or rows from the spreadsheet. The interesting formulas are in the B3:F7 range. Let's look at the formula in C3:

```
=IF(ISBLANK(A3),"",document.stockticker.quote(A3).LastSale)
```

The formula first checks to see whether the leftmost cell in the row (A3) is blank. If it is, the formula puts a blank string into the cell. If not, the formula establishes a property binding with a control that has the ID "stockticker". (For a refresher on the property-binding syntax, see Chapter 2.) The formula binds to the LastSale property of the object returned from the stock ticker's Quote method. The Quote method accepts a stock symbol as a parameter and returns a Quote object for that symbol. I will describe the Stock Ticker control and the Quote object in more detail in the next section. In the meantime, note that you can use cell references in a property binding. In this case, I use the value from A3 as the parameter to the Quote method. When the Spreadsheet control requests the current value of the LastSale property, it passes the current value of A3 as the input argument to the Quote method. If the value of A3 changes, this cell (C3) is considered a dependent and the Spreadsheet control will automatically recalculate C3, passing the new value of A3.

The portfolio section of the spreadsheet uses the VLOOKUP function to find the symbol you entered in column A and retrieve the symbol description and current price. For example, the formula in cell B11 looks like this:

```
=IF(ISBLANK(A11),"",VLOOKUP(A11,$A$3:$B$7,2,FALSE))
```

If the value in the leftmost cell in the row (A11) is blank, this formula makes B11 blank as well. If A11 contains a symbol, the formula passes four arguments to the VLOOKUP function: the value of A11, the range where the real-time symbols and descriptions lie ($A$3:$B$7), the column index 2, and a flag indicating that I want an exact match. The second argument to the VLOOKUP function is a range. VLOOKUP searches the first column in this range for the value passed to the first argument. If it finds a match, it returns the corresponding value in the second column of the range, which in this case is the symbol description.

THE STOCK TICKER CONTROL

The stock portfolio spreadsheet is quite simple, and the only thing required to make new data values appear in the spreadsheet is the property-binding formula syntax I illustrated earlier. However, implementing the source control that actually gets the data and notifies the Spreadsheet control when values have changed is more difficult.

For this solution, I implemented a control (Stock Ticker) in Visual Basic 6 that screen-scrapes stock information from HTML pages returned by the Microsoft Investor web site. This was an approach of last resort, and I would not at all recommend this technique as a reliable way for obtaining live data. The Stock Ticker control needed an easy way to obtain live stock price information, and the few COM controls I found that claimed to deliver this information required complex setups or did not work through a firewall. Thus, I was left with extracting data from an HTML page, but this is littered with limitations.

First, the solution will work only as long as the Microsoft Investor web site retains its current structure and page layout. If the source URL I use in the Stock Ticker control no longer returns stock information, the control will no longer know how to obtain data. If the Investor site inserts a new column in its data results tables, the Stock Ticker control will also fail. Why is this control so fragile? The answer to this question helps us understand why XML and XSL (Extensible Stylesheet Language) were invented. Indeed, the correct future implementation of this kind of control should be XML-based.

Second, HTML is a presentation format. In HTML, data and formatting are mixed together into one stream of text, and extracting just the data values is problematic because they are not explicitly marked. HTML is also an inefficient way to transmit only data values because all the extra formatting and layout information is unnecessary when the requesting program is simply interested in the data values. In many ways, HTML is a step back toward mainframe and minicomputer terminals, and all the lessons learned from client-server computing are now being repeated in the world of Internet technologies—which brings us to XML and XSL.

XML and XSL represent an attempt to separate data from its presentation. XML defines a mechanism for expressing structured and semistructured data as a hierarchical set of nodes. XSL offers a way to translate those nodes into another set of nodes, most commonly in HTML format. The Stock Ticker control is the perfect example of a component that is interested only in the data portion and therefore needs only the XML nodes. This component could extract the values it needs by finding the appropriate node in the hierarchy by name, and it would not have to rely on a specific, physical onscreen layout.

Furthermore, data expressed in XML can be locale-independent, transmitting numbers and dates in ISO standard formats that programs can accurately interpret no matter what the source and destination locales are. For example, a date transmitted as HTML is generally formatted in some friendly manner because users viewing a web page do not want to see dates formatted as 03-01-1999T00:00:00. However, date formatting is extremely locale specific. If the data source is in the UK, I might get dates in the dd/mm/yy format; however, a U.S. machine expects those dates in mm/dd/yy format. If the source sends a date such as 03/01/99, the receiving program has no way of knowing whether to interpret it as January 3, 1999, or March 1, 1999. Formatted numbers pose a similar problem. If the source sends the number 1,001, the receiving program has no way of knowing whether to interpret it as "one thousand and one" or as "one and one-one thousandth." Because XML and XSL separate the data from its presentation, dates and numbers can be expressed in ISO standard formats in XML but formatted in a locale-specific manner with XSL. Programs requiring the raw data values can accurately interpret dates and numbers from the XML, while users viewing the content in a web browser will see a nicely formatted display.

Unfortunately, I was not able to find any site on the Web that distributes stock information in XML. When considering how to get the real-time data for your solution, think about using XML instead of attempting to scrape data values from formatted HTML as I did in this solution. Let's look at how I got the stock information the hard way.

Getting Stock Quote Information the Hard Way

The Stock Ticker control (StockTicker.ctl) has two other COM controls inside it: an Internet Transfer control and a standard Visual Basic Timer control. The first control provides a mechanism for obtaining the results of a URL. The second provides a polling heartbeat by which the Stock Ticker control fetches new data. The timer's interval can be set through the RefreshRate property of the Stock Ticker control. When the timer fires, the Stock Ticker control uses the Internet Transfer control to get the results of a specific URL exposed from the Microsoft Investor web site. Let's look at the code in the Timer event:

```
Private Sub Timer1_Timer()
    Dim fSuccess As Boolean
    If m_colQuotes.Count > 0 Then
        fSuccess = GetQuotes(True, m_fFakeData)
        If fSuccess Then
            UserControl.PropertyChanged "LastUpdated"
            RaiseEvent NewData(False, "")
        Else
            RaiseEvent NewData(True, m_sLastErrText)
        End If
    End If
End Sub 'Timer1_Timer()
```

The first thing this code does is check the internal collection of Quote objects to make sure there is at least one quote. The control maintains a collection of Quote objects in the variable m_colQuotes and adds a new object for each distinct symbol requested by a client. If there are no Quote objects, the client has not requested any quotes and there is no need to fetch any new data.

If there are quotes, the code calls the GetQuotes function (which I will describe shortly) to populate the Quote objects with new information. The code passes the data member m_fFakeData, which is set by the control's SimulatedData property. A client application with no connection to the Internet can use this value to specify that data be simulated. If the GetQuotes function returns True (indicating success), the code first calls the PropertyChanged method exposed by the base UserControl object to send a property change notification. I will describe how to raise property change notifications in Visual Basic in more detail in the next section; for now, just understand that the change notification is sent at this point. Next, the code raises the Stock Ticker control's NewData event, passing True (error) or False (no error) and the last error text.

Now let's dive into the GetQuotes method itself:

```
Private Function GetQuotes(Optional Notify As Boolean = True, _
Optional FakeData As Boolean = False) As Boolean
    Dim sURL As String          ' URL to get
    Dim sHTML As String         ' Returned HTML
    Dim ss As Spreadsheet       ' Spreadsheet for parsing returned HTML
    Dim nPos As Long            ' Start position marker
    Dim nPosEnd As Long         ' End position marker
    Dim sFind As String         ' String to find in overall returned HTML
    Dim q As Quote              ' Quote iterator
    Dim ct As Long              ' Generic loop counter
    Dim fCancel As Boolean      ' Cancel flag for BeforeNewData event

    On Error GoTo Err_GetQuotes

    fCancel = False
    RaiseEvent BeforeNewData(fCancel)

    If fCancel Then Exit Function

    ' Check the FakeData flag
    If FakeData Then
        ' If the user wants simulated data, generate it
        For Each q In m_colQuotes
            If Len(q.LastSale) = 0 Then
                ' New quote; initialize with random values
                q.Description = "Simulated Data!"
                q.LastSale = GenRandomValue(1, 100)
                q.Change = "0"
                q.PercentChange = "0%"
                q.Volume = GenRandomValue(5000, 1000000)
            Else
                ' Existing quote; adjust values based
                ' on a randomly generated delta
                q.Description = "Simulated Data!"
                q.LastSale = GenRandomValue(1, 100)
                q.Change = "0"
                q.PercentChange = "0%"
                q.Volume = q.Volume
            End If
        Next q

        ' Return True
        GetQuotes = True
        ⋮
```

The GetQuotes function begins by declaring a slew of variables you will see throughout the code that follows. It then raises the Stock Ticker control's BeforeNewData event, passing the fCancel variable, giving the client application a chance to stop fetching new data. Because I declared the BeforeNewData event's parameter to be passed ByRef (that is, by reference), the client application can set this parameter to True and my code in the control can check the parameter value after the event to determine whether it should retrieve new data or cancel the operation.

Next the code checks the FakeData flag and, if it is True, stuffs each Quote object full of randomly generated values. Because this is stock price information, I didn't even attempt to make the values look plausible, and I change them wildly with each refresh. This way, it will be obvious that the data is simulated. Otherwise, readers might mistakenly rush to their phones to sell their stocks based on erroneous data.

The GetQuotes function continues processing the Else case:

```
    ⋮
Else
    ' Get real data from the Investor web site

    ' Hack: Due to an Internet Explorer 5 bug, we have to ignore the
    ' first call to GetQuotes. If you use the WinInet control to get a
    ' URL while Internet Explorer is still loading and initializing
    ' the page, it will cause bad things to happen in the
    ' Spreadsheet control's AutoFit code.
    ' (You usually see a black area around the control and
    ' the control doesn't size correctly, and then
    ' the control often crashes upon closing.)
    If m_fIgnoreGet Then
        m_fIgnoreGet = False
        GetQuotes = True
        Exit Function
    End If

    ' Get out of here if we're still fetching
    If m_fFetching Then Exit Function
    ⋮
```

The first part of this code is the direct result of a long debugging session and an extremely long bug report that bounced between the Internet Explorer and OWC teams. Before I included this code, this solution failed to load properly about 50 percent of the time: the Spreadsheet control did not autofit correctly, black areas appeared where the scroll bars were supposed to be, and the solution often crashed when I closed Internet Explorer. After considerable investigation, our developers discovered a timing-related problem in Internet Explorer that manifested itself only in this specific circumstance. Suppose you had a page containing a control that attempted to automatically adjust its size while the page loaded (the Spreadsheet control's AutoFit feature). If at the same time, another control attempted to execute another URL through the Internet Transfer control (which eventually uses WinInet and URLMon, two components also used by Internet Explorer), Internet Explorer would get confused and improperly handle the control's resize request.

After further investigation, we determined that it was possible to work around the problem by simply delaying the Stock Ticker control's first URL request until after its timer fired once. This gives the Spreadsheet control time to complete its resize request and gives Internet Explorer time to process it. Once the Spreadsheet control performs its initial resize, the Stock Ticker control can begin requesting URLs and everything will work properly thereafter. To accomplish this little code dance, I use a data member called m_fIgnoreGet. The variable is initialized to True in the Stock Ticker control's Initialize event. The first time the GetQuotes function runs, it notices that this flag is set to True, sets it to False, and exits successfully. The Stock Ticker control then waits for the next timer event and thereafter fetches stock information.

After this beautiful hack, the GetQuotes method continues like so:

```
    ⋮
' Create the spreadsheet in memory
Set ss = New Spreadsheet

' Build the URL, adding all the symbols
' Put one symbol on there to begin with so that we get the
' multiquote return page
' even if we have just one symbol in the list
sURL = "http://investor.msn.com/quotes/quotes.asp?" & _
    "QUICKQUOTE=Quote&Symbol=msft"

For Each q In m_colQuotes
    sURL = sURL & "," & q.Symbol
Next q

' Get the data
m_fFetching = True

' Set the timeout for twice as long as the refresh rate
Inet1.RequestTimeout = ((Timer1.Interval * 2) / 1000)
sHTML = Inet1.OpenURL(sURL)

m_fFetching = False
    ⋮
```

This section of the function builds the URL that will return all the information for all the stock symbols in one request. The Quotes.asp page on the Microsoft Investor web site can process any number of symbols separated by commas, but it will generate different results if you ask for just one symbol instead of two or more. Because I need to have a reliable format to parse, I always add one hard-coded symbol to the front of the URL so that I am guaranteed to have more than one. (As you will remember, the code in the timer event made sure that I had at least one Quote object in my collection.) Luckily, I do not need to worry about which symbol I use, as the Investor site will happily return the same quote information for two identical symbols.

After building the URL, I set the Internet Transfer control's request timeout value so that it is twice as long as our refresh rate. URL requests can take a while to process, but the Quotes.asp page usually returns within a second on a fast modem connection. If you find that the requests are constantly timing out, try setting the Stock Ticker control's refresh rate to a higher value. You can do this by setting the value in the RefreshRate <param> tag. (The solution is coded to refresh every 3 seconds.)

After setting the timeout, I use the Internet Transfer control's OpenURL method to get the results of the URL I built earlier. This method is executed synchronously, so this line of code will block until the results return or until the request times out. A request timeout is considered an error, so a timeout will cause the execution to jump to the error-handling block at the bottom of the GetQuotes function. If the results return successfully, the code continues like so:

```
    ⋮
' Find our known string within the results table
sFind = "quotes.asp?Symbol=msft"">"
nPos = InStr(1, sHTML, sFind, vbTextCompare)

' If we found it, get the symbol data
If nPos > 0 Then
    ' Look backward for the beginning of the closest table
    nPos = InStrRev(sHTML, "<table", nPos, vbTextCompare)

    ' Look forward for the end of the table
    nPosEnd = InStr(nPos, sHTML, "</table", vbTextCompare)
    nPosEnd = nPosEnd + 8 '=Len("</table>")

    ' Load the spreadsheet, and let it parse the table
    ss.HTMLData = Mid(sHTML, nPos, nPosEnd - nPos)
    ⋮
```

This is where the code gets somewhat tricky and is most subject to failure. When building the solution, I looked at the HTML source returned from the Quotes.asp page and saw that I could find the HTML table containing the quote information by searching for the string "quotes.asp?Symbol=msft">". This was part of a hyperlink (<a>) tag returned for the first hard-coded symbol in my URL. I knew that if I found this in the HTML string, I could back up to the opening <table> tag and find the closing </table> tag, allowing myself to extract the whole results table.

I next needed a way to parse the HTML table of results. At first I tried parsing the text myself, but I quickly found that the Investor site sometimes includes <font> tags when it needs to format numbers, such as when it shows negative values in red. Instead of handling all the strange cases that might come back, I decided to let the Spreadsheet control parse the table for me. As noted in Chapter 2, you can set the HTMLData property to an HTML table and the Spreadsheet control will load the table cells into the corresponding spreadsheet cells. I could then simply walk the spreadsheet cells to get the various quote information, as shown here:

```
    ⋮
' Load the quote objects
ct = 3
For Each q In m_colQuotes
    ' Set the Notify flag to whatever was passed in
    q.Notify = Notify

    q.Description = ss.Range("b" & ct).Value
    q.LastSale = ss.Range("c" & ct).Value
    q.Change = ss.Range("d" & ct).Value
    q.PercentChange = ss.Range("e" & ct).Value
    q.Volume = ss.Range("f" & ct).Value

    ' Reset the Notify flag to True
    q.Notify = True

    ct = ct + 1
Next q

GetQuotes = True
m_sLastErrText = ""
    ⋮
```

The HTML table of results contains one row per stock symbol, with the columns Symbol, Symbol Description, Last Sale, Change, Percent Change, and Volume Values, appearing in that order. Since I already have the symbol itself, I load the other values into the quote object. I also assume that the results table uses the same order as the symbols in the requested URL, so I can simply iterate over the Quotes collection matching each quote to a row in the table.

So what happens when a new symbol is not valid? The Investor site will of course return a page, but it will not include the normal results table. Instead it will return a page stating that one of the symbols was invalid. So if the previous code does not find that special string (quotes.asp?Symbol=msft">) in the resulting HTML page, the code falls into this Else block:

```
    ⋮
Else
    ' Find string was not found--site has changed,
    ' error has occurred,
    ' or the symbol was invalid

    ' Remove the last quote because if it was invalid,
    ' it would cause this condition
    If m_colQuotes.Count > 0 Then
        m_colQuotes.Remove m_colQuotes.Count
    End If

    GetQuotes = False
    m_sLastErrText = "Symbol not found, or Investor " & _
                     "has changed its site layout!"
End If 'Find string was found
    ⋮
```

There are two reasons why the code might not find the special string: the most recent symbol might be invalid, or the results table returned from the Investor site might have changed its layout. The more likely case is that the symbol is invalid. Since I would be totally out of luck if the site had changed, I attempt to correct the condition by removing the quote that was most recently added from the Quotes collection. I know that the quote most recently added must be the invalid one because previous quotes would not have caused this code to run (or else those quotes already would have been removed).

The other type of error condition is an error that occurs during the URLOpen method. If that happens, the code execution jumps to the error handler code block, shown here:

```
    ⋮
Err_GetQuotes:
    ' Error!
    m_sLastErrText = Err.Description
    GetQuotes = False

    ' Set all values to error
    For Each q In m_colQuotes
        q.Description = "Error Retrieving Values!"
        q.LastSale = "#VALUE!"
        q.Change = "#VALUE!"
        q.PercentChange = "#VALUE!"
        q.Volume = "#VALUE!"
    Next q

    Exit Function
    ⋮
```

In this case, I set all values of all Quote objects to "#VALUE!". This special string is interpreted by the Spreadsheet control as an error value, and all cells dependent on a cell set to "#VALUE!" are also set to "#VALUE!". This guarantees that a user does not see stale data values in the event of an error. I also put the Err.Description string into my last error string variable so that I can return it in the NewData event raised from the timer event shown earlier.

Raising Property Change Notifications in Visual Basic

Raising property change notifications from your Visual Basic control is fairly straight-forward. However, there are some interesting tricks to raising them from public classes. Let's look at both cases.

To raise a property change notification from a Visual Basic control, you should write code like this:

```
UserControl.PropertyChanged "LastUpdated"
```

UserControl is the base class for any control created in Visual Basic, and a number of common methods and properties required for control development are exposed from this class. The PropertyChanged method provides you with a mechanism for raising property change notifications. The first and only parameter to this method is the name of the changed property. The code above, taken from the Stock Ticker control's timer event, notifies a client that the LastUpdated property has changed.

Raising property change notifications from a public class uses a similar mechanism, but it requires one extra step that is hardly obvious. By default, the Visual Basic compiler will not allow code that calls the PropertyChanged method in a public class. For example, if you type this line of code into a newly created public class, the compiler will generate an error when you try to enter the line:

```
PropertyChanged "LastSale"
```

Without the ability to enter a line of code like this, it would seem that you cannot raise property change notifications from a public class. However, the compiler will allow the previously mentioned line of code if you set the class's DataBindingBehavior property to vbSimpleBound. The class properties are exposed in Visual Basic's property sheet when the class's code window is open and active. Figure 10-4 shows where to find this property.

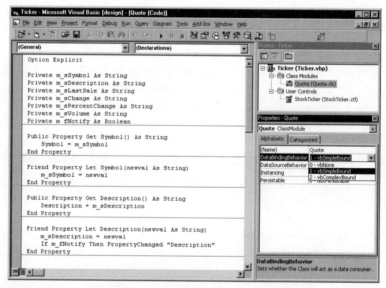

Figure 10-4. *Setting the DataBindingBehavior property.*

After setting this property, call the PropertyChanged method to send a property change notification from your public class. This allows a Visual Basic control to act as a factory for public classes that expose properties with change notifications, just as I have done in the Stock Ticker control.

HANDLING ERRORS IN THE HTML PAGE

Any control obtaining real-time data from a remote source must be prepared to deal with communication errors. As noted earlier, the Stock Ticker control sets the Internet Transfer control's RequestTimeout property to ensure that the HTTP request eventually returns. If the request times out, it passes the error information back to the web page through the NewData event. Let's look at how the HTML page handles the error condition:

```
Sub StockTicker_NewData(fError, ErrText)
    If fError Then
        Dim nReponse
        window.status = "Problems obtaining new stock information!"
        nResponse = MsgBox("Unable to load new stock information " & _
            "because..." & _
            vbCrLf & vbCrLf & ErrText & vbCrLf & vbCrLf & _
            "Would you like to work off line with simulated data?", _
            vbYesNo + vbCritical)

        If nResponse = vbYes Then
            rbOffline_onClick
        End If
    Else
        window.status = "Completed loading new stock data."
    End If
End Sub 'StockTicker_NewData()
```

The Stock Ticker control itself does not display error information in a message box. This is intentional because you should always pass error information up to the highest user interface level possible, allowing that level to display the error. In this case, the higher user interface level is the web page.

The web page's NewData event handler checks the error flag, and if True, it sets the browser's status bar to indicate that an error has occurred and displays the error text returned from the Stock Ticker control in a message box. It wraps a question around the error text, asking the user if he or she wants to work off line instead. If the user responds with a "yes," the code sets the Stock Ticker control's SimulatedData property to True by calling the Click event handler of the Simulate Data radio button. If the error flag was False, the code simply updates the status bar to reflect a successful fetching of new data.

SUPPORTING SAVESNAPSHOT

So far, we have discussed how the Stock Ticker control obtains new data and how the Spreadsheet control updates the stock portfolio with new data as it arrives. However, assuming a user has taken the time to enter a set of symbols to watch and filled out the portfolio section of the spreadsheet, it is also helpful to let the user save the current portfolio so that he or she can open the page later and see current data inputs to the complete portfolio. To enable this, we can save a user's portfolio to a server using the technique described in Chapter 8; however, many users would be leery of letting a program save their private financial information to a network server. Instead, most users prefer to save the portfolio to their local file system.

At first, this might seem as easy as telling a user to choose the File|Save As menu item and save the page on his or her computer. But if you try this with a page of your own, you will find that Internet Explorer saves the page *as it originally arrived from the web server.* Any changes made to the spreadsheet after it was loaded will not be saved because Internet Explorer does not ask the controls on the page to repersist themselves. Instead, Internet Explorer persists the <object> and <param> tags as they originally came from the web server, losing all changes made since.

The Internet Explorer team realized that this was not optimal, and they also wanted to enable developers to save the current contents of other HTML controls such as text boxes, check boxes, and drop-down lists. To allow controls to save their current state when the user saves a page to his or her local machine, Internet Explorer defined a new behavior in version 5 called *saveSnapshot.* Behaviors are a whole new area of functionality for Internet Explorer 5, and discussing behaviors in general is beyond the scope of this book. However, I will explain here how the saveSnapshot behavior works and how you can include it in your web pages to support saving the current state of an OWC control.

In Internet Explorer 5, when the user chooses the File|Save As menu item, the browser examines all elements on the page, looking for any that the developer indicated should have the saveSnapshot behavior. For each control marked with the saveSnapshot behavior, Internet Explorer asks the control to persist its current state into a property bag, which is the standard mechanism used to save and load control properties. Internet Explorer saves the control's current property values in the page written to the local machine, enabling a user to open the page later and resume working.

To enable this behavior, the Internet Explorer documentation says you must include a specific <meta> tag in the <head> section and add the saveSnapshot behavior to each control that needs the ability to save its current state. I have found that the <meta> tag seems to be optional—Internet Explorer seems to save snapshots whether this tag is included or not. However, it is always a good idea to follow directions in these cases since you never know when such a tag will suddenly be required. The <meta> tag looks like this:

```
<head>
<!-- Other head section information omitted -->

<meta content=snapshot name=save>
```

After adding this <meta> tag, you next need to add the saveSnapshot behavior to your various controls. When adding a behavior to many controls at once, it is often useful to define a style class in your <style> section:

```
<style>
<!-- Other style information omitted -->

.saveSnapshot
{
    behavior: url(#default#saveSnapshot)
}
</style>
```

You can implement behaviors by using the new behavior style attribute. The saveSnapshot behavior is one of Internet Explorer's built-in behaviors, so I set the value of the behavior style attribute to url(#default#savesnapshot), which is the syntax for naming built-in behaviors. This style block defines a style class called saveSnapshot (though you can call it anything you want), which I can now use as the class attribute of any HTML element I want to have saved. If you want to do so with the Spreadsheet control, you need to use HTML that looks like this:

```
<div id=div1 class=saveSnapshot>
<object classid="clsid:0002E510-0000-0000-C000-000000000046"
id="Spreadsheet1" width="576" height="288">
<!-- <param> tags omitted -->
</object>
</div>
```

The astute reader is probably wondering why I used the saveSnapshot style class on a <div> tag surrounding the Spreadsheet control's <object> tag. Theoretically, you should be able to use the class on the <object> tag itself and not include a <div> at all. However, the <div> tag is a required workaround to another Internet Explorer problem. Internet Explorer does not notice when the saveSnapshot behavior is used on an <object> tag, so you must wrap another HTML tag around your <object> tag.

The easiest and least obtrusive tag to use is <div> because it has no visible manifestation and provides only a logical grouping of elements. Attaching the saveSnapshot style to the <div> tag causes Internet Explorer to persist all tags within <div>, which in this case is the Spreadsheet control's <object> tag. It's a hack, but it works. Perhaps the Internet Explorer development team will fix this in their next version.

You can also include the saveSnapshot behavior style attribute on each control or element instead of defining a style class. To do so, include the following style attribute on any HTML element you want to have saved:

```
style="behavior:url(#default#savesnapshot)"
```

Keep in mind that the saveSnapshot behavior is new to Internet Explorer 5. Previous versions of Internet Explorer will safely ignore this behavior.

SUMMARY

Property binding introduces a push model into the Spreadsheet component. By implementing a control that raises property change notifications, you can push new data values into a spreadsheet model as they become available, without writing any script to coordinate the two controls. Nonprogramming users authoring pages in FrontPage can use your control and the Spreadsheet control to build solutions such as the real-time stock portfolio described in this chapter.

However, remember that property binding works only if you are building your solution in Internet Explorer. Also, if you just want to expose custom calculations to a spreadsheet model, property binding is not necessary and you will instead want to implement a custom function library. Chapter 11 explains how to do that and shows you some interesting functions that extend the Spreadsheet component to work with other kinds of data sources, such as a multidimensional database.

Chapter 11

Building Custom Spreadsheet Function Add-Ins

In Chapter 10, I showed you how to create a real-time data source object to which you can bind cells in your spreadsheet model. In this chapter, I will show you the other side of custom calculations: function add-ins. Although property binding and function add-ins can produce similar results, there is an appropriate time to use each.

ABOUT THE SOLUTION

The Spreadsheet component offers a staggering number of built-in functions, but for many users, this set is one or two functions shy of all the functions they will ever need. Many disciplines have specific functions that are commonly used or that deviate from the Spreadsheet component's built-in functions. Furthermore, some businesses have specific, top-secret calculations that they want to let their employees use. However, those businesses do not want those calculations to be shipped as part of the Spreadsheet component because the calculations give them a technical advantage over their competitors.

To accommodate these cases, the Spreadsheet component allows you to develop custom function add-ins. A function add-in is simply a COM object that supports IDispatch. Once you add the object into the Spreadsheet component (using the AddIn method), every public method on that class becomes a viable function. You or your users can utilize the public method as if it were a built-in function, passing cell or range references to it and using it in the middle of an encompassing formula.

The possibilities are enormous. Custom functions can perform literally any task, from simple calculations to complex Monte Carlo algorithms or other statistical analyses. Custom functions can also access network resources such as databases and core business systems, pulling critical business data into your spreadsheet models. Furthermore, custom functions can retrieve data from other data sources such as your e-mail inbox, your contacts list, a local lookup file—anything you can accomplish in a COM object can be exposed to the Spreadsheet component as a custom function.

It is not terribly hard to implement simple function add-ins, but as soon as you want to work on ranges of cells or require a specific editor to help users build a parameter list for your function, implementation can get a bit more complex. The solution in this chapter is a custom function add-in that contains some simple example functions; some more powerful, range-based analysis functions; and a function designed to look up a cell value from an OLAP data source, complete with its own function-editing user interface. These illustrate the various types of functions you might want to implement in a custom function library, providing you with a starting point from which to implement your own custom functions.

TECHNIQUES ILLUSTRATED IN THIS SOLUTION

Like the solutions you have seen so far, the Custom Function Library solution demonstrates a number of techniques. Table 11-1 lists the various techniques and the source file in which each is implemented. Although I might not discuss each technique listed here, you can use this table to find the appropriate source file and examine the implementation on your own. You can also use it as a quick reminder of the techniques illustrated in this solution.

Technique	*Source File*
Adding a custom function library into the Spreadsheet component.	FuncTest.frm
Implementing a simple calculation function.	CustomFunctions.cls
Exposing Microsoft VBA functions as custom functions.	CustomFunctions.cls
Working with ranges in custom functions.	CustomFunctions.cls
Retrieving a single aggregate from an OLAP cube.	CustomFunctions.cls
Designing a custom function-editing user interface for complex functions.	OLAPLookupWiz.frm, FunctionWizards.cls, OLAPLookupDef.cls
Enumerating cubes, dimensions, and members using Microsoft ActiveX Data Objects Multidimensional (ADO MD).	OLAPLookupWiz.frm

Table 11-1. *Techniques illustrated in the Custom Function Library solution.*

RUNNING THE SOLUTION

The Custom Function Library solution is entirely based in Microsoft Visual Basic 6. Although all the previous solutions ran in web pages, I wanted to show you in this last solution how to use the Microsoft Office Web Components in a Visual Basic application. This also makes it easy to test the function add-in DLL by stepping through each function as the Spreadsheet component evaluates it.

To run this solution, open the FuncLibTestGrp.vbg project group in Visual Basic 6 or a later version. The project group consists of two projects: the analysis function library DLL project and the function library test EXE project. If you like, you can set breakpoints and run the application to step through the custom functions line by line.

Alternatively, you can run the prebuilt executables on the companion CD by following these steps:

1. Copy the AnalysisFuncLib.dll file from the Chap11 folder to your hard disk and register it by running Regsvr32.exe, passing the DLL name as the command-line parameter.

2. Run the FuncLibTest.exe program from the Chap11\Test folder.

ADDING A CUSTOM FUNCTION LIBRARY TO THE SPREADSHEET COMPONENT

Before you can use any of your custom functions, you must use the Spreadsheet component's AddIn method to pass the instance pointer of your COM object to the Spreadsheet component. You should do this in whatever event your container raises when the form or page is initialized. In a Visual Basic form, this is the form's Load event. The following code comes from that event in the custom function test form:

```
' Create the custom function library, and
' add it into the Spreadsheet control
Set m_flCustom = New CustomFunctions
ssTest.AddIn m_flCustom
```

The CustomFunctions class is a public class in the analysis functions library. It is a COM object that supports IDispatch, as are all public classes defined in a COM DLL or COM EXE Visual Basic project. Because the Spreadsheet component needs a live instance of your COM object, this code first creates an instance, assigning it to the form-level variable m_flCustom. It then passes the instance pointer to the Spreadsheet component's AddIn method.

When you call the AddIn method, the Spreadsheet component examines all unknown function references in the model and resolves them if they are public functions in the class you just added. This enables you to enter references to your custom functions in a designer (as I have done in the custom function test form), even though your code has not yet added the custom function library.

You can add as many custom function COM objects as you want, and the Spreadsheet component merges all public methods into one flat namespace. The Spreadsheet component resolves functions by searching through the add-in object list in the order in which the objects were added and stopping when it finds a match. For example, if you define a function named MyFunction in two different classes, the Spreadsheet component will bind a reference to MyFunction to the first object added using the AddIn method. The Spreadsheet component also checks its own function library before looking at custom function libraries, so it is not possible to override any of the built-in functions.

IMPLEMENTING SIMPLE FUNCTIONS

In this chapter, I will use the term "simple functions" to describe functions that take only scalar values (not ranges) for inputs and do not need a custom function-editing user interface. These are the most common functions, and thankfully, they are quite easy to implement. Let's take a look at the two simple functions I implemented in the custom function library: DoubleIt and DateAdd.

DoubleIt—The "Hello World" of Custom Functions

Every programming book has a "Hello World" demo in it somewhere, and this is mine. To illustrate defining a custom function in the simplest context possible, I wanted the first function we discuss to be so trivial that you will not focus on the implementation of the function itself. The DoubleIt function merely multiplies the input value by 2, catching the appropriate error conditions:

```
Public Function DoubleIt(Number As Variant) As Variant
    On Error GoTo Err_DoubleIt

    If IsNumeric(Number) Then
        DoubleIt = Number * 2
    Else
        ' Return #NUM! if not numeric
        DoubleIt = "#NUM!"
    End If
    Exit Function

Err_DoubleIt:
    DoubleIt = "#VALUE!"
    Exit Function
End Function 'DoubleIt()
```

To call this function in a cell formula, use the following formula syntax:

```
=DoubleIt(C3)
```

HOW CAN I USE MY EXISTING XLL ADD-INS IN THE SPREADSHEET COMPONENT?

Long ago, Microsoft Excel defined a model for custom functions and add-ins referred to as XLLs, which are DLLs that implement certain function entry points so that Excel can generically inspect the DLLs and invoke functions exposed from them.

The Spreadsheet component uses the COM standard to enable function add-ins. If you have existing XLLs that expose custom functions, you can easily use these functions with the Spreadsheet component by wrapping them in a COM object. You do not need to reimplement your functions—you only need to repackage them as a COM object.

If you specify a cell reference as an input argument to your custom function, the Spreadsheet component will pass the current value of that cell to your custom function. The Spreadsheet component will also note that the cell containing your function is dependent on the referenced cell (C3, in this case) and will automatically recalculate the function whenever the referenced cell's value changes.

As you can see, defining a custom function is as easy as defining a public function in a class module. However, I want to impart a few tips for implementing a good custom function.

First, the Spreadsheet component is Variant-based, meaning that all cell values are inherently Variants. A cell can just as easily contain a string, a date, or a Null, Empty, or Error value as it can contain a number. Therefore, it is typically better to type your function input arguments as Variants and check their type and value in your code than to rely on the Spreadsheet component to convert the cell value to the type you declare. If you type an input argument as a stronger type such as String or Long, the Spreadsheet control will attempt to coerce the input value into that type before calling your function. If the Spreadsheet control cannot coerce an input value into the type you request, the control will resolve the function to "#VALUE!" without ever calling your function. If you want to handle those conditions in a more graceful way, type your input parameters as Variants and return a more appropriate value if the input is not the required type. You can use the VBA functions that start with "Is" to determine whether the Variant is a certain type.

Second, it is helpful to include an error handler in any custom function. The Spreadsheet control will gracefully handle any errors generated by a custom function, displaying "#VALUE!" and ignoring the error, but you might want to display the error text in a fashion that lets your users know the nature of the failure. In the OLAPLookup function discussed later in the chapter, I return the Err.Description property in the event of an error so that the error description text is actually inserted into the cell.

The last tip is that you can return any of the error strings (such as "#VALUE!") to set the cell value to an error. Other error values include "#NULL!" for returning a Null value, "#NUM!" to indicate a problem with an input argument, and "#N/A!" to indicate that some information is missing or the function's result is not applicable given the inputs or current conditions.

Exposing Powerful VBA Functions

There are many kinds of simple functions you might want to implement, but often, the function you need is already implemented in the programming language you use to create your COM object. For example, VBA exposes many complex and highly useful functions for working with dates, strings, and even the file system. You can expose these functions to the Spreadsheet component by simply wrapping them in a public method of your COM class. For example, let's look at the DateAdd function in the CustomFunctions.cls file:

```
Public Function DateAdd(Interval As String, Number As Double, _
StartDate As Date) As Variant
    On Error GoTo Err_DateAdd

    If IsDate(StartDate) Then
        DateAdd = VBA.DateAdd(Interval, Number, StartDate)
    Else
        ' Return #NUM! if not a date
        DateAdd = "#NUM!"
    End If
    Exit Function

Err_DateAdd:
    DateAdd = "#VALUE!"
    Exit Function
End Function 'DateAdd()
```

This function simply wraps the VBA version of the function (called by using the VBA library qualifier), performing some initial error checking and returning the appropriate error values. You can use this same technique to expose any programming language's functions or any other function not already exposed as a method of a COM object. To try this, run the project in Visual Basic and adjust the various inputs to DateAdd in the Simple Functions section of the test spreadsheet. Try setting the Interval value to "yyyy" to see the result of adding a number of years to the start date.

A custom function can return only a scalar value, meaning you cannot return other COM objects, arrays, structures, or binary data. If you do, the Spreadsheet component will either display "#NAME!" or the token "<Binary Data>". The rule of thumb is that if you can type the value into the cell, you can return it from a custom function. Although it would be nice to load a range of cells with an entire table of data, you can do this through the programming model only by using the Range object, not by returning a value from a custom function.

IMPLEMENTING RANGE-BASED FUNCTIONS

As I noted earlier, simple functions take scalar input values and do not require custom user interface editors. In this section, I will show you how to implement custom functions that accept ranges of values for input arguments. Working with a range parameter is somewhat tricky, so let's examine how it is done.

The IXRangeEnum Interface

Although you might expect the Spreadsheet component to pass a Range object for a range parameter, it does not. Instead it passes an IXRangeEnum interface. This interface is marked as hidden in the OWC type library, so you can view it by choosing to show hidden members in your Object Browser. (In Visual Basic, right-click the Object Browser and choose Show Hidden Members.)

This interface is streamlined for the task of retrieving the values from the range's cells. Typically, you need to use only the ColCount, RowCount, and Next methods on this interface. The interface also contains other methods for converting values from one Variant type to another using the Spreadsheet component's internal type conversion routines, which occasionally differ slightly from the type conversion routines in OLE Automation. You can usually ignore these methods, but C++ developers might find them handy if they want more detailed control over type conversions.

Getting Cell Values from IXRangeEnum

To get cell values from the IXRangeEnum interface, you typically use the Next method. The following function, taken from CustomFunctions.cls, shows how to extract cell values in VBA:

```
Private Function GetCellValues(Range As IXRangeEnum) As Variant()
    Dim ctCols As Long          ' Number of columns
    Dim ctRows As Long          ' Number of rows
    Dim objRange As Object      ' IDispatch interface

    ' QI for the IDispatch interface so that we can use
    ' the unsigned longs
    ' This is dangerous, but we know that the
    ' number of rows or columns in a range won't be
    ' greater than the maximum value for a signed long
    Set objRange = Range

    ' Performing nasty, dangerous casting from unsigned to
    ' signed longs here!
    ctCols = objRange.ColCount
    ctRows = objRange.RowCount

    ' Allocate an array of Variants for all the values, and get them
    ReDim vRngValues((ctRows * ctCols) - 1) As Variant
    objRange.Next ctRows * ctCols, vRngValues(0), vbNull

    ' Return it
    GetCellValues = vRngValues
End Function 'GetCellValues()
```

The IXRangeEnum interface was really defined for C++ developers, so the interface is littered with properties and parameters of type unsigned long. This type is not directly supported in OLE Automation (only signed longs are), and you will receive compile errors if you try to access these properties or pass values to these parameters. However, you can work around this nasty limitation by using the IDispatch interface of the object implementing IXRangeEnum. This function accesses the IDispatch interface by declaring a variable of type Object and then setting it equal to the IXRangeEnum parameter. Visual Basic will use the QueryInterface method to get the IDispatch interface of the source object because the destination variable is typed as Object. Once you have the IDispatch interface, your code can access unsigned long values and assign them back to variables declared as Long.

Although there is a potential for error when assigning unsigned long values to signed long values, it is highly unlikely that the column or row count of a range is larger than the maximum signed long value, which is around 2 billion. The Spreadsheet control itself supports a maximum of 702 columns and 65,536 rows.

Whenever you implement a function that accepts a range, you can use the GetCellValues function shown earlier to obtain a one-dimensional Variant array full of the values from the specified range. Your code can then use the UBound and LBound functions to determine the dimensions of the returned array and iterate over the values.

The SumTopN and SumBottomN Functions

To illustrate how to implement a range-based function, I created two functions in my custom function library: SumTopN and SumBottomN. The SumTopN function adds up the top *N* numbers in the range, and the SumBottomN adds up the bottom *N* numbers. Since these functions are similar, much of their implementation is shared; the only major difference is in which direction I sort the data values before adding up the first *N* items. Let's take a look at the SumTopN function:

```
Public Function SumTopN(ByVal Range As IXRangeEnum, ByVal N As Long) _
As Double
    Dim vRngValues() As Variant
    Dim colSorted As Collection

    If N > 0 Then
        ' Get the cell values
        vRngValues = GetCellValues(Range)

        ' Sort the elements into a collection
        Set colSorted = SortValues(vRngValues, flSortDescending)
```

(continued)

```
        ' Calculate the SumTopN
        SumTopN = SumNElems(colSorted, GetRealN(colSorted, N))
    Else
        SumTopN = 0
    End If 'N > 0
End Function 'SumTopN()
```

This function takes two parameters: a range of values and the number of top values to sum. Because the first parameter is a range, I type it as IXRangeEnum. To enable a parameter to accept a range of values, you must declare its type as IXRangeEnum. If you do not, the Spreadsheet component will fail to bind to the function and will resolve the function to an error value.

The function first checks whether N is greater than zero. If it is not, the function simply returns a zero right away because, by definition, the sum of zero items is zero and I can avoid the overhead of sorting the values. If N is greater than zero, I use the GetCellValues function to obtain all the cell values in the range as a Variant array. I then use another helper function called SortValues to sort the Variant array (in descending order) into a Collection object full of Variants. The code then uses two other helper functions: GetRealN and SumNElems. The first gets the real N value (which I will explain later), and the second adds up that many elements in the collection. Finally, the function returns the sum to the Spreadsheet control. Let's first look at the SortValues function:

```
Private Function SortValues(vRngValues(), Optional SortDir _
As SortDirEnum = flSortAscending) As Collection
    Dim ctCells As Long              ' Number of cells
    Dim fInserted As Boolean         ' Inserted flag
    Dim nCell As Long                ' Cell index
    Dim colSorted As Collection      ' Sorted collection
    Dim nSortElem As Long            ' Current sort element
    Dim vVal As Variant              ' Temporary Variant

    ctCells = UBound(vRngValues) + 1

    ' Do an insertion sort using a collection
    Set colSorted = New Collection
    For nCell = 0 To (ctCells - 1)

        nSortElem = 1
        fInserted = False

        If colSorted.Count = 0 Then
            colSorted.Add vRngValues(nCell)
```

```
        Else
            For Each vVal In colSorted
                If SortDir = flSortAscending Then
                    If vRngValues(nCell) < vVal Then
                        colSorted.Add vRngValues(nCell), , nSortElem
                        fInserted = True
                        Exit For
                    End If
                    nSortElem = nSortElem + 1
                Else
                    If vRngValues(nCell) > vVal Then
                        colSorted.Add vRngValues(nCell), , nSortElem
                        fInserted = True
                        Exit For
                    End If
                    nSortElem = nSortElem + 1
                End If
            Next vVal

            If Not fInserted Then colSorted.Add vRngValues(nCell)

        End If 'colSorted.Count = 0
    Next nCell

    ' Return the sorted collection
    Set SortValues = colSorted
End Function 'SortValues()
```

The SortValues function is an extremely simple insertion sort, and I do not even pretend to think that this is an optimized sorting algorithm. You can easily improve on this function (for example, by performing a binary search when inserting a new value), but it does perform the job for medium-sized N values. The function builds a new Collection object by inserting each value in the Variant array into its sorted position in the collection. When the function finishes, the returned collection contains a sorted list of items, ready to enumerate and total.

It is quite amazing that VBA still does not offer any built-in sorting functions, especially considering the existence of the qsort function in the C runtime library. Alas, we are left to implement our own sorting in VBA. Maybe someday we will get built-in functions for sorting arrays and collections, especially when they contain homogenous scalar types.

After sorting the values, the SumTopN function first calls the GetRealN function in the process of calling the SumNElems function. The GetRealN function determines how many items actually constitute the top *N* items. The following page shows what the code for the GetRealN function looks like.

```
Private Function GetRealN(colSorted As Collection, ByVal N As Long) _
As Long
    ' If N > the count of elements, set N = to the count
    If N >= colSorted.Count Then
        N = colSorted.Count
    Else
        ' Figure out our real N (check for N and N + 1 being equal)
        Do While colSorted(N) = colSorted(N + 1)
            If N >= colSorted.Count Then
                N = colSorted.Count
                Exit Do
            End If

            N = N + 1
        Loop
    End If 'N > colSorted.Count

    ' Return it
    GetRealN = N
End Function 'GetRealN()
```

As I discussed in Chapter 2, top or bottom N functions can actually include more than N items in the result if the N and $N + 1$ items are equal. If you asked for the top three items in the set {3, 4, 5, 5, 6, 7}, which 5 would you include? You have to include both 5s (a total of four items) because both are within the top three values. The GetRealN function compares the N and $N + 1$ values, and if they are equal, keeps looping to find the point at which the N and $N + 1$ values are no longer equal or until it falls off the end of the collection. It then returns the real N value, which is passed to the SumNElems function:

```
Private Function SumNElems(colSorted As Collection, N As Long) As Double
    Dim vVal As Variant        ' Temporary Variant
    Dim nResult As Double      ' Result
    Dim nSortElem As Long      ' Index of current element

    ' Start at element one
    nSortElem = 1
    nResult = 0

    ' Sum up the values
    ' Use For Each and short circuit as this is a
    ' faster way to iterate over a collection
    For Each vVal In colSorted
        nResult = nResult + vVal
        nSortElem = nSortElem + 1
```

```
        If (nSortElem - 1) = N Then
            Exit For
        End If
    Next vVal

    ' Return it
    SumNElems = nResult
End Function 'SumNElems()
```

This fairly straightforward function enumerates the collection of sorted values, adding each value to a running total. As soon as the code adds up the *N* elements, it exits and returns the sum to the SumTopN function, which in turn passes it back to the Spreadsheet control.

The SumBottomN function works exactly the same way as SumTopN, except that it sorts the range values in ascending order instead of in descending order:

```
Public Function SumBottomN(ByVal Range As IXRangeEnum, ByVal N As Long) _
As Double
    Dim vRngValues() As Variant
    Dim colSorted As Collection

    If N > 0 Then
        ' Get the cell values
        vRngValues = GetCellValues(Range)

        ' Sort the elements into a collection
        Set colSorted = SortValues(vRngValues, flSortAscending)

        ' Calculate the SumBottomN
        SumBottomN = SumNElems(colSorted, GetRealN(colSorted, N))
    Else
        SumBottomN = 0
    End If 'N > 0
End Function 'SumBottomN()
```

Using these functions in the spreadsheet model is just like using the built-in SUM function, except that you pass one extra parameter for the N value:

```
=SumTopN(B9:B14,E9)
=SumBottomN(B9:B14,E9)
```

You pass a range to a custom function the same way you pass a range to any other built-in function. The Spreadsheet control will also allow users to semi-select (click on a cell to paste its cell reference into the current formula) the range reference while building the formula, so your custom function should look and feel built in. To try these functions, run the project in Visual Basic and adjust the inputs in the Analysis Functions section of the test spreadsheet.

IMPLEMENTING COMPLEX FUNCTIONS WITH USER INTERFACE BUILDERS

The functions I have described so far are all fairly easy to type directly into a spreadsheet cell. All references passed are to other cells on the spreadsheet, and the set of parameters is fairly easy to understand. However, many kinds of custom functions are not as easy to type directly into the spreadsheet. Functions that reference resources outside the current spreadsheet (such as shared data sources) or functions that allow a user to graphically select part of that reference might need to display custom user interfaces for creating and editing formulas that use those custom functions. The final function I implemented in the custom function library is such a function.

The OLAPLookup function fetches a single aggregate from a multidimensional data source. As I discussed in Chapter 4, a multidimensional database defines an *N*-dimensional structure containing values. Each value is the result of an intersection of *N* members (one from each dimension), and the logical address of that value's cell is the member *tuple*. A tuple is a fancy word that simply means a set of related attributes, which in this case is a set of unique member names that define a data point intersection.

The OLAPLookup function is a useful mechanism for pulling a few specific aggregates into your spreadsheet model to use either as inputs to a forecasting model or as values you want to analyze using other built-in or custom functions. Although the PivotTable component can obtain many aggregates from an OLAP data source, the Spreadsheet component offers no direct support for retrieving these as part of a model. Furthermore, it is often useful to have absolute control over where the aggregates display in the spreadsheet, allowing you to customize the presentation of your data any way you please.

To get this aggregate, the OLAPLookup function needs three pieces of information: the connection string for the OLAP data source, the name of the cube you want to query within that data source, and the cell's coordinates defined by a tuple of member unique names. Although you can type all this information into your spreadsheet formula, it is much better to offer your users a graphical wizard that helps them specify these parameters. It is highly unlikely that your users will know how to construct an OLE DB connection string and even less likely that they will know the unique names for the various members they want to use in the coordinates. The OLAPLookup Function wizard provides that graphical user interface, and it also provides an example of how to build a reentrant function-editing wizard.

The OLAPLookup Function

Before we discuss how the OLAPLookup Function wizard works, let's look at the code for the OLAPLookup function itself:

```
Public Function OLAPLookup(ConnectionString As String, _
CubeName As String, CellCoordinates As String) As Variant
    Dim cn As Connection        ' Connection to OLAP database
    Dim cset As New Cellset     ' OLAP cellset

    On Error GoTo Err_OLAPLookup

    ' Get a connection to the specified database
    Set cn = GetConnection(ConnectionString)

    ' If connected
    If Not (cn Is Nothing) Then
        ' Execute the MDX query to get the single cell
        cset.Open "select from " & CubeName & _
            " where (" & CellCoordinates & ")", _
            cn

        ' Get the value for the single cell
        OLAPLookup = cset.Item(0).Value

        ' Close up
        cset.Close
        Set cset = Nothing

    End If 'Connection valid

    ' Success
    Exit Function

Err_OLAPLookup:
    ' Error! Return the error description for debugging purposes.
    OLAPLookup = Err.Description
    Exit Function
End Function 'OLAPLookup()
```

Retrieving a single aggregate from a cube is surprisingly easy. After getting a connection to the OLAP data source, the OLAPLookup function builds a simple MDX statement that will return just one cell. The code uses the CubeName parameter for the FROM clause and the CellCoordinates parameter for the WHERE clause. By definition, a full set of coordinates will return just one cell, so the code executes the MDX statement and returns the first (and only) cell in the cellset. It then closes the cellset, releases it, and exits.

To optimize the OLAP database connections, I implemented a function called GetConnection, which checks a collection of cached connections and returns an opened connection if one already exists for the same connection string. The code looks like this:

```
Private Function GetConnection(sConnString) As Connection
    Dim cn As Connection

    ' Try to get an existing connection
    On Error Resume Next
    Set GetConnection = m_colConns.Item(sConnString)

    ' If there was no existing one
    If Err.Number <> 0 Then
        ' Create a new connection, and open it
        On Error GoTo 0
        Set cn = New Connection
        cn.Open sConnString

        ' If it connected OK
        If Err.Number = 0 Then
            ' Add it to the collection
            m_colConns.Add cn, sConnString
            Set GetConnection = cn
        Else
            Set GetConnection = Nothing
        End If
    End If
    On Error GoTo 0

End Function 'GetConnection()
```

The function first tries to get an open Connection object from the m_colConns collection using the requested connection string as the key value. If a connection exists, the Err.Number value is set to zero and the function returns the Connection object. If the Err.Number value is not zero, no connection exists yet, so the code creates a new Connection object, opens it, and then adds it to the m_colConns collection using the connection string as the key value. Finally, the function returns the new or existing Connection object, which is in turn used by the OLAPLookup function to execute an MDX query to get the requested aggregate.

You might wonder why I didn't implement this function as a pool, checking out connections and returning only connections that are not currently used by other callers. Because the function library itself is apartment model–threaded, and because the Spreadsheet control evaluates functions in a serialized manner, two threads can never enter the OLAPLookup function at the same time. Since I use the Connection object only in the context of the OLAPLookup function, I do not need to mark the Connection object as "in use" because there is no danger of another client requesting the same Connection object while the first client is using it. If I implemented this function in a free-threaded library, I would have to rewrite this function to pool connections instead, or I could use the built-in connection pooling provided by the Microsoft Data Access Components (MDAC).

The OLAPLookup Function Wizard

To make it easier for a user to enter or edit an OLAPLookup formula, I created a custom user interface wizard. This wizard is exposed from the same DLL as the custom functions, so any application using the OLAPLookup function can also use the wizard without additional files. To try the wizard yourself, run the project in Visual Basic, select the cell you want to contain the function, and click the OLAP Cube toolbar button. You should then see a wizard user interface that looks like Figure 11-1.

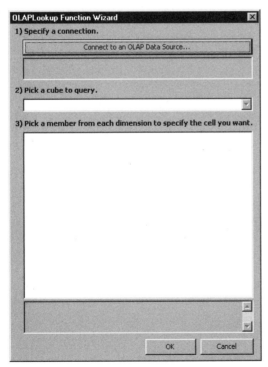

Figure 11-1. *The OLAPLookup Function wizard.*

I realize that my use of the term "wizard" here is rather loose, as this is a single page dialog box. However, three clear steps are required and they must be performed in order. I could have implemented this as a three-page wizard with Next and Back navigation buttons, but the first two steps require so little screen real estate that it seemed like a waste.

To connect to a data source, click the top button on the wizard. This will launch the prompting dialog box from the Microsoft SQL Server OLAP Services provider (you can easily change the code to use another OLAP provider), in which you can enter a server name or a path to a cube file, such as the cube file in the Data folder on your companion CD. After connecting to the data source, you can select a cube within the data source. After selecting a cube, the wizard loads the tree view with the dimensions and first-level members and checks the default member from each dimension. The result should look like Figure 11-2.

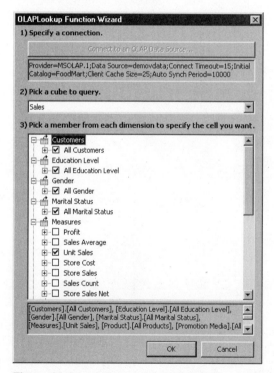

Figure 11-2. *Selecting a cube cell with the OLAPLookup Function wizard.*

You can now change the selected member for any dimension, and the unique member name tuple displayed below the tree view should change to reflect the new selection. When you exit the wizard using the OK button, it returns a fully constructed

OLAPLookup formula that the test application inserts into the selected spreadsheet cell. The Spreadsheet control then calls the OLAPLookup function I showed you earlier, and the resulting aggregate displays in the cell. The first time you access the data source, a slight delay will occur while the OLAPLookup function opens a new connection; however, further recalculations should happen almost instantaneously.

Often, a user will also want to edit this new formula and select different cell coordinates. The OLAPLookup Function wizard is reentrant, meaning it can edit an existing OLAPLookup formula. To try this, select the cell in which you inserted a new OLAPLookup function and press F2 to start editing the cell. After confirming that you want to use the wizard to edit the cell, the wizard displays with the same settings you had when you created the formula. You can then change cell coordinates or even the data source or cube name and click the OK button to change the function. To see how I automatically invoke the wizard when a user attempts to edit the cell, see the ssTest_StartEdit event handler in the test form's code module.

Accomplishing the reentrancy was rather difficult, and the solution at which I eventually arrived involved using another object to hold a structured definition of an OLAPLookup formula. This object is an instance of the OLAPLookupDef class in the OLAPLookupDef.cls file.

The OLAPLookupDef Class

OLAP member unique names are strange beasts. Each OLAP provider determines the format of a unique name, and client applications are never supposed to assume anything about the contents of a unique name. To the client application, the unique name is just an opaque string of characters. The provider can easily determine which member the unique name refers to, as well as the dimension in which the member exists. However, there is no easy or efficient way to determine a parent dimension given a member unique name.

This makes reentrancy in the wizard difficult. The OLAPLookup function takes a member unique name tuple as the last parameter. The tuple is just a set of unique names separated by commas. It is relatively easy to parse this apart using the Split function in VBA, but this is not totally reliable because a provider can embed a comma inside a member unique name that is framed by identifier tokens (such as "[" and "]"). Additionally, ADO MD offers no function to return a parent dimension name given a member name. You could iterate over all members in the cube until you found the member, but that would be exceedingly slow.

To combat these problems, I took the approach of creating a structured definition of an OLAPLookup function. Client programs pass this object to the OLAPLookup Function wizard and then hold onto it in case the user wants to edit the formula. On the next page, we'll take a look at the class definition for the OLAPLookupDef class.

```
Public ConnectionString As String
Public CubeName As String
Public CellCoordinates As Dictionary


'---------------------------------------------------------------------
' Class Init
'---------------------------------------------------------------------
Private Sub Class_Initialize()
    Set CellCoordinates = New Dictionary
End Sub
```

The various member unique names that make up a cell's coordinates are stored as separate items in a dictionary. I use the parent dimension name as the key to the item. The client application (in this case, the test form) can store a set of these classes, each one associated with the address of the cell in which the user has inserted an OLAPLookup function. I accomplish this in the test form by using another Dictionary object that stores OLAPLookupDef objects using the address of the spreadsheet cell as the key.

When the test form edits an OLAPLookup function using the wizard, it checks this dictionary and hands back the existing definition object if it finds one. This code segment, taken from the EditOLAPLookup function in the test form, performs the necessary work:

```
    ⋮
' If the range has a formula
If rng.HasFormula Then
    ' Check whether there is a stored OLAPLookupDef for
    ' the selected range
    If m_dictOLDefs.Exists(rng.Address) Then
        Set oldef = m_dictOLDefs.Item(rng.Address)
    End If
End If

' Invoke the OLAPLookup Function wizard to create
' or edit the formula (modal)
sFmla = m_wizFunctions.OLAPLookupWiz(oldef)
    ⋮
```

If the selected spreadsheet cell has an associated OLAPLookupDef object, the code fetches it from the m_dictOLDefs dictionary and passes it to the wizard object's OLAPLookupWiz function. When the wizard finishes, the code continues and stores the newly edited OLAPLookupDef object back in the dictionary, using the address of the spreadsheet cell as the key:

```
    ⋮
' If the returned formula is not an
' empty string
If Len(sFmla) > 0 Then
    ' Set the range's formula
    If rng.HasFormula Then
        ' Surgically replace OLAPLookup formula
        rng.Formula = ReplaceOLAPLookup(rng.Formula, _
            sFmla)
    Else
        rng.Formula = sFmla
    End If

    ' Add or update the OLAPLookupDef to the
    ' dictionary so that we'll know to edit it next time
    If m_dictOLDefs.Exists(rng.Address) Then
        Set m_dictOLDefs.Item(rng.Address) = oldef
    Else
        m_dictOLDefs.Add rng.Address, oldef
    End If 'Update dictionary
End If 'Wizard not canceled
    ⋮
```

Note that my use of the HasFormula property is critical to the proper operation of this routine. If the user has cleared the contents of a cell that once contained an OLAPLookup function, an OLAPLookupDef object will remain in the dictionary associated with the cell address. However, the HasFormula property will now return False because the cell no longer contains a formula. In this case, the code will hand an empty OLAPLookupDef object to the OLAPLookupWiz function and happily replace the old, invalid OLAPLookupDef object when the wizard returns.

The OLAPLookupWiz Function

The OLAPLookupWiz function is implemented in the FunctionWizards class and is the entry point for displaying the OLAPLookup Function wizard user interface. The function looks like this:

```
Public Function OLAPLookupWiz(Optional oldef As OLAPLookupDef = Nothing) _
As String
    Dim frmWiz As frmOLAPLookupWiz      ' Wizard instance
    Set frmWiz = New frmOLAPLookupWiz

    ' Create the OLAPLookupDef if necessary
    If oldef Is Nothing Then
        Set oldef = New OLAPLookupDef
    End If
```

(continued)

```
' Pass the OLAPLookupDef to the wizard
Set frmWiz.OLAPLookupDef = oldef

' Show the wizard modally
frmWiz.Show vbModal

' Pass back the wizard's outputs if not canceled
If Not frmWiz.WizardCanceled Then
    ' Grab the new OLAPLookupDef object
    Set oldef = frmWiz.OLAPLookupDef

    ' Return the new function
    OLAPLookupWiz = "=OLAPLookup(""" & _
        oldef.ConnectionString & """, ""[" & _
        oldef.CubeName & "]"", """ & _
        GetCoords(oldef) & """)"
Else
    ' Wizard canceled; send back empty string
    OLAPLookupWiz = ""
End If 'Wizard canceled

End Function 'OLAPLookupWiz()
```

The function starts by creating an instance of the wizard's form and sets the OLAPLookupDef public property exposed from that form. This seeds the form with the OLAPLookupDef object that the wizard will edit. Next the function calls the Show method of the form, telling it to display modally. When displayed modally, the Show method will block until the form is dismissed—meaning that the line after the Show method is not executed until the user has clicked OK, clicked Cancel, or closed the form using the Close button on the title bar.

After the Show method, the function looks at another public property of the form, WizardCanceled, to determine whether the user canceled the wizard or chose the OK button. If the wizard was not canceled, the code builds a complete OLAPLookup formula from the OLAPLookupDef properties and returns it. If the wizard was canceled, the code simply returns an empty string and the test form checks the return value for an empty string to determine whether it should update the formula of the selected spreadsheet cell.

The OLAPLookup Wizard Form

Since there is quite a bit of code (about 440 lines) in the OLAPLookupWiz form, I do not have time to discuss it all here. I will cover only the highlights in this section; however, you can refer to the OLAPLookupWiz.frm file on the companion CD to see the rest of the code.

As I noted in the previous section, the wizard form has a few public properties. The most important is the OLAPLookupDef property, which allows the caller to hand the wizard form an OLAPLookupDef object for editing. The property procedures follow:

```
Public Property Get OLAPLookupDef() As OLAPLookupDef
    Set OLAPLookupDef = m_oldef
End Property 'OLAPLookupDef Get

Public Property Set OLAPLookupDef(newval As OLAPLookupDef)
    Set m_oldef = newval
End Property 'OLAPLookupDef Set
```

These are simple procedures that get and set a class variable called m_oldef, which I will use throughout the rest of the form's code.

When the form is displayed, the form's Load event handler runs. Here is what that event handler's code looks like:

```
Private Sub Form_Load()
    m_fCancel = True

    cbxCube.Enabled = False
    tvwMembers.Enabled = False

    ' If the OLAPLookupDef is valid
    ' and has a connection string
    ' try to reload all the information
    If Not (m_oldef Is Nothing) Then
        If Len(m_oldef.ConnectionString) > 0 Then
            Connect
            SelectCbxItem cbxCube, m_oldef.CubeName
            txtCoords.Text = GetCoords()
        End If
    End If
End Sub 'Form_Load()
```

This code defaults the cancel flag to True (this flag is set to False in the btnOK button's Click event handler) and performs some initial disabling of the cbxCube drop-down list and tvwMembers tree view control. Then it determines whether the OLAPLookupDef object is valid and whether the ConnectionString property is not blank. If both conditions are true, the code calls the Connect method to connect to the data source, attempts to select the cube named in the CubeName property of the OLAPLookupDef, and sets the txtCoords text box to display the current cell coordinates.

WATCH OUT FOR THE
NON-SHORT-CIRCUITING IF CONDITIONS IN VBA!

You might think that I could have shortened part of the code I just discussed to something like this:

```
If Not (m_oldef Is Nothing) And _
Len(m_oldef.ConnectionString) > 0 Then
    Connect
    SelectCbxItem cbxCube, m_oldef.CubeName
    txtCoords.Text = GetCoords()
End If
```

But in fact I cannot do so without risking a runtime error when m_oldef is Nothing. "If" conditions in VBA do not short circuit, meaning VBA attempts to evaluate every subcondition and then determines whether the overall condition is True. In C, the code would never evaluate the second part of this condition if the first part evaluated to False—False And (*anything*) will always be False, so there is no need to evaluate the remainder of the condition. To prove that "If" conditions in VBA do not short circuit, try running the following code in Visual Basic:

```
Sub Main()
    Dim obj As Collection

    If (Not (obj Is Nothing)) And (obj.Count > 5) Then
        MsgBox "You'll never get here!"
    End If
End Sub
```

When you run this program, the message box will never appear. You will get a runtime error on the If line because VBA attempts to evaluate the subcondition *obj.Count > 5* even though the first part is False.

Let's now take a look at the Connect method, called from the form's Load event handler or when the user clicks the Connect To An OLAP Data Source button on the wizard:

```
Private Sub Connect()
    On Error GoTo Err_Connect

    ' If the connection string is blank
    If Len(m_oldef.ConnectionString) = 0 Then
```

```
    ' Default the provider to msolap (OLAP Services)
    ' You can change this to another provider because the rest of
    ' the code is generic ADO MD code
    m_cnOLAP.Provider = "msolap"
Else
    ' Connect using the connection string defined in
    ' the OLAPLookupDef object
    m_cnOLAP.ConnectionString = m_oldef.ConnectionString
End If 'Len(m_oldef.ConnectionString) = 0

' Set the prompting property to prompt if necessary
m_cnOLAP.Properties("Prompt") = adPromptComplete

' Open the connection
m_cnOLAP.Open

' Get the fully completed connection string
m_oldef.ConnectionString = m_cnOLAP.ConnectionString
txtConnString.Text = m_oldef.ConnectionString

' Load the cube's drop-down list
LoadCubes

' Disable the connect button
btnConnect.Enabled = False

' Exit successfully
Exit Sub

Err_Connect:
    ' Error connecting!
    txtConnString.Text = "Error Connecting!"
    Exit Sub
End Sub 'Connect()
```

This method first checks the ConnectionString property of the OLAPLookupDef object to see whether it is blank. If it is, the method sets the Provider property of the Connection object to "msolap" so that ADO knows what OLE DB provider to load. The "msolap" provider name signifies the provider for OLAP Services. You can change this to use any other OLE DB for OLAP provider because the rest of the wizard and OLAPLookup function code should work against any OLE DB for OLAP provider.

The code then sets the Prompt property of the underlying OLE DB provider to adPromptComplete. The Prompt property is exposed only through the Properties collection because it is actually a property of the underlying OLE DB provider rather than ADO itself. The adPromptComplete setting tells the provider to prompt the user for more connection information only if necessary. If the connection string contains everything the provider needs, it does not prompt for more information and connects to the data source.

This method next attempts to open the Connection object. If successful, it uses the LoadCubes method to load the cube drop-down list with the names of all the available cubes in the data source. Let's now take a look at the LoadCubes method:

```
Private Sub LoadCubes()
    Dim cdef As CubeDef

    Set m_ctlg.ActiveConnection = m_cnOLAP

    cbxCube.Clear

    For Each cdef In m_ctlg.CubeDefs
        cbxCube.AddItem cdef.Name
    Next cdef

    cbxCube.Enabled = True
    If Me.Visible Then cbxCube.SetFocus
End Sub 'LoadCubes()
```

The LoadCubes method uses ADO MD objects to enumerate the available cubes in the current data source. To accomplish this, the method sets the ActiveConnection property of the m_ctlg variable (an ADOMD.Catalog object) to the newly opened Connection object. After doing so, the code enumerates the cubes using the CubeDefs collection and adds each cube's name to the cbxCube drop-down list. After loading the list, the code enables the control, and if the form is visible, sets focus to it so that the user can immediately select a cube. Always remember to check the form's visible setting before calling SetFocus—calling SetFocus while the form is invisible (which it still is during the form's Load event) will generate a runtime error.

Now that the cbxCube drop-down list is populated, the user can select a cube and begin selecting members to build the OLAP cell coordinates. When the user selects a cube, the form runs the LoadMembers method to populate the tvwMembers tree view with the list of dimensions and first-level members. The first part of this method follows:

```
Private Sub LoadMembers()
    Dim cdef As CubeDef        ' CubeDef object
    Dim dm As Dimension        ' Dimension object
    Dim hier As Hierarchy      ' Hierarchy object
    Dim mem As Member          ' Member object
    Dim ndHier As Node         ' Node for the hierarchy
```

```
Dim ndMem As Node            ' Node for the member
Dim idxImage As Variant      ' Index of the node's image

' Clear the tree view and the CellCoordinates if necessary
tvwMembers.Nodes.Clear
If cbxCube.Text <> m_oldef.CubeName Then
    m_oldef.CellCoordinates.RemoveAll
    txtCoords.Text = ""
End If

' Get out if the cube name is blank
If Len(cbxCube.Text) = 0 Then Exit Sub

' Get the CubeDef object for the selected cube
Set cdef = m_ctlg.CubeDefs(cbxCube.Text)
⋮
```

The method begins by clearing the tree view of any existing nodes and also clearing the dictionary of coordinates if the cube name has changed. (Coordinates from another cube would no longer be relevant.) It then gets the ADOMD.CubeDef object for the selected cube, which it uses to obtain the list of dimensions and first-level members in the cube:

```
⋮
' Loop over all dimensions in the cube
For Each dm In cdef.Dimensions
    ' Get the first hierarchy in the current dimension
    Set hier = dm.Hierarchies(0)

    ' Add a node for the hierarchy; use UniqueName for the key
    Set ndHier = tvwMembers.Nodes.Add(, , dm.UniqueName, _
        dm.Name, 1, 1)

    ' Expand the hierarchy node
    ndHier.Expanded = True

    ' Set the hierarchy node's tag to the dimension object
    Set ndHier.Tag = dm

    ' If no coordinate exists for this dimension yet
    If Not (m_oldef.CellCoordinates.Exists(dm.UniqueName)) Then
        ' Add the default member as the coordinate
        m_oldef.CellCoordinates.Add dm.UniqueName, _
        hier.Properties("DEFAULT_MEMBER").Value
    End If 'No coordinate for dimension
```

(continued)

```
' Loop over the members in the first level of the hierarchy
For Each mem In hier.Levels(0).Members
    ' If the member is the current coordinate for
    ' this dimension
    If mem.UniqueName = _
        m_oldef.CellCoordinates.Item(dm.UniqueName) Then
            ' Use the check node icon
            idxImage = "Check"
    Else
            ' Use the unchecked node icon
            idxImage = "UnCheck"
    End If 'Member is the current coordinate

    ' Add the member to the tree view
    Set ndMem = tvwMembers.Nodes.Add(ndHier, tvwChild, _
        , mem.Caption, idxImage, idxImage)

    ' Set the node's tag to the member object
    Set ndMem.Tag = mem

    ' Add a fake node below the new node so that an expand
    ' indicator shows
    tvwMembers.Nodes.Add ndMem, tvwChild, , FAKE_NODE

    Next mem
Next dm
```

There are two critical aspects of this code segment you should notice. First, I use the Tag property of the tree view node to hold an instance of an ADO MD object that the node is representing. Because the Tag property is a Variant, it can hold an object instance, which makes it easy to retrieve the object that the node represents later when Visual Basic passes a Node object in a tree view event.

Second, I preset the selected member for each dimension to the *default member* of that dimension. In an OLAP data source, one member in each dimension must be declared as the default member. When you execute an MDX query, any dimension not used on the result axes is implicitly included in the WHERE clause as a slicing dimension. If you do not explicitly name a member from such a dimension, the OLAP query processor will use the default member as the slicing member. Because the OLAPLookup Function wizard needs a member from each dimension, the logical choice is to use the default member for the dimension until the user chooses a different member. To obtain the default member of a dimension, use the DEFAULT_MEMBER property in a Hierarchy object's Properties collection. In this code, I use the first hierarchy defined in the dimension.

VARIANTS AND OBJECT DEFAULT MEMBERS: A DEADLY COMBINATION

While building this wizard, I spent about three hours debugging a seemingly impossible situation. When I attempted to use the wizard to edit an existing OLAPLookupDef object, I received a runtime error when the code attempted to access an item in the CellCoordinates dictionary. The runtime error indicated that "the object was no longer valid," which seemed odd considering that I thought I was putting strings into the dictionary. (Strings should never expire during a program and produce an error like this.) The key phrase here is *I thought* I was putting strings into the dictionary.

After becoming completely befuddled by this, I used the TypeName function to ask the dictionary what type it thought the item was. I of course expected to see String come back. Instead, the TypeName function returned Property, and then it all became clear. The previous code used to look like this:

```
' If no coordinate exists for this dimension yet
If Not (m_oldef.CellCoordinates.Exists(dm.UniqueName)) Then
    ' Add the default member as the coordinate
    m_oldef.CellCoordinates.Add dm.UniqueName, _
        hier.Properties("DEFAULT_MEMBER")
End If 'No coordinate for dimension
```

The important piece missing was the Value property on the end of the *hier.Properties("DEFAULT_MEMBER")* line. Value is the default member of the ADODB.Property object, so you would expect this to still work fine. However, my problems were due to the often misunderstood behavior that occurs when you combine Variants and members that return objects with default members.

The Dictionary.Add method takes a Variant for the second parameter. Because a Variant can hold an object reference, you can pass an object to this parameter and the dictionary will happily store a reference to the object returned from the Properties collection. In this case, it does not store the value of the default member. So the whole time, I was building a dictionary full of Property objects rather than member unique name strings. The rest of my code worked fine because whenever I compared the dictionary entry to another string, VBA knew to retrieve the default member and compare using it, because comparing a string to an object makes no sense. However, when I exited the wizard, the OLAP Connection and Catalog objects were destroyed. This automatically marks the Property objects as *zombied,* which means they still exist as objects but all calls to methods and properties produce a runtime error like the one I saw. The moral of the story: Don't rely on default members. Always qualify your statements using the property name even if it is the default property.

The LoadMembers method loads only the first-level members from each dimension. Loading all members can take quite a while, especially if your dimensions contain numerous members. Instead, I use the tree view's Expand event to dynamically load the child members for the member the user is about to expand. Using this technique I load only as many members as the user views, which typically is not a large number. The Expand event calls the LoadChildMembers method, shown here:

```
Private Sub LoadChildMembers(mem As Member, nd As Node, _
sDimName As String)
    Dim memChild As Member      ' New child member
    Dim ndChild As Node         ' New child tree view node
    Dim idxImage As Variant     ' Node image index

    ' Loop over all the children for the specified member
    For Each memChild In mem.Children
        ' If the member is the currently selected coordinate
        ' for the dimension
        If memChild.UniqueName = _
            m_oldef.CellCoordinates.Item(sDimName) Then
            ' Use the check node icon
            idxImage = "Check"
        Else
            ' Use the uncheck node icon
            idxImage = "UnCheck"
        End If 'Member is current coordinate

        ' Add the new child member to the tree view
        Set ndChild = tvwMembers.Nodes.Add(nd, tvwChild, _
            , memChild.Caption, idxImage, idxImage)

        ' Set the new node's tag to the child member
        Set ndChild.Tag = memChild

        ' Add the fake node to get the expand indicator
        tvwMembers.Nodes.Add ndChild, tvwChild, , FAKE_NODE
    Next memChild
End Sub 'LoadChildMembers()
```

This method enumerates the parent member's Children collection, which contains a Member object for each child member. The method loads each child member into the tree view as a child node of the parent node. The method also checks whether this child member is the currently selected member for the dimension. If it is, the method sets the child's image to reflect that. Finally, the method sets the child node's Tag property to the Member object instance so that you can access it again from the tree view node.

The last bit of code I will describe executes when the user clicks a node in the tree view. If the user clicks a member node that is not the currently selected member for the dimension, the wizard must update the CellCoordinates dictionary to note the new member unique name for the dimension. This is accomplished in the NodeClick event handler of the tree view:

```
Private Sub tvwMembers_NodeClick(ByVal Node As MSComctlLib.Node)
    Dim ndDim As Node
    Dim ndOld As Node

    ' If the node is a member and not a hierarchy
    If Node.Image <> 1 Then

        ' Uncheck the current member for the parent dimension
        Set ndDim = GetParentDim(Node)
        Set ndOld = FindNode(ndDim, m_oldef.CellCoordinates(ndDim.Key))
        If Not (ndOld Is Nothing) Then
            ndOld.Image = "UnCheck"
            ndOld.SelectedImage = "UnCheck"
        End If

        ' Set the new node as the new coordinate, and check it
        m_oldef.CellCoordinates.Item(ndDim.Key) = Node.Tag.UniqueName
        Node.Image = "Check"
        Node.SelectedImage = "Check"

        txtCoords.Text = GetCoords()
    End If 'Node is not a hierarchy
End Sub 'tvwMembers_NodeClick()
```

The code first checks whether the clicked node is a member node and not a node representing the whole dimension. To do so, it checks the node's Image property, which returns the index of the image used for the node. Dimension nodes use the first image, so if the node's image does not equal 1, the code continues.

The code next finds the tree view node associated with the previously selected member for the current dimension. It does this by finding the parent dimension node and then finding the member node that matches the member unique name in the CellCoordinates dictionary for that parent dimension. Once it finds the tree view node, it sets that node's Image and SelectedImage properties to the unchecked image.

The code continues by updating the entry in the CellCoordinates dictionary for the current dimension. It then sets the Image and SelectedImage properties for the clicked node to the check image. Finally, it updates the txtCoords text box to show the updated cell coordinates.

Because this event keeps the CellCoordinates dictionary updated with the current selections, when the user closes the wizard, the function calling the wizard can iterate over the coordinates and build a complete OLAPLookup formula.

SUMMARY

This chapter showed you how to build a custom function add-in for the Spreadsheet component. I discussed how to implement simple functions, functions that take ranges for input arguments, and functions that access external resources and have their own function-editing user interfaces. Using these techniques, you can build powerful function add-in libraries for the Spreadsheet component, providing your users with your own advanced analytics.

This is the last chapter that describes a complete solution involving the Office Web Components. Chapter 12, the final chapter of the book, will describe how to deploy solutions using the components, including how to make the components automatically download and install in a web-based application.

Chapter 12

Deploying
the Components

Now that you know how to build complex business solutions involving the Microsoft Office Web Components, the last topic I want to discuss is how to deploy the components to the people using your solutions. Although the Office Web Components are COM controls, the way you deploy them and the manner in which they are installed is slightly different than for most COM controls. This chapter will explain your options for deployment, give you step-by-step instructions on how to configure a page to automatically download and install the components, show you how to detect whether the components are already installed, and provide you with a complete list of files required by the Office Web Components and Microsoft Data Access Components (MDAC) version 2.1.

RELATIONSHIP TO OFFICE 2000

As I mentioned in Chapter 1, the Office Web Components have no technological tie to Office 2000. Our team statically linked all the common code from Office into the Office Web Components so that there would be no technological dependency. This enables you to deploy the components in your custom solutions before your organization deploys Office 2000. We also specifically designed the components to coexist with Office 95 and 97 so that it is safe to deploy the components on a client machine running a previous version of Office.

Although OWC has no *technological* dependency on Office 2000, it does have a *licensing* dependency. The OWC library is licensed as part of Office 2000, so any client machine using the components at either design time or runtime must have an Office 2000 license. The client machine does not have to install any other part of Office 2000, but it does need a valid Office 2000 license (which is just a piece of paper). Corporations that purchase site licenses for Office 2000 can freely redistribute the OWC library within the corporation, which is by far the easiest approach for developing and deploying information systems using the components.

Because the OWC library is licensed as part of Office 2000, it is automatically installed when a client installs Office 2000. Deploying Office 2000 is actually the easiest way to deploy the OWC library to client desktops, but this is often an unrealistic option for large corporations with many client desktops. To facilitate the advance rollout of only the Office Web Components and MDAC 2.1, our team developed a separate installation and a special installer control known as the Web Installer.

USING THE WEB INSTALLER

If your target runtime environment is a web browser (or the Web Browser COM control in a Microsoft Visual Basic or C++ application), you can configure your application to automatically download and install the Office Web Components using the special Web Installer provided in the Office 2000 setup. Using the Microsoft Windows Installer technology, the Web Installer deploys only the OWC library and MDAC 2.1 files to the client, leaving the rest of Office 2000 on the file server.

Creating a Network Install Image

To use the Web Installer, you must first create an Office 2000 network install image on a file server. Most large corporations already do this because it provides the opportunity to preconfigure the Office setup experience and the initial application options to match company policies. If your corporation has created such an install image, you can use it as the source for the Office Web Components installation.

If your company has not set up an image, you can either use the Office Resource Kit or you can simply run the Office 2000 setup wizard using the /a command-line switch. For example, if your CD drive is D:, insert CD 1 from your Office 2000 CD set and type the following command:

```
D:\setup.exe /a
```

The setup wizard will run in administrative setup mode, allowing you to specify a file location for the network install image. The wizard will copy all the files from CD 1 to this directory, which consumes about 554 MB. Unfortunately, neither the

Office Resource Kit nor the administrative setup allows you to copy only the subset of files needed for the Office Web Components; however, the file lists at the end of this chapter will help you determine which files you actually need. The Web Installer was built to find the necessary files in the directory structure defined on the CD and copy them to the client machine, so you cannot simply copy some of the files from the CD into a directory structure of your own choosing.

Specifying the Codebase Attribute

After creating your network install image, the next step in enabling the automatic download of the components is to add the codebase attribute to all your object tags. The codebase attribute is the key to making Microsoft Internet Explorer automatically download and run the Web Installer—if you omit the codebase attribute, Internet Explorer will fail to load the controls and will instead display the alternate HTML defined for the <object> tag.

The codebase tag tells Internet Explorer the location from which it should install a component that is not yet installed on the client's system. If the class ID defined in the <object> tag's classid attribute is not registered, or if the existing version is older than the requested version, Internet Explorer automatically uses the URL specified in the codebase attribute to download and install the component. A typical <object> tag and codebase attribute look like this:

```
<object id="Spreadsheet1"
  classid="CLSID:0002E510-0000-0000-C000-000000000046"
  codebase=
  "file:\\OfficeInstallServer\InstallShare\Msowc.cab#version=9,0,0,2710"
>
```

The first part of the codebase attribute (the part before the hash symbol [#]) in this example points back to a file path on a mythical file server called OfficeInstallServer with a mythical share called InstallShare. This path should point directly to the Office network install image I described earlier. The Msowc.cab file is the file your codebase attribute should reference, and it is in the root of the Office network install image.

The second part of the codebase attribute (the part after #) specifies an explicit version of the OWC library. This part of the codebase tag is optional, but it is extremely useful for forcing clients to automatically upgrade to a newer version of the library. When you include the version number, Internet Explorer checks the existing version of the component implementing the specified class ID to make sure it is the requested version or higher. If not, Internet Explorer automatically downloads the newer version and installs it.

Because of the licensing restrictions on the Office Web Components, the value in the codebase attribute must be a file: path rather than an http: path. The Web Installer will ensure that the codebase attribute starts with "file:" before installing the OWC library. If the Web Installer allowed downloading of the OWC library over the Internet, you could not guarantee that the client machine had an Office 2000 license. You can still take advantage of clients that do have the Office Web Components installed by simply writing pages without codebase attributes and offering the user a choice between static or interactive content, as I demonstrated in Chapter 9.

Running the Web Installer

As you might have noticed, the Msowc.cab file is actually quite small—86 KB to be exact. This is because this file contains only the Web Installer itself. When Internet Explorer starts an automatic download of the OWC library using the codebase attribute, it first downloads and installs the Web Installer. The Web Installer then registers itself as implementing all the class IDs of the Office Web Components so that it can masquerade as if it were the components themselves.

Internet Explorer then creates an instance of the Web Installer for each Office Web Component used in the page. Instead of displaying the real OWC control, the Web Installer displays a watermark and begins the process of installing the OWC library (and MDAC 2.1 if you do not already have it installed). When you first start the installation process, your page will look something like Figure 12-1.

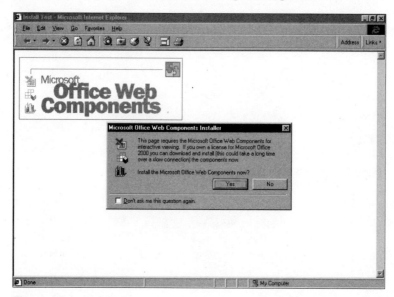

Figure 12-1. *The Web Installer starting a dynamic install.*

The opening screen of the Web Installer verifies that the user does want to install the Office Web Components, describes the Office 2000 license requirement, and warns the user that the full download (including MDAC 2.1) can take a while over a slow connection. If the user chooses Yes in this dialog box, he or she is then shown the full end user license agreement for the components, which is depicted in Figure 12-2.

Figure 12-2. *The Web Installer's End User License Agreement Dialog Box.*

The content displayed in this dialog box comes from the License.txt file located in the root directory of the Office 2000 network install image you created earlier.

After the user accepts the license agreement, the Web Installer ensures that the Windows Installer—the new install engine in Office 2000 and Windows 2000—is present on the system (downloading it if necessary) and then uses that engine to install the OWC library and the MDAC 2.1 files if they are not already on the system. The Windows Installer displays a dialog box with a progress meter that informs the user how long it will take to complete the install. This dialog box is depicted in Figure 12-3.

Figure 12-3. *The Windows Installer deploying the Office Web Components.*

After the Web Installer finishes, it notifies Internet Explorer to reload the current page. Now that the real Office Web Components are registered, Internet Explorer creates the real controls and displays them in the page.

The Web Installer begins the download process before any code in your window_onLoad event handler executes. After the install, Internet Explorer reloads the page and then fires the window_onLoad event, giving you the opportunity to initialize the controls. Note that if the user chooses No in the first dialog box, the Web Installer halts the installation process and your window_onLoad event handler will run. However, because the controls were not installed, script that references properties and methods of the controls will fail. If you are enabling an automatic download through the Web Installer, you should use one of two methods to ensure that the controls were indeed installed:

■   Use the On Error Resume Next declaration, and then try to read one of the properties from the control, such as MajorVersion. If the control was not installed, this will fail and Err.Number will return a nonzero value.

■   Use the TypeName function to ask for the type name of the control. For example, the code TypeName(Spreadsheet1.Object) will return "Spreadsheet" if the Spreadsheet control was properly installed; otherwise, it will return "IWebInstCtl", which is the class name of the Web Installer.

Note that if any file being installed is currently in use, the Web Installer will notify the user that he or she must reboot the system before running the page. Because the Office Web Components are new to Office 2000 and since they do not upgrade existing Office 95 or 97 files, it is necessary to reboot only when another application is using one of the MDAC files. Because the Data Access Group chose to keep all its DLL names the same, it is possible that another application will be using an older version of an MDAC file, and the Web Installer cannot simply overwrite a DLL that is in use. Because forcing a reboot can be disruptive to the user, you might consider creating a special installation page, as described in the next section.

Creating an Installation Page

An installation page is a special page in your web site that knows how to check the client machine to see whether the Office Web Components are already installed. If the components have not been installed, this page will ask the user whether he or she wants to install them and will let the user continue after the installation finishes. Checking for the presence of the OWC library is also an easy way to dynamically determine whether you should return a page with an interactive control or a page with static information from a web site on the Internet.

I have implemented a simple installation page in the InstallOWC.asp file located in the Chap12 folder on the companion CD. You can use this file as is or customize it to fit the look and feel of your particular site. To call this page, use the following URL syntax:

```
InstallOWC.asp?ContinueTo=URL&Codebase=CodebaseURL
```

In this line, *URL* is the URL that you want the page to navigate to if the OWC library is installed (or after it is installed), and *CodebaseURL* is the value you would normally put in the codebase attribute, as I described earlier. The page will check for the existence of the OWC library—if it is installed, the page will immediately navigate to the URL specified in the ContinueTo parameter. If not, the page will return a page containing the Chart control, placing the value from the Codebase parameter into the <object> tag's codebase attribute.

Let's take a look at how this page works. The Microsoft Active Server Pages script will emit this HTML and client-side script fragment when first checking for the presence of the OWC library:

```
⋮
<p id=lblChecking>Checking whether the Microsoft Office 2000 Web
Components are installed...</p>

<script language=vbscript>
Option Explicit

' Attempt to create an Office Web Component as
' an object in memory to determine whether the OWC
' library is installed
On Error Resume Next
Dim objOWC
Set objOWC = CreateObject("OWC.Chart.9")
' If this was successful
If Err.number = 0 Then
    ' And if the object reference is something
    If Not(objOWC Is Nothing) Then
        ' Check the MinorVersion and BuildNumber to make
        ' sure it is the required version
        ' (Note: Change these values if you want to require
        ' a version other than the version
        ' released with Microsoft Office 2000)
        If objOWC.MinorVersion >= 0 And _
            StrComp(objOWC.BuildNumber,"2710") = 0 Then
            window.navigate "<%= Request("ContinueTo") %>"
        End If 'Correct version
    End If 'Components installed
End If 'No error on create
</script>
⋮
```

The script block attempts to create the object OWC.Chart.9, and if successful (if Err.Number is 0), the script checks that the version number is acceptable. If all this checks out, the script navigates the window to the URL specified in the ContinueTo parameter and your user continues to work with your web site. Note that because the Office Web Components are marked as safe for initialization and safe for scripting, this code will not produce security warnings, meaning it is extremely unobtrusive.

If the CreateObject function fails or if the version number is not correct, the page continues by emitting this HTML fragment:

```
<p id=lblInstall style="display:none">
<b>You need to install the Microsoft Office 2000 Web Components.</b>
</p>
<p>
Installing the components might take some time over a slow connection.
To make the installation as easy as possible, you should close
any other applications you have running before starting
the installation.
</p>
<a href="InstallOWC.asp?ContinueTo=<%= Request("ContinueTo") %>
&Codebase=<%= Request("Codebase") %>&Install=True">
<img src="PoweredByMSOWC.gif" border=none>
<b>Click here to install the Microsoft Office 2000 Web Components.</b>
</a>

<script language=vbscript>
Option Explicit
lblChecking.style.display = "none"
lblInstall.style.display = ""
</script>
```

This HTML warns the user that the download might take some time and encourages him or her to shut down all other applications in case any of the MDAC files are in use. The HTML then provides a hyperlink that returns to the same ASP page, but this time it passes the Install=True query string attribute, which causes the page to emit the following HTML and client-side script fragment:

```
<p>Installing the Microsoft Office 2000 Web Components...</p>
<p id=lblClick>When you see the chart, click it to continue.</p>
<object id=cspace
width="50%" height="50%"
classid="clsid:0002E500-0000-0000-C000-000000000046"
codebase="<%= Request("Codebase") %>"
>
</object>
```

```
<script language=vbscript>
'-------------------------------------------------------------------
' Window Load Event Handler
'
Sub window_onLoad()
    Dim cht      ' Temporary WCChart reference
    Dim c        ' Constants object reference
    Dim ser      ' Temporary WCSeries reference

    ' Check for successful download
    On Error Resume Next
    Dim nMajorVer
    nMajorVer = cspace.MajorVersion
    If Err.number <> 0 Then
        Exit Sub
    End If
    On Error Goto 0

    ' Create a simple literal data chart
    Set c = cspace.Constants
    Set cht = cspace.Charts.Add()
    cht.HasLegend = True
    cht.SetData c.chDimSeriesNames, c.chDataLiteral, _
        Array("Forecasted Sales", "Actual Sales")
    cht.SetData c.chDimCategories, c.chDataLiteral, _
        Array("Quarter 1", "Quarter 2", "Quarter 3", "Quarter 4")

    Set ser = cht.SeriesCollection(0)
    ser.SetData c.chDimValues, c.chDataLiteral, _
        Array(100000, 110000, 120000, 130000)

    Set ser = cht.SeriesCollection(1)
    ser.SetData c.chDimValues, c.chDataLiteral, _
        Array(110000, 140000, 170000, 190000)
End Sub

'-------------------------------------------------------------------
' Chart Space Click Event Handler
'
Sub cspace_Click(evtinfo)
    window.navigate "<%= Request("ContinueTo") %>"
End Sub 'cspace_Click()

'-------------------------------------------------------------------
' Chart Space MouseMove Event Handler
'
```

(continued)

```
Sub cspace_MouseMove(evtinfo)
    lblClick.style.fontWeight = "Bold"
End Sub 'cspace_MouseMove()


'--------------------------------------------------------------------
' Document MouseOver Event Handler
'
Sub document_onMouseOver()
    lblClick.style.fontWeight = ""
End Sub
</script>
```

The HTML fragment contains an <object> tag for the Chart control, specifying the codebase attribute so that Internet Explorer will begin the download process and invoke the Web Installer. When the Web Installer finishes, Internet Explorer fires the window_onLoad event and the code in that event's handler adds some literal data to the chart. When the user clicks the Chart control, the client-side code navigates the window to the URL specified in the ContinueTo parameter and the user continues to use your web site as normal.

CUSTOMIZING DEPLOYMENT SETTINGS

For a custom-written solution, you can control the file path used in the codebase attribute and you can control what is written in the alternate HTML section of your <object> tags. However, if your solution allows users to publish interactive content from Microsoft Excel 2000, you might want to control the codebase path and alternate HTML automatically inserted by Excel.

Excel, Microsoft FrontPage, and Microsoft Access all use the contents of a registry key for the value of the codebase attribute. The key is found under:

HKEY_CURRENT_USER\Software\Microsoft\Office\9.0\Common
Internet\LocationOfComponents

Changing the contents of this key will alter what Excel, FrontPage, and Access write for the codebase attribute of any Office Web Component.

When publishing interactive content, Excel 2000 will insert a short HTML fragment into the alternate HTML section of any <object> tag for a Spreadsheet, Chart, or PivotTable control. By default, the English version of this HTML is as follows:

```
<p style='margin-top:100;font-family:Arial;font-size:8.0pt'>
To use this Web page interactively, you must have Microsoft Internet
Explorer 4.01 or later and the Microsoft Office Web Components
<span style="mso-spacerun: yes"> </span>See the
```

```
<a HRef="http://officeupdate.microsoft.com/office/redirect/
fromOffice9/MSOWCPub.htm?&amp;HelpLCID=1033">
Microsoft Office Web site</a> for more information.</p>
```

This text has a hyperlink to the Microsoft Office Update web site for more information, but in your solution, you might want to instead direct users to the installation page discussed earlier. To substitute your own text, add the following registry key and set the key's value to your custom text:

HKEY_CURRENT_USER\Software\Microsoft\Office\9.0\Common
Internet\MissingComponentText

Unfortunately, I discovered in my own testing that this value is always HTML encoded when written into the published page. HTML encoding transforms an HTML tag such as <a> into <a> so that it is no longer an HTML tag but is instead interpreted as literal text. This means you cannot include HTML tags in the value for this registry key because they will not be correctly written to the page. Therefore, you are limited to plain text without any hyperlinks or formatting.

OFFICE WEB COMPONENTS FILES

Tables 12-1 through 12-4 list the OWC files installed by the Web Installer. The files listed in Table 12-3 are installed for each locale directory, so although this table lists the files for the 1033 folder (U.S. English), the same files are deployed for the other locale folders, except that the contents will be localized.

File	*Description*
Msowc.msi	This file is renamed to a numeric value after installation and is used only by the Windows Installer.

Table 12-1. *File installed to the Windows(Winnt)\Installer folder.*

File	*Description*
Msowc.dll	Main OWC Library.
Msowcf.dll	Extended Spreadsheet function library.

Table 12-2. *Files installed to the Program Files\Microsoft Office\Office folder.*

File	Description
Msowc.sll	Property Toolbox contents file.
Msowci.dll	Locale-specific resources for the OWC library.
Msowcdpl.chm	PivotTable component design-time user help file.
Msowcdss.chm	Spreadsheet component design-time user help file.
Msowcrdp.chm	Data Access Pages runtime help file.
Msowcrpl.chm	PivotTable component runtime user help file.
Msowcrss.chm	Spreadsheet component runtime user help file.

Table 12-3. *Files installed to the Program Files\Microsoft Office\Office\1033 folder.*

File	Description
Msoeuro.dll	Euro conversion Spreadsheet component functions.

Table 12-4. *File installed to the Program Files\Common Files\Microsoft Shared\Euro folder.*

MDAC 2.1 FILES AND CORE OFFICE AND SYSTEM FILES

This list contains all the other files installed as part of MDAC 2.1 or as core Office and system files. Most of these files are part of MDAC 2.1 and will be installed only if MDAC 2.1 is not already on the client machine.

12520437.cpx	Hhctrl.ocx	Msorcl32.dll	Msxml.dll	Odbctrac.dll
12520850.cpx	Instcat.sql	Mspbde40.dll	Mtxdm.dll	Oddbse32.dll
Asycfilt.dll	Itircl.dll	Msrclr40.dll	Mtxoci.dll	Odexl32.dll
Cliconfg.dll	Itss.dll	Msrd2x40.dll	Odbc16gt.dll	Odfox32.dll
Cliconfg.exe	Jeterr40.chm	Msrd3x40.dll	Odbc32.dll	Odpdx32.dll
Dbmsadsn.dll	Mscpxl32.dll	Msrdo20.dll	Odbc32gt.dll	Odtext32.dll
Dbmsrpcn.dll	Msdatsrc.tlb	Msrecr40.dll	Odbcad32.exe	Oleaut32.dll
Dbmsshrn.dll	Msexch40.dll	Msrepl40.dll	Odbcbcp.dll	Olepro32.dll
Dbmssocn.dll	Msexcl40.dll	Msrpjt40.dll	Odbccp32.cpl	Rdocurs.dll
Dbmsspxn.dll	Msjet40.dll	Msrtedit.dll	Odbccp32.dll	Sqlsrv32.dll
Dbmsvinn.dll	Msjint40.dll	Mstext40.dll	Odbccr32.dll	Sqlstr.dll
Dbnmpntw.dll	Msjter40.dll	Msvcrt40.dll	Odbccu32.dll	Sqlwid.dll
Ds16gt.dll	Msjtes40.dll	Mswdat10.dll	Odbcint.dll	Sqlwoa.dll
Ds32gt.dll	Msjtor40.dll	Mswstr10.dll	Odbcji32.dll	Stdole2.tlb
Expsrv.dll	Msltus40.dll	Msxbde40.dll	Odbcjt32.dll	Vbajet32.dll

SUMMARY

In this chapter, I described how to deploy the Office Web Components using the Web Installer and showed you an easy way to detect whether they are installed on a client machine before navigating the client to a web page. The Web Installer provides an easy mechanism for downloading and installing the Office Web Components with your solutions before your corporation actually rolls out all of Office 2000.

Index

A

absolute range references, 17

Access 2000
  data access pages, 12, 147, 156
  OWC controls and, 6

Access Data Sources Across Domains security
    setting, Internet Explorer 5, 156

ActiveX, 6. *See also* COM (Component Object
    Model)

ActiveX Data Objects Multidimensional (ADO
    MD) objects, 218, 219, 327, 334, 336

AddIn method, 35, 36, 312

Add method of PageFields collection, 161

AddTotal method, 125, 142, 260

ADO Error object, 165

ADO MD. *See* ActiveX Data Objects
    Multidimensional (ADO MD) objects

ADO Recordset objects. *See* Recordset objects

AllowFiltering property, 49, 136

AllowGrouping property, 136

AllowPropertyToolbox property
  PivotTable control, 136
  Spreadsheet control, 46

Alvarez, Cesar, 21

Analysis ToolPak (ATP), 15

apartment threading model, 173

Area charts, 65–66, *66*

areas, in PivotTable component, 116

ASP (Microsoft Active Server Pages), 5
  current directory of, 178
  generating a server-side chart, 174, 175,
      177, 178
  in Helpdesk Reporting solution, 172, 173,
      180, 181
  in Sales Analysis and Reporting solution,
      203, 204, 206, 207, 212

auto-expansion behavior, 140

AutoFilter.Apply method, 48

AutoFilter.Filters property, 48

AutoFilter user interface, Spreadsheet
    component's, 23, *23*

AutofitColumns method, 246

AutoFit feature (or property), 143, 236, 293
  PivotTable component, 133
  Spreadsheet component, 38, 46
  in Visual Basic and FrontPage, 30

AutoLayout method, 120, 215
  OLAP data sources and, 121, 124, 142

AutoTitlePivot method, 216–17

axes, 58, *58*
  adjusting scaling attributes of, 90
  areas as, 116
  labels of, 85
  titles of, 82–84

B

bands, 148

Bar charts, 62–64, *62, 63*

BeforeCommand event, 51

BeforeNewData event, 298

BeginUndo method, 23, 50

<bgsound> tag, 250

bindable properties, 289–90

BindCharts method, 237

BindChartToSpreadsheet method, 77

binding. *See* data binding; property binding

bottom *N* filtering, in Sales Analysis and
    Reporting solution, 217–21

Browscap.ini, 269, 270

browser, determining client browser
    capabilities, 268. *See also* Internet
    Explorer 5

BrowserType object, 268–69, 272

Bubble charts, 67, *67, 68*
  data points in, 56–57
  values in, 57

Index

DAVE STEARNS

Dave Stearns started his career as a software developer in Microsoft's Information Technology group, building internal systems. Coincidentally (or maybe ironically), his first project involved building a client/server sales analysis and reporting system for Microsoft Press using Microsoft SQL Server 1.1 and Microsoft OS/2 (when it was still *Microsoft OS/2*) on the server and PowerBuilder 1.0 on the client (Microsoft Windows 3.0). Dave eventually became a development lead in the IT group, heading the team that built the C++-based client application for Microsoft's central customer and product registration database. Dave then became a program manager in Microsoft's Visual Basic group, designing the database features in the Enterprise Editions of Visual Basic 4.0 and 5.0. After a brief stint designing the Microsoft ADO (ActiveX Data Objects) programming interfaces, Dave joined a newly formed team in the Microsoft Office organization to help design and build the first version of the Office Web Components. Dave is currently working on the next version of the Office Web Components.

Dave lives in Seattle with his wonderful wife, Chelle. When he's not working, he makes a vain attempt at playing his saxophones and other miscellaneous woodwinds. He aspires to one day play the only woodwind instrument louder than the saxophone—the bagpipes.

The manuscript for this book was prepared using Microsoft Word 97. Pages were composed by Microsoft Press using Adobe PageMaker 6.52 for Windows, with text in Garamond and display type in Helvetica Black. Composed pages were delivered to the printer as electronic prepress files.

Cover Graphic Designer

Girvin | Strategic Branding & Design

Cover Illustrator

Glenn Mitsui

Interior Graphic Artist

Joel Panchot

Principal Compositor

Paula Gorelick

Principal Proofreader/Copy Editor

Roger LeBlanc

Indexer

Maro Riofrancos

Editorial Assistant

Denise Bankaitis

Here's the
key to building
dynamic
Web applications

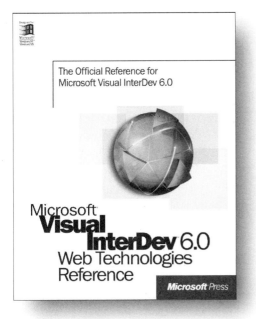

Achieve
dynamic
new effects
on the Web

Microsoft Press offers *comprehensive* learning solutions to help new users, power users, and professionals get the most from *Microsoft technology.*

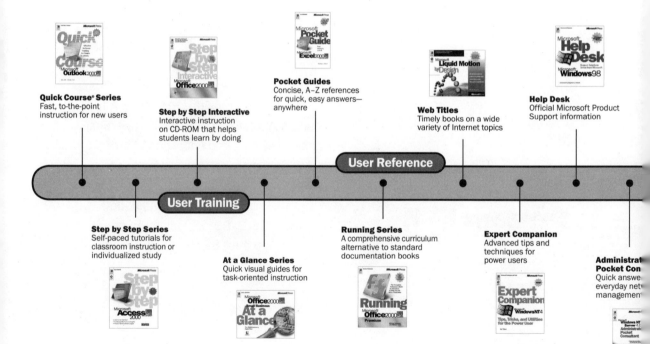

Quick Course® Series
Fast, to-the-point
instruction for new users

Step by Step Interactive
Interactive instruction
on CD-ROM that helps
students learn by doing

Pocket Guides
Concise, A–Z references
for quick, easy answers—
anywhere

Web Titles
Timely books on a wide
variety of Internet topics

Help Desk
Official Microsoft Product
Support information

User Reference

User Training

Step by Step Series
Self-paced tutorials for
classroom instruction or
individualized study

At a Glance Series
Quick visual guides for
task-oriented instruction

Running Series
A comprehensive curriculum
alternative to standard
documentation books

Expert Companion
Advanced tips and
techniques for
power users

**Administrat
Pocket Con**
Quick answe
everyday net
managemen

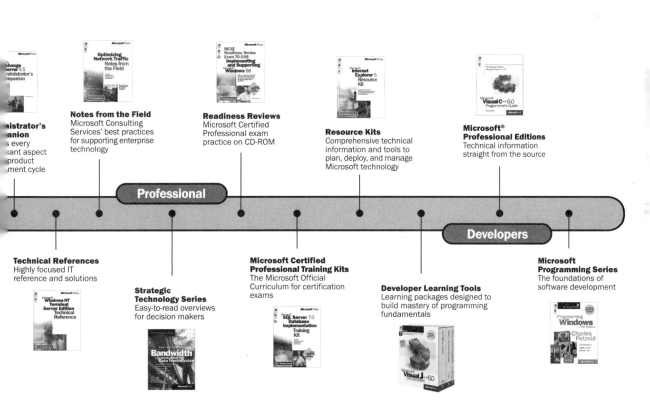

MICROSOFT LICENSE AGREEMENT
Book Companion CD

IMPORTANT—READ CAREFULLY: This Microsoft End-User License Agreement ("EULA") is a legal agreement between you (either an individual or an entity) and Microsoft Corporation for the Microsoft product identified above, which includes computer software and may include associated media, printed materials, and "online" or electronic documentation ("SOFTWARE PRODUCT"). Any component included within the SOFTWARE PRODUCT that is accompanied by a separate End-User License Agreement shall be governed by such agreement and not the terms set forth below. By installing, copying, or otherwise using the SOFTWARE PRODUCT, you agree to be bound by the terms of this EULA. If you do not agree to the terms of this EULA, you are not authorized to install, copy, or otherwise use the SOFTWARE PRODUCT; you may, however, return the SOFTWARE PRODUCT, along with all printed materials and other items that form a part of the Microsoft product that includes the SOFTWARE PRODUCT, to the place you obtained them for a full refund.

SOFTWARE PRODUCT LICENSE

The SOFTWARE PRODUCT is protected by United States copyright laws and international copyright treaties, as well as other intellectual property laws and treaties. The SOFTWARE PRODUCT is licensed, not sold.

1. **GRANT OF LICENSE.** This EULA grants you the following rights:

   a. **Software Product.** You may install and use one copy of the SOFTWARE PRODUCT on a single computer. The primary user of the computer on which the SOFTWARE PRODUCT is installed may make a second copy for his or her exclusive use on a portable computer.

   b. **Storage/Network Use.** You may also store or install a copy of the SOFTWARE PRODUCT on a storage device, such as a network server, used only to install or run the SOFTWARE PRODUCT on your other computers over an internal network; however, you must acquire and dedicate a license for each separate computer on which the SOFTWARE PRODUCT is installed or run from the storage device. A license for the SOFTWARE PRODUCT may not be shared or used concurrently on different computers.

   c. **License Pak.** If you have acquired this EULA in a Microsoft License Pak, you may make the number of additional copies of the computer software portion of the SOFTWARE PRODUCT authorized on the printed copy of this EULA, and you may use each copy in the manner specified above. You are also entitled to make a corresponding number of secondary copies for portable computer use as specified above.

   d. **Sample Code.** Solely with respect to portions, if any, of the SOFTWARE PRODUCT that are identified within the SOFTWARE PRODUCT as sample code (the "SAMPLE CODE"):

      i. **Use and Modification.** Microsoft grants you the right to use and modify the source code version of the SAMPLE CODE, *provided* you comply with subsection (d)(iii) below. You may not distribute the SAMPLE CODE, or any modified version of the SAMPLE CODE, in source code form.

      ii. **Redistributable Files.** Provided you comply with subsection (d)(iii) below, Microsoft grants you a nonexclusive, royalty-free right to reproduce and distribute the object code version of the SAMPLE CODE and of any modified SAMPLE CODE, other than SAMPLE CODE, or any modified version thereof, designated as not redistributable in the Readme file that forms a part of the SOFTWARE PRODUCT (the "Non-Redistributable Sample Code"). All SAMPLE CODE other than the Non-Redistributable Sample Code is collectively referred to as the "REDISTRIBUTABLES."

      iii. **Redistribution Requirements.** If you redistribute the REDISTRIBUTABLES, you agree to: (i) distribute the REDISTRIBUTABLES in object code form only in conjunction with and as a part of your software application product; (ii) not use Microsoft's name, logo, or trademarks to market your software application product; (iii) include a valid copyright notice on your software application product; (iv) indemnify, hold harmless, and defend Microsoft from and against any claims or lawsuits, including attorney's fees, that arise or result from the use or distribution of your software application product; and (v) not permit further distribution of the REDISTRIBUTABLES by your end user. Contact Microsoft for the applicable royalties due and other licensing terms for all other uses and/or distribution of the REDISTRIBUTABLES.

2. **DESCRIPTION OF OTHER RIGHTS AND LIMITATIONS.**

   - **Limitations on Reverse Engineering, Decompilation, and Disassembly.** You may not reverse engineer, decompile, or disassemble the SOFTWARE PRODUCT, except and only to the extent that such activity is expressly permitted by applicable law notwithstanding this limitation.

   - **Separation of Components.** The SOFTWARE PRODUCT is licensed as a single product. Its component parts may not be separated for use on more than one computer.

   - **Rental.** You may not rent, lease, or lend the SOFTWARE PRODUCT.

   - **Support Services.** Microsoft may, but is not obligated to, provide you with support services related to the SOFTWARE PRODUCT ("Support Services"). Use of Support Services is governed by the Microsoft policies and programs described in the user manual, in "online" documentation, and/or in other Microsoft-provided materials. Any supplemental software code provided to you as part of the Support Services shall be considered part of the SOFTWARE PRODUCT and subject to the terms and conditions of this EULA. With respect to technical information you provide to Microsoft as part of the Support Services, Microsoft may use such information for its business purposes, including for product support and development. Microsoft will not utilize such technical information in a form that personally identifies you.

- **Software Transfer.** You may permanently transfer all of your rights under this EULA, provided you retain no copies, you transfer all of the SOFTWARE PRODUCT (including all component parts, the media and printed materials, any upgrades, this EULA, and, if applicable, the Certificate of Authenticity), **and** the recipient agrees to the terms of this EULA.

- **Termination.** Without prejudice to any other rights, Microsoft may terminate this EULA if you fail to comply with the terms and conditions of this EULA. In such event, you must destroy all copies of the SOFTWARE PRODUCT and all of its component parts.

3. **COPYRIGHT.** All title and copyrights in and to the SOFTWARE PRODUCT (including but not limited to any images, photographs, animations, video, audio, music, text, SAMPLE CODE, REDISTRIBUTABLES, and "applets" incorporated into the SOFTWARE PRODUCT) and any copies of the SOFTWARE PRODUCT are owned by Microsoft or its suppliers. The SOFTWARE PRODUCT is protected by copyright laws and international treaty provisions. Therefore, you must treat the SOFTWARE PRODUCT like any other copyrighted material **except** that you may install the SOFTWARE PRODUCT on a single computer provided you keep the original solely for backup or archival purposes. You may not copy the printed materials accompanying the SOFTWARE PRODUCT.

4. **U.S. GOVERNMENT RESTRICTED RIGHTS.** The SOFTWARE PRODUCT and documentation are provided with RESTRICTED RIGHTS. Use, duplication, or disclosure by the Government is subject to restrictions as set forth in subparagraph (c)(1)(ii) of the Rights in Technical Data and Computer Software clause at DFARS 252.227-7013 or subparagraphs (c)(1) and (2) of the Commercial Computer Software—Restricted Rights at 48 CFR 52.227-19, as applicable. Manufacturer is Microsoft Corporation/One Microsoft Way/Redmond, WA 98052-6399.

5. **EXPORT RESTRICTIONS.** You agree that you will not export or re-export the SOFTWARE PRODUCT, any part thereof, or any process or service that is the direct product of the SOFTWARE PRODUCT (the foregoing collectively referred to as the "Restricted Components"), to any country, person, entity, or end user subject to U.S. export restrictions. You specifically agree not to export or re-export any of the Restricted Components (i) to any country to which the U.S. has embargoed or restricted the export of goods or services, which currently include, but are not necessarily limited to, Cuba, Iran, Iraq, Libya, North Korea, Sudan, and Syria, or to any national of any such country, wherever located, who intends to transmit or transport the Restricted Components back to such country; (ii) to any end user who you know or have reason to know will utilize the Restricted Components in the design, development, or production of nuclear, chemical, or biological weapons; or (iii) to any end user who has been prohibited from participating in U.S. export transactions by any federal agency of the U.S. government. You warrant and represent that neither the BXA nor any other U.S. federal agency has suspended, revoked, or denied your export privileges.

DISCLAIMER OF WARRANTY

NO WARRANTIES OR CONDITIONS. MICROSOFT EXPRESSLY DISCLAIMS ANY WARRANTY OR CONDITION FOR THE SOFTWARE PRODUCT. THE SOFTWARE PRODUCT AND ANY RELATED DOCUMENTATION ARE PROVIDED "AS IS" WITHOUT WARRANTY OR CONDITION OF ANY KIND, EITHER EXPRESS OR IMPLIED, INCLUDING, WITHOUT LIMITATION, THE IMPLIED WARRANTIES OF MERCHANTABILITY, FITNESS FOR A PARTICULAR PURPOSE, OR NONINFRINGEMENT. THE ENTIRE RISK ARISING OUT OF USE OR PERFORMANCE OF THE SOFTWARE PRODUCT REMAINS WITH YOU.

LIMITATION OF LIABILITY. TO THE MAXIMUM EXTENT PERMITTED BY APPLICABLE LAW, IN NO EVENT SHALL MICROSOFT OR ITS SUPPLIERS BE LIABLE FOR ANY SPECIAL, INCIDENTAL, INDIRECT, OR CONSEQUENTIAL DAMAGES WHATSOEVER (INCLUDING, WITHOUT LIMITATION, DAMAGES FOR LOSS OF BUSINESS PROFITS, BUSINESS INTERRUPTION, LOSS OF BUSINESS INFORMATION, OR ANY OTHER PECUNIARY LOSS) ARISING OUT OF THE USE OF OR INABILITY TO USE THE SOFTWARE PRODUCT OR THE PROVISION OF OR FAILURE TO PROVIDE SUPPORT SERVICES, EVEN IF MICROSOFT HAS BEEN ADVISED OF THE POSSIBILITY OF SUCH DAMAGES. IN ANY CASE, MICROSOFT'S ENTIRE LIABILITY UNDER ANY PROVISION OF THIS EULA SHALL BE LIMITED TO THE GREATER OF THE AMOUNT ACTUALLY PAID BY YOU FOR THE SOFTWARE PRODUCT OR US$5.00; PROVIDED, HOWEVER, IF YOU HAVE ENTERED INTO A MICROSOFT SUPPORT SERVICES AGREEMENT, MICROSOFT'S ENTIRE LIABILITY REGARDING SUPPORT SERVICES SHALL BE GOVERNED BY THE TERMS OF THAT AGREEMENT. BECAUSE SOME STATES AND JURISDICTIONS DO NOT ALLOW THE EXCLUSION OR LIMITATION OF LIABILITY, THE ABOVE LIMITATION MAY NOT APPLY TO YOU.

MISCELLANEOUS

This EULA is governed by the laws of the State of Washington USA, except and only to the extent that applicable law mandates governing law of a different jurisdiction.

Should you have any questions concerning this EULA, or if you desire to contact Microsoft for any reason, please contact the Microsoft subsidiary serving your country, or write: Microsoft Sales Information Center/One Microsoft Way/Redmond, WA 98052-6399.

Register Today!

Return this
Programming Microsoft® Office 2000 Web Components
registration card today

Microsoft® Press
mspress.microsoft.com

For information about Microsoft Press®

products, visit our Web site at

mspress.microsoft.com

Microsoft *Press*